The Struggles of Post-Independence Nigeria

The Struggles of Post-Independence Nigeria

Missed Opportunities and a Continuing Crisis

Ucheoma Nwagbara

LEXINGTON BOOKS
Lanham • Boulder • New York • London

Published by Lexington Books
An imprint of The Rowman & Littlefield Publishing Group, Inc.
4501 Forbes Boulevard, Suite 200, Lanham, Maryland 20706
www.rowman.com

86-90 Paul Street, London EC2A 4NE, United Kingdom

British Library Cataloguing in Publication Information Available

Library of Congress Cataloging-in-Publication Data

Names: Nwagbara, Ucheoma, 1959- author.
Title: The struggles of post-independence Nigeria : missed opportunities and a continuing crisis / Ucheoma Nwagbara.
Description: Lanham : Lexington Books, 2021. | Includes bibliographical references and index.
Identifiers: LCCN 2021043312 (print) | LCCN 2021043313 (ebook) | ISBN 9781793633750 (cloth) | ISBN 9781793633767 (epub)
Subjects: LCSH: Political corruption—Nigeria. | Nigeria—Economic conditions—1960- | Nigeria—Politics and government—1960-
Classification: LCC HC1055 .N86 2021 (print) | LCC HC1055 (ebook) | DDC 330.9669—dc23
LC record available at https://lccn.loc.gov/2021043312
LC ebook record available at https://lccn.loc.gov/2021043313

Dedicated to My Beloved Children
Ijeoma and Ucheoma Jr.

ALSO THE BOOK IS A GIFT TO MY GENERATION

Those conceived in the heat of the struggle for Nigerian independence
Born into the promise of independence
Tempered by the Nigeria-Biafra Civil War
Encouraged by the peace
Betrayed by the postwar Nigerian leadership

Contents

List of Tables

Foreword

Nigeria Gets Much-Needed Scrutiny by an Expert

A. B. Assensoh, LLM, PhD

Professor Emeritus (Indiana University) and Courtesy Professor Emeritus (University of Oregon)

The West African nation of Nigeria is considered to be one of the largest countries on the second largest continent (Africa). It is also deemed to be among the most populous as well as the most well endowed in natural and human resource terms. Indeed, it is an important oil-rich nation, which is an active member of the Organization of the Petroleum Exporting Countries (OPEC).

Yet, Nigerian scholars and commentators have vociferously written about countless maladies, which have afflicted their post-independent country, ranging from rampant corruption, abject poverty of a large section of the citizenry, and very transparent greed on the part of several of the country's former and current leadership. To help in issuing a clarion call about the foregoing shortcomings of the oil-rich country, Dr. Ucheoma Nwagbara has taken the time to write his very useful book, *The Struggles of Post-Independence Nigeria*; as a remarkable researcher, he has as well offered a prescription to help his beloved Nigeria find a way to solve the multitude of problems, if his work is taken seriously by the elected rulers of the country.

Dr. Nwagbara, who hails from the Igbo ethnic group in Nigeria, earned his terminal doctoral (PhD) degree in the area of public policy from Southern University and A&M College, Baton Rouge, Louisiana, USA. Apart from his academic concentration, Dr. Nwagbara has also researched and written so widely that his varied writing interests have evolved around policies that touch on health, economic development, overall public policy, Nigerian political economy, leadership as well as governance, governmental reform and innovation, bureaucracy, globalization and, indeed, modernization.

The Struggles of Post-Independence Nigeria is a well-researched and detailed book, in which Dr. Nwagbara offers his readers analyses of Nigeria at a glance in five very solid chapters. Specifically, the chapters deal with the following: a well-documented Preface; "The Economy: Shattered" (chapter 1); High Cost of Governance: "The Nigerian Factor" (chapter 2); "Corruption" (chapter 3); "Leadership: The Missing Link" (chapter 4); and "Summary and Conclusions" (chapter 5). Also, there are very copious references and notes, coupled with a List of Tables; List of Abbreviations to aid the reader; dedications to his children (Ijeoma and Ucheoma Jr.) and also as a gift to his generation.

Described as a Nigerian patriot's cri de coeur, the author uses *The Struggles of Post-Independence Nigeria* to bring to a sharp focus the crisis of leadership, endemic corruption, excruciating poverty, and very appalling economic conditions in Nigeria amid enormous oil wealth. Dr. Nwagbara relies on very up-to-date sources of information and research articles, including very prestigious and credible newspaper reports to share some of the sad details that readers of the book are to be confronted with. For example, readers, in the preface, are to come across such informative details as the following poignant observation from the *Punch* publication: "Nigeria has been run by dreadful governments for so long" (*Punch*, December 4, 2013). This statement is forcefully demonstrable in the forlorn condition of both the Nigerian state and people. Consequently, in order to analyze the past and mobilize for Nigerian future, the idea to write this book was conceived after a thorough and in-depth reflections on the developmental, leadership, globalization, modernization, and nation building challenges facing Nigeria and the possible pathways forward.

Since the sweetness of the pie lies in obtaining and eating it, I urge readers to obtain copies of this very readable publication in order to share in Dr. Nwagbara's expertise. In fact, I commend the author for informing his readers from the onset about the factors, which motivated him to write the book, most certainly including the following:

> There are three motivating factors for writing this book. First, to offer invaluable insights and nuanced understanding as to why Nigerians, especially the middle class and the poor, in spite of Nigeria's huge oil wealth, are worse-off today than they were at independence in 1960. Second, to provide additional evidence and knowledge in the literature to further buttress the fact that successive Nigerian leaderships have failed to utilize the country's enormous resources to improve the country and extend economic opportunities, especially, to the middle class and the poor. Furthermore, this book will deepen and widen the literature on

Nigeria, particularly on the subjects of leadership and governance, economy and development; serve as a resource for academics, students, practitioners, policymakers, analysts, researchers, planners, development partners and agencies, foundations, and the global public. Third, this book combines theoretical analysis and practical illustrations and draws on various pertinent subject matters to explain and offer cutting-edge commonsense solutions to the Nigerian problems, and in the process help to pave a way for a better country, per se to restore hope to Nigeria and its citizens.

It is, indeed, not an exaggeration to point out the fact that the publication of this book is very timely, hence I expect academics, students, the general reader and, also, policymakers in Nigeria and in other African countries to obtain copies for perusal and guidance. I very much agree with Dr. Nwagbara, as he, inter alia, wrote that it has been necessary for him to pen such a candid book, especially as he pointed out that "while there are many studies on Nigeria, apparently none has focused exclusively on the socio-economic and political developments in Nigeria since independence, including highlighting especially the unprecedented 20 years of un-interrupted democracy that is supposed to make Nigerian lives better from 1999 to the present. [It is certainly the longest period of democracy in Nigeria's post-independence history]. This book is expected to fill the yawning gap in the existing literature on the subject matter."

Without equivocation, I again encourage readers to obtain copies of this very useful book. For example, apart from the thematic four chapters, the author has, as well, utilized the final chapter (chapter 5) to offer Summary and Conclusions, which should be very useful for policymakers as well as the general reader. I commend Dr. Nwagbara for deeming it necessary to produce such an important book, *The Struggles of Post-Independence Nigeria*, which will certainly stand the test of time, as I expect it to play an important role in helping to rebuild Nigeria.

After all, in the past, such eminent Nigerian writers as Professors Chinua Achebe, Wole Soyinka, J. F. Ade Ajayi and famous journalists-cum-commentators like Peter Enahoro (Peter Pan), Lateef K. Jakande, Alade Odunewu (Allah Dey), Tai Solarin, and others wrote extensively to offer their own critiques as well as prescriptions for the betterment of Nigeria. In 1983, for example, Professor Achebe gave to his fellow Nigerians, just like a mirror, his very small but crucial book, *The Trouble with Nigeria*, in which he discussed unambiguously that his home nation suffers from dearth in leadership. Subsequently, his intellectual brethren—Professor Soyinka—two years later penned *Of Africa* (2013), a Yale University Press-published book that was a biting indictment of the continent with specific criticisms of some particular nations, including his own Nigeria. A follow-up was *Then Spoke the Thunder*, which became Nigeria and Africa's foremost and respected journalist Peter Enahoro's long-awaited autobiography, a 730-page tome. It is his account as well as reflections on the crisis of leadership in Nigeria, a topic that Dr. Ucheoma Nwagbara treats very well in *The Struggles of Post-Independence Nigeria.*

In his own famous column, "Thinking with You" (published by *Daily Times* newspaper), the late Dr. Tai Solarin, then principal of Mayflower Secondary School at Ikenne, Ogun State, Nigeria, critiqued the ills of Nigerian society in his column. At the time of his death in July 1994, he had become very famous for his unrelenting crusade against corruption and other socioeconomic maladies of his beloved Nigeria. It is remarkable that Dr. Nwagbara is following the footsteps of these bold and selfless Nigerian citizens, who demonstrated unabashedly, in their penchant critiques of Nigeria, that the pen is, indeed, mightier than the sword!

Preface

This carefully researched book, *The Struggles of Post-Independence Nigeria*, is my cri de coeur as a Nigerian patriot. In the publication, I have endeavored to bring to sharp focus the crisis of our country's leadership, which transparently includes sheer endemic corruption, excruciating poverty, and appalling economic conditions engulfing Nigeria as a nation of enormous oil wealth. The research for this publication has brought to the fore the reality that, over the years, Nigeria has been degraded for a long time as a result of what the late celebrated writer, Chinua Achebe, has described as lack of high quality leadership. Indeed, the reality of the country's deplorable state of affairs, including the leadership quagmire, has very obviously been manifested in the forlorn economic stagnation of the Nigerian state and the forlorn conditions of the people.

Consequently, I felt the urgent need to analyze the past and, in the process, to mobilize for Nigeria's future, a situation that prompted the idea to write this book in the context of a thorough and in-depth reflection on the developmental, leadership, globalization, modernization, and nation building challenges facing Nigeria. In the process, I have utilized my expertise and policy training to provide a modern-day blueprint for policy in order to unearth possible pathways forward in Nigeria, the most populous nation of Africa, the world's second largest continent behind Asia.

Most certainly, there are three motivating factors for writing this book. The first is to offer invaluable insights and nuanced understanding as to why Nigerians, especially the middle class and the poor, are worse-off today than they were at independence in spite of the country's huge oil wealth. Second, it is to provide additional evidence and knowledge in the literature to further buttress the fact that successive Nigerian leaderships have, over the years, failed to utilize the country's enormous natural and human resources to develop the country and also to extend economic opportunities to the citizenry, especially to the middle class and the poor.

Furthermore, it is to deepen and widen the literature on Nigeria with respect to the subjects of leadership and governance, economy as well as overall development; to serve as a resource for academics, students, practitioners, policymakers, analysts, researchers, planners, developmental partners and agencies, foundations, and the global public. Third, my book clearly combines theoretical analysis and practical illustrations and draws on various pertinent subject matters to explain cutting-edge, common sense solutions that are relevant to the Nigerian problems and, in the process, to help to pave a way for a better country and, per se, to restore hope to Nigeria and its citizenry.

Therefore, I wish to underscore the fact that the writing of this book is not only timely but also very necessary because, in spite of the fact that there are many studies on Nigeria, it is apparent that none has focused exclusively on the socioeconomic and political developments of Nigeria since independence. Comparatively, this work, in particular, makes it a point to highlight the unprecedented 20 years of uninterrupted democracy that is supposed to make Nigerian lives better between 1999 and the present, which is the longest period of democracy in Nigeria's post-independence history. In the end, my book is expected to fill the yawning gap in the existing literature on the topic or subject matter the publication dwells on.

Writing a book is not an easy undertaking, when it is especially combined with the burden of my regular full-time work schedule and, also, my doctoral program, which included overall school work and its such inherent responsibilities as regular classes; periodic exams; completing research papers and projects, coupled with presentations; conferences; advisor meetings; proposal formulation and defense of selected topic; the final comprehensive examination; dissertation research, writing, and the final defense to attain the golden fleece. As I still recall, a lot has gone under the bridge, so to point out, as the foregoing was my lot before I began researching and writing this book, in the midst of my full doctoral studies, which I started in the Fall of 2016 and, in fact, graduating with my doctoral (PhD) degree in the Spring of 2019. In fact, the love and support of my family, loved ones, sympathizers, colleagues, professors, and the Almighty God were of inestimable value as I completed this book and, also, my doctoral program. I, in fact, thank each and everyone of them all from the bottom of my heart.

As I did earlier, this book has been dedicated to my beloved children, Ijeoma and Ucheoma Jr., both of whom were born and raised in the United States of America, a nation of unlimited opportunities. It is my ardent belief that both of my children hope to see a better Nigeria of their father and heritage, where working hard and playing by the rules should bring about ultimate success, and that Nigeria of their dreams will become a place, where political leaders are to be held accountable, and that there is shared prosperity, level playing field, coupled with better opportunities, and for zero tolerance for corruption to be the overall enshrined norm.

I am eternally grateful to Professor Damien Ejigiri, dean, Nelson Mandela College of Government and Social Sciences, Southern University and A&M College, Baton Rouge, Louisiana, USA, indeed, for his magnanimous assistance in his college with graduate assistantship to help me defray most of the costs of my doctoral education. Also, I am forever grateful to him for his pivotal role as the project advisor for this book. He was generous with his time and unlimited with his encouragement. Although any errors are mine, I am also particularly grateful to Professor Damien Ejigiri (Southern University and A&M College, Baton Rouge, Louisiana, USA) and Georges Nzongola-Ntalaja, professor of African, African American, and Diaspora Studies, at the University of North Carolina at Chapel Hill, USA, for reviewing the first draft of the manuscript. Their comments, suggestions, and wisdom were immeasurable, as they greatly improved the manuscript for this book.

I as well extend my gratitude to Indiana University's Emeritus Professor Akwasi B. Assensoh for writing the Foreword for the book manuscript. Above all, I very much thank my brother, Professor Onyinye Nwagbara, for his general brotherly support. Finally, I owe a special debt of gratitude to my beloved late parents, Mr. Fred Nwagbara and Mrs. Onyemata Nwagbara, as their inspirations were invaluable in my overall scholarship and in completing the manuscript for this book.

Ucheoma Nwagbara
Baton Rouge, Louisiana, USA
Summer 2021

List of Abbreviations

ADB	African Development Bank
AIDS	Acquired Immunodeficiency Syndrome
ATA	Agricultural Transformation Agenda
AU	Africa Union
BBC	British Broadcasting Corporation
BPE	Bureau of Public Enterprises
CASS	Center for Advanced Social Sciences
CBN	Central Bank of Nigeria
CCB	Code of Conduct Bureau
CLEEN	Center for Law Enforcement Education of Nigeria
DMO	Debt Management Office
DRC	Democratic Republic of the Congo
ECOWAS	Economic Community of West African States
EFCC	Economic and Financial Crimes Commission
EIU	Economist Intelligence Unit
FDI	Foreign Direct Investment
FEC	Federal Executive Council
FERMA	Federal Roads Maintenance Agency
FME	Federal Ministry of Education
FRSC	Federal Road Safety Corps
GDP	Gross Domestic Product
GIFMIS	Government Integrated Financial Management Information System
GNP	Gross National Product
ICPC	Independent Corrupt Practices Commission
IMF	International Monetary Fund
INEC	Independent National Electoral Commission

ING	Interim National Government
IPP	Independent Power Producers
IPPIS	Integrated Payroll and Personnel Information System
MPLA	Popular Movement for the Liberation of Angola
NAIRA	₦ (Nigerian currency)
NASS	National Assembly
NBS	National Bureau of Statistics
NCP	National Council on Privatization
NEITI	Nigeria Extractive Industries Transparency Initiative
NIPP	National Integrated Power Project
NNPC	Nigerian National Petroleum Corporation
NPDC	Nigerian Petroleum Development Company
NSO	Nigeria Standard Organization
OECD	Organization for Economic Cooperation and Development
OPEC	Organization of the Petroleum Exporting Countries
RMAFC	Revenue Mobilization Allocation and Fiscal Commission
SUBEB	State Universal Basic Education Board
TSA	Treasury Single Account
UAE	United Arab Emirates
UBEC	Universal Basic Education Commission
UNDP	United Nations Development Program
UNESCO	United Nations Educational, Scientific, and Cultural Organization
UNICEF	United Nations International Children's Emergency Fund
UNODC	United Nations Office on Drugs and Crime
USAID	United States Agency for International Development
USIP	United States Institute of Peace
WHO	World Health Organization

Introduction

Nigeria attained its independence from the colonial rule of Britain in 1960. Yet, Nigerian leadership continues to be mired in what critics see as a charade and wanton corruption, coupled with abuse of office, lack of vision, and total disconnect from or with the citizenry. Therefore, Nigerian leadership, for all practical purposes, is considered to be an alternate reality: thus acceleration without speed, movement without motion and, most certainly, walking but without the expected steps. Most obnoxious of all, in spite of the massive oil and gas reserves of the country, are the mounting economic stagnation and the widening of inequality. Furthermore, successive Nigerian leaderships have, inexcusably, failed to utilize the country's huge natural resources as a game changer to shape the destiny of the nation as well as to alleviate poverty, improve the citizens' living conditions, bolster security, and extend economic opportunities, especially when it comes to the middle class and the abjectly poor of the country.

The French scholar, Rene Dumont, saw as a "false start" (Dumont, 1966) Africa's emergence as a continent with independent nations; in Nigeria, for example, the very ideals behind the struggle for independence have utterly been betrayed by the emergent indigenous post-decolonization leadership, which continues today to steer the ship of state in the wrong direction and, also, in favor of personal rule and utter greed while many Nigerians fall behind. The children of post-independent Nigeria including the author of this book were known to have dreamed of better days and great things after independence have been dealt a bad hand and let down by the leadership. The scholar, Richard Joseph (2013), lamented the following words about Nigeria's post-independence foibles: "The glorious future of unlimited possibilities has been constricted into a bleak vista of regret and recrimination."

Then, as the author of this book, my generation and others have regrettably become "the lost generation" rather than being the leading and upbeat generation. And since the Nigerian leadership could not fashion out visionary ways to make the country better, many of the independence era generation have been forced into diasporic exile of sort, often as "economic migrants" (Achiume, 2019, p. 1524) and adventurist nomads. And their skills and talents are benefiting as well as improving their host countries instead of Nigeria. Walter Carrington, former American ambassador to Nigeria (1993–1997), has offered a proof of this "flight of human resource" (Carrington, 2013) in the following words:

> My country and others around the world profit from Nigeria's greatest export—her accomplished people. I often ask Nigerians, who are legally in the U.S., why they remain. The two major obstacles to going back [home], which they cite, are their fears of the omni presence of corruption and the growing insecurity. They cringe whenever they hear Nigeria belittled on television comedies because of 419 schemes. They have so much to contribute to their homeland and ways must be found to create the environment which will invite them to return and reverse the brain drain which does so much damage to the body politic. . . . Over 3 million Nigerians live and work in the United States and Canada, and not to say of the large numbers in the United Kingdom. They excel everywhere in their contributions to all sectors of our society [America]. (Carrington, 2013)

As owners of the country, Nigerians must reclaim their country by demanding accountability from the present and future leadership of their country. For far too long, leaders of Nigeria in Abuja, the capital, have created a government that, proverbially, "comes at the people instead of a government that comes from the people." This, in the minds of many Nigerians, must change. However, if Nigerians do not rise to the occasion, nobody else can do the job for them. In this regard, perhaps, Acemoglu, Verdier, and Robinson (2004, p. 162) view is apt, "members of society need to cooperate in order to depose a kleptocrat [bad leaders]." Sadly, the Nigerian system has been corrupt and adrift because the citizens have not exercised their responsibilities as owners. The esteemed Edmund Burke (1729–1797), the British statesman and political theorist, once said: "The greatest impetus for evil to triumph is for good people to do nothing." In Nigeria, the silent majority has kept quiet for too long. Now is the time to be heard or never. However, it is often said that it takes two to tango, hence elite corruption, abuses, and misgovernance of Nigeria cannot occur without the complicity and indulgence of ordinary Nigerians.

Meanwhile, popular resistance to the current gridlock will succeed only if Nigerians come to terms with their predicament and, in the process, hasten the struggle for popular democracy and the construction of a more inclusive Nigerian state (Amuwo, 2010, p. 425). For that to occur, Nigerians must disavow their docility (or what Olson (1965) referred to as "collective action problem"), unite, and go to the extent of demanding real change through political and social activism. That, in a large measure, is the only way to save the country and subsequently free Nigerians from the grip of corrupt, greedy, and discredited leaders.

In the Nigerian situation, the most disturbing are the statistics on economic decline and as well as social decay. That, to a large extent, is why more than 70% of Nigerians remain trapped in poverty, while not less than 60% of the population subsists on less than $1.90 a day, according to the World Bank. While the country's economy is sputtering, the overall economic outlook itself remains bleak. The Economist Intelligence Unit (EIU) of the *Economist* of London had its latest forecast for Nigeria released in November 2019, and it indicated that "severe instability, interventionism by the central bank and government and corruption will be major obstacles to economic development over 2020–24" (*The Economist*, November 20, 2019). The EIU is not alone in its conclusions.

For example, a 2019 World Bank's survey, titled "Nigeria Opinion Survey Report," revealed the following: only 28% of Nigerians are very optimistic about the future of their country; nearly 50% (49% to be exact) think that economic opportunities are decreasing; almost 70% (69% exact) see terrorism as the most serious global challenge, which is also facing Nigeria; 5.0 mean rate trust Nigerian governments (State And Federal) to do the right thing, compared to 7.3, 7.1, and 6.9 for the World Bank, United Nations, bilateral organizations/international civil society, respectively (World Bank, 2019, pp. 8, 12–13) (mean rate: "1= to no degree at all," 10= "to a very significant degree").

While Nigeria's unemployment numbers remain depressing, inflation has as well remained at double digits for several years; also, budget deficit persists; external debt remain a big problem; the domestic debt continues to pile up; crime rate, including escalating violent insurgency, continues to climb. The specter of corruption has made investors tepid, while their faith in the system has terribly shaken and, very sadly, business scams that target foreigners remain a pervasive problem. The *Economist* of London has stated that Nigeria "has become a byword for swindle and fraud" (*The Economist*, April 14, 2011). The *New York Times*, one of America's major newspapers, added its own voice: "Nigeria has notoriety as a source of global flimflam" (Roberts, 2015) and as "one of the world's most difficult business environments" (Page & Okeke, 2019, p. 1).

Security for life and property is constantly begging for attention, as it was poignantly manifested by the outrageous abduction and reported enslavement of innocent school girls from Chibok, Borno State, in the Northeast by the militant Islamic sect, Boko Haram, in April 2014. The kidnappings at Chibok are only one part of Nigeria's security problems. The real kicker is that in spite of the more than $20 billion security budget/military expenditure between 2010 and 2019 (Stockholm International Peace Research Institute, 2020), and presidential "declaration of State of emergency in May 2013" (*Punch*, May 7, 2014) in Boko Haram's enclaves of "Adamawa, Borno, and Yobe States," and that "Boko Haram has been technically defeated" (*BBC News*, December 24, 2015) in December 2015, Boko Haram has grown bolder and deadlier. According to the Institute for Economics and Peace (Australian think tank) "2015 Global Terrorism Index" (Institute for Economics and Peace, 2015) and "2020 Global Terrorism Index" reports, respectively, "Boko Haram has become the world's deadliest terrorist group," causing "Nigeria 1,245 deaths in 2019 from terrorist activity . . . ranking 3 among the 5 most terrorist impacted countries in the world (Afghanistan 1, Iraq 2, Syria 4, Somalia 5)" out of 162 countries covered (Institute for Economics and Peace, 2020, p. 2, 8).

The Boko Haram violence continues unabated with frightening audacity. On November 19, 2018, for example, Boko Haram terrorists overran a military base in Metele, Borno State, and killed dozens of soldiers (some reports say more than 100 soldiers) including the military commander (*Vanguard*, November 21, 2018). Also, in March 2020, "50 Nigerian soldiers were killed in a deadly Boko Haram ambush in Yobe State" (Umar, 2020). Furthermore, in February 2018, Boko Haram abducted more than 100 schoolgirls in Dapchi, Yobe State (*BBC News*, February 26, 2018); additionally, in December 2020, Boko Haram abducted more than 300 schoolboys in Kankara, Katsina State (Paquette, 2020). On top of this, IHS Markit, a London-based information analytics firm, in its 2021 latest "Nigeria Economics and Country Risk" report warned, "Islamist militants are in the ascendant against a demoralized and poorly resourced Nigerian army" (IHS Markit, 2021, p. 4). "In all of these," according to a recent report by SB Morgen, a Nigeria-based data analytics firm, "the spate of kidnapping is a feature in all parts of Nigeria. Kidnap for ransom is a lucrative business in Nigeria . . . between June 2011 and March 2020, not less than $18 million was paid in ransom money to kidnappers" (SB Morgen, 2020, pp. 3–4).

Apart from Boko Haram and kidnapping, other insecurities and problems abound. Millions of Nigerians have neither adequate health care nor a decent and affordable housing (Adeyemo, 2005; Reich, 2016; Ibem, 2010; Ugochukwu & Iwuagwu, 2015). Many work harder than they used to but earn less and can only meet a fraction of their family needs with their incomes. Education is crumbling and the future of a Nigerian child is anything but bright (Nwagwu, 1997; Olatoun, 2010). Public infrastructures particularly electricity and roads are at advanced stage of decay (Akinwale, 2010; Obialor, 2017).

To a large extent, Nigeria's problems are not difficult to identify. However, their solutions call for hard choices, sacrifice, immediate action, and bold and effective leadership. The time of waiting and vacillation is over. The grim winter of despair must be turned into optimistic spring of hope. The national mood must be upbeat once again and confidence must be restored in the people. More jobs and wealth must be created; parents must be assisted to educate their children; Nigerian children must have the opportunity to reach their potentials; Nigeria must plug into the global knowledge economy. The civil service must be transformed from the diehard practices of waste, fraud, and incompetence into one that provides services for the people in which service, affordable and quality health care, and decent housing must be within the reach of every Nigerian; Nigeria must be able to feed itself; the national leadership must be honest, strong, and visionary. These are the critical "New Deal" (Schlesinger, 1958[1]) elements that would move Nigeria forward as she advances in the twenty-first century.

Estimated 70% of Nigerians now live in poverty, compared to 30% at independence, according to the World Bank. The International Crisis Group (ICG), a Belgium-based nongovernmental organization, released the following about Nigeria: "Nigeria is a fractured state. It is rich but Nigerians are poor, many extremely so" (ICG, 2014). Corruption, a boom and bust cycle of oil prices, and failure to diversify the economy have left the country in "a development trap" (ICG, 2006; Bach, 2005, p. 54). It added that "in the absence of checks and balances," "the state has failed to fulfill most of its major functions, and large segments of the public have ceased to expect social services, public utilities, infrastructure, security or administration from it." Many groups have resorted to self-help measures through ethnic, religious, community or civic organizations (ICG, 2006). The situation has taken a turn for the worse in recent times as poll after poll and research show escalating poverty, distress, insecurity, and despondency among Nigerians.

A recent survey by the Gallup Poll (USA) disclosed:

> About 6 in 10 Nigerians (59%) said there had been times in the past year when they didn't have enough money to buy food for their families. Four in 10 (40%) said there had been times when they did not have enough to provide adequate shelter. Both figures are significantly higher than the median results among countries surveyed in sub-Saharan Africa. (Crabtree, 2012)

The Gallup Poll is not alone in its assessment and conclusions. For example, a 2013 NOI Polls (a Nigerian survey agency that partners with the Gallup Poll) reported that "majority (88%) of Nigerians believe that the country is worse-off today than it was at independence and, another 72% do not think that the vision of the founding fathers have been achieved in the first 100 years." (In 1914, the British colonial administration unified the Northern and Southern Protectorates of Nigeria to form the single entity of Nigeria.)

However, in spite of rebasing Nigeria Gross Domestic Product (GDP) in 2014 from ₦42.4 trillion to ₦80.2 trillion ($510 billion, to become Africa's largest economy) and 20 years of democratic rule that is supposed to make peoples' lives better, the World Bank lists Nigeria among the "five severely poor countries in which two-thirds of the world's extremely poor are concentrated" (Udo, 2014). The *Guardian* proclaimed: "Democratic governance has not delivered the desired dividends. Nigerians remain largely poor; in fact, among the poorest in the world" (*Guardian*, November 25, 2013).

Sadly, it is a transparent fact that, in Nigeria, there has been an amalgam of bad leadership as well as economic decline, social malaise, corruption and mismanagement, insidious bureaucracy, and moral decay that have devastated the country, thereby leaving the citizens to be exasperated and pauperized. As former American president Franklin D. Roosevelt once said at the height of America's Great Depression in the 1930s, "it is only a foolish optimist who can deny the harsh realities of the moment" (Roosevelt, 1933) in Nigeria. A December 2014 *Punch* newspaper editorial put it dramatically:

> Today, Nigeria is farther from a new nation more than at any other time in its chaotic history. In the last 15 years, we have completely missed our national goals to build a tolerant, free, liberal, democratic and pluralistic society. Security of life and property, which is the most fundamental purpose of any government, has virtually collapsed. In many parts of the country, felons, including terrorists, armed robbers and kidnappers, now question the authority of the state, brazenly killing fellow citizens. A large part of the North-East zone is bleeding from a brutal siege by Boko Haram terrorists.

Again, the *Economist* noted: "On the whole, the country [Nigeria] is tottering along, acclaimed as much for its massive potential as for its actual achievements. It is still a sick man all the same" (*The Economist*, April 13, 2013).

More than half of a century after independence, Nigeria remains a walking billboard of misrule, drift and decay, corruption, poverty, insecurity, and conflict (Clapham, 1996; Suberu & Diamond, 2002). This observation is not out of the ordinary. Benjamin Nwabueze, a constitutional lawyer, also deemed it necessary to weigh in his own voice, "Nigeria is fast turning into a failed state" (Edike, 2013). Former president Obasanjo again declared "Nigeria is sitting on a keg of gunpowder" (Nwogu, 2013). John Campbell, erstwhile American ambassador to Nigeria (2004–2007), wrote: "Nigeria is dancing on the brink" (Akinloye, 2014). Nigerian leadership in particular has become the people's worst nightmare and worry. They remain odious, "prebendal" (Joseph, 1987[2]), and temperamental. And instead of being dutiful, they are unruly and show laxity and bravado to governance, and disdain for accountability. Instead of pursuing policies that will uplift the country, they continue to poison the well of collective progress and care for personal survival only. Nigerian leaders see something and do not say something; they hear something and do not do anything. The net effect is that in the eyes of the world Nigeria is an unstable and corrupt country governed by out of touch, rapacious, and money hungry kleptocrats.

PLAN OF THE BOOK

This book is divided into five chapters. Chapter 1 examines the Nigerian economy and its failure to improve the lives of Nigerians in spite of the vast oil wealth and quality human capital. General economic condition remains terrible especially for the middle class and the poor who have been literally squeezed to the breaking point (Kerry & Edwards, 2004[3]). People are flat on their back and need help. The economy remains sluggish, unemployment is a big problem, and signs of recovery are not in sight. Windows of economic opportunity are shrinking and have already been closed for many. The industrial base has all but collapsed. The country is increasingly sliding back into a stifling debt burden, and worse, high budget deficits and prodigal spending including wayward official remunerations continue to be a drag on economic growth. Nigeria's infrastructures are not only inadequate, but they are also at advanced stage of decay, if not at the verge of total collapse.

Chapters 2 and 3 look at the high cost of governance and corruption. Nigerian government costs too much and delivers little. Nigerian leaders pay more heed to their own personal survival and offshore bank accounts than to the welfare of their people. There is a fierce pursuit for anything the leadership sharks could grab from, skim, or fleece out of the system, and corruption is widely used as an instrument of statecraft while the nation drifts into darkness. This government for sale behavior of Nigerian leaders has psychological effects on the populace. Nigerian people have come to view government as something of a country club, good for members but dismissive of nonmembers. And this feeling has seriously chipped away at the sacred trust that binds Nigerians with their government, subsisting on Berlin Wall like barricade of cynicism and disconnection. High cost of governance and corruption are inextricably linked.

No doubt the elevation of corruption to a national pastime tops the list of Nigeria's woes. Nigeria's oil riches have inadvertently given vent to the corruption monster and the use of official position and political power for unbridled personal gains, especially at the upper echelon of influence and apogees of power. The culture of mandatory Federal handouts and paternalistic subsidies from oil receipts is so embedded in the public psyche that it has become a national obsession. This practice has over the years created a dependency syndrome, whereby State and Local governments virtually depend on monthly Statutory Allocations from the Federal Treasury to run their respective jurisdictions. Consequently, it has all but robbed States and Local authorities of their fiscal independence, blighted the ability to attract new businesses, and crippled public incentives to create new private sector jobs. Most damaging of all, it has foisted a choking culture of fraud and patronage network on the country and the benefiting elite and their cronies will not let go. As the author, Nigeria must break away from this deeply flawed fiscal arrangement and be on the path of true federalism, economic diversity, agricultural revival, technological prowess, transparency, global respect, and integrity.

Along the foregoing line of thinking, chapter 4 of my book examines the issue of leadership in Nigeria. As Chinua Achebe wrote in his celebrated book (*The Trouble with Nigeria*), about the country's leadership shortcomings, I totally agree that bad leadership is at the root of the Nigerian dilemma. The ideals behind the struggle for independence have been betrayed by the emergent indigenous leadership, which continues to do wrong and care for personal survival only. It will be in order to expatiate on the expected ideals that underlay the struggle for Nigerian independence.

Upon independence, Nigerians expected from their leaders the ideals of dedicated and accountable leadership, transparent institutions, political stability, affordable health care, quality education, reliable infrastructure, robust economy, poverty eradication, assured security to life and property, to mention just a few. In fact, as Lofchie (1968, pp. 4–5) concurs, "there was a generally widespread sense of optimism about the future in Africa [Nigeria] . . ." and "the general sense of Africa's [Nigeria] political future as stable and predictable" upon independence or "termination of colonial authority." Nigeria in particular was "once expected to become black Africa's economic showpiece and continental powerhouse" (Hoffman, 1995, p. 146) and seen as "emerging power in Africa" (Sklar, 1963) after independence. Polhemus (1977, p. 43) "when Nigeria became independent on October 1, 1960 there was good reason to regard it as potentially the most powerful State." The above statements are preponderantly true, because Nigeria has the largest population in Africa, a good agricultural and mineral resource base, including large deposits of petroleum (Polhemus, 1977, p. 43). Additionally, as Robert W. July (1983, p. 119) enunciated, "If political independence had any purpose beyond its own self, African [Nigerian] political leaders stated that it was meant to bring the fruits of economic growth and modernization, long stinted under colonial controls. All this seemed appropriate enough."

However, for "Africa [Nigeria] the prognostications" for the expected juicy fruits of "independence were altogether more uncertain" (Clapham, 1996, p. 809) and disappointing. This is because as Ake (1993, p. 240) forcefully articulated, "the foundation upon which Africa's [Nigeria] democracy [leadership] movement is based is the bitter disappointment of independence and post-independence plans. . . . Poor leadership and structural constraints have turned the high expectations of the independence movement into painful disappointment." Consequently, "throughout Africa [Nigeria] ordinary people are demanding a second independence, this time from the indigenous leadership whose economic mismanagement, together with brutal repression, have made mere survival all but impossible." Ake is not alone, bordering on injurious colonial legacies and policies. Lofchie (1968, pp. 4–5) noted:

> Part of the blame for the failures could be placed squarely on the shoulders of an unenlightened and short-sighted colonial policy . . . even there was an unspoken premise that civil societies would endure and that a generally representative political environment would be maintained . . . concepts and categories drawn from the western political experience have, of course, been bitterly criticized. . . . The suggestion has been made repeatedly that such terms as "constitutionalism," "rule of law," "representation," and "consent" have no meaning or place in the African context and that they are, for all practical purposes, as alien to Africa as the parliamentary institutional arrangements left behind by western colonial powers.

Ihonvbere and Ekekwe (1988, p. 273) weighed in from the economic front, harkening back to Nigeria,

> Thus, Nigeria, the creation of Western imperialism, inherited a highly distorted, disarticulated, underdeveloped and dependent political economy at independence in 1960. The state had a tenuous hegemony and legitimacy and lacked control over the social formation. The economy was under the full control and domination of profit and hegemony-seeking transnational corporations. The local dominant forces were subservient, dependent, corrupt, and largely irresponsible and marginalized in the internal power, production and exchange systems.

This disjunction between the promises of independence and post-independence realities and afflictions has become "African independence fiction" (Lazarus, 1986, p. 49), as the "inability of most African states [including Nigeria] to find a political [leadership] norm compatible with the exigencies of independence is by now a truism" (Chazan, 1978, p. 15). In the same conundrum, "decolonization involved a unique, but temporary, opportunity to form viable states in Africa. Because colonial territories were poorly integrated, a fluid situation existed which could never be recaptured" (Rothchild, 1970, p. 509), not to mention the lingering leadership crisis in Africa including Nigeria. Yagboyaju and Akinlola (2019) "over the decades, there has been a recurrent and sustained argument that the Nigerian state . . . underperforms due to lack of state capacity to deal with the contemporary complexities of governance."

As a result of this atmosphere of persistent leadership crisis "Nigeria has been at a crossroads all its history and the confusion is far from over. . . . Nigeria is far from being a nation at peace with itself . . . acrimonious ethnicity in national life, regional power imbalance, and unrelenting official corruption" (Uwazurike, 1996, p. 3 and 1). Much earlier, Nixon (1972, p. 473) had concluded, "in the history of post-colonial Africa no country has suffered a more tragic experience than Nigeria." And the worst "tragic experience" of Nigeria is that the wind of effective and accountable leadership is yet to take effect in country, so Nigeria remains a country "caught in a vicious circle of [leadership] decay, and one whose [leadership] aspirations remain hostage to the sway not of [broad based] consensus but of cliquism, casuistry, and command" (Othman, 1989, p. 212). By implication, "it is essential to develop a set of concepts based on African history and traditions in order to have a truly relevant and meaningful analysis of African [Nigerian]" (Lofchie, 1968, p. 5) leadership crisis. And this book has provided an opening for that analysis and discussion.

Aside the disappointments of independence, Nigerians are all appalled and share collective sense of loss and outrage due to what several commentators and observers have concluded to be criminal mismanagement of oil wealth by unaccountable, predatory, and compradorial leadership over the years. The huge oil revenues in the last 60 years could have afforded Nigeria adequate ways and means to sustain growth, beef up prosperity, and upgrade the country.

According to available statistics from OPEC, in the most recent 10 years—between 2009 and 2018, as shown in Table 1.19, for example, Nigeria alone earned close to $600 billion in petroleum exports, which also excluded $293 billion in royalty payments from oil and gas companies operating in the oil-rich country. These figures have, indeed, been confirmed in the 2015 report of Nigeria Extractive Industries Transparency Initiative (NEITI) (Ejoh, 2015). Yet, such a huge fortune was squandered by the Nigerian political leadership while the developmental needs of the people were either neglected or left to suffer without any cogent reason. This, of course, to some extent, was expected if one looks at the proverbial "oil curse" phenomenon suffered by other oil-rich nations on the continent, including Libya under its assassinated president.

> Furthermore, Nigeria's return to civilian rule in 1999 held a lot of promise for the nation and its citizenry; yet, that did not bring Nigerians the economic improvements they either anticipated or hoped for in their lives, sadly not from their duly elected leaders, from who campaigned for their offices with unlimited promises, as captured by several of the local newspapers in editorial and op-ed commentaries. (*Guardian*, May 29, 2013)

Chapter 5 of the book is very crucial for its readers, as it ties together as well as it recaptures the "narratives of the policy gaps and missing links" in Nigeria's quest for development as has been fully documented and analyzed in the entire publication.

As developmental experts like Rene Dumont, a French expert on Africa, have confirmed in their scholarship about Africa in general, there is no doubt that 60 years of political autonomy and indigenous leadership has not brought Nigeria the expected or desired changes in its national life. For example, the system of governance and political leadership of the West African nation are still in a mess and without the expected vision. Indeed, over the years, the Nigerian leadership, like the disobedient biblical prophet Jonah, has done what it was not supposed to be done and left undone what is supposed to be done, a situation that has left the country and its citizenry both desolate and traumatized.

Very interestingly, the Nigerian middle class and the abjectly poor populace are yet to share in the prosperity that they deserve from Nigeria's obviously robust oil wealth. Instead, the nation's economy is battered and essential infrastructures are in dire straits as well. Very sadly, too, corruption and mismanagement on the part of the ruling elite, coupled with extravagant governance, greed, and thievery continue to undermine the overall economic prosperity and also wreak havoc on the country. The state of affairs remains so hopeless in a variety of ways in Nigeria that poverty, disease, and instability stalk the otherwise oil-rich nation.

The foregoing sad state of affairs reminds readers of Bill Moyers, the celebrated American journalist, who instructively said that "a democracy can die of [from] too many lies" (Stelter, 2019). A priori, the greatest danger or existential threat to the Nigerian democracy-cum-state may not be elite plunder and abuses, leadership betrayal and excesses, lack of chivalry and integrity of public officials, self-dealing of the political class, imperialist and neocolonialist intrigues and conspiracy theories as well as comprador exploitation, compromised institutions and arbitrary processes, invasion by a foreign army, gay/lesbian controversy, religious schism, ethnic tensions, tribal balkanization, debt wallop, and disease pandemic. Rather, I believe, the lethal attunement and utter resignation of Nigerians to misrule, bad leadership, and corruption, or what the *Punch* referred to as "supine acquiescence of Nigerians to oppression" (*Punch*, December 11, 2019) as accepted ways of life and doing business. Of course, this must change, as the preamble to the 1999 Nigerian Constitution began with this apt invocation, "We the people of the Federal Republic of Nigeria."

As such, every difference should be subordinated to what the constitution has expressed, including all aspects of and also irrespective of such man-made nuances of party or partisan politics, tribal or ethnic jingoism, regional or geopolitical zone backgrounds, state or local governmental allegiances, place of provenance or residence as well as language or dialect considerations, and religious or belief systems; "we the Nigerian people" must come together and demand effective and accountable leadership, good governance, better rule of law as they continue to strive to tackle the challenges of development, nation building, globalization, and modernization. In doing so, we can easily conclude that, after all, it is not all gloom and pain in Nigeria.

As the research for this book has amply confirmed, there are signs of hope, promise, and change in Nigeria. Nigeria has clearly made a solid transition back to democracy and civilian government, and the military has retained respect since its withdrawal from politics (USAID, 2015, p. 7). In addition, as civil society and independent media outlets emerge, enhanced by Nigeria's reputed vibrant press and the power of the social media revolution, Nigerians are increasingly voicing their concerns about the ills of the country and the need to do things better—this emerging voice of public opinion offers hope that the elements for a change are underway.

Recent efforts to deregulate and privatize the economy show promise. Since the return to civil rule in 1999, for example, the deregulation of the telecommunication sector and consolidation of the banking sector have improved communication and stabilized the financial system, respectively (Mailafia, 2008; Ajakaiye, 2008; Oji & Agu, 2008). There are recent improvements in railway construction and modernization to help ease transportation difficulties across the country (Ndukwe, 2017). Furthermore, as the World Bank has pointed out in its records, there is improved road access in new construction, upgrade, rehabilitation, and maintenance, which has helped to reduce transportation costs and boost business development (World Bank, 2016). As specific examples, in 2015, the Buhari administration announced a $25 billion national fund for infrastructure, which includes $1.4 billion for roads, with a pledge to complete 200 roads by the end of 2016 (Oxford Business Group, n.d.).

Then, in 2005, the electricity sector was deregulated and the frameworks of Independent Power Producers (IPPs) and the National Integrated Power

Projects (NIPPs) were established to boost electricity generation in the country (Okedu et al., 2018). Happily, the Bureau of Public Enterprises (BPE), established in 1999 as a part of governmental reform exercises, is also implementing government privatization program (Walkenhorst, 2007; Azubuike, 2005; Soludo, 2008), which is transferring loss making state enterprises[4] to private hands, thereby freeing subsidies and raising capital[5] for other development needs.

Most certainly, the introduction of the Integrated Payroll and Personnel Information System (IPPIS) and the 2007 Government Integrated Financial Management Information System (GIFMIS) has helped to check ghost worker problems and payroll fraud in the civil service. The evidence follows.

Tunji Olaopa (n.d.) confirms "investments in IPPIS and GIFMIS have delivered significant results in the reduction of payroll cost and increasing transparency and efficiency of the finance and budgeting process." Okafor, Abada, and Omeh (2018, p. 32) also echoed similar sentiments, "introduction of IPPIS and computerization exercise has ethically exposed and blocked the holes through which the government treasuries were siphoned and it has also enhanced quality planning and budgeting." The above assertions are not without merit because reports indicate that IPPIS has recorded "encouraging successes thus far" (Mede, 2016), especially in financial savings for the Nigerian government, which can be used to meet pressing budget priorities. Nigeria, for example, has recorded the following financial savings advantage as a result of the IPPIS protocol (Mede, 2016): about ₦12 Billion ($60.9 million) from IPPIS pilot implementation between 2007 and 2009 (the pilot program was funded with $4.99 million World Bank loan), about ₦160 Billion ($812.18 million) and over 60,000 ghost workers removed as at 2014; about ₦220.8 Billion ($1.12 Billion) cumulatively, and 391 MDAs with a total employee enrollment of 288,858 were captured on the IPPIS platform, by December 2015. Also, according to the Office of the Accountant General of the Federation, because of the IPPIS initiative, "over 80,000 ghost officers were disrupted at the Nigerian Police Force" (Udo, 2018), with attendant salary bills relief for Nigerian taxpayers. The IPPIS and GIFMIS are not without criticisms, however, especially from academic labor unions.

The Academic Staff Union of Universities (ASUU) in Nigeria has been one of the most vociferous critics of the IPPIS regime, and in several occasions have embarked on work stoppage actions to drive home its point. ASUU complains that IPPIS "infringes on universities autonomy" (Kolawole, 2020) (Universities Autonomy Act No. 1, 2007), since Section 2AAA of the said Act states as follows: "The Governing Council of a University shall be free in the discharge of its functions and exercise of its responsibilities for the good management, growth and development of the university." In conjunction, ASUU complains that "IPPIS is not backed by law" (Kolawole, 2020), because it is at odds with Section 2AA of the referenced Act that states: "The powers of the Council shall be exercised, as in the Law and Statutes of each University and to this extent establishment circulars that are inconsistent with the Laws and Statutes of the University shall not apply to the Universities." For ASUU, the foregoing provision of the referenced Act "makes IPPIS unnecessary and inapplicable to the universities" (News Agency of Nigeria, October 29, 2019). Furthermore, ASUU claims that IPPIS is not a "home grown initiative," but rather, an outside measure imposed on the Nigerian university system by the World Bank, which ASUU perhaps views with suspicion, and may stir the specter of undue outside interference into Nigeria's domestic higher education affairs (News Agency of Nigeria, October 29, 2019).

Meanwhile, ASUU has set up (awaiting government approval) its own alternative individual university-based system called University Transparency and Accountability Solution (UTAS), as opposed to the unified IPPIS platform. The onus of the UTAS system is to include all personnel information as well as a payroll system, but it will be domiciled in each institution, and monitored by the Federal government to ensure transparency and proper tracking of allocated and disbursed funds (Kolawole, 2020).

Then, the Fiscal Responsibility Act (FRA) adopted in 2007 and amended in 2011 has brought some sanity "against financial rascality and reckless spending by the government." Nigeria adopted the FRA in 2007 as a tool to enhance fiscal prudence and public expenditure transparency because fiscal profligacy of the government has become a major contributor to state corruption and macroeconomic instability in Nigeria (Ushie, 2010). Broadly, the kernel of FRA is to "improve fiscal prudence by placing statutory obligations on governments (Federal, State, and Local) to commit to transparent fiscal and budget practices that can be evaluated over time" (Ushie, 2010, p. 7), especially "in a fast deteriorating macroeconomic environment as Nigeria" (World Bank, 2017, p. 3). The International Monetary Fund (IMF) also had this to say, "fiscal responsibility laws are permanent institutional devices aiming to promote fiscal discipline in a credible, predictable, and transparent manner" (Corbacho & Schwartz, 2007, p. 58).

In the Nigerian case proper, in a nutshell, the FRA provides for

> prudent management of the nation's resources, ensure long-term macroeconomic stability of the national economy, secure greater accountability and transparency in in fiscal operations within a medium-term policy framework, and the establishment of the Fiscal Responsibility Commission to ensure the promotion and enforcement of the nation's economic objectives; and other related matters. (Fiscal Responsibility Act, 2007)

"Prior to the enactment of FRA," Ndan (2013, pp. 82–83) stated:

> Nigeria's fiscal policies were generally characterized by poor planning, massive waste and wrong priorities. The situation was so bad that budget indiscipline was the order of the day. In fact, monies were spent for items not budgeted for and those budgeted releases were delayed or denied. Government at different levels obtained loans indiscriminately. Some loans were obtained even when it was clear there was no need for them. More often than not, they were uncoordinated and not properly documented or accounted for.

Then, the FRA adopted in 2007 and amended in 2011 has brought some sanity "against financial rascality and reckless spending by the government" (Ndan, 2013; Ushie, 2010; World Bank, 2017; IMF, 2010) in Nigeria. This positive development is substantiated pursuant to the impacts brought to bear by the efficacy of and adherence to fiscal prudence measures contained in the FRA. It will be in order to mention some of the key provisions of the FRA that have influenced better accountability and transparency in public finance administration and management in Nigeria:

> The FRA 2007, Part II (Sections 11–17) provides for Medium Term Expenditure Framework (MTEF) (for brevity partial list is below).
>
> Section 11 (1) (a) of the FRA mandates that the "Federal Government after consultation with the States shall cause to prepare and lay before the National Assembly (NASS) for consideration and approval an MTEF for the next three financial years."
>
> Section 11 (3) (a) of the FRA mandate that the "MTEF shall contain a Macroeconomic Framework setting out the macro-economic projections, for the next three financial years, the underlying assumptions for those projections and an evaluation and analysis of the macroeconomic projections for the preceding three financial years."
>
> Section 12 (1) mandates that the "estimates of aggregate expenditure and the aggregate amount appropriated by the National Assembly for each financial year shall not be more than the estimated aggregate revenue plus a deficit, not exceeding three per cent of the estimated GDP or any sustainable percentage as may be determined by the National Assembly for each financial year."

Section 13 of the FRA mandates the

> Minister of Finance to prepare the MTEF after consultation with some MDAs such as the CBN, National Planning Commission, National Economic Commission, National Assembly, Revenue Mobilization Allocation and Fiscal Commission, National Bureau of Statistics, NGOs, the press, civil society organizations, organized private sector, and approved by the Federal Executive Council (FEC) before transmission to the National Assembly.

Section 17 of the FRA mandates the "Federal Government to assist States and Local Governments who so desire to manage their fiscal affairs within the medium-term framework." In other words, Section 17 of the FRA recognizes the constitutional autonomy of the States and Local governments within the context of the Federal system Nigeria operates to manage its public finances in unfettered way (Ndan, 2013, p. 81).

Section 18 of the FRA mandates that "annual budgets of the Federal Government, including the MDAs, shall be derived from the MTEF as approved by the National Assembly pursuant to section 81 (1) of the Constitution." The MTEF is prepared every year and submitted to the National Assembly not later than August every year proceeding the next three financial years.

In 2015, the government approved the Treasury Single Account (TSA) program, which consolidated disparate government revenue collection points. The TSA is "expected to block all loopholes and leakages of financial resources of the government and also ensure a robust financial management system" (Isa, 2016, p. 66). And the TSA seems to be making an impact. According to one report, the TSA saved Nigeria ₦56.4 billion in bank overdraft charges in 2016–2017 (Okwe, 2017).

Meanwhile, very successful periodic elections and due process in the resolution of election disputes are deepening democracy and building institutional trust as well (see, for example, Owen & Usman, 2015, pp. 455–471). According to the United States Institute of Peace (USIP), while "Nigeria still has significant work to do in improving national, State, and Local governance. . . . National and State elections in 2019 were deeply competitive, with scattered instances of violence amid a mostly peaceful process. . . . Overall, Nigeria has made major strides in its democratic development" (United States Institute of Peace, 2019). The USIP is not alone.

Several studies substantiate the thesis that periodic elections can advance and do have positive effect on democracy, due process, and build institutional trust, and this could lead to what Carbone and Cassani (2016, p. 52) called a "virtuous cycle" in governance. In essence, Diamond (2005, p. 14) stated, "the indispensable requirement for a country to be a democracy is that all its principal positions of political power be decided by regular, meaningful, free and fair elections," thereby deepening democracy. Lindberg (2006, p. 140) found that "there is a value inherent in the holding of elections." In Africa [Nigeria] particularly, Lindberg found that elections have been largely beneficial to democratization—"elections in Africa shows that an uninterrupted series of competitive elections imbues society with certain democratic qualities. Repeated elections, regardless of their relative freeness or fairness appear to have a positive impact on human freedom and democratic values" (Lindberg, 2006, p. 140; Lindberg, 2009). Carbone and Cassani (2016, p. 36) also apprised that "elections are indicators of democracy and even potential drivers of democratic progress."

In support of USIP's findings, Carbone & Cassani (2016, p. 33) found that "reiteration of elections can be instrumental in the advancement and institutionalization of democracy in Nigeria" and Africa in general. Voting does not always advance democratization, but it sometimes does (Carbone & Cassani, 2016). The 2015 election in Nigeria, in particular, demonstrated opportunity for democratic progress through elections. As Carbone & Cassani (2016, p. 34) rightfully summarized:

> Marking an unprecedented watershed in the history of Nigeria, opposition candidate Muhammadu Buhari soundly defeated incumbent president Goodluck Jonathan. Africa's most populous country and largest economy joined the limited number of sub-Saharan states whose voters had been able to oust a sitting president and hand power to the opposition. While political continuities are bound to hamper Nigeria's political renewal and its tortuous progress towards democratic politics, the achievement of a government turnover via elections represents a new cornerstone upon which to continue building. Its full importance is best understood when interpreted in light of the electoral path that the country has followed since 1999, and compared with the trajectories experienced by other African countries over the past 25 years.

By this singular act, Nigeria has demonstrated unambiguously that "positive political change remains possible even after years of apparent stagnation. . . . In Nigeria, previous electoral rounds proved fundamental to instilling respect for term limits, presidential successions, to improving electoral administration, and to gaining familiarity with the game of ballot-box competition" (Carbone & Cassani, 2016, pp. 50–51), and by extension entrenching democracy.

It is very important to point out that, in spite of its oil-rich status, in 2005, Nigeria secured $18 billion debt write-off, indeed out of the $30 billion it owed to the Paris Club. In 2017, in the midst of mounting challenges, the Buhari administration developed economic blueprint titled "Economic Recovery and Growth Plan 2017–2020" aimed at improving the economy. Very importantly, the government also introduced the Agricultural Transformation Agenda (ATA) between 2010 and 2014 as part of its Agricultural Sector Strategy, which is geared toward reforms in agricultural infrastructure as a way to boost agricultural productivity, food and nutrition security, wealth creation, and value chain development (Federal Ministry of Agriculture and Rural Development, n.d). Report shows that during the 2010–2014 interval, the ATA program boosted food production by 21 million metric tons, food import bill fell to ₦635 billion in 2013 from ₦3.2 trillion in

2011, while direct farm employment rose by 3.56 million during the period (*Guardian*, January 26, 2017).

As pointed out before, Nigeria is still a land of promise, which is blessed with abundant material and human resources that the oil-rich country and its leadership can utilize to soar and bring about prosperity for all and sundry in the country. What is lacking, however, is a proper focus of the country's hopes and aspirations, policies that emphasize social justice and shared prosperity as well as true rule of law, root out corruption, stabilize the economy, and ensuring better services and security and, most importantly, accountable and effective leadership.

In this book, I use data and information from various sources for analyzing the dimensions and the effects of the Nigerian crisis, cataloged as touching all aspects of the nation, including the following: economy, budget, spending, poverty, leadership, corruption, infrastructures, insecurity, and so on. In fact, simple back-of-the-envelope calculations and analysis have shown consistent and irrefutable evidences that Nigerian leaders have been mismanaging as well as squandering of the nation's riches, hence its citizenry is worse-off today than they were at independence.

Other sources of information for the book come from native country knowledge of the author, which came from personal manuscripts and records; through reading, study, research; available books, newspapers, periodicals; think tanks, journals, Internet; professional links, public square discussions, oral histories, and government documents. Additional sources include such international organizations and government agencies as the World Bank, IMF, United Nations (UN), OPEC, United States (U.S.), among others.

Unlike any other period in Nigerian history, in the decade of unprecedented oil receipts, more than 20 years of uninterrupted democracy, and according to a 2013 World Bank report, "of why a decade of rapid GDP growth by official statistics, concentrated in the pro-poor areas of agriculture and trade, failed to bring stronger welfare and employment benefits to the population" (World Bank, 2013, p. 1). This book provides both the diagnosis and prognosis of the Nigerian condition in a lucid and unromanticized manner, a situation that makes this book to be of a compelling interest and relevance in African and global issues.

NOTES

1. New Deal—the domestic program of the administration of U.S. president Franklin D. Roosevelt between 1933 and 1939, which took action to bring about immediate economic relief as well as reforms in industry, agriculture, finance, waterpower, labor, and housing, vastly increasing the scope of the Federal government's

activities. *Encyclopedia Britannica*. http://www.britannica.com/EBchecked/topic/411331/New-Deal. The programs were in response to the Great Depression and focused on what historians call the "3 Rs": Relief, Recovery, and Reform. That is Relief for the unemployed and poor; Recovery of the economy and agriculture to normal levels; and Reform of the financial system to prevent a repeat depression.

2. Richard Joseph is usually credited with first using the term prebendalism to describe patron-client or neo-patrimonialism in Nigeria. He wrote: "According to the theory of prebendalism, state offices are regarded as prebends that can be appropriated by officeholders, who use them to generate material benefits for themselves and their constituents and kin groups" (Joseph, 1987).

3. While not dealing with but instructive for Nigeria. Excerpts from "A Contract with America's Middle Class," In John Kerry and John Edwards, *Our Plan for America*. Public Affairs Reports, New York, 2004 (pp. 203–207).

4. "Of the $100 billion expended by the Federal government for the acquisition of 590 public enterprises between 1975 and 1995, only 160 are in economic activities" (*Vanguard*, April 20, 2003: 3pp). "Nigeria has in the past few years invested about ₦800 billion in public-owned enterprises but has within the period realized far below ₦80 billion from such enterprises" (*Vanguard*, March 19, 2004:2pp).

5. "Federal Government may have saved close to $4 billion in 2004 alone for embarking on the privatization of some of the huge public enterprises" (*This Day*, April 28, 2005:2pp). "The BPE has realized ₦26. 9 billion from the sale of Federal Government shares in public enterprises since inception of the program in 1999" (*This Day*, November 26, 2003:4pp).

Chapter 1

The Economy

Shattered

Foremost economist, Adam Smith (1723–1790), averred, "the final measure of an economy is the wellbeing of the people." Franklin D. Roosevelt (1882–1945), former American president, said, "the test of our progress is not whether we add more to the abundance of those who have much, it is whether we provide enough for those who have too little" (Roosevelt, 1937). Joseph Stiglitz, former World Bank chief economist (from 1997 to 2000), argued, "inequality is not inevitable, it is a choice we make with the rules we create to structure our economy" (Stiglitz, 2015, p. 7).

The above quotations attest to several aspects of the ways of life of the Nigerian citizenry that I have chosen to discuss in this chapter irrespective of the fact that those being quoted were non-Nigerians. After all, their words are apt and very much applicable to the varied ways in which Nigerians have found themselves, whether in the arena of one's well-being, the gaping abundance of the wealthy, or the inequality that stares in the face of the abjectly poor in Nigeria. Meanwhile, this opening chapter of the book examines the Nigerian economy and its failure to improve the lives of Nigerians, especially the middle class and the abjectly poor. This state of affairs is, indeed, in spite of the nation's huge oil wealth and talented human capital.

The sad state of affairs is also in spite of the prevailing excruciating poverty even though the 1999 Nigerian Constitution—under the "Fundamental Objectives and Directive Principles of State Policy" (Chapter II) section 14 (2) (b)—provides that "the security and welfare of the people shall be the primary purpose of Government," and section 17 (3) (g) adds that the "provision is made for public assistance in deserving cases or other conditions of need"; yet, "social protection programs remain extremely small scale in the context of high numbers of poor people" (Holmes et al., 2011, p. 1) (World Bank, n.d.[1]). Unfortunately, this state of prevailing poverty among the people is despite the rising popularity of social protection as an antipoverty intervention in Africa and, as confirmed by experts, social protection is still inadequate in Nigeria (Umukoro, 2013). Respective Nigerian governments have been slow to adopt social assistance as a major redistributive program in spite of the deepening poverty profile; furthermore, Nigeria's investment in social assistance has been quite meager, indeed at 0.001% of the GDP (Aiyede et al., 2015). Yet, if Nigeria were to utilize its resources well, the citizens would be better off. Instead, according to President Buhari, Nigerians are subjected to a situation to "beg to survive" (Atoyebi, 2015). Very promptly, one can conclude unequivocally that Nigeria's economic performance, since independence, has been decidedly unimpressive (Iyoha, 2008). To illustrate, the following statement is both apt and instructive:

> It is estimated that Nigeria received over US$228 billion from oil exports between 1981 and 1999 (Udeh, 2002, p. 168), and yet the number of Nigerians living in abject poverty, subsisting on less than US$1 a day more than doubled between 1970 and 2000, and the proportion of the population living in poverty rose from 36 percent to 70 percent over the same period. At official exchange rates, Nigeria's per capita income of US$260 in 2000 was precisely one third of its level in 1980. Meanwhile, during this period, Nigeria's external debt rose almost continuously, as did the share of its GDP owed annually in debt service. (Iyoha, 2008, p. 1)

From the available statistics, a vast majority of Nigerians are poor, not by choice or indolence, but as a result of the incompetence and obdurate failure of the leadership to use the nation's enormous resources to empower the people, ease their sufferings, and eradicate poverty. The ICG, a Belgium-based nongovernmental organization, has therefore proclaimed: "Nigeria is a fractured state. It is rich but Nigerians are poor, many extremely so" (ICG, 2014). This situation echoes what Milton Friedman, an economics Nobel laureate, often described as the "paradox of great need on the one hand and unused resources on the other" (Breit & Hirsch, 2004). At the same time, "corruption, a boom and bust cycle of oil prices and failure to diversify the economy" have left Nigeria in what some experts have described as a "development trap" (ICG, 2006; Bach, 2005, p. 54). Also, "in the absence of checks and balances" (ICG, 2006), one can underscore the fact that the state has failed to fulfill most of its major functions, and large segments of the public have ceased to expect social services, public utilities, infrastructure, security, or administration from it. Many groups have resorted to self-help measures through ethnic, religious, community, or civic organizations (ICG, 2006).

THEORIES

The presentation of the cited theories in the book in this section of the book, chapter 1, is important because it offers the reader, from the onset, a one stop and very concise-optimized version of the theories used in this book to help address and explain Nigeria's developmental and leadership challenges, as they have been analyzed throughout the book. While it complements the overall efforts, it does not replace the theories already prodigiously and lucidly enumerated in the book. In addition, this segment is simply a converged summary of cited theories, which has been done to curtail if not totally eliminate the drudgery for the reader of voluminous and disparate details. Furthermore, it is to offer the reader an alternative nimble reading choice, while, at the same time, preserving and drawing attention to the broader detailed backdrop of social, economic, and political developments in Nigeria covered in the entire book. Perhaps most important, the theories indicate that contemporary Africa [Nigeria] leadership and development problems cannot be explained within the context of a single theoretical perspective (Bradshaw & Tshandu, 1990). Instead, scholars must combine and modify existing theories of international political economy (IPE) to explain and reflect the unique challenges facing modern Africa [Nigeria] (Bradshaw & Tshandu, 1990).

Meanwhile, the listing of these theories is not by themselves the silver bullet to Nigeria's myriad problems; instead, it presents a correct and fair understanding, as possible, of the available theoretical options for analyzing and explaining Nigeria's challenges of leadership, development, modernization, globalization, and nation building.

Colonialism Theory

Colonialism theory suggests "there are significant disparity of power between those who govern and those on whom foreign rule is imposed" (Emerson, 1969, p. 3). It holds that it is for economic reasons that colonial powers justify their presence (Balandier & Cunneen, 1952), and for "any colony to be of value to the mother country it must contribute revenue to her" (Kittrell, 1965, p. 190). According to colonialism theory, "the colonial policy was born of monopoly, of the exportation of capital and the search for economic zones of influence" (Julien, 1948, quoted in Balandier & Cunneen, 1952, p. 15), and hence "colonies exist for the economic benefit of the mother country and are useless unless they help to achieve profit" (Nowell, Webster, & Magdoff, 2020). Furthermore, the colonialism theory explains that the colonial system is an extra-economic hegemonial relationship designed only for exploitation (Gottheil, 1977). In this context, the disposition and problems of contemporary African politics and underdevelopment are believed to have taken roots from and been shaped by colonialism (Osaghae, 2006).

From the foregoing, it is indisputable that "modern African politics for the most part is a product of the colonial experience" (Ekeh, 1975, p. 93). Walter Rodney (1972, p. 29) puts it in a vivid context: "In order to understand the present economic conditions in Africa, one needs to know why it is that Africa has realized so little of its natural potential, why so much of its present wealth goes to non-Africans who reside for the most part outside of the continent." In response, Heldring and Robinson (2013) revealed "Africa is poorer today than it would have been had colonialism not occurred," and Rodney (1972) enjoined "European colonialism underdeveloped Africa." Also, in Martin's (1982, p. 221) thought "colonialism is one of the major causes of the continued state of underdevelopment and dependency in Africa in spite of its enormous wealth and tremendous economic potential." Concomitantly, "colonialism financed the development of the West and enabled colonial 'primitive accumulation' for West's economic-industrial take-off" (Dossa, 2007, p. 891). In this milieu, Karl Marx pointed out that colonialism foisted "the extirpation, enslavement and entombment in the mines of the indigenous Americans, the start of the conquest and plunder of East Indies [India], and the conversion of Africa into a preserve for the commercial hunting of black skins," that is, black slavery (Marx, 1867, *Capital* vol. I, Chapter 31—The Genesis of Industrial Capitalism, p. 533; Dossa, 2007, p. 891).

Bias against Africa Theory

The "bias against Africa" theory explains that (French, 2014, para. 5 and 6)

> global development experts who control development agenda have systematically betrayed underdeveloped countries [including African nations] . . . technocratic advisers attach scant importance to the histories of the countries they work on. . . . They disregard evidence indicating that the highest benefits to a society come from the spontaneous, uncoordinated actions of mostly small actors whose talents are allowed to flourish, as opposed to top-down initiatives involving the state or outside donors.

In support, the Malawian economist Thandika Mkandawire (2014, p. 174) argued that the bias against Africa problem impinges on development and raised "concerns about the competence and ideas of expatriate planners who were imposed on Africa as technical assistants or plan ghost writers." These conclusions reinforce Rajan and Subramanian's (2005) thought that "for aid to be effective in the future, the aid apparatus will have to be rethought." Therefore, it is consequential that bias against Africa's theoretical framework must be brought to bear on explaining African development challenges, but also, it is pertinent to measuring the effectiveness, or otherwise, of foreign aid and development assistance from the West to Africa, vis-à-vis, Nigeria.

It is important to note that William Easterly, a former World Bank economist with extensive work experience in Africa, is a chief proponent of the bias against Africa theory. His theory is particular on the shortcomings of Western sponsored aid to Africa; he famously asks, "Can Foreign Aid Buy Growth?", "Can the West Save Africa?" Easterly is of the view that West's foreign aid-financed "Big Push" paradigm for Africa, instead of helping Africa to boost development and mitigate poverty, has not only failed to spur growth and development in Africa, but also has made Africa to fall deeper into the "poverty trap" (Easterly, 2007). In a similar view prior, maybe not in the same term and circumstance, but nonetheless insightful, Boone (1995) found "foreign aid does not significantly increase investment and growth, nor benefit the poor as measured by improvements in human development indictors." More recently, Clapham (2018, p. 1157) argued "whatever the formal ideologies of donors . . . at an operational level donors are driven largely by 'value for money' criteria that emphasize the visible returns on their investments."

Ethnic Fragmentation Theory

The ethnic fragmentation theory stresses that "greater ethnolinguistic fractionalization can produce corruption" (Cerqueti, Coppier, & Piga, 2008, p. 19), "impede national integration and nation building, and significantly endanger prospects for peaceful coexistence" (Mbaku, 2018, p. 7). Ethnic fragmentation theory further informs that "ethnic tensions are common around the world and it is an important factor in explaining poor economic policymaking, low quality of government, and delays in development" (Alesina & Zhuravskaya, 2008). For instance, a popular explanation of sub-Saharan African states' failures is the linguistic and ethnic fragmentation of many countries in the continent (Easterly & Levine, 1997). To expatiate, Easterly and Levine (1997, p. 1203) contend that "ethnic diversity not only contribute to Africa's growth tragedies," concurrently, "it explains a significant part of the problems of low schooling, political instability, underdeveloped financial systems, distorted foreign exchange markets, high government deficits, and insufficient infrastructure in Sub-Saharan Africa." In turn, the ethnic fragmentation is often a result of absurd boundaries left by former colonizers (Alesina & Zhuravskaya, 2008), or, what Easterly and Levine (1997, p. 1213) described as the "tragicomic determination of the borders of African nations by European powers in the nineteenth century that split up ethnic groups and worsened pre-existing high levels of ethnic and linguistic diversity." Nigeria is no exception.

About Nigeria, specific, Chudi Uwazurike (1996, p. 1) wrote: "The single most critical factor that has spun a red ribbon across most of Nigeria's travails, remains malignant ethnicity." (Osaghae, 2003, p. 1) also aptly observed:

> The pervasiveness of ethnic politics in Nigeria is taken to be symptomatic of the aggravated crisis of legitimacy that has engulfed the state, and is explained in terms of the proven efficacy of the ethnic strategy, the weakness of alternative identities and political units, the prevailing milieu of lawlessness that has enveloped the country's political landscape, and the inability of the state to act as an effective agency of distributive justice.

Okwudiba Nnnoli (1993, p. 34) added ethno-nationalism [ethnic fragmentation] in Nigeria is "associated with cultural prejudice and social discrimination." One of the most egregious example of the ethnic fragmentation problem in Nigeria is the obnoxious "indigene and non-indigene" state government policy in Nigeria whereby citizens are marginalized and discrimination against based on their ethnic background or "traditional roots, regardless of the fact that they may have lived" or worked and paid taxes "in a particular locality for generations" (Campbell & Page, 2018, p. 10).

In this respect, from the foregoing, Campbell and Page (2018, p. 10) argued "all Nigerians are not created equal before the law." It is worth recalling a 2006 report by Human Rights Watch:

> As a matter of government policy, many states refuse to employ non-indigenes in their state civil services, and most if not all of Nigeria's thirty-six states deny them the right to compete for academic scholarships. State universities generally discriminate against non-indigenes in their admissions policies and charge higher fees to non-indigene students who do manage to secure admission. Non-indigenes must also contend with a range of less formal discriminatory practices, such as barriers to political participation and discrimination in the provision of basic services and infrastructure to their communities that government does nothing to stop or even discourage.

In this situation, scholars Rotimi Suberu and Larry Diamond (2002) in a paper on ethnic conflict in Nigeria argued "ethnic fragmentation" reinforces "socioeconomic underdevelopment" and polarization "in Nigeria." No surprise, Uwazurike (1996, p. 11) argued that "Nigeria's geo-ethnic injustice is a strong delegitimizing current."

Disease Factor Theory

The disease factor theory associates Africa's economic devastation and underdevelopment with diseases. Several studies suggest that the problem may have root in colonialism (Acemoglu, Johnson, & Robinson, 2000; Turshen, 1977; Turshen, 1984; Janssens, 1980; Lorcin, 1999). Tilley (2016, p. 749) stated:

> The end of colonial rule in sub-Saharan Africa involved its own forms of structural and real violence. . . . European governments also withdrew medical personnel, cut funding for health services, and allowed disease control efforts to lapse . . . epidemiological challenges remained and sometimes increased. . . . State health systems were also typically understaffed and underfunded, making it difficult to fulfill their mandate and raising questions about distributive justice . . . colonial rule marginalized forms of care and therapy that made sense to many people.

Coghe (2020) is also of the view that

> there is little doubt that colonialism itself had aggravated the burden of disease[malaria] . . . military conquest, oppressive economic policies, and increased labor mobility facilitated the spread of infectious diseases such as smallpox, sleeping sickness, or TB: these factors worsened the social determinants of health and hence increased Africans' general susceptibility to "disease" and underdevelopment.

Malaria, specifically, has been found to be a major threat to public health and economic development in Africa (Ntuomi et al., 2004; CDC, 2021; WHO, 2020; Gallup & Sachs, 2001; Sachs & Malaney, 2002), with Nigeria included. In this connection, Dumett (1968, p. 153) noted that "malaria is the most pernicious malady of the tropics." Medical historian, Randall Packard, added that "malaria clearly imposes microeconomic costs on those it afflicts" (Packard, 2009, p. 54), "malaria blocks development," and "it enslave populations, preventing economic growth" (Packard, 2001, p. 593) including in tropical Africa. According to World Health Organization (WHO), Africa carries a disproportionately high share of the global malaria burden, with 94% of the global malaria cases and deaths in 2019, the most recent data available (WHO, 2020). In 2019, the three countries with highest malaria cases in the world are in Africa: Nigeria (27%), Democratic Republic of the Congo (DRC) (12%), and Uganda (5%) (WHO, 2020, p. xiv). Likewise, the top three countries with the highest global malaria deaths are in Africa: Nigeria (23%), DRC (11%), and Tanzania, 5% (WHO, 2020, p. xv).

A 2001 influential study by economists John Gallup and Jeffrey Sachs, "The Economic Burden of Malaria," found that "poverty and malaria are intimately connected in Africa (Africa is intensively malarial)," and Nigeria is no exception. The cross-country regressions of 150 countries for the 1965–1990 period found that countries with intensive malaria grew 1.3% less per person per year, and a 10% reduction in malaria was associated with 0.3% higher growth (Gallup & Sachs, 2001). In fiscal terms, the average GDP per capita for the malarial countries was $1,526, compared with an average income of $8,268 in the countries without severe malaria, five times higher (Gallup & Sachs, 2001). Most recently, according to Johns Hopkins Bloomberg School of Public Health (2021), the economic impact of malaria is estimated to cost Africa $12 billion yearly, in health care costs, absenteeism, days lost in school, decreased productivity because of brain damage from cerebral malaria, and loss of investment and tourism. Overall, households in Africa lose estimated 25% of their income to malaria annually. In Nigeria, specifically, according to Nigeria's Federal Ministry of Health (2010, 2014), malaria induces estimated ₦132 billion (about $364 million) losses annually in the form of treatment costs, prevention, and lost work hours.

Globalization Theory

Globalization is broadly defined as the "economic integration of the world economy" (IMF, 2008, p. 2). At the heart of globalization are open markets—free trade, unrestricted movement of people, capital, goods, and services across national boundaries. Globalization is not a new concept, because it is a well-established economic practice expressed in various forms, such as international trade, foreign direct investments (FDIs), capital market flows, and trade bloc alliances. Not to mention the rise of Internet giants, such as Amazon, Apple, Facebook, Google, Netflix, and Microsoft (Winseck, 2017) which have revolutionized commerce and global interaction. Yet, not until the dawn of the 1990s did the concept of globalization begin to take hold. Since then, global markets and institutions continued to grow in importance. Several studies (Reye, 2001; Guillén & Suárez, 2005; World Bank, 2016) indicate that the major cause of this development is the increasing flexibility of technology to connect people around the world, especially the emergence of the Internet, the "greatest information and communications revolution in human history" (World Bank, 2016, p. xiii).

The central element of the globalization theory is that it takes global perspective in determining the unit of analysis, as opposed to focusing strictly on the nation-state (Reyes, 2001). In that encompassing mode, the globalization theory also assumes that the Internet has increasingly enabled global integration and interaction and has created new environment for carrying out global economic transactions (Reye, 2001) influenced by market economies, rightfully warranting the appellation of the Internet as "a global digital market" (World Bank, 2016, p. 297). Meanwhile, in the process, globalization has created both "winners and losers," and left-behinders, manifested in rising inequality and poverty, with associated anger, resistance, and "discontent" (Stiglitz, 2002). In other words, in spite of the "digital dividends of the Internet" (World Bank, 2016), optimism gave way to disappointment as it became apparent that the benefits of globalization had been minimal (Nissanke & Thorbecke, 2010), especially to those who feel that the "game is rigged." Africa is not immune to the maladies of globalization.

As Nissanke and Thorbecke (2010) noted, "despite the enormous potential of globalization in accelerating economic growth and development through integration into the world economy, the transfer of technology, and the transmission of knowledge . . . concerns have been raised as to why globalization, so far, has not contributed more to poverty alleviation in Africa." In essence, in Africa, suffice it to say, globalization has "not gone beyond platitude in minimizing the risk of unintended negative consequences" (Acemoglu & Robinson, 2008, p. 1). Africa carries more burden of the losers, or left-behinders, from globalization. The rapid spread of the "third wave" (Huntington, 1991) of democratization to sub-Saharan Africa in the 1990s represented the most significant political change in the continent since the independence period in the 1960s (van de Walle, 1999). On the impetus of this unprecedented wave of democratization, "most economies in Africa significantly liberalized their trade and investment policy regimes" (Nissanke & Thorbecke, 2007), not only as a way to attract much needed FDIs and capital, but also as a means to undergo structural economic transformation to better integrate into the global economy. In a relative term, this could be similar to what political sociologist, Seymour Martin Lipset, called "some social requisites of democracy" (Lipset, 1959, p. 69)—those factors especially "economic development and political legitimacy" that could help to sustain democracy.

Globalization has been found to be an additive factor of Africa's underdevelopment, because "African countries have benefited less from the positive effects of globalization compared to other parts of the world in terms of economic growth and development" (Nissanke & Thorbecke, 2007). This is because as Umezurike (2012) explained, "economic reforms in Africa have been largely volatile and contradictory primarily because they respond both to the laws of the free market [globalization] and to domestic social struggle," and in the process have "wreaked havoc on African economies" (Umezurike, 2012), exemplified in escalating poverty, inequality, and underdevelopment, and thereby may have "consigned many to irredeemable misery" (Clapham, 1996, p. 809) in Africa. Additionally, it has been suggested, perhaps, globalization has precipitated "a race to the bottom in wages, regulatory standards, and social protections" (Drezner, 2004, p. 477), if not "another form of re-colonization of African countries" (Lere, 2014, p. 153), especially given Africa's weak clout and disproportionate vulnerability in the global configuration.

Resource Curse Theory

The resource curse theory is a body of political and economic literature, which examines the link between resource abundance and poor economic growth (Matti, 2010). In addition, the resource curse theory also helps researchers and scholars to understand and analyze how "resource-exporting countries are negatively affected by political, economic, and social distortions" (Mahler, 2010, p. 7).

Take illustration from Nigeria from the spectrum of petroleum and natural gas resources induced negative economic impact, especially through the influence of corruption on institutional quality and standard of living. Sala-i-Martin and Subramanian (2013, p. 570) argued, "The Nigerian experience provides a telling proof of this aspect of natural resources. Waste and corruption from oil rather than Dutch disease has been responsible for its poor long run economic performance." Prior, the authors alluded "Nigeria has been a disastrous development experience" (Sala-i-Martin & Subramanian (2003), demonstrated "very robustly" on how "oil in particular exert a negative and nonlinear impact on growth via their deleterious impact on institutional quality" through corruption.

Although partly divergent, but nonetheless related, resource curse theory can also be applicable to explain the "oil-violence link" (Mahler, 2010) in the Niger Delta region of Nigeria. The oil factor influences the occurrence of violence in the Delta region and represents yet another example of the curse natural resources can engender, further contributing to underdevelopment and instability in Nigeria. In a systematic way, it shows both the endogenous and exogenous contextual factors pertinent to explaining the "dynamics of an economy of violence, with the involvement of security forces, politicians, and corporate entities in illegal oil theft, and inherently perpetuating violent conflicts" (Mahler, 2010), which further undermines "economic growth" (Auty, 1993, 2008; Sachs & Warner, 2001; Ross, 2004, 2006; Fearon, 2004; Fearon & Laitin, 2003) and nation building. In this respect, the assumptions of the rentier state theory, vis-à-vis resource curse theory, concerning the usual socioeconomic distortions in petro-states due to the self-privileging of the elites instead of productive reinvestment (Beck, 2007, p. 46 quoted in Mahler, 2010, p. 29) apply strongly to the case of Nigeria (Mahler, 2010, p. 29).

Institutional Theory

Institutional theory "emphasizes the quality of regulatory framework, the capacity of government institutions to enforce compliance with standards and ensure credibility, the rule of law and fighting corruption, protection of property rights, and government effectiveness" (Desta &Hirsch, 2012, p.

133). Also, institutional theory views institutions as "equilibrium constraints . . . non-technologically determined constraints that influence social interactions and provide incentives to maintain regularities of behavior" (Greif, 1998, p. 80). In other words, governance quality, political stability, transparent institutions, anticorruption, rule of law, and accepted behavior bear positively on economic growth (Barro, 2003, 2013; Fukuyama, 2008, 2011, 2014; Acemoglu & Robinson, 2008; Acemoglu, 2008; North, 2008; Rodrik, 2008).

Ancient Greek philosopher Aristotle (384 BC–322 BC) wrote: "Where the laws [institutions] are not supreme, there demagogues spring up" (*Politics*, Book IV, Chap 4, p. 179). Acemoglu and Johnson (2005, p. 950) and others (Dani Rodrik; Douglas North) have also confirmed, "good institutions will simultaneously support private contracts and provide checks against expropriation by the government or other politically powerful groups." Rodrik (2008) stated: the quality of institutions "holds the key to prevailing patterns of prosperity around the world." North (1991, p. 97) stated: "institutions are the humanly devised constraints that structure political, economic and social interaction. . . . Institutions provide the incentive structure of an economy; as that structure evolves, it shapes the direction of economic change towards growth, stagnation, or decline." A priori, "institutions as a key determinant of incentives have a major effect on economic outcomes, including economic development, growth, inequality, and poverty" (Acemoglu & Robinson, 2008, p. 2).

However, many developing countries lack the capacity to perform vital institutional tasks (such as fighting corruption and protection of property rights), and when they do they can be murky and prone to corruption and abuses (Myrdal, 1968). Africa including Nigeria is no exception. According to Desta and Hirsch (2012, p. 127), "African poverty and stagnation is the greatest tragedy of our time" and Africa's weak internal institutions and external factors are partly to blame (Collier & Gunning, 1999; Sachs & Warner, 1997). Hence, Africa's [Nigeria] weak institutions and related political development have adverse impact on economic development and social progress in Africa (Nwagbara, 2019), and at the same time, "pose challenges to those who wish to solve the problem of development and poverty in Africa" (Acemoglu & Robinson, 2008, p. v).

Cost Disease Theory

The American economist, William Baumol, advanced the "cost disease" theory (Baumol & Bowen, 1965; Baumol, 1967; Baumol, 2012). The underlying premise of Baumol's theory is that innovation enables workers to produce more output in different sectors of the economy, such as in agriculture and in manufacturing, which pushes up wages nationwide. The cost disease theory, in reverse, is fit to explain and analyze the high cost of governance in Nigeria.

In the Nigerian case proper, the factor that pushes up the cost of government is not innovation in the governmental process or service delivery, but rather, it is because of the impact of deep-rooted systematic cost disease problem known as the "Nigerian factor," particularly the abuse of office and official position for personal gain. Ameh (2017, p. 678) offered a corroboration of this phenomenon: "Nigerian factor is a corrupt value system and mind-set which are learnt either consciously or unconsciously, which propels an individual to seek for self-gratification against the collective interest and growth of the nation." High cost of governance in Nigeria is particularly fueled by the headwinds of fraud, waste, abuse, corruption, and theft. Campbell and Page (2018, p. 2) summarized it vividly,

> If Nigeria is a democracy, it is also a kleptocracy, a nation characterized by a type of corruption in which government or public officials seek personal gain at the expense of those being governed. Throughout the post-independence period, wholesale looting of the state by members of the political class has accelerated. . . . Kleptocracy and government dishonesty have corrosive effects on popular confidence in governance.

Prebendal Theory

The scholar, Richard Joseph (1987), has argued forcefully that the prebendalism concept offers a useful theoretical framework to analyze and understand the dynamics of Nigerian politics and government, especially concerning the endemic problem of corruption, and the games the political class and "overdetermined interest group" (Uwazurike, 1996, p. 10) play to "gain a decisive advantage" (Nugent, 1989, p. 222). The German sociologist, Max Weber (1864–1920), popularized the concept of prebendalism, historically rooted in feudal societies. By way of definition, a "prebend" "is a public office procured by an individual in return for loyal service to a lord and retained for his personal use and for benefiting his own followers" (Mozaffar, 1989, p. 500). In other words, prebendalism invariably also means the use of official position for personal gain. Nigeria offers a perfect example because of its odious history of corruption, especially governmental corruption.

From this purview, in the Nigerian case, Joseph's work "demonstrates the centrality in the Nigerian political economy of the fierce struggle for control of state power and its spoils" (Othman, 1989, p. 211). This tendency is premised on the "justifying principle that public offices should be competed for and then utilized for the personal benefit of office-holders as well as of their reference or support group" (Joseph, 1987, p. 8), invariably putting personal benefit over public purpose. This process has been widely understood as part of a process of appropriation and assimilation by African [Nigerian] elites and their followers in the modern state structures presumably created at independence (Hoffmann & Nolte, 2013). "Thus Nigeria," according to Uwazurike (1996, p. 4), "with an elite segment anchored in a system of prebendalism and similar privileges, is turned into a rentier state where its most dynamic core exchanges state patronage for real production and a stake in the world market beyond their narrow base." Similarly, Joseph contends that "prebendalism in Nigeria is socio-culturally rooted in clientelism, which links individuals from similar as well as different factions, classes and ethnic groups in hierarchical relations centered around the exchange of political support for material resources" (Mozaffar, 1989, p. 501). Consequently,

> a prebendal system will be seen not only as one in which public offices are allocated and then exploited as benefices by the office holders, but also as one where such a practice is legitimated by a set of political norms according to which the appropriation of such offices is not just an act of individual greed, or, ambition but concurrently the satisfaction of the shorter objectives of a subset of the general population. (Joseph, 1987, p. 67)

Hence, to aptly generalize, "to a large extent, prebendalism has become a national identity-shaper" (Uwazurike, 1996, p. 15) and a zero-sum game in Nigeria, where "patron-based fiscal administration" (Suberu, 2018, p. 184) and "illicit kleptocratic accumulation by the well-connected" (Uwazurike, 1996, p. 11) are increasingly and dangerously shaping the destiny of the country, further escalating mass poverty, economic decline, and anxiety.

State Failure Theory

There is plenty of literature on state failure in Africa (Bates, 2008a; Bates, 2008b; Bates, 2008c; Hagmann & Hoehne, 2009; Herbst, 1997; Herbst & Joseph, 1997; Jackson & Rosberg, 1982; Milliken, 2003; Krause, 2002). Nigeria provides "a unique and disturbing opportunity to explore" (Bates, 2008, p. 297) the state failure hypothesis because her post-independence history (except for the short interval of Murtala Mohammed's leadership) reveals successive leadership failures. In addition, the "human tragedies caused" (Herbst, 1997, p. 120) by leadership failures in Nigeria and the "profound economic and political" (Herbst, 1997, p. 120) impacts compel the application of state failure theory to explain Nigeria's leadership crisis.

By these lines of reasoning, state failure theory proposes that Nigeria is a nation at risk, and the "trouble with Nigeria" is bad leadership and poor governance manifested worst in the virtual inability of government to protect life and property (which is the most fundamental purpose of any government: mandated in the 1999 Nigerian Constitution—under the "Fundamental Objectives and Directive Principles of State Policy" (Chapter II) section 14 (2) (b)—provides that "the security and welfare of the people shall be the primary purpose of Government"). A prime example of the inability of the Nigerian government to deliver on security to life and property is acutely shown in the more than a decade Boko Haram deadly insurgency in the country that has left thousands dead, displaced, and livelihoods disrupted. The galling impunity of Boko Haram attacks and feeble government responses, if not, total helplessness to fight the insurgency, increasingly question state authority and subject citizens to live in constant fear.

In addition, state failure theory holds that Nigeria "has fallen prey to an array of destructive forces" (Hagmann & Peclard, 2010, p. 540) foisted by the country's leaderships since independence, exhibited by mutually reinforcing governmental corruption and abuses, malfeasance, bureaucratic dysfunction, mute value, unaccountability, economic mismanagement, perversion to provide for the common good, tepid checks and balances, playing the ethnic card, political instability, citizens disconnect and cynicism, all which has eroded the bright hopes widely held for Nigeria at independence. Furthermore, the state failure theory explains that greed and the political and economic interests of Nigeria's leadership elite are the chief sources of the mismanagement and underdevelopment of the Nigerian state, and have left the country near completely incapable of progress. This alarming situation is poignantly demonstrated by excruciating poverty in the midst of abundant oil and gas wealth, Nigeria became the only member of OPEC to be listed among the world's poorest countries (Carrington, 2015), to the extent that more than 70% of Nigerians are trapped in poverty, half of what it was at independence, according to the World Bank.

Modernization Theory

To keep it simple, some definitional perspectives of modernization theory will be in order. Modernization theory casts development as a uniform evolutionary route that all societies follow, from agricultural, rural, and traditional societies to postindustrial, urban, and modern forms. In other words, all societies, once engaged in the modernization process, follow a predetermined sequence of developmental stages: traditional economies, transition to take-off, take-off itself, drive to maturity, age of high consumption, and postindustrial society (Ynalvez & Shrun, 2015).

Modernization is a process that involves industrialization, urbanization, rationalization, bureaucracy, mass consumption, and adoption of democracy. During this process, traditional societies transform into modern societies

(Crossman, 2019). Modernization theory is the belief that industrialization and economic development lead directly to positive social and political change (Berman, 2009). The basic assumption of modernization theory, in any of its versions, is as follows:

> Modernization consists of a gradual differentiation and specialization of social structures. . . . The specific causal chains consist of sequences of industrialization, urbanization, education, communication, mobilization, and political incorporation, among innumerable others: a progressive accumulation of social changes that ready a society to proceed to its culmination, democratization. (Przeworski & Limongi, 1997)

NIGERIA AT INDEPENDENCE

A diverse body of research shows that, at independence, Nigeria had a strong and impressively growing economy. In his remarkable book, *Foundations of an African Economy: A Study of Investment and Growth in Nigeria*, the economist, Ojetunji Aboyade (1966, p. 25) stated:

> By the time of political independence in 1960, the Nigerian economy appeared to have come a long way from the state of substantial external trade dependence existing at Amalgamation in 1914. The formal process of political consolidation and the evolution into national sovereignty was complete. The foundation for "translating political to economic independence" was now laid. There was a working governmental apparatus for guiding and aiding the economy. Planning, no matter how rudimentary, had become an almost inevitable feature of public debate. With varying degree of effectiveness, the basic structure for improved economic performance was being placed in position—the public utilities, universities, industrial estates, statistical intelligence, experimental research, banking institutions and social welfare schemes. There was a pervasive atmosphere of national self-confidence, rising expectation, acquisitive zeal and infectious enthusiasm. It was an optimistic image of a country that was, so to say, "going places."

The Nigerian historian, Kenneth Dike (1956, pp. 41, 49, and 57; 204–205), also documented the "vigor" of the Nigerian economy and the "striking progress made" before the advent of amalgamation in his seminal book *Trade and Politics in the Niger Delta 1830–1885:*

> Indeed, historians of the 19th Century Nigeria have amply demonstrated the vigor of the economy under stimulating impact of pacification, consolidation

> of indigenous kingdoms, introduction of new crops, promotion of foreign trade and expansion of domestic markets . . . for the nineteenth century the most important trading organization was connected with the trade in palm oil. Early in the century the oil trade was developing and in 1830 had become more vital to the economy of the city-states than the trade in men. . . . The area from which the bulk of the oil was derived lay immediately within the Delta hinterland. The famous "oil markets" which loomed so large in the consular reports of the last century were situated in the palm belt, at the heads of creeks and rivers linking the interior to the coast. . . . Over half of the oil handled in the Delta was sold at Bonny, all of which came from the exclusive markets of Essene, Obunku, Imo, Akwete, Urata, Azumiri, Ohambele, Ngwa (landing port, Aba), and Ndele. . . . The approximate quantity of produce shipped from the Niger valley for the year 1878 was as follows: 5,000 tons of palm oil at £39 a ton (£195,000), 65 tons of ivory at £800 a ton (£52,000), 1,500 tons of shea butter at £39 a ton (£58,000), 150 tons of beri-seed at £24 a ton (£3,600), 50 tons of groundnuts at £12 a ton (£600).

Also, Eicher (1967, pp. 1160–1161) documented:

> It is important to point out that Nigeria produced a sizable agricultural surplus prior to 1900, mainly in the form of cotton and oil palm products. Export data also indicate rapid response of Nigerian farmers to price incentives in the nineteenth century. For example, the volume of cotton exported from Lagos rose fivefold during and after the American Civil War when world supplies were tight, then dwindled later as the world price declined (Berry, 1967, p. 22). Also, the technique of tapping wild rubber trees in the rain forest was brought to Nigeria from Ghana in the early 1890s; rubber exports increased from 5,867 to 5,069,577 lbs. in one year 1894–1895. In brief, Nigeria already had established extensive coastal trade with Western Europe and had developed an overland Saharan desert trade for two centuries prior to becoming a British colony in 1900.

The scholar, James Coleman (1960, pp. 65–66), in his seminal work *Nigeria: Background to Nationalism*, also wrote:

> Several groups in Nigeria had had centuries of contact with Western economic forces prior to the formal establishment of British administration in 1900. For at least three centuries the coastal groups were deeply involved in a semi commercialized economy, first through slave trade, and later, during the latter part of the nineteenth century, through legitimate trade in palm oil and other products. In the far north, sizable commercial communities had grown up around such centers as Kano city, which had been linked with Mediterranean cities via caravan trade

> since the Middle Ages. . . . Within the Northern Region alone at least fourteen basic commodities are produced in one area for consumption in other areas. Between the Northern Region and southern regions, a very active trade has developed; the north ships dried fish, skins, leatherwork, cloth, and cattle to the south and receives kola, citrus, and other foodstuffs in return. The Middle Belt in the Northern Region is a food surplus area supplying yams to food deficit areas such as the plateau mining areas in the north and cocoa growing areas in the Western Region. Coal from the Enugu mines in the Eastern Region supplies the whole country. In addition, there has grown up in almost every area where urbanization has occurred, or where there is a heavy dependence on an export economy, a rather extensive exchange of goods between urban centers and rural areas.

The scholar Peter Bauer (1954) in his notable book, *West African Trade*, which evaluated (at the behest of the British Colonial Office) the organization of trade in the former British West Africa, cataloged the "pervasive economic advance in West Africa," including that of Nigeria; it indicated, "most notably in Southern Nigeria and the Gold Coast (Ghana)"; and he also wrote in one article:

> Before 1885, there was not a single cocoa tree in British West Africa. By the 1930s, there were millions of acres under these and other export crops, the bulk of them owned and operated by non-Europeans. But while I knew this and a good deal else about local conditions, I was nevertheless surprised by much of what I saw, including the extensive economic transformation occurring in large areas and the vigor of economic life of much of the local populations. . . . In this region (West Africa) there were (and are) no European-owned plantations. The large area under cocoa, groundnuts, cotton, and kola nuts has been entirely occupied by farms established, owned, and operated by Africans. The extensive capital involved was made available partly by European trading firms which financed local traders, and partly by direct investment by Africans, the latter in important instances carried out by migrant farmers in regions far from their homes. . . . The traders made available consumer goods and production inputs, and provided the outlets for the cash crops. Their activities stimulated investment and production. The rapid economic progress generally in these areas, of which the large-scale capital formation in agriculture by the local people was a major component, cannot be squared with the idea of the vicious circle of poverty and stagnation. (Bauer, 1984, pp. 28–30)

Kilby (1969, p. 7), in his own important book, *Industrialization in an Open Economy: Nigeria 1945–1966*, noted:

> In 1900 when the British Government took over from the Royal Niger Company, the jurisdiction and administration of the Niger basin, the 373,250

> square miles that would in 1914 be called Nigeria, comprised thousands of largely self-sufficient communities engaged in the traditional production of food, clothing and utensils. Exports in 1900 were £1.7 million, of which palm oil and palm kernels (purchased by European traders operating in the coastal "oil rivers") constituted 90%. With establishment of law and order by the colonial administration, the development of a communications network and the presence of intermediary European traders, the Nigerian economy underwent a process of integration both internally and with the world economy. New crops were introduced—groundnuts, cotton, rubber, cocoa, and cassiterite (tin ore) and coal deposits were uncovered and exploited.

The Caribbean scholar and economics Nobel laureate Arthur Lewis (1969, 1970) provided consummate insight into the "rapid development of the tropical world from 1880–1913," including her "aspects of tropical trade between 1883 and 1965 (including West Africa vis-à-vis Nigeria)":

> Between 1883 and 1913 the exports of tropical trade grew 3.6% annually, slightly higher compared to the 3.2% average growth in the four leading countries, the USA, Britain, Germany, and France. Between 1913 and 1950 the tropics passed through a long depression, associated with world wars and adverse terms of trade. The rate of growth of tropical trade fell to 2.2% per annum between 1913 and 1955. However, since 1955 the volume of tropical trade has again grown very rapidly, namely, by 4.5%. Indeed, it has grown as rapidly as industrial production in the OECD countries. (Lewis, 1969, p. 8)

Lewis continued:

> The demand for tropical produce increased at the same pace as world trade as a whole. The market was especially buoyant for cotton, oilseeds, cocoa, coffee, tobacco, hard fibers, bananas, rubber, and various minerals. . . . For the tropics as a whole food supply kept pace with population growth, while exports increased at an average rate of 36% per annum, with purchasing power in terms of manufactures exactly the same in 1908–12 as in 1879–83. In addition there was a considerable expansion of services, improvements in housing, schooling, etc. . . . The myth spread that economic development was more difficult to achieve in the tropics than in the temperate zones, and writers invented many kinds of structural and ideological explanations, which were left high and dry after 1950, when world trade revived. The truth is the reverse: but for the great depression of 1913 to 1950, several tropical countries would already have reached self-sustaining growth by 1950. When all is said, it remains indisputable that the expansion of exports in tropical countries raised net national income per head between 1880 and 1913. (Lewis, 1970, pp. 13–45)

There are abundant and well documented empirical evidences to support the assertions of Aboyade, Dike, Coleman, Bauer, Kilby, and Lewis. While growth was noticed in several sectors in Nigeria's colonial economy, three areas, namely: (1) commodity exports (specifically palm produce, cocoa, and groundnuts); (2) GDP expansion; and (3) national income growth stood out and shall be evaluated and discussed as performance indicators. This is mainly because, as Aboyade pointed out, "given the relative simplicity of the economy coupled with absence of a comprehensive quantitative data, it become defensible to look at developments in the foreign trade sector in estimating the broad trend of events, at least before the first National Accounts study for 1950" (Aboyade, 1966, p. 3). Aboyade further stated: "In the broad sweep of events between Nigerian Amalgamation in 1914 and her political independence in 1960, the world had experienced two catastrophic wars, a severe depression and a protracted boom. Thus, we have a good platform from which to observe the main trends in the colonial economy" (Aboyade, 1966, p. 3).

In respect to GDP (with reference to the value of final goods and services produced in a country in a given period of time) and national income indicators, their salience, as core components and benchmark measures of national economic accounting, cannot be overemphasized. The U.S. Bureau of Economic Analysis (BEA), for example, noted:

> Because these accounts [GDP and national income] provide a detailed picture of economic activity at a given time, as well as a consistently defined series of measures over time, they are indispensable to researchers, forecasters, government officials, academics, and investors who use them for a wide array of academic, public policy, and other purposes. (U.S. Bureau of Economic Analysis, 2007, p. 1)

In encore, backdrop to the United States but with global disposition:

> GDP is one of the most comprehensive and closely watched economic statistics: It is used by the White House and Congress to prepare the Federal budget, by the Federal Reserve to formulate monetary policy, by Wall Street as an indicator of economic activity, and by the business community to prepare forecasts of economic performance that provide the basis for production, investment, and employment planning. (U.S. Bureau of Economic Analysis, 2014, p. 1)

Of crucial importance is the discussion of Nigeria's identified growth indicators, which have been undertaken below. It starts with the base year of 1900, which was chosen as the beginning period to report on Nigerian cash crops' export data because according to Coleman (1958, p. 4) "it was the year Nigeria emerged as a political unit known to the world and to the people living within its boundaries"; the process paved the way for a better information gathering and reporting, and the concomitant availability of comparable data. Also, as this new book is, in the main, a study of the historical roots of Nigeria's underdevelopment, earlier data on economic performance and growth must be examined, analyzed, and compared to the present economic decline.

Furthermore, Nigeria's pre-independence economic growth and successes must be interpreted against the wider background of social, economic, and political developments of the country. But first and foremost, awareness of the aggregate commodity exports' value, during the period under review, is quite welcome. Before the American Great Depression, which started in 1929, wreaked global economic havoc and brought commodity export trade to a screeching halt, Nigeria recorded rapid export growth and vitality. Helleiner (1966, pp. 5–6; also see Ijere, 1974; Burns, 1963, p. 299) provided granular telescopic insight into the Nigerian exports dynamo in the following words:

> Between 1900 and 1929 great strides were made in the development of the Nigeria export economy. Export volumes and values rose by leaps and bounds. By 1929 export value had increased more than sevenfold, export volume fivefold, implying compounded annual growth rates of 7 and 51/2 percent respectively. Export production in 1929 probably amounted to 5 to 7 percent of gross domestic product. New cash crops such as groundnuts, cocoa, rubber, and cotton brought more and more peasants into contact with the world market and with outside ideas, and reduced Nigeria's former extreme export dependence upon oil palm produce. . . . During these thirty years Nigeria outgrew its original status as a collection, accidentally enclosed within artificial foreign-made boundaries of small, traditional, largely self-sufficient agricultural communities possessing a few, relatively insignificant trading links with North Africa and Europe, though still far from an effective national unit, it now emerged as a group of much larger Regional economies, each increasingly tying itself to the world economy.

However, Nigerian commodity export trade did not only rebound bullishly after World War II; instead, "export prices were also extremely favorable" (Helleiner, 1966). In fact, Bauer described the growth in commodity export trade, at the material time, as "rapid," "phenomenal," and, "in a class by themselves" (Bauer, 1963, p. 195). This was clearly borne out by hard data stemming from export volume and receipts as Helleiner (1966, pp. 30–31) noted:

> In 1952, at which time export volume was roughly 50% higher than its 1945 level, the export price index was over four times the level of 1945. Import prices

rose too during this period but not nearly rapidly, so that the net barter terms of trade moved strongly in Nigeria's favor. As the value of exports soared from £17.2 million in 1945 to £146.2 million by 1954, the import purchasing power of exports rose fourfold. . . . By 1964 the value of exports totaled £210 million. These later increases in export value, unlike those of the immediate postwar years, were achieved mainly through the already mentioned great expansion of the volume of exports.

Now back to the discussion of the earmarked growth indicators. Firstly, [it was] agriculture commodity exports, beginning with palm products.

Agricultural Commodity Exports

The oil palm tree (*Elaeis guineensis*) is native to tropical West Africa and grows wild throughout southern Nigeria (then Eastern, Western, and Midwestern Regions, now, Southeast, South-South, and Southwest) (Helleiner, 1996). The oil palm is a tree crop requiring over 10 years under normal conditions (3–4 years on plantations) to attain maturity (Helleiner, 1996). Oil palm trees may live to be 60–70 years, output usually declining after about 35 years (Helleiner, 1996).

While Nigeria's export trade in palm oil has always existed, the profile rose gigantically following British abolition of the slave trade in the mid-1800s, and palm oil, used in soap making (also used as a cooking oil), became the principal item of trade between Nigeria and the rest of the world (Helleiner, 1996, p. 96). Dike (1956, pp. 49–50) contended:

> With increasing population at the time of the industrial revolution in Britain came changes in social customs and industrial requirements. As British people began to take washing seriously, the demand for soap rose considerably, and palm oil was the chief constituent in its manufacture. The substitution of metal for wooden machinery and the development of railways caused a steep rise in the use of oil as a lubricant. The existing sources of animal fats were not only inadequate but sometimes unsuitable. West African palm oil was found to satisfy these needs. In 1830 the [Niger] Delta was known to be the chief source of this commodity. Henceforth to the British merchant prohibited by the law to deal in men, the slave coasts gained a new prominence as the oil rivers.

Table 1.1 shows foreign trade movements of palm kernels and palm oil exported from Nigeria between 1900 and 1960. Palm kernels' exports volume grew at an average of 6.5% per annum, while palm oil exports rose average of 5.0% per annum, in the same time period.

Table 1.1 Quantity of Palm Products Exports, 1900–1960 (Tons)

Year	*Palm Kernels*	*Palm Oil*	*Year*	*Palm Kernels*	*Palm Oil*
1900	85,624	45,508	1931	254,454	118,179
1901	114,046	56,766	1932	309,061	116,060
1902	132,556	64,167	1933	259,945	128,696
1903	131,898	54,257	1934	289,447	112,773
1904	139,788	57,947	1935	312,746	142,628
1905	108,822	50,562	1936	386,145	162,778
1906	113,347	57,260	1937	337,749	145,718
1907	133,630	65,473	1938	312,048	110,243
1908	136,558	70,460	1939	299,943	121,042
1909	158,849	82,130	1940	235,521	132,723
1910	172,907	76,851	1941	378,124	127,778
1911	176,390	79,387	1942	344,569	151,287
1912	184,625	76,994	1943	331,292	135,268
1913	174,718	83,090	1944	313,530	124,829
1914	162,452	72,531	1945	292,588	114,199
1915	153,319	72,994	1946	277,242	100,885
1916	161,439	67,422	1947	316,376	125,954
1917	185,998	74,619	1948	327,174	139,204
1918	205,167	86,425	1949	375,835	170,145
1919	216,913	100,967	1950	415,906	173,010
1920	207,010	84,856	1951	347,013	149,752
1921	153,354	52,771	1952	374,163	167,288
1922	178,723	87,609	1953	402,872	201,345
1923	223,173	99,439	1954	464,111	208,482
1924	252,847	127,083	1955	433,234	182,143
1925	272,925	128,113	1956	451,069	185,235
1926	249,100	113,267	1957	406,200	166,200
1927	257,206	113,240	1958	441,228	170,508
1928	246,638	127,111	1959	430,608	163,692
1929	251,477	131,845	1960	418,176	183,360
1930	260,022	135,801			

Source: Gerald Helleiner, 1966.

Table 1.2 presents the annual value of palm kernels and palm oil exported from Nigeria between 1900 and 1960. Palm kernels' exports value grew at an average of 50.4% per annum, while palm oil exports receipts climbed average of 32.6% per annum in the same time frame. As at 1960, palm kernels' exports fetched £26.062 million up 3,025% from 1900, while palm oil garnered nearly £14.0 million in external trade, up 1,953% from 1900. One important observation was made in the primary commodity export trade flows, particularly, in the 1933–1943 decade. Meanwhile, that is, while export volume increased from the prior decade, export revenue accruals dropped. During this time, palm kernels' and oil export volume rose 25% (700,000 ton) and 15% (200,000 ton), respectively, from the previous decade, while exports receipts for the former were £26 million, down 38% from £42 million in the prior

Table 1.2 Value of Palm Products Exports, 1900–1960 (£000)

Year	Palm Kernels	Palm Oil	Year	Palm Kernels	Palm Oil
1900	834	681	1931	2,132	1,542
1901	948	813	1932	2,696	1,514
1902	1,274	958	1933	1,899	1,384
1903	1,094	848	1934	1,591	885
1904	1,278	929	1935	2,245	1,656
1905	1,090	858	1936	3,637	2,079
1906	1,194	1,002	1937	3,648	2,364
1907	1,658	1,314	1938	2,172	984
1908	1,425	1,155	1939	1,873	930
1909	1,816	1,447	1940	1,500	1,099
1910	2,451	1,742	1941	2,283	1,047
1911	2,574	1,697	1942	2,458	1,427
1912	2,797	1,655	1943	3,117	1,587
1913	3,110	1,854	1944	3,637	2,030
1914	2,541	1,572	1945	3,496	1,894
1915	1,693	1,462	1946	4,164	2,052
1916	1,740	1,403	1947	9,491	5,038
1917	2,582	1,883	1948	11,451	9,048
1918	3,226	2,704	1949	16,913	11,910
1919	4,948	4,246	1950	16,694	12,072
1920	5,718	4,677	1951	20,059	12,949
1921	2,832	1,656	1952	22,767	17,091
1922	2,810	2,676	1953	22,185	13,020
1923	3,741	2,982	1954	22,791	13,431
1924	4,461	3,911	1955	19,196	13,151
1925	4,937	4,166	1956	20,440	14,866
1926	4,440	3,616	1957	17,959	13,801
1927	4,439	3,375	1958	20,450	12,663
1928	4,423	3,751	1959	25,971	13,808
1929	4,265	3,767	1960	26,062	13,982
1930	3,679	3,250			

Source: Gerald Helleiner, 1966.

decade, and the exports receipts for the latter were £15 million, down 57% from £35 million in the preceding decade. The scenario that played out was that due to the vicissitudes of the seismic event of World War II (1941–1945), commodity prices crashed, and ipso facto reduced export receipts in primary commodity export dependent countries including Nigeria. Also, fluctuations in the business activities level in the principal consuming countries (North America, United Kingdom, and Western Europe) (Helleiner, 1966) and the "big dip for war preparations in 1938" (Aboyade, 1966, p. 4) further reduced export earnings.

Aside from exports, a large amount of palm oil is consumed locally in Nigeria, and it is an "important source of Vitamin A"—good for vision, immune system, and cell growth (National Economic Council, *Economic*

Survey of Nigeria 1959). Also, the oil palm tree is tapped to provide palm wine, which contains the vitamins of the B complex—helps body energy, boosts nerve cells, produces red blood cells, and so on (National Economic Council, *Economic Survey of Nigeria 1959*). Furthermore, palm oil and kernels are used to make soap; palm oil and kernels were sold to the then marketing boards (government appointed buyers), who in turn supplied to local soap manufacturers and other vendors (National Economic Council, *Economic Survey of Nigeria 1959*).

Above all, in ending the discussion on palm oil and kernels, it is noteworthy to stress that, by 1961, Nigeria was the largest exporter of palm kernels and oil, and provided nearly 60% of the world commerce in kernels and almost 30% in palm oil (table 1.3).

Cocoa (*Theobroma cacao*) is native to the Americas (World Cocoa Foundation, n.d.). It was introduced to Nigeria in the late nineteenth century (Amelonado and Amazon are the two principal varieties grown). It is mainly grown in the "cocoa belt" of the then Western Region (now Southwest), principally, in the areas of Abeokuta, Ibadan, Akure, Ife, and Ilesha, where the climate is very conducive for the crop (Helleiner, 1966). Under the Nigerian environment, production does not start until 5–7 years after planting, becomes significant in 7–10 years, and peaks between the 10th and 15th years of the tree's life (Helleiner, 1966). Cocoa is used in producing chocolate, cocoa butter, and different types of cocoa drinks. Table 1.4 shows foreign trade movements of cocoa exported from Nigeria between 1900 and 1960.

Since 1910, exports rose exponentially by nearly 20-fold to more than 52,000 tons by 1930. This was followed by a period of steady and substantial growth, interrupted periodically by "bad weather and blights," which undercut exports to 90,000 tons by 1940. The growth was attributable mainly to increased land

Table 1.3 Shares of World Oil and Kernels Exports, Selected Years

	1938		*1954*		*1961*	
	tons 000's	*%*	*tons 000's*	*%*	*tons 000's*	*%*
Palm Kernels						
Nigeria	312	45.5	464	56.7	411	58.1
West Africa*	521	75.9	674	82.4	615	88.1
World Total	686	100.0	818	100.0	698	100.0
Palm Oil						
Nigeria	110	22.5	208	36.5	165	29.3
West Africa*	136	27.9	226	39.6	192	34.0
World Total	488	100.0	570	100.0	564	100.0

*Gambia, Ghana, Nigeria, Sierra Leone, Cameroon, Benin (Dahomey), Guinea, Côte d'Ivoire (Ivory Coast), Liberia, Guinea Bissau (Portuguese Guinea), Equatorial Guinea (Spanish Guinea), Togo.

Source: Gerald Helleiner, 1966.

Table 1.4 Quantity of Cocoa Exports, 1900–1960 (Tons)

Year	*Qty*	*Year*	*Qty*
1900	202	1931	52,806
1901	206	1932	71,039
1902	307	1933	60,737
1903	281	1934	77,982
1904	531	1935	88,143
1905	470	1936	80,553
1906	723	1937	103,216
1907	933	1938	97,104
1908	1,366	1939	113,841
1909	2,241	1940	89,737
1910	2,932	1941	104,681
1911	4,401	1942	59,937
1912	3,390	1943	87,487
1913	3,621	1944	70,051
1914	4,939	1945	77,004
1915	9,105	1946	100,186
1916	8,956	1947	110,793
1917	15,442	1948	91,449
1918	10,219	1949	103,637
1919	25,711	1950	99,949
1920	17,155	1951	121,478
1921	17,944	1952	114,731
1922	31,271	1953	104,671
1923	32,821	1954	98,373
1924	37,205	1955	88,413
1925	44,705	1956	117,133
1926	39,099	1957	135,300
1927	39,210	1958	87,648
1928	49,163	1959	142,800
1929	55,236	1960	154,176
1930	52,331		

Source: Gerald Helleiner, 1966.

under cultivation, the increased use of insecticides, fungicides, improved seedlings, subsidies, credit programs, extension services by the Western Regional Marketing Board, the Western Region Development Corporation, and the Regional Ministry of Agriculture (Helleiner, 1966). During the war years, there was a slump in the volume of exports, while prices tumbled due to the disruptions of the war and depressed producer prices of the war period. However, at the end of hostilities and the removal of price ceilings by major buyers, especially the United States and United Kingdom, exports recovered and surged, doubled from 77,000 tons in 1945 to more than 154,000 tons by 1960.

Table 1.5 shows the sum of money value of cocoa exports during the 1900–1960 period from Nigeria. Export revenues climbed profoundly during

Table 1.5 Value of Cocoa Exports, 1900–1960 (£000)

Year	*Amount*	*Year*	*Amount*
1900	9	1931	1,093
1901	8	1932	1,461
1902	11	1933	1,144
1903	10	1934	1,290
1904	19	1935	1,584
1905	17	1936	1,997
1906	27	1937	3,660
1907	48	1938	1,572
1908	51	1939	1,776
1909	72	1940	1,583
1910	101	1941	1,769
1911	165	1942	1,043
1912	131	1943	1,542
1913	157	1944	1,338
1914	172	1945	2,150
1915	314	1946	3,780
1916	393	1947	10,650
1917	499	1948	17,879
1918	236	1949	14,697
1919	1,068	1950	18,984
1920	1,238	1951	31,381
1921	436	1952	28,666
1922	871	1953	24,858
1923	922	1954	39,261
1924	980	1955	26,188
1925	1,484	1956	23,985
1926	1,363	1957	26,036
1927	1,999	1958	26,668
1928	2,421	1959	38,289
1929	2,306	1960	36,772
1930	1,756		

Source: Gerald Helleiner, 1966.

the first 20 years of the century, fell briefly in the early 1920s, and regained momentum until the onset of the Great Depression of the 1930s. Except the brief revival in 1936–1937, cocoa exports receipts remained sluggish at a peak well below the previous high until the end of World War II. Thereafter, growth accelerated, rising from a total value of £2.1 million in 1945 to £39.3 million in 1954, a peak that was only repeated again in 1964.

Table 1.6 shows Nigerian share of global cocoa exports for the representative years. Except for the inconsequential dip in 1954, Nigeria supplied an average of almost 20% of world's total cocoa exports volume. The country's total exports volume rose immensely from 105,000 tons in 1937–1939 to 184,000 tons in 1961, a jump of more than 75%. In the West Africa

Table 1.6 Shares of World Cocoa Exports, Selected Years

	Average, 1937–1939		1954		1961	
	tons 000's	%	tons 000's	%	tons 000's	%
West Africa*	477	69.2	451	67.2	777	79.3
Nigeria	105	15.2	98	14.6	184	18.8
World Total	689	100.0	671	100.0	980	100.0

*Nigeria, Ghana, Côte d'Ivoire (Ivory Coast), Cameroon, Togo, Equatorial Guinea (Spanish Guinea), Gabon, São Tomé and Príncipe.
Source: Gerald Helleiner, 1966.

subregion, Nigeria contributed nearly 25% of the region's total world cocoa exports.

Groundnuts or peanuts (*Arachis hypogaea*) are believed to have been originally introduced into West Africa by the Portuguese and are produced in Northern Nigeria (Helleiner, 1966). Groundnuts are an annual crop, requiring annual planting and replanting and considerable amount of care in cultivation (Helleiner, 1966). They are legumes (soil manure boosters) and the seeds ripen underground. Groundnut has many uses. It is used as edible oil with high protein content, and nutritional value as a foodstuff (Helleiner, 1966).

Table 1.7 shows external trade movements of groundnut exported from Nigeria between 1900 and 1960. The completion of the rail link from the coast to the groundnut growing areas in 1911–1912 induced instantaneous surges in the volume of groundnuts produced for export (Helleiner, 1966). Prior to this time, groundnut exports did not exceed 2,000 tons per year. However, by 1916, Nigeria was exporting over 50,000 tons, surged to more than 146,000 tons of the product per year by 1930, except for the decline in the 1922–1923 period, compared to the 1916–1918 period.

Growth, in peanut production, continued to expand even during the Great Depression, indeed reaching 245,000 tons in 1934 and climbed to 326,000 tons in 1937. The lower prices and other difficulties of the war years resulted in lower export levels, but growth resumed after the war (Helleiner, 1966). From 1946 to 1960, growth held steady topping half a million tons per year in 1958, except for the decline in the 1950–1951 period; however, this was attributed to "groundnut crop failure in 1950–1 and the payment of low prices to producers" (Bauer, 1963, p. 196).

Table 1.8 shows the aggregate money value of groundnuts' exports during the 1900–1960 period from Nigeria. By 1900, Nigeria earned a miniscule £4,000 from groundnut exports. However, by 1913 with the impetus of the railway that eased groundnut transportation in the North, the volume of groundnut exports increased rapidly from then on to 1929, representing 14% of total Nigerian exports as against only 2.6% of the total in 1913 (Helleiner, 1966). The Great Depression had less devastating impact on groundnut

Table 1.7 Quantity of Groundnut Exports, 1900–1960 (Tons)

Year	*Qty*	*Year*	*Qty*
1900	599	1931	159,739
1901	210	1932	188,123
1902	322	1933	204,606
1903	468	1934	244,886
1904	777	1935	183,993
1905	790	1936	218,389
1906	1,661	1937	325,929
1907	1,936	1938	180,136
1908	1,654	1939	147,263
1909	1,615	1940	169,480
1910	995	1941	247,176
1911	1,179	1942	194,190
1912	2,518	1943	142,152
1913	19,288	1944	156,194
1914	16,997	1945	176,242
1915	8,910	1946	285,668
1916	50,368	1947	255,866
1917	50,334	1948	245,155
1918	57,554	1949	378,321
1919	39,334	1950	311,221
1920	45,409	1951	141,359
1921	50,979	1952	260,444
1922	23,890	1953	326,725
1923	22,887	1954	427,868
1924	78,266	1955	396,904
1925	127,226	1956	448,084
1926	126,799	1957	302,388
1927	90,773	1958	513,180
1928	103,161	1959	498,228
1929	147,379	1960	332,916
1930	146,371		

Source: Gerald Helleiner, 1966.

exports earnings; in fact, groundnut exports' receipts actually did well, reaching a high of £4.1 million in 1937, but plummeted thereafter through 1943 except for 1941. The early postwar period witnessed a huge upswing in export value. Even though

> a large proportion of the increase in world oilseed prices was withheld from Nigeria by the British Government through the West African Produce Control Board and later the price agreements, sufficient increases were passed along, together with increases in export volume, to produce an increase in the value of groundnut exports from £2.7 million in 1945 to £18.9 million in 1949 and a peak of £29.9 million in 1954. Export instability in this immediate postwar period was as great as ever; in 1951, for example, the value of groundnut exports fell to

Table 1.8 Value of Groundnut Exports, 1900–1960 (£000)

Year	*Amount*	*Year*	*Amount*
1900	4	1931	1,511
1901	1	1932	1,874
1902	2	1933	2,064
1903	3	1934	1,860
1904	5	1935	2,093
1905	7	1936	2,847
1906	13	1937	4,056
1907	18	1938	1,308
1908	15	1939	1,048
1909	15	1940	1,476
1910	9	1941	2,140
1911	10	1942	1,688
1912	19	1943	1,475
1913	175	1944	2,013
1914	179	1945	2,696
1915	72	1946	5,676
1916	474	1947	6,397
1917	710	1948	9,806
1918	920	1949	18,916
1919	699	1950	15,237
1920	1,120	1951	6,321
1921	1,112	1952	22,114
1922	481	1953	24,928
1923	403	1954	29,900
1924	1,461	1955	23,134
1925	2,394	1956	27,764
1926	2,343	1957	20,139
1927	1,630	1958	26,948
1928	1,849	1959	27,472
1929	2,466	1960	22,878
1930	2,196		

Source: Gerald Helleiner, 1966.

> only £9.3 million. After 1954, as groundnut prices drifted downward, the value of their exports fluctuated to roughly the levels of the early 1950s from 1961 to 1964; however, with record volumes, the value of Nigerian groundnut exports reached new peaks—as much as £36.6 million (plus another £6.5 million of groundnut oil) in 1963. (Helleiner, 1966, p. 116)

In the context of the Nigerian economy, table 1.9 shows the Nigerian share of global groundnut exports for the representative years. By 1938, the West African nation supplied almost half of the West African subregion's groundnut exports, accounting for almost 10% of total exports. By 1954, exports from Nigeria alone took a quantum leap to nearly 430,000 tons, representing more than 50% of West Africa's total combined. In 1961, it was estimated

Table 1.9 Shares of World Groundnut Exports, Selected Years

	1938		1954		1961	
	tons* 000's	%	tons* 000's	%	tons* 000's	%
West Africa**	389	18.2	707	63.6	1,002	76.7
Nigeria	180	8.4	428	38.5	494	37.8
World Total	2,138	100.0	1,111	100.0	1,307	100.0

*Shelled equivalent.
**East Cameroon, Benin (Dahomey), Burkina Faso (Upper Volta), Chad, Côte d'Ivoire, Gambia, Ghana, Guinea, Guinea Bissau (Portuguese Guinea), Mali, Niger, Nigeria, Senegal, Togo.
Source: Gerald Helleiner, 1966.

that nearly 80% of internationally traded world groundnut supplies were West African in origin (see table 1.9), with Nigeria supplying between 22% and 40% of the world total (Helleiner, 1966, p. 114).

GDP

As expected, the GDP matrix is employed to measure the growth as well as the performance of Nigerian pre-independence economy. From table 1.10 we can observe that the GDP grew 32.4% between 1950 and 1957 (in monetary terns from £687 million to £910 million). Some components of activity grew faster than the overall economy, namely, manufacturing, public utilities, building and civil engineering construction, transport, and government each stood in 1957 at over 200% of the 1950 output measured at 1957 prices (Okigbo, 1962). By contrast, some of the large sectors, particularly agriculture and livestock, grew at a much slower rate than the economy (Okigbo, 1962).

In pari passu, there was a broad pattern of more than 4% average annual growth in the economy, and in the first half of the decade, the performance was much higher than the average, as it actually rose to nearly 8% in 1951 and 1954, respectively (table 1.11). In the second half, the growth rate slowed, and worsened to nearly 3% negative in 1956 (table 1.11). This was not totally surprising, as Aboyade confirmed in the following words:

> To some extent, such growth variation is not surprising for an economy substantially dependent on agriculture which is sensitive to the vagaries of nature and the unsteady fortune of world commodity prices. Although it is reasonable to expect that the dependence of the GDP on movement in the level of external trade would be less in the 1950s than before World War II, the structure of the economy had not really become significantly oriented toward internal dynamic forces to minimize and absorb external shocks. (Aboyade, 1966, p. 16)

Table 1.10 Components of the GDP by Output at 1957 Constant Prices (£m)

Category	*1950*	*1951*	*1952*	*1953*	*1954*	*1955*	*1956*	*1957*	*% Change 50–57*
Agriculture	377.6	415.0	430.5	446.0	471.3	483.9	459.8	471.4	24.8
Livestock	60.1	57.7	52.5	53.5	55.7	56.5	57.6	57.7	–4.0
Fishing	9.7	9.8	9.9	10.0	10.2	10.3	12.6	13.3	37.1
Forest products	9.4	12.0	10.1	11.9	12.3	13.4	13.6	14.6	55.3
Mining and Oil exploration	7.6	7.6	8.2	7.9	8.1	9.0	9.6	9.4	23.7
Mfg & Public Utilities	3.9	4.0	5.8	6.3	7.9	8.7	12.0	13.1	235.9
Communications	2.7	2.7	3.0	2.9	2.6	2.4	2.6	3.1	14.8
Bldg & Civil Engineering	20.3	25.4	19.4	25.9	37.8	38.3	36.5	43.0	111.8
Ownership of buildings	8.9	9.1	9.2	9.4	9.6	9.7	9.8	10.3	15.7
Transport	28.6	34.0	35.3	45.4	50.9	60.2	65.1	74.6	160.8
Crafts	15.8	15.9	16.0	16.1	16.2	16.4	16.5	16.7	5.7
Missions	6.9	7.0	7.6	7.8	8.7	11.4	12.7	15.9	130.4
Government	15.0	16.4	19.9	16.5	17.6	23.4	28.7	30.5	103.3
Marketing Boards	41.0	10.5	28.0	28.8	42.7	25.0	44.9	11.7	–71.5
Banking, Insurance & Prof.	1.5	1.2	1.3	1.7	1.7	2.1	2.2	2.5	66.7
Domestic Services	4.4	4.4	4.4	4.7	4.8	5.0	5.7	5.5	25.0
Miscellaneous	0.9	1.0	1.1	1.1	1.2	1.5	1.9	2.0	122.2
Land development	8.2	8.2	8.2	8.2	8.2	8.2	8.2	8.2	0.0
Distribution, Res. Error	64.6	98.3	122.6	105.7	104.7	112.7	74.1	106.5	64.9
GDP at Factor Cost	687	740	793	810	872	898	874	910	32.4

Source: Pius Okigbo, 1962.

Table 1.11 Components of the GDP Annual Growth Rates at 1957 Constant Prices

	Percentage Change in One Year over Previous Year							*Average Annual Rate*		
Category	*51–50*	*52–51*	*53–52*	*54–53*	*55–54*	*56–55*	*57–56*	*54–50*	*57–54*	*57–50*
Agriculture	9.9	3.7	3.6	5.7	2.7	−5.0	2.5	5.7	1.5	3.3
Livestock	−4.0	−9.0	1.9	4.1	1.4	1.9	0.2	−1.7	1.9	−0.5
Fishing	1.0	1.0	1.0	2.0	1.0	22.3	5.6	1.3	7.7	4.8
Forest products	27.7	−15.8	17.8	3.4	8.9	1.5	7.4	8.3	5.3	7.3
Mining and Oil exploration	0.0	7.9	−3.7	2.5	11.1	6.7	−2.1	1.7	4.6	3.2
Mfg & Public Utilities	2.6	45.0	8.6	25.4	10.1	37.9	9.2	20.4	20.7	19.8
Communications	0.0	11.1	−3.3	−10.3	−7.7	8.3	19.2	−0.6	2.4	2.5
Bldg & Civil Engineering	25.1	−23.6	33.5	45.9	1.3	−4.7	17.8	20.2	15.1	13.6
Ownership of buildings	2.2	1.1	2.2	2.1	1.0	1.0	5.1	1.9	2.3	2.1
Transport	18.9	3.8	28.6	12.1	18.3	8.1	14.6	15.9	13.3	14.9
Crafts	0.6	0.6	0.6	0.6	1.2	0.6	1.2	0.6	0.9	0.8
Missions	1.4	8.6	2.6	11.5	31.0	11.4	25.2	6.0	19.8	13.1
Government	9.3	21.3	−17.1	6.7	33.0	22.6	6.3	5.1	17.1	11.7
Marketing Boards	−74.4	166.7	2.9	48.3	−41.5	79.6	−73.9	35.8	3.1	15.4
Banking, Insurance &Prof.	−20.0	8.3	30.8	0.0	23.5	4.8	13.6	4.8	10.5	8.7
Domestic Services	0.0	0.0	6.8	2.1	4.2	14.0	−3.5	2.2	4.2	3.4
Miscellaneous	11.1	10.0	0.0	9.1	25.0	26.7	5.3	7.6	16.5	12.4
Land development	0.0	0.0	0.0	0.0	0.0	0.0	0.0	0.0	0.0	0.0
Distribution, Res. Error	52.2	24.7	−13.8	−0.9	7.6	−34.3	43.7	15.5	4.0	11.3
GDP at Factor Cost	7.7	7.1	2.1	7.7	3.0	−2.7	4.1	6.2	3.0	4.2

Source: Pius Okigbo, 1962.

Table 1.12 Nigerian National Income (GDP), 1950/1951 and 1956/1957 (£m)

Sector	*1950/1951 at 1950/1951 Prices*	*1956/1957 at 1956/1957 Prices*	*% Change*
Agriculture	407.6	501.0	22.9
Minerals	7.8	9.7	24.4
Industry	9.4	14.5	54.3
Construction & Civil Engineering	41.6	89.4	114.9
Public Utilities	1.6	4.0	150.0
Services	100.4	139.1	38.5
Ownership of Houses	5.1	6.3	23.5
Government	19.2	44.9	133.9
Intra-Household Services	4.0	4.0	0.0
Earnings of Assets Abroad	3.0	6.9	130.0
Total GDP (A)	599.7	819.8	36.7
Less Interest and dividends (B)	−6.3	−7.5	−19.0
GDP of Nigeria (A−B)	**593.4**	**812.3**	**36.9**

Source: National Economic Council, *Economic Survey of Nigeria, 1959*, p. 109.

National Income

In the context of national income and expenditure paradigm, national income vis-à-vis per capita income is a marquee measure of standard of living. From table 1.12, we can notice that national income rose sharply, up 37% with £218.9 million from £593.4 million in 1950/1951 to £812.3 million in 1956/1957. Some elements of activity, including industry, services, and overseas investments, grew faster than the overall GDP, while construction and civil engineering, public utilities, and government not only outperformed the general GDP, but also each stood in 1957 at over 100% of the 1950 GDP measured at 1957 prices. Also, the national income increased in real terms (inflation adjusted) by not less than 4% per year between 1950/1951 and 1956/1957 (*Economic Survey of Nigeria*, 1959, p. 17). And after allowing for population increases, this represents an increase of £3 per person over the six years at 1950/1951 prices, or 10 shillings (2.5%) per annum (*Economic Survey of Nigeria*, 1959, p. 17).

Meanwhile, further analysis indicated that the national income for 1956/1957 (i.e., £812.3 million) averaged between £25 and £29 per capita (*Economic Survey of Nigeria*, 1959, p. 17). Then, national aggregate, per capita income of between £25 and £29, is small by the standard of industrialized nations; however, it is not particularly low when compared to other countries,

Table 1.13 Comparative National Income for Selected Countries, 1956/1957 (£m)

*Country**	*Aggregate National Income (£million)*	*National Income per Capita (£)*
Nigeria	812–965	25–29
Uganda	112	20
Kenya	159	26
Tanganyika (Tanzania)	136	16
Rhodesia and Nyasaland (Zimbabwe)	331	46
Ghana	261	56
Union of South Africa	1,721	124
Jamaica	146	93
Ceylon (Sri Lanka)	364	41
Pakistan	1,556	19
India	8,558	22
United Kingdom	16,538	323

*Except in respect of Nigeria all figures of aggregate national income and of the populations used in calculating the national income per head are those included for 1956 in the United Nations Monthly Bulletin of Statistics for July 1959.

Source: National Economic Council, *Economic Survey of Nigeria, 1959*, p. 18.

which are mainly dependent on agriculture as Nigeria was at the time, regardless of the fact that Nigeria's population makes her total national income larger relative to other African countries (*Economic Survey of Nigeria*, 1959, pp. 17–18). Table 1.13 (refer only to countries within the sterling area in 1956/1957) offers a useful basis for comparison.

Invariably, the analysis of the performance of Nigerian pre-independence economy gets better. For, in 1950/1951 and 1956/1957, Nigeria did not only enjoy expansion in its GDP and national income, but also the proceeds of her foreign investment at home and remittances from abroad (*Economic Survey of Nigeria*, 1959, p. 18). In 1956/1957 (without borrowing), Nigeria used its return inflows from overseas investments as well as increase in the yield of indirect taxes and foreign investments in Nigeria (£79.7 million total) to pay for increases in public expenditure, including provision for gross domestic investment (*Economic Survey of Nigeria*, 1959, p. 20).

From table 1.14 it can be deduced that Nigeria's imports and home produced private consumption represented £516.7 million (or 85%) in 1950/1951, while the same categories accounted for £729.3million (or 87%) in 1956/1957. At 87% consumption rate in 1956/1957, this proportion is not only high, but it also unequivocally demonstrated improved level of living and disposable income; most of all, it compared favorably with the reported ratios for other countries in table 1.15.

From table 1.15 we can plausibly conclude that, in 1957, "it was true that all of the named countries did have a considerably higher National Income

Table 1.14 Nigerian Consumption Expenditures, 1950/1951 and 1956/1957 (£m)

Category	*1950/1951*	*%*	*1956/1957*	*%*
Imports	86.5	14	196.4	23.5
Home produced	430.2	71	532.9	63.5
Government (noncapital)	18.1	3	46.1	5.5
Gross Domestic Investment	40.4	6.5	95.6	11.5
Investment Overseas	42.6	7.0	48.6	
Other	5.7	1.0	6.9	1
Sub-Total	623.5	103	877.9	105
Less Indirect Taxes	15.3	2.5	37.8	5
Total	**608.2**	**100**	**840.1**	**100**

Source: National Economic Council, *Economic Survey of Nigeria, 1959*, p. 19.

Table 1.15 Comparative Consumption Expenditures for Selected Countries

Country	*Year*	*Percent*
Belgian Congo (DRC)	1955	62
Ghana	1956	86
Rhodesia and Nyasaland (Zimbabwe)	1955	60
United Kingdom	1956	66
Union of South Africa	1955	64

Source: National Economic Council, *Economic Survey of Nigeria, 1959*, p. 21.

per capita than Nigeria; as a result, it could, therefore divert a larger proportion of available resources to domestic investment without restricting so severely immediate increases in the standard of living" (*Economic Survey of Nigeria*, 1959, p. 21). It strongly suggests that, aside from all difficulties and uncertainties, Nigeria was moving in the right direction and, at the same time, it exercised prudent management of the limited resources at its disposal at the material time for the benefit of the majority of Nigerian people, indeed to the point of notably rubbing shoulders with more affluent countries. As underscored by an official source, if successive Nigerian leaderships had, as quoted,

> continued to devote the same proportion of available resources to increasing the immediate standard of living, the capital required for future generation of wealth would have depended to a considerable extent on internal savings being mobilized for use in Nigeria and on investment overseas. (*Economic Survey of Nigeria*, 1959, p. 21)

Oil Discovery and Agricultural Neglect in Nigeria

According to Sala-i-Martin and Subramanian (2008, p. 61), "Nigeria has been a disastrous development experience. On just about every conceivable metric,

Nigeria's performance, since independence, has been dismal." The economy is no exception and, in fact, no better example illustrated the tragedy of Nigeria's post-independence economy than the impact of oil on agriculture. According to Daramola et al. (2007, p. 2), agriculture constituted 60–70% of Nigeria's exports in the 1950s and in the 1960s. As a result, Nigeria was a major exporter of cocoa, cotton, palm oil, palm kernel, groundnuts, and rubber (Daramola et al., 2007, p. 2). Also, the bulk of governmental revenue came from agriculture. All that impressive agricultural sector performance changed for the negative with the discovery of oil.

As shown in table 1.16, agriculture's share of the GDP fell by nearly half from 41.3% in 1970 to 23.4% in 1980, and it was only 18.3% of the GDP in 2010. It rebounded slightly to 25% of the GDP in 2017. The sector recorded moderate growth of 3.0% between 2013 and 2014.

As shown by figures in table 1.16 between 1970 and 1975, agricultural exports, as a percentage of total exports in Nigeria, fell hugely from about 30% to 4.5%. From 1980 to 2000, the average annual growth rate of agricultural exports declined by nearly 80%. By 2017, agriculture accounted for only 0.2% of exports and, as a share of non-oil exports, agriculture plummeted by

Table 1.16 Nigeria's Agricultural Exports 1960–2017

Year	*Amount*	*Total Export Earnings % Share Agriculture*	*% Share Agriculture Non-Oil export*	*% Share Agriculture of GDP*
1960	£113.904 million			
1964	£113.994 million			
1970	₦265.2 million	29.7	70.9	41.3
1975	₦230.6 million	4.5	65.9	25.5
1980	₦340.1 million	2.4	61.3	23.4
1985	₦259.8 million	2.2	52.3	40.3
1990	₦2,429.3 million	2.2	74.5	39.6
1995	₦15,512.0 million	1.6	67.2	38.6
2000	₦9,322.2 million	0.5	37.5	40.4
2005	₦38,588.1 million	1.2	48.1	41.2
2010	₦142.00 billion	1.6	35.7	18.3
2011	₦260.00 billion	6.1	54.1	31.2
2013	₦338.00 billion	3.2	47.0	53.6
2014	₦370.00 billion	0.4	38.7	55.2
2015	₦331.20 billion	n.a.	48.9	48.0
2016	₦270.56 billion	0.2	40.0	24.4
2017	₦336.37 billion	0.2	31.3	25.1

n.a. not available.
Source: Central Bank of Nigeria, Annual Report, Various Years.
World Bank.
Adebiyi Daramola et al. (2007).
Author calculation.

more than half from 71% in 1970 to 31% in 2017. Ordinarily mineral discovery should not have undermined agriculture output, especially in export crops' dependent countries, of which Nigeria was one. Unfortunately, that is what occurred in Nigeria. Huge oil find in the country, coupled with the subsequent oil boom, has been largely linked to the neglect of agriculture in the political economy of the proverbial oil curse.

Sadly, oil discovery has been disastrous for Nigerian agriculture and its long-term impact on economic development and growth. The downside of the oil boom was the gradual decline in the other non-oil sectors, especially the agricultural sector that received limited attention (Sertoglu et al., 2017, p. 549). The reasons for this are many and, as expected, they have been well documented. Particular attention is paid to the role played by the Dutch Disease (Karl, 1997; Auty & Evia, 2001; Rodiquez & Sachs, 1999; Auty, 1994, Caselli & Michaels, 2009; Mikesell, 1997; Forsyth & Kay, 1980; Van der Ploeg, 2011; Stevens, 2015) syndrome in agricultural decline and the overall economy. As such, the analysis of Nigeria's structural economic problems is fully developed by using the basic Dutch disease model (Herbst & Olukoshi, 1994, p. 457). Daramola et al. (2007, p. 3), Shaxson (2005, p. 312), and the World Bank (1994, p. vii) offer nested consensus:

> The major cause of the decline in agricultural exports was the oil price shocks of 1973–74 and 1979, which resulted in large inflows of foreign exchange and neglect of the agricultural sectors ("Dutch disease"). The consequence of this phenomenon was that, owing to the reduced competitiveness of agriculture, Nigeria began to import some of those agricultural products it formerly exported and other food crops that it had been self-sufficient in. For example, between 1970 and 1982, Nigeria lost over 96.6 per cent of her exports in nominal terms. Domestic food production also declined substantially, causing the food import bill to attain a high of about $4 billion in 1982. The astronomical increase in imports was financed by oil revenues. . . . By 1986, the situation had reached crisis stage, dramatizing the ineffectiveness of the policy of industrialization through import substitution. This strategy, conferring protection on import-competing manufacturing by imposing high duties on finished imports and low duties on raw materials and intermediate goods, taxed the exportable goods (agricultural) sector of the economy so that, by the time the oil market crashed, many manufacturing concerns could no longer operate because of lack of foreign exchange to import raw materials.

Shaxson (2005, p. 312) confirmed:

> Large inflows of foreign exchange cause real exchange rates to rise and to damage local non-oil production in an effect called the "Dutch Disease"; expansion

> in the oil sector does not compensate populations for this because it creates so few jobs, even indirectly; dependence on oil revenues can dangerously distort institutions and politicians' incentives and behavior; and competition for resources can provoke conflicts. Secrecy and arbitrary power are important for private accumulation; this, of course, has anti-democratic effects. Rulers lose interest in citizens. Another problem is volatile oil prices. Revenue volatility hampers planning, boosts deficits, and tends to raise debt. Volatility depresses economic growth by increasing both interest rates and uncertainty.

The World Bank (1994, p. vii) offered the following brief analysis:

> In a classic case of the Dutch disease, Nigeria's resources shifted from the production of non-oil traded goods (mostly agricultural) to that of non-traded goods (mostly public services). The impact on the agricultural sector—Nigeria's major source of GDP and export revenues before oil was especially pronounced. In the manufacturing sector, import duties and prohibitions favored imports of intermediate goods and parts for assembly into consumer durables and capital goods.

In contrast to the pre-independence era, profound economic successes, and contrary to reasonable expectations, post-independence Nigerian economy has grossly underperformed relative to the country's enormous resource endowment and its peer nations. The recent Nigerian government *Economic Recovery & Growth Plan 2017–2020* (2017, p. 10) captured the trajectory vividly in the following words:

> Nigeria has the potential to become a major player in the global economy by virtue of its human and natural resource endowments. However, this potential has remained relatively untapped over the years. After a shift from agriculture to crude oil and gas in the late 1960s, Nigeria's growth has continued to be driven by consumption and high oil prices. Previous economic policies left the country ill-prepared for the recent collapse of crude oil prices and production. The structure of the economy remains highly import dependent, consumption driven and undiversified. . . . Majority of Nigerians remain under the burden of poverty, inequality and unemployment. General economic performance was also seriously undermined by deplorable infrastructure, corruption and mismanagement of public finances. Decades of consumption and high oil price-driven growth led to an economy with a positive but jobless growth trajectory.

For a better understanding of Nigerian post-independence economic problems, a suggestion is to examine Nigerian economy in the general context of Africa's political economy framework, and that is for several reasons. First,

Nigeria is widely regarded as the "giant of Africa" and the largest economy, in 2019 with $448 billion GDP, South Africa second with $351 billion GDP, and Egypt third with $303 billion GDP (World Bank, 2021) and the most populous country (more than 195 million people) in Africa. Second, Nigeria has traits common to many African countries that plague its progress and stability, including history of colonialism, political instability, commodity shocks, unfavorable terms of trade, leadership crisis, institutional decay, conflicts, corruption and governmental mismanagement, poverty, insecurity, poor health outcomes, to name just a few.

Third, Claude Ake (1985, p. 1), among other details, noted that "political economy approach has led to the increased understanding of the importance of studying the state as the key to understanding socio-economic formations, particularly their configuration of social forces and the possibilities of their transformation." Thus, findings in Nigerian political economy situation could help to understand Africa's development crisis and, at the same time, to suggest ways or the means to address it.

POLITICAL ECONOMY OF UNDERDEVELOPMENT IN NIGERIA AND AFRICA

Kenyan-born political scientist, Ali A. Mazrui, among other details, wrote: "Much of contemporary Africa is in the throes of decay and decomposition. . . . War, famine, and ruin are the postcolonial legacy for too many Africans" (Mazrui, 2003, p. 339). Also, Decalo, another scholar, reiterated that the unrealistic formula guaranteeing the establishment of a viable and integrative political order has eluded many African states (Decalo, 1985, p. 209). As a backdrop, Herbst argued (2014 quoted in Nunn, 2007, p. 27) that this is "because of a lack of significant political development during colonial rule." Meanwhile, Hersbt, too, pointed out: "Africa's post-independence leaders inherited nation states that did not have the infrastructure necessary to [uplift their countries]." Hersbt (1997, p. 120) further surmised that "after independence, Africa's diverse political heritage was brushed aside in the rush by nationalists to seize the reins of power of the nation-states as defined politically and geographically by their European colonizers." The economy is no exception in the "brush aside."

Africa's economic history, since 1960 (the decade most African countries gained independence from colonial rule), fits the classical definition of tragedy: potential unfulfilled, with disastrous consequences (Easterly & Levine, 1997). Ayittey (2002, p. 1) stated: "Africa's deteriorating economic situation is baffling. The continent's untapped mineral wealth is immense and its tourism potential is enormous. Yet, it is inexorably mired in steaming squalor, misery, deprivation, and chaos." Romer (2006, p. 6) pointed out that "many countries of Sub-Saharan Africa had growth disasters compared to growth miracles of East Asia." At the same time,

> the pattern of growth found in Africa appears to be poverty-increasing, as the growth path these countries have followed since independence has given rise to an unacceptable level of unequal income/asset distribution with a most unequal access for the majority of the population to essential services required for their mere survival. No doubt, the high level of poverty and inequality and the deteriorating trends on both accounts poses a great challenge to policy-makers in Africa in their efforts for reversing the trends and overcoming this debilitating condition. (Nissanke & Sindzingre, 2006, p. 355)

Of all the regions in the world for which the World Bank tracks economic data, none has had a more disappointing economic performance than sub-Saharan Africa (Clapham, 1996). In addition, many sub-Saharan Africa countries depend on primary commodity and foreign investment flows (loans, private investment, and development aid) for development (Mbaku, 1994). As such, "the economic development produced by the collusion between African economies and foreign capital creates significant inequalities in income distribution, increased levels of unemployment, and domestic unrest" (Mbaku, 1994, p. 248). Furthermore (Mbaku, 2000, p. 29), "today, most African countries are unable to generate the wealth they need to deal fully and effectively with mass poverty and deprivation, and, as a result, must depend on the industrial North for food and development aid." In fact, "Africa remains the suffering object of external exploitation" (Clapham, 1996, p. 810). Collier and Gunning (1999) asked "Why Has Africa Grown Slowly" in spite of the fact that "in the 1960s, Africa's future looked bright." Hall and Jones (1999) asked in rather different terms "why do some countries produce so much more output per worker" than Africa. The *Economist* (May 13, 2000) dubbed Africa the "hopeless continent."

Scholars like Ucheoma Nwagbara and Kingsley Esedo have provided valid comments by relying on data available from such renowned agencies as the UN, World Bank, Organization for Economic Cooperation and Development (OECD), and other world bodies. To them, such development indicators as the GDP, personal incomes, and social improvement indexes are rising (Nwagbara & Esedo, 2017). Therefore, in 1990–2015, global regional GDP growth increased dramatically by an average of more than 300% (World Bank, *World Development Indicators 2017*). During the same time period, the physical quality of life index gap was cut in half: lowered infant mortality (21.7 per 1,000 live births vs. 41.6 per 1,000 live births), increased life expectancy (73.2 years vs. 68 years), and rising literacy rates (77.8% vs. 62.0%) (World Bank, *World Development Indicators 2017*). Even in "hopeless Africa" things appear to be improving. As Meagher (2016, p. 483) observed: "The resurgence of growth in African economies since the early 2000s, coupled with leaner prospects in OECD countries and rising competition from Asia, has encouraged investors and development experts to look at Africa with new eyes."

Though the debate in the literature about Africa's underdevelopment is big and often regurgitated, it will be proper to discuss some topical factors responsible for Africa's development distress using theoretical models approach. The advantage of this approach is that as Eisenhart (1991, p. 205) explained "theoretical framework is a structure that guides research by relying on a formal theory . . . constructed by using an established, coherent explanation of certain phenomena and relationships." Similarly, Sarter (2005, p. 494) noted of the "limited usefulness of findings and conclusions" when a study is not justified by a theoretical framework (Grant & Osanloo, 2014). Most certainly, several factors have stymied African development and frustrated the pursuit of effective and relevant development agenda (Mazrui, 1975; Nzongola-Ntalaja, 2002). Seven factors stand out, namely, colonialism, flawed policies, ethnicity, disease, globalization, resource curse, and faulty institutions.

Legacy of Colonialism

According to various scholars, including Loomba, colonialism is the most complex and traumatic relationship in human history (Loomba, 2005, p. 8). Clapham (1985, p. 12) argued:

> The ultimate aim of colonialism was technological (invention of ship to facilitate travel to reach other parts of the world), and its principal motive was economic. . . . Even those societies which retained their independence were obliged to come to terms with a world in which European influence was dominant, and to adapt their own domestic political structures and economies to meet the European prerequisites of statehood.

Achiume (2019, p. 1510) was of the following view: "European colonialism . . . global interconnection and political subordination [of Africans], initiated over the course of this history [colonialism] . . . entailed . . . the flow of natural and human resources across the globe, for the benefit of Europe and Europeans." Lonsdale (1981, p. 139) also averred: "European colonialism was a living denial of the ability of Africans to organize their own sovereignties." "Our Common Interest" *Report of the Commission for Africa*[2] is very revealing, adding the following (pp. 25–26):

> The railways and roads put in place in colonial times were primarily designed to transport minerals and other raw materials from the African interior to its ports for shipping to Europe. They were not designed to join one part of the continent to another or generate more links to the East. . . . The colonial era brought other problems. The division of Africa into its present countries was the product of Western interests not African minds. The lines drawn on a map by the great European powers in Berlin in 1884 still have profoundly disruptive consequences. Many traditional communities of people are now divided between two, three or even four countries. Elsewhere disparate groups, some of whom were traditional enemies, are yoked together in uneasy union, many of them lacking a common language with which to speak to one another. . . . The legacy of all this is that Africa had a very weak starting point in the race for development.

Report of the Commission for Africa is not alone in decrying the shortcomings of the continent. For example, the Nigerian historian, J. F. Ade Ajayi, posited (2002, p. 5):

> My argument is that development remains elusive in Africa, not merely because of the misrule and warped personalities of many African leaders, but because Africa had been damaged severely, first by the slave trade, then by the colonialism which grew out of the slave trade. Further, that Africa cannot rejoin the development train in the world until the damage is repaired as much as possible. When that is done, it will be of immense benefit not only to Africa, but also to the whole world.

Meanwhile, there is "a knock-on effect" on African development, indeed as Benjamin Mkapa, the former president of Tanzania portrayed:

> The effect of colonial rule on African politics, economics, and social life has remained strong, and not just because Africans were taught and pressed to think and speak in the languages of their colonizers. It is also because at independence Africans inherited, with a few variations, the political and economic systems of their colonizers. Every white man, woman, or child was made out to be superior in all respects, including color and culture, and the black man, woman, or child was made to feel inferior. African confidence and dignity were deliberately undermined. Humiliation was pervasive. This is a historical fact. Slavery, which in itself was an enforced inferiority on the black people, was superseded by colonial administration that made little if any effort to disabuse

> the black people of such imposed inferiority. In other words, Africans were protected from slavery abroad, but were condemned to be an underclass at home. (Mkapa, 2010, p. 24)

Meanwhile, several scholars, including Olúfémi Táíwò, have argued that practices of colonial rule hindered the emergence of modernity in Africa (Taiwo, 2010; see also Ake, 1981; Rodney, 1973; Rodney, 1967). Consequently, to awaken and meet the challenges of globalization and modernity, Taiwo (2014, p. xii) did insist that "Africa Must Be Modern" since "colonialism promised but denied Africans modernity as recompense for bearing its burden while colonialism lasted." Other scholars, in Pan-Africanist mode, underscored important theories; in *The Price of Civilization* (Sachs, 2011) echoed Taiwo's words.

Furthermore, reflecting on Africa's post-colonial economic subjugation, political conflicts, and institutional fragility, former Ghanaian president, Kwame Nkrumah, penned an entire book *Neo-colonialism: The Last Stage of Imperialism*. In fact, Nkrumah (1968, p. 1), among other details, charged: "Africa is a paradox which illustrates and highlights neo-colonialism. Her earth is rich, yet the products that come from above and below her soil continue to enrich, not Africans predominantly, but groups and individuals who operate to Africa's impoverishment." In the particular Nigerian context, Falola and Ihonvbere (1985, pp. 83–84) theorized:

> And to understand underdevelopment one must take into cognizance the impact of colonialism, the nature of the neocolonial rentier state and the character of the Nigerian national proto-bourgeoisie. Over five decades of British colonial rule and exploitation left Nigeria in 1960 a spatially distorted, underdeveloped and peripheral capitalist country in the international division of labor. It is difficult to identify a sector of the economy which experienced positive development as a result of deliberate colonial policy. . . . At independence in 1960, the country was backward in all respects. As a primary producer for the world market, the country's cash crop exports and imports were concentrated on western (particularly (EEC) markets. . . . The colonial state had ensured that the oil, banking, import-export and the limited manufacturing sectors were all dominated by transnational corporations such as Shell-BP, Barclays Bank (now Union Bank), UAC, Leventis, etc.

Similarly, Peel (2006, p. 2) argued that "in common with many other African countries, Nigeria is the product of colonial exploitation and gerrymandering, in this case by the British . . . nation state was imposed rather than agreed." Meanwhile, with respect to Nigeria and its size, Oyovbaire (1983, p. 13) argued that

> the amalgamation of 1914 was largely for reasons of economic complementarity of the two colonially delimited halves of the country. The compelling force of economic complementarity continued well beyond the 1940s. . . . In a sense therefore, and without implying any theory of class conspiracy, the Nigerian nation-state is rooted in the class character of the political economy, the interests of the British.

Jega (2000, p. 16), in the following words, further explained the Nigerian economy and development as they were shaped by the country's colonial legacy:

> The colonial state pursued a capitalist development strategy initially through the promotion of primary commodity production for export, through which foreign commercial interests established a firm footing in the Nigerian economy, in the post-second world war period, manufacturing enterprises controlled by foreign capital burgeoned, with the growing comprador classes playing supporting role. . . . The role of the indigenous comprador class in the capitalist production processes and accumulation increased in the era decolonization, a foreign capital sought willing partners to protects its investment, and then even more swiftly in the post-independence period when the post-colonial state became a prime mover of capitalist development.

Indeed, Amuwo (2010, p. 429) complemented Falola and Ihonvbere, Oyovbaire, and Jega's observations based on what he described as "repercussions of structural imperialism," and that was regarding the nature and character of Nigeria's post-colonial economy. He added:

> The Nigerian state was sucked, at independence, into the vortex of unequal relations and false partnership with former colonial (and other Western) powers at the expense of a genuine social compact with the Nigerian people. Two, as an archetypal neo-colony, Nigeria has appeared trapped since independence between two social logics: the imperative of popular democratization and people-friendly and genuine development on the one hand, and the stranglehold of structural imperialism and neo-colonialism, on the other. Fifty years on, the latter logic remains ascendant.

Beckman (1982, p. 39) corroborated the above arguments and concluded,

> The Nigerian state is an organ of international capital of imperialism. [Nigeria] Independence is seen as largely formal. Real control over the economy remains with foreign capital. Nationalist leaders have been co-opted by imperialism.

> They 'inherited' the colonial state, a state imposed by imperialism for its own purposes. The nature of the state itself therefore did not change fundamentally. The nationalists never really challenged the pervasive domination of the economy by imperialism. They were placed in a position where they were left to administer the state on behalf of foreign capital.

Colonialism and interrelated imperialism left its mark in Africa in general. Ake (1981, p. 19) argued, "To date, the experience of Western imperialism, particularly colonization, remains the most decisive event in the history of Africa." Consequently, Ake (1996) formulated the post-colonial "political conditions" theory to explain Africa's development failures. To Ake the problem is not that development failed in Africa, but to begin with, development was never really pursued because of the disingenuous and vicious nature of African politics after independence. Ake further posited: "The problem is not so much that development has failed as it was never really on the agenda in the first place. By all indications, political conditions in Africa are the greatest impediment to development" (Ake, 1996, p. 1).

While other factors are at work, Ake maintained that cutthroat and malevolent political competition legacy of colonial rule was one of the most destructive forces to visit African development:

> Colonial rule left most of Africa a legacy of intense and lawless political competition amidst an ideological void and a rising tide of disenchantment with the expectation of a better life. . . . It is easy to see that the political environment at independence was profoundly hostile to development. The struggle for power was so absorbing that everything else, including development was marginalized. . . . Besieged by a multitude of hostile forces that their authoritarianism and exploitative practices had engendered, those in power were so involved in the struggle for survival that they could not address the problem of development. (Ake, 1996, pp. 6–7)

Ake integrated "political conditions" (1996) theory with "dialectical materialism" (1981) (Marx, 1905, 1910; Marx, 1867;[3] Marx & Engels, 1984; Foley, 2008) model of analysis to further explain Africa's post-colonial underdevelopment. According to Ake (1981, p. 1), "dialectical materialism is a method which gives primacy to material conditions, particularly economic factors, in the explanation of social life." In this regard, Ake argued that a major cause of Africa's underdevelopment is the lack of what he called "authentic productive forces—labor power, objects of labor and means of labor" (Ake, 1981, p. 11) which were haphazardly developed during colonialism and have remained largely the same since after. Thus according to Ake:

> The productive forces express the overall productive capabilities of the society. They tend to develop at all times. When one talks of the development of productive forces one may be thinking of the quantitative and qualitative improvements in labor power, for instance, when people acquire more scientific education and technical skills, one could be thinking of the improvements of natural assets such as irrigation of arid lands to make it arable.

Despite the manifestation of these problems, according to Udoko (1993, p. 21)

> the various regimes that usurp the state power in Nigeria basically are not yet committed to question the appropriateness of the inherited colonial capitalist development philosophy or to make rational changes when necessary . . . the economic conditions usually remain the same or worsen.

Continuing Udoko added that

> "the present Nigeria economy is structurally disarticulated as a satellite colonial capitalism or a peripheral political economy still dominated by the center," and as a result, "like most post-colonial states that adopted the metropolitan strategies of development but historically failed, Nigeria is not capable in its present setting of take off into economic development. Its development "strategies and tactics" lack authenticity or clear indigenous base. (Udoko, 1993, p. 22)

Before Ake and Udoko, Caribbean-born Walter Rodney (1973) drew early attention to the adverse impact of colonialism on African development by offering a perspective on the colonialism theory in his remarkable book *How Europe Underdeveloped Africa*. To Rodney, contemporary Africa's underdevelopment is inextricably linked to deliberate exploitation and underdevelopment by European colonial regimes. Rodney further observed:

> All of the countries named as "underdeveloped" in the world are exploited by others; and the underdevelopment with which the world is now preoccupied is a product of capitalist, imperialist and colonialist exploitation. African and Asian societies were developing independently until they were taken over directly or indirectly by the capitalist powers. When that happened, exploitation increased and the export of surplus ensued, depriving the societies of the benefit of their natural resources and labor. That is an integral part of underdevelopment in the contemporary sense. . . . The situation is that Africa has not yet come anywhere close to making the most of its natural wealth, and most of the wealth now being produced is not being retained within Africa for the benefit of Africans. (Rodney, 1973, Chap. 1, pp. 19–20, and 29)

Not only that colonialism perpetuated the economic exploitation of Africa, it was reinforced with force and violence (Ajayi, 1974; Ake, 1981; Ake, 1986; Young, 1994; Volpato & Licata, 2010; UNESCO, 1989–1999), further undermining development. Colonialism was based on exploitation, manifested in the form of collecting taxes, mobilizing people for labor, or forcing them to plant cash crops (Rodney, 1985, p. 338 quoted in Muiu, 2010, p. 1313). As Muiu (2010, pp. 1311 and 1313) reminds us:

> From its inception, the colonial state acted with impunity in all aspects of life . . . colonialism was based on violence. No colonial power consulted Africans as to whether or not they wanted to be colonized. Brutal force was required first to control the population and second, to impose the will of the colonial powers. . . . Relations between the colonial state and its subjects were marked by extreme tension and suspicion that required the constant use of military force. . . . Such a state had to be authoritarian for it to be efficient. It was a top-down model where the colonial officer gave the orders. . . . For maximum economic efficiency, it was very important that the colonies serve as plantations for the colonial powers. Whatever the colonial power needed—from cocoa, coffee, peanuts, minerals to rubber—the colony was forced to produce without any regard to human rights.

Acemoglu et al. (2001, p. 1370) reinforced Rodney's formulations. "European powers set up 'extractive states,' exemplified by Belgian colonization of the Congo. . . . In fact, the main purpose of the extractive state was to transfer as much of the resources of the colony to the colonizer." Engerman and Sokoloff (2005, p. 1) observed that "colonial powers leveraged their imbalance of power to impose institutional arrangements on the colonies that were adverse to their long-term development." Also, Ndulo (2003, p. 320 quoted in Muiu, 2010, p. 1314) aptly observed: "Colonial powers imposed unfavorable terms of trade and strongly skewed economic activities towards extractive industries and exportation of primary goods. These conditions stimulated little demand to improve skills and educational levels of the work force, a situation that continued into post-independence states." While the interpretation of Rodney's central premise has evolved over the years, with the preponderant criticism that it downplayed other historical factors consequential to colonialism, however, what is indisputable is that "imperialism [colonialism] was a hegemonic ideology" (Newell, 2016, p. 307), in which Rodney's work according to Soyinka (1994, p. 206) "the issue of [under]development was rendered most explicitly, and that apparent vacuum that was hollowed out of Africa."

Irrespective of the analytical context, Rodney's work was considered to be groundbreaking not only because it was among the first to shine light on the impact of colonialism on Africa's underdevelopment, but also, Soyinka said, "he was clearly one of the most solidly ideologically situated intellectuals ever to look colonialism and exploitation in the eye and where necessary, spit in it" (quoted in Lee Wengraf, 2017). Inextricably linked to colonialism as a factor in Africa's underdevelopment was the deleterious impact of slave trade, especially the Trans-Atlantic slave trade (Ajayi & Uya, 2010; DuBois, 1896; Franklin, 2010; Rodney, 1970; Rodney, 1967; Inikori, 2000; Austen, 1979; Afigbo, 2009; Smithsonian, n.d.; Nunn, 2007).

Wolfe (2006, p. 388) argued that "enslaved people [Africans] augmented their owners' wealth." Lovejoy (2012) added "African slaves were used extensively for production" in Europe to the "detriment of African societies." Nunn (2007, p. 1) "found a robust negative relationship between the number of slaves exported from a country and current economic performance . . . together the evidence suggests that slave trade have had an adverse effect on economic development" in Africa. Bairoch (1993, p. 8 quoted in Nunn, 2007, p. 1) stated: "there is no doubt that a large number of negative structural features of the process of economic underdevelopment have historical roots going back to European colonialism." Manning (1990, p. 124 quoted in Nunn, 2007, p. 2) echoed Bairoch's sentiment and wrote: "slavery was corruption: it involved theft, bribery, and exercise of brute force as well as ruses. Slavery thus may be seen as one source of pre-colonial origins for modern corruption." M'baye (2006, p. 607) observation is preponderantly apt: "The Atlantic slave trade radically impaired Africa's potential to develop economically and maintain its social and political stability. The arrival of Europeans on the West African Coast and their establishment of slave ports in various parts of the continent triggered a continuous process of exploitation of Africa's human resources, labor, and commodities." This conclusion bore out what Wolfe (2006, p. 387) describes as "settler colonial logic of elimination of the native" perhaps in a different terms.

Policy Bias

The former development economist at the World Bank, William Easterly has pushed what he called the "bias against Africa" (Easterly, 2007) theory. The "bias against Africa" theory is based on the premise that (French, 2014, para. 5 and 6)

> experts in charge of the global development agenda have systematically betrayed underdeveloped countries [including African nations] . . . technocratic advisers attach little importance to the historical background of the countries they work on. . . . These advisers also ignore evidence saying the greatest benefits to a society come from the spontaneous, uncoordinated actions of mostly

> small actors whose talents are allowed to flourish, as opposed to top-down initiatives involving the state or outside donors.

Also, the Malawian economist, Thandika Mkandawire (2014, p. 174) has noted that this problem impinge on development and raised "complaints about the competence and ideas of expatriate planners who were imposed on Africa as technical assistants or plan ghost writers."

On Africa, for example, attaining the UN championed Millennium Development Goals (MDGs), Easterly (2007, p. 19) wrote that

> a series of arbitrary choices made in defining "success" or "failure" as achieving numerical targets for the Millennium Development Goals made the attainment of MDGs less likely in Africa than in other regions even when its progress was in line with historical or contemporary experience of other regions (p. 1). . . . The negative picture matters because it is demoralizing to African leaders and activists, and because it might have real consequences for things like private foreign investment to reinforce the stereotype that "Africa always fails."

On foreign aid, William Easterly asked, "Can Foreign Aid Save Africa?" (Easterly, 2005). While not negating the importance of aid in stimulating economic growth, he expressed concerns that foreign aid contributes to African underdevelopment, mainly because of problems of poor accountability, donor laxity, and bureaucracy (Easterly, 2002). The right response is to shift the paradigm and the money away from top-down plans by "experts" to "bottom-up researchers—like Nobel Peace Prize winner and microcredit pioneer Mohammad Yunus—who keep experimenting until they find something that works for the poor on the ground. The right response is to get tough on foreign aid, not to eliminate it, but to see that more of the next $2.3 trillion does reach the poor."

Dambisa Moyo (2009), as an economist, shares in Easterly's sentiments. In her thought-provoking book, *Dead Aid*: *Why Aid Is Not Working and How There Is a Better Way for Africa*, she questioned the continuing relevance of West's aid to Africa. Moyo's contention was that the "effectiveness"[4] of aid as a driver of development has increasingly come under scrutiny (Easterly, 2007; Moyo, 2009; Edwards, 2014; Chiripanhura & Nino-Zarazua, 2015). And contrary to popular belief, the billions of dollars in development assistance from rich nations to Africa in the past decades has done more harm than good and has not improved the life of Africans. Instead, in her estimation, "overreliance on aid has trapped developing nations in a vicious circle of aid dependency, corruption, market distortion, and further poverty, leaving them with nothing but the 'need' for more aid."

Sachs and Warner (1997) are known for their related and often cited study on the sources of slow economic growth in Africa based on international cross-country framework during the period 1965–1990; in it, they found that the combination of poor policies, inhibited international markets, and geographical factors such as lack of access to the sea and tropical climate predispose Africa to slow growth. These factors are what Collier and Gunning (1999) called Africa's "domestic destiny."

Ethnic Fragmentation

Similarly Easterly and Levine (1997, p. 1203) propounded the "ethnic fragmentation theory" to explain "Africa's growth tragedy." The authors contend that Africa's "high ethnic fragmentation" is associated with "low schooling, political instability, underdeveloped financial systems, distorted foreign exchange markets, high government deficits, and insufficient infrastructure." These factors they argued "account for about two-fifths of the growth differential between the countries of Sub-Saharan Africa and fast growing East Asia" (p. 1205). In addition, Alesina, Easterly, and Matuszeski (2006, p. 2) correlated Africa's underdevelopment with what they called the "artificial states" syndrome. (Artificial states are those in which political borders do not coincide with a division of nationalities desired by the people on the ground.)

The fact that ethnic diversity is an inhibitor to growth, detractor to sustainable development, and crisis provocateur cannot be overemphasized. According to Ojie and Ewhrudjakpor (2009, p. 1), "ethnic diversity is the albatross of many nations, and has caused conflicts and wars all over the world," and the "elites might manipulate ethnic markers for their own survival or gain" (Esteban & Ray, 2008, p. 2185) to the disadvantage of the larger society. About Nigeria, specific, Osaghae (2003, p. 1) wrote:

> The pervasiveness of ethnic politics in the country is taken to be symptomatic of the aggravated crisis of legitimacy that has engulfed the state, and is explained in terms of the proven efficacy of the ethnic strategy, the weakness of alternative identities and political units, the prevailing milieu of lawlessness that has enveloped the country's political landscape, and the inability of the state to act as an effective agency of distributive justice.

Earlier, Nnoli's (1978) seminal study *Ethnic Politics in Nigeria* shed light on the corrosive effects of ethnicity on Nigeria from the standpoint of colonialism. He contended that "colonial exploitative tendency and divide and rule policy" which foisted intense elite competition for economic and political advantages in negation of the common good and in the process induced lack of economic unity, regional inequalities, rivalry in the provision of amenities, among other ills (Ukiwo, 2005).

Blanton et al. (2001) also noted that the British colonial style of indirect decentralized rule in Africa (e.g., Nigeria) fostered an unranked system of ethnic stratification . . . and because unranked systems engender competition between ethnic groups which can readily spiral into conflict, the "British colonial legacy is positively correlated to both the frequency and intensity of ethnic conflict" which does not augur well for development. The trio of Osaghae's, Nnoli's, and Blanton et al.'s strictures reinforce the crux of the assertion by Easterly and Levine (1997, p. 1206) that "ethnic diversity may increase polarization and thereby impede agreement about the provision of public goods and create positive incentives for growth-reducing policies, such as financial repression and overvalued exchange rates, that create rents for the groups in power at the expense of society at large."

Disease

The disease factor theory also helps to explain Africa's underdevelopment. It is simply the association of diseases with Africa's economic devastation. Malaria, for example, is a major threat to public health and economic development in Africa (Ntuomi et al., 2004), with Nigeria included. Malaria accounted for 16% of deaths in Africa (Akachi & Atun, 2011). Also, the cost of malaria control and treatment drains African economies, slowing economic growth by about 1.3% a year (UNICEF, 2018). According to Johns Hopkins Bloomberg School of Public Health (2021), the economic impact of malaria is estimated to cost Africa $12 billion every year, in health care costs, absenteeism, days lost in school, decreased productivity due to brain damage from cerebral malaria, and loss of investment and tourism. Overall, households in Africa lose estimated 25% of their income to malaria annually.

Gallup and Sachs (2001) put forward an analytical framework in their study titled "The Economic Burden of Malaria." It tested for the impact of malaria on economic growth in malaria-intensive countries relative to malaria free countries. The influential study found a correlation between malaria and poverty in such malaria-intensive areas as the Africa tropical zone. According to the study,

> cross-country regressions for the 1965–1990 period confirm the relationship between malaria and economic growth. Controlling for many other tropical diseases does not change the correlation of malaria with economic growth, and these diseases are not themselves significantly negatively correlated with economic growth. (Gallup & Sachs, 2001, p. 85)

Forty-four of the 150 countries examined (or 29%) have intensive malaria and 35 of these 44 countries are in Africa (Gallup & Sachs, 2001, p. 86). The average GDP per capita in 1995 for the malarial countries was $1,526, compared with an average income of $8,268 in the countries without severe malaria, five times higher (Gallup & Sachs, 2001, p. 86). Of the 119 poorest countries, all but 12 have some incidence of malaria, while the richest 31 countries are free of malaria consistent to the study (Gallup & Sachs, 2001, p. 86). In Nigeria, for example, according to the Federal Nigeria's Ministry of Health (2010, 2014), malaria induces estimated ₦132 billion (about $364 million) losses annually in the form of treatment costs, prevention, and lost work hours.

Meanwhile, the top three countries in Africa with the highest global malaria cases are Nigeria (27%), DRC (12%), and Uganda (5%); bottom three countries in Africa with the lowest global malaria cases are Mozambique (5%), Niger (5%), and Malawi (2%) (World Health Organization, hereafter WHO, 2020, p. xiv). Likewise, the top three countries in Africa with the highest global malaria deaths are Nigeria (23%), DRC (11%), and Tanzania (5%); bottom three countries in Africa with the lowest global malaria mortality are Burkina Faso (4%), Mozambique (4%), and Niger (4%) (WHO, 2020, p. xv).

Globalization

Globalization is broadly defined as the "economic integration of the world economy" (IMF, 2008, p. 2). At the core of globalization are open markets—free trade, unrestricted movement of people, capital, goods, and services across national boundaries. In addition, Nwabueze (2004, p. 239) suggested that globalization vis-à-vis "economic liberalization is a necessary basis for democracy." Globalization is not a new phenomenon. In fact, it is a well-established economic practice expressed in various forms, such as international trade (imports and exports), FDIs (firms investing in other countries), capital market flows (foreign and domestic sources of funds including bonds, equities, loans), region-specific market bloc alliances (e.g., North American Free Trade Agreement, Free Trade Area of the Americas, European Union, Economic Community of West African States (ECOWAS)), and global trade pacts (e.g., the World Trade Organization (WTO), etc.) (Nwagbara, Buehlmann, & Schuler, 2002). Yet, not until the dawn of the 1990s did the concept of globalization begin to take hold. Since then, global markets and institutions continued to grow in importance. Several studies indicate that the chief cause of this development is technological progress, especially, the emergence of the Information Age epitomized by the Internet (Nwagbara, Buehlmann, & Schuler, 2002) and the "availability of cheap, rapid, and reliable communications that have cut both communication and transportation costs" (Williamson, 1998).

Trade is at the heart of the IPE of globalization, market economies have winners and losers, and globalization has influenced that (Nwagbara & Esedo, 2017). Resistance and anger associated with globalization has centered on rising inequality and stagnating incomes within countries, and the feeling that the "game is rigged" (Nwagbara & Esedo, 2017), Joseph Stiglitz, economics Nobel laureate, aptly captured it in his remarkable book, appropriately titled *Globalization and Its Discontents*.

The spread of the "third wave" (Huntington, 1991; Shin, 1994) of democratization (global democratic revolution and expansion of freedom in the late twentieth century, consequent particularly to the end of the Cold War) to sub-Saharan Africa in the early 1990s represented the most significant political change in the continent since the independence period three decades earlier (van de Walle, 1999, p. 21). Williams (1994, p. 214) explained that the democratic "wave" was triggered mainly "by the inability of governments to secure their fiscal bases and to satisfy the multiplicity of demands of their various constituents undermined their legitimacy and led to the emergence of popular movements demanding democratic reforms, and encouraged some regimes to embark in haste on strategies to transfer power to elected successors."

Umezurike (2008, 2009, 2012, n.d.) conceptualized that the wave of "democratic transitions" has wreaked havoc on African economies provoked especially by economic globalization. Umezurike (2012, p. 26) enjoined that the "forces of globalization via the economic reforms of the Nigerian state have been undermining democracy in this society [Nigeria]" vis-à-vis the economy. He postulated that "economic reforms in Africa have been largely volatile and contradictory primarily because they respond both to the laws of the free market [globalization] and to domestic social struggle" (Umezurike, 2012, pp. 26–27). Haggard and Kaufman (1995, p. 152) reiterated that the "new democratic governments [in Africa] face exceptionally strong distributive pressures, both from groups reentering the political arena after long periods of repression and from established interests demanding reassurance."

To further demonstrate the "domestic social struggle" between the elite and the masses over the economic benefits induced by globalization, Rita Edozie (2008) constructed a theoretical model that examined the relationship between capitalism and democracy in three democracies in Africa (Nigeria, South Africa, and Kenya). She found that a democratic crisis in each country is associated with an economic crisis intertwined with the negative fallouts from economic globalization. Consequently, this feeds into the "weakness of Nigeria in the global political economy and the limited democratic value of domestic petty bourgeois governance" (Umezurike, 2012, p. 27).

This tendency is contextualized in what Turner (1980) described as the "comprador character" of the political economy of the Nigerian state, which have contributed to undermine Nigerian development. Turner says (1980, p. 204), "From independence, Nigeria has been governed by a neo-colonial comprador state which lacks coherence and stability. . . . Representatives of this class occupy government posts and control the state."

Onimode (1978) reinforced the "neo-colonial comprador state" theory in Nigeria as elsewhere in Africa rather in a different way as the handiwork of multinational corporations. He argued that the activities of these monopoly "sharks" (multinational corporations) are important to the understanding of the ways through which Third-World countries are exploited, manipulated, and perpetuated as the collective "wretched of the earth." He further added:

> The historical origin of this collective malaise is nineteenth and twentieth century colonization of Nigeria by British imperialists. . . . In particular, after independence in 1960, the carefully recruited and cultivated pro-imperialist privileged classes articulated an "open door policy" for the free inflow and outflow of foreign monopoly capital. These elite also continued their colonial role of imperialist collaboration and willing integration of Nigeria into the orbit of world capitalism as a neocolonial state. (Onimode, 1978, pp. 207–208)

Consequently, Davidson (1974, pp. 4–5) posited,

> What already exists, in this meaning and context, is either an inheritance from a world that is past, or the merely peripheral fragment or fragments of an international system built and controlled for the benefit of non-Africans. On the one hand, the past cannot be recalled, however valid it may once have been.

Resource Curse

The "resource curse" (Lynn, 1997; Ross, 2001) concept is also a suitable unit of analysis for interpreting Africa's underdevelopment. The theory is a body of political and economic literature, which examines the link between resource abundance and poor economic growth (Matti, 2010, p. 402). Auty (1993) first used it as a term in the formal literature. Since then, a cornucopia of studies on resource curse has emerged, for example on conflict, war, and militancy (Le Billon, 2001; Janus, 2012; Fearon, 2005; van der Ploega, 2012, 2017; Morelli, 2015; Obi, 2010; "Blood Diamond"[5]); environmental degradation (United Nations Development Program, *Niger Delta Human Development Report*, 2006; Zabbey et al., 2017; Sam et al., 2017; Babatunde et al., 2017; Allison et al., 2018); prevalence of poverty (Ross,

2012; Auty, 1994; Sarraf and Jiwanji, 2001; Humphreys, Sachs and Stiglitz, eds., 2007); political change and democracy (Auty, 2001; Armadov, 2013; O'Connor et al., 2018; Prichard et al., 2018; Ross, 2001). What is resource curse?

While there are several definitions of resource curse available, the following by Michael Ross (2013, p. 1) is clear and concise: "The resource curse can be defined as the perverse effects of a country's natural resource wealth on its economic, social, or political well-being." The idea that natural resource wealth can have undesirable consequences is not new. For Example, Adam Smith (1723–1790), in his seminal work, *The Wealth of Nations*, stressed the danger of pursuing mineral wealth in the following words:

> Of all those expensive and uncertain projects, however, which bring bankruptcy upon the greater part of the people who engage in them, there is none perhaps more ruinous than the search after new silver and gold mines. It is perhaps the most disadvantageous lottery in the world. . . . They are the projects, therefore, to which of all others a prudent lawgiver, who desired to increase the capital of his nation, would least choose to give any extraordinary encouragement. (Smith, [2007] (1776), Volume I, Book IV, chapter 7, p. 435)

Smith is not alone. David Ricardo (1772–1823), who pioneered the modern concept of economic rents, saw limited social or economic benefits from mining silver or gold (Ross, 2013). In his book *On the Principles of Political Economy and Taxation*, he notes that Spain and Portugal, for example, were Europe's greatest producers of gold and silver; yet, the author (Ross, 2013, p. 3) explained:

> This increase of the quantity of those metals, however, has not, it seems, increased that annual produce; has neither improved the manufactures and agriculture of the country, nor mended the circumstances of its inhabitants. Spain and Portugal, the countries which possess the mines, are, after Poland, perhaps, the two most beggarly countries in Europe. (Ricardo, [1817] (1911, chapter 28, par.10. Quoted in Ross, 2013, p. 3)

According to Ross (1999, p. 297), "there is strong evidence that states with abundant resource wealth perform less well than their resource-poor counterparts." He offered four economic explanations as to why this is the case: "decline in the terms of trade for primary commodities, the instability of international commodity markets, the poor economic linkages between resource and non-resource sectors, and an ailment commonly known as the 'Dutch Disease'" (Ross, 1999, p. 298). Original work by Sachs and Warner

(1995) on the inverse relationship between resource abundance and growth stimulated much of the debate about the resource curse phenomenon.

It is generally assumed that large revenues accruing from the sale of hydrocarbon resources should promote economic growth and reduce poverty (Stevens, 2015, p. 3). But that is not necessarily the case. In fact, oil and mineral wealth has caused more harm than good in African countries. Annan (2000, p. 5) explained further that "instead of being exploited for the benefit of the people, Africa's mineral resources have been so mismanaged and plundered that they are now the source of our misery." Obi (2014, p. 1) added that "abundant oil endowment in Africa has largely been associated with high levels of violence and corruption based on the political economy of an oil curse" and by extension has induced economic underdevelopment and setbacks in Africa. Aryeetey and Asham (2011) stated: "oil, gas and mineral wealth [in Africa] have instead become associated with high poverty rates, weak state institutions, corruption and conflict." Ross et al. (n.d. p. 1) stated: "there is not a strong empirical relationship between oil rents and development in African countries." To buttress Tuokuu (2012) and Ross et al. (n.d.) noted:

> Even though some African countries are endowed with large and rare natural resources, 22 out of 24 nations in 2009 that were identified as having "Low Human Development" according to the United Nations' Human Development Index, were located in Sub-Saharan Africa. . . . For example, the Democratic Republic of Condo (DRC) is richly endowed with mineral and forest resources. It is estimated that the Congo basin alone can produce enough food to feed nearly half the global population. (Quoted in Ross et al., n.d.)

In spite of these resources, the average Congolese earns an annual income of less than US$100 and State revenue is less than US$1billion (Ross et al., n.d.). It is also common for productive agricultural and manufacturing sectors to move away from their successful operations toward mining production (Ross et al., n.d.). For example, the cocoa farms in Ghana are now used for mining activities (Ross et al., n.d.). Not only does this impact on the production and exports of cocoa, but it also affects the landowner's future prospects (Ross et al., n.d.). "Students whose families farmed with cocoa could apply for scholarships from the Cocoa Marketing Board. Now that the land is no longer used for cocoa production, students are no longer eligible for these scholarships. Other African countries with similar statistics include Sierra Leone, Chad, Nigeria, Angola and Mozambique" (Ross et al., n.d. pp. 1–2).

Ross (2013, p. 5) indicated that

> two types of resources have been consistently correlated with lamentable outcomes: petroleum, which is the key variable in the vast majority of the studies

that identify some type of curse; and alluvial diamonds, which in several careful studies have been associated with civil conflict.

Take illustration from Nigeria from the spectrum of petroleum resources induced negative economic impact, especially through the influence of corruption on institutional quality and standard of living.

Meanwhile, Sala-i-Martin and Subramanian (2003) of Columbia University and IMF, respectively, in their paper "Addressing the Natural Resource Curse: An Illustration from Nigeria" showed "very robustly" how "oil in particular exert a negative and nonlinear impact on growth via their deleterious impact on institutional quality" through corruption. They further argued: "The Nigerian experience provides telling confirmation of this aspect of natural resources. Waste and corruption from oil rather than Dutch disease has been responsible for its poor long run economic performance. . . . Nigeria has been a disastrous development experience." On just about every conceivable metric, Nigeria's performance since independence has been dismal. Sala-i-Martin and Subramanian (2003):

> In purchasing power parity (PPP[6]) terms, Nigeria's per capita GDP was US$1,113 in 1970 and is estimated to have remained at US$1,084 in 2000. The latter figure places Nigeria amongst the 15 poorest nations in the world for which such data are available. In terms of GDP growth since 1960, Nigeria fared worse than the average country. . . . Nigeria, unfortunately, fares much worse on measures of poverty and income distribution. Between 1970 and 2000, the poverty rate, measured as the share of the population subsisting on less than US$1 per day increased from close to 36 percent to just under 70 percent. . . . To illustrate: whereas in 1970 the top 2 percent and the bottom 17 percent of the population earned the same total amount of income, in 2000 the top 2 percent had the same income as the bottom 55 percent. . . . These developments, of course, coincided with the discovery of oil in Nigeria. (Abstract; para. 1, 2, 3, 5)

Finally, Sala-i-Martin and Subramanian contended that while the literature on resource curse has identified the tripartite factor of trade volatility, overvaluation of the real exchange rate, institutional quality and associated Dutch Disease as influential to growth, in the particular Nigerian case, they

> provide evidence suggesting that Dutch disease is an inadequate explanation for Nigeria's growth performance. The waste explanation, on the other hand, appears to be overwhelming, with oil a key factor causing a whole series of pathologies that have led to the waste. (Sala-i-Martin and Subramanian (2003))

Institutions

It is now widely recognized that domestic institutions play a pivotal role in economic development (Desta & Hirsch, 2012, p. 132). The institutional perspective theory emphasizes the quality of regulatory framework, the capacity of government institutions to enforce compliance with standards and ensure credibility, the rule of law and fighting corruption, protection of property rights, and government effectiveness (Desta & Hirsch, 2012, p. 133). As Acemoglu and Johnson (2005, p. 950; see also Acemoglu & Robinson, 2008, 2010; Osman, Alexiou, & Tsaliki, 2011; Fukuyama, 2008; North, 1990) added that "good institutions will simultaneously support private contracts and provide checks against expropriation by the government or other politically powerful groups." Also, Rodrik (2008) noted that the quality of institutions "holds the key to prevailing patterns of prosperity around the world." Okigbo (1989, pp. 6–7) added: "The maintenance of internal law, order and justice is an important part of the economic environment . . . the provision of law and order has a great bearing on the freedom of the individual to engage in economic activity." Also, more than 200 years ago, Adam Smith's thought on the role of institutions in fostering trade and commerce was very apt:

> Commerce and manufactures can seldom flourish long in any state which does not enjoy a regular administration of justice, in which the people do not feel themselves secure in the possession of their property, in which the faith of contractors is not protected by law, and in which the authority of the state is not supposed to be regularly employed in enforcing the payment of debts from all those who are able to pay. Commerce and manufactures, in short, can seldom flourish in any state in which there is not certain degree of confidence in the justice of government. (Smith, 1776, *Wealth of Nations*, Book V, Chapter III, Of Public Debts, p. 710)

Recent development studies indicate that markets and institutions are interwoven, and that markets do not exist in isolation of an institutional framework (Desta & Hirsch, 2012, p. 133; Rapley, 2007). Research has shown that corruption by government officials depresses economic growth and overburdens the poor (Zhang, 2000; Na, Kang, & Kim, 2018; World Bank, 2018). Also, "corruption is bad for development due to its adverse effects on the incentives, prices and opportunities that private and public agents face" (Blackburn, Bose, & Haque, 2004, p. 3). Consequently, countries with lower corruption levels tend to have higher levels of GDP per capita (Higbee & Schmid, 2004); similarly, higher levels of corruption are associated with lower government revenues, lower GDP, lower expenditures on operations and maintenance, and a lower quality of public infrastructure (Tanzi & Davoodi, 1997; Mensah, 2016; Aidt, 2009).

ECONOMIC CHANGES AND DECLINE IN NIGERIA

No sooner had Nigeria gained independence in 1960 than her economic fortunes began to unravel. Iyoha (2008, p. 4) offers an explanation:

> The economy had relied heavily on export-driven primitive agriculture, small-to-medium scale manufacturing, and petty trading. However, with crude oil becoming the dominant product in Nigeria's exports, political elites and their administrations failed to harness the receipts from oil for a proper diversification of the export base of the economy. Instead they engaged in capital flight and massive importation of consumer goods, to the detriment of the balance-of-payments position.

This situation can be explained by the dependency theory concept of underdevelopment, as, "historically third-world economic dependence is tied to Western European capitalist expansion and imperialism" (Jack et al., 2016, p. 206). The integration of dependency into Africa's IPE at independence has continued to undermine wealth creation and economic success in Africa (Shaw, 1975, 1982; Mlambo, 2018). Santos (1970, p. 231) defined dependence as a "situation in which the economy of certain countries is conditioned by the development and expansion of another economy to which the former is subjected." McGowan and Smith (2009, pp. 179–180) added:

> Dependency refers to an asymmetrical structure of control relations wherein a controller, such as a state, multinational enterprise, or parent, regularly and hence predictably, changes or maintains the behavior of a controlee, such as another state, an economic sector, or a child. Viewed from the perspective of the controller, such asymmetrical control relationships represent dominance, whereas for the controlled they represent dependency and often exploitation.

In essence, according to Ake (1981, p. 55) "an economy is dependent to the extent that its position and relations to other economies in the international system and articulation of its internal structure make it incapable of auto-centric development." That being the case, first, according to Ekekwe (1985, p. 53), "the post-colonial state in Nigeria, being a creation of imperialism, has followed a developmental strategy dictated by the interests of imperialism and its local allies, not by those of the majority of the indigenous population."

Then, "the colonial state, through deliberate administrative manipulation and discrimination, underdeveloped indigenous entrepreneurship and relegated it to a compradoral role in the economy" (Akeredolu-Ale, 1975, quoted in Falola & Ihonvbere, 1985 p. 84). Third, from the mid-1960s,

Nigeria progressively shifted from cash crops production to oil production, and by the mid-1970s oil had become the major foreign exchange earner and chief source of budget revenues (oil revenues increased significantly from ₦3.4 million in 1960 to ₦4,190 million in 1975) (Falola & Ihonvbere, 1985, p. 87). Furthermore, dependency on commodity exports and attendant volatility of prices of raw materials in the world capitalist exchange predisposes resources to fluctuations in the world market (Falola & Ihonvbere, 1985, p. 84).

Everywhere you look in Nigeria there is poverty amid oil wealth, deprivation amid elite opulence or what Thorstein Veblen called "conspicuous consumption" (Veblen, [1899] 1979), and social decay amid profligate public spending. And most certainly, the economic maelstrom must be swiftly and forcefully tackled for the good of the country.

Nigerians ought to enjoy salubrious economic prosperity on the backs of the country's vast resource endowments. But that is not occurring. Rather Nigeria's economic profile is that of poverty, squandered riches, missed opportunities, debts, and borrowing. According to Thomas and Canagarajah (2002) of the IMF, "Nigeria is a case of poverty in a wealthy economy:" They further add (pp. 4–6):

> Nigeria is endowed with land, oil, and natural resources, but a substantial of portion of its population remains very poor because of its failure to manage its wealth effectively. Between 1970 and 1990, Nigeria earned almost $200 billion (primarily through exports), some of which was locally invested. However, these investments had very little impact on the population's welfare. . . . Among Sub-Saharan African countries, Nigeria had the second largest export income (after South Africa) in 1994. Nigeria earned about $9 billion while South Africa earned about $23 billion. On a per capita basis, Nigeria had the fourth largest export income per capita, after South Africa, Angola and Zambia. This clearly shows the wealth of the Nigerian economy and its potential for effectively alleviating or reducing poverty.

Years of economic mismanagement, corruption, and unaccountable leadership have taken their toll and have left the economy reeling and in a stupor or torpor. While Nigeria's peers in Asia with vast oil resources, for example, Indonesia (Lewis, 2007; Tirtosudarmo, Henly & Fuady, 2012), have become economic juggernauts anchored on a thriving middle class, dynamic labor force, good jobs and rising wages, mega social progress, economic diversity, smart technology, strong manufacturing, robust exports, bullish stock market, and effective leadership, Nigeria has lagged and became an economic basket case. The nation's economic crisis is particularly unique in not only its longevity but also its continued severity.

Mismanagement

One of the major objectives of development planning in Nigeria, according to the five-year Third National Development Plan (1975–1980), for example, "is to spread the benefit of economic development so that the average Nigerian would experience a marked improvement in his [her] standard of living" (p. 29). This objective did support the third core national objective of the Plan, that is, "to establish Nigeria firmly as a just and egalitarian society."

In essence, rapid economic and social development of Nigeria should be mixed with even development of the country and by equality of access to political and economic power (Idang, 1978, p. 999). Regardless, it is too evident that there is little dispute that executive economic mismanagement has hampered the "spread of the benefit of economic development" in Nigeria. While mismanagement transcends virtually all segments of governance in Nigeria, executive economic mismanagement has been the worst. Peter Lewis (2007, pp. 77–78) offers an explanation here:

> The failure of Nigerian development stems above all from the absence of a political and institutional center to serve as a principal of economic change. Nigeria's elites, divided along communal and factional lines, have not consolidated stable political regimes or fostered capable state organizations. . . . Nigeria embodies a striking absence of central authority, whether arising from a strong leader, a governing party, the military, or the bureaucracy, to furnish public goods and enforce institutional prerogatives. Nigeria's poor economic performance is linked to this central problem of collective action.

Earlier, Osayimwese and Iyare (1991, p. 89) surmised up that "Nigeria's economic difficulties are due primarily to public-sector mismanagement worsened by the dynamics of federalism and state creation and by the growth in centralized Federal power." Also, "monetary policy has been inadequate, fiscal policy has benefited state governments but misaligned their spending policies with their own resources and with national economic objectives, and resources have been consistently misallocated, mainly because of the principle of" "Federal character" (Osayimwese & Iyare, 1991, p. 89; Idike et al., 2019). Suberu (2010, p. 459) also contended that "many influential commentators" see the "current centralized system of federalism in Nigeria as a veritable source of, rather than a credible solvent for, the country's multifaceted crises of unity, democracy, and development." Asefa and Huang (2015, p. 1) buttressed "sustainable development requires good governance that is predictable, open, enlightened, accountable, inclusive of all citizens, and operates under the rule of law." Hence, "to understand economic performance," according to Brautigam (1999, p. 1), "it is important to factor in the political role of government," especially in a developing country such as Nigeria where the government is expected to do more for the citizens, as Lewis (1955, p. 376) also noted that "no country has made economic progress without positive stimulus from government."

Brautigam (1992, p. 1) asserted that

> governments determine how well, or how poorly, markets function . . . if governments are assumed to be neutral, and committed to serving the public good, then deviations from optimum economic performance can generally be corrected simply through policy reform, or through improving information systems.

"The central argument" according to Lewis (2007, p. 27) "is that differences in long term economic performance are determined by variations in the ability of states to make credible commitments to market participants. Such commitments include policy stability, secure property rights, and a conducive setting for contracting, which together enable capital accumulation."

Unfortunately in Nigeria the motto of Nigerian leaders is at variance with the chapter's opening quotes and both Lewis's and Brautigam's insights. The well-being of the nation according to the Nigerian leadership is how many politicians and public officials looted and abused his or her position most. It seems Nigerian leaders loathe the idea that economic growth "promotes the general welfare" (Rushefsky, 2013, p. 47). Economic growth induces a number of benefits: increased personal income, resources for investment, new job opportunities, and enhanced support for government and incumbents (Gosling & Eisner, 2014). A review of the Nigerian economy from 1980 to the present confirms the Nigerian motto for seeking leadership.

The year 1980 was a watershed moment in Nigeria's post-independence economic history because it witnessed the initial slump in world oil prices (with oil being the backbone of Nigeria's economy); oil prices went from "$40 a barrel in 1980 to $14 a barrel in 1987" (*The Economist*, 1992). The oil bust had devastating impacts on the economies of oil exporting countries including Nigeria. And since oil prices dictate the health of Nigeria's economy, this seismic economic jolt sent the Nigerian economy into a tailspin. The 1980's oil price slumps led to drop in Nigeria's oil revenues from $25 billion in 1980 to $12 billion in 1982 to $6 billion in 1986 (Aliyu, 2006). External shocks were chiefly to blame for the price slump. For example, energy conservation and improved technology in the industrialized economies decreased the demand for oil (Campbell & Marston, 1999, p. 544). Also, new sources of oil in the North Sea and Alaska and overproduction, especially by non-OPEC countries, resulted in oil surplus (Campbell & Marston, 1999, p. 544). Also, "the changes in the economic directions abroad result in changes in the direction of economic activities in Nigeria due mainly to the fact that Nigeria economy seems to lack its own internal dynamic" (Kalu, 1996, p. 231).

The collapse in world oil market did not only deal a devastating blow to the Nigerian economy, but it also exposed the soft underbelly of Nigeria's oil-dependent economy to the volatility of international energy prices. At the same time, "inefficient planning sharply distressed the Nigerian economy in a context in which agriculture was not only in decay, but had clearly suffered serious neglect with consequences for peasants, labor and the masses" (Kalu, 1996, p. 234). Therefore, Olukoshi (1993, p. 3) argued:

> The collapse of the world oil market which resulted in Nigeria's oil earnings falling dramatically from a peak of ₦10.1 billion in 1979 to about ₦5.161 billion in 1982 immediately triggered a major crisis in industry and the rest of the economy. At the level of industry, many firms either suspended production or scaled down capacity utilization drastically because of inability of the state to continue to meet their foreign exchange needs. It is generally reckoned that about 50 percent of the total number of manufacturing establishments operating in Nigeria stopped production for some time with adverse consequences for workers who were retrenched in their thousands. An inflationary spiral also took hold in the economy as there emerged an acute shortage of consumer goods and imported food items like rice. (Quoted in Kalu, 1996, p. 234)

While the drop in oil price was a major cause of Nigeria's economic travails beginning in the 1980s, other factors including wasteful consumption, the incompetence, and the lack of vision of the Nigerian leadership to ameliorate the effects of, or, head-off completely, this economic blizzard in spite of the ample resources at their disposal were also in play and no less devastating. Of wasteful consumption, for example, out of the 63 projects undertaken in the 1980s for which $2.6 billion was borrowed only one project was viable (Aliyu, 2006), tying into what Ansar et al. (2016, p. 360) referred to as "overinvesting in unproductive projects which results in build-up of debt, monetary expansion, instability in financial markets, and economic fragility," semblance of the Nigerian experience, maybe not in exact words.

Shagari and the Economy

The Nigerian military deposed President Shagari's government in 1983 accusing it of massive corruption, financial mismanagement, failure to appropriately address the country's poverty, and continued marginalization of the rural population (Agbese, 1992; quoted in Mbaku, 1994, p. 259). According to Ihonvbere (1991, p. 607),

> it was clear to all that the military was bound to intervene: students did not receive their scholarships, workers were unpaid at the state and federal levels for several months, food and essential commodities became scarce, armed robbery increased, there were daily demonstrations, riots, strike actions, and attacks against the agents and agencies of the state.

In a meeting with foreign diplomats shortly after the coup, the new military head of state, General Buhari, said this of the ousted Shagari administration: "Nigeria had been enslaved by a handful of people who had been sharing the wealth among themselves and who were determined to stay in office at any cost" (May, 1984). Shagari's administration presided over the most serious economic mismanagement crisis Nigeria had faced (Ekwe-Ekwe, 1985, p. 613). Osaghae (1998, pp. 155–156) offered an elaboration:

> Of all the failings of the Second republic, the one on which commentators are agreed, and which the military gave for a fresh intervention, was the gross mismanagement of the economy, especially by the NPN controlled Federal government. The indicators of this mismanagement were all too clear. From average annual growth rate of 6–7 percent between 1975 and 1980, GDP fell by 8.5 percent in real terms between 1981 and 1983, while consumer prices increased by over 20 percent. Agricultural production, especially of cash crops, declined from 4.0 percent in 1979 to 3.4 in 1981 and 2.7 percent in 1982, although domestic food output rose by 7 percent at the end of 1983 (due largely to good harvests in those years). Foreign exchange reserves declined from ₦5.462 billion in 1980 to ₦798.5 million which was barely enough to pay for one month's imports in 1983, while total external debt rose from about US$9 billion in 1980 to about US$18 billion in 1983.

Olukoshi and Abdulraheem (1985, p. 95) did offer in more graphic details of the parlous state and mismanagement of the economy under Shagari:

> In December 1983, when the Buhari coup took place, the Nigerian economy was in a dire state. About 50 per cent of the industrial capacity of the country had been lost owing to the closure of factories unable to obtain foreign exchange to import raw materials and spare parts. As a result about one million workers had been retrenched from the manufacturing sector between 1980 and 1983. The country's GDP fell by 4.4 per cent in 1983 after a decline of 2 per cent in 1982 and the budget deficit for 1983 was ₦6.231 billion, representing more than 50 per cent of total government expenditure. The foreign exchange current account recorded a deficit of ₦4.9 billion in 1982 and ₦2.9 billion in 1983. For an economy which spent ₦9.095 billion on imports in 1980, rising to ₦3.59 billion in 1981, the foreign exchange earnings principally from crude petroleum

> exports, fell from ₦10.1 billion in 1979 to ₦5.161 billion in 1982. . . . The real incomes of workers and peasants were undermined as the prices of basic commodities like milk, sugar, rice, beans and yams escalated beyond their reach, and that was if and when they were available. On top of this, the level of foreign indebtedness reached a peak of ₦15 billion in 1983 while the country's backlog of trade payments stood at ₦5 billion in 1983. The parlous state of affairs was worsened by the collapse of basic social services like hospitals, rural health clinics and schools.

"Shagari made no serious attempt to improve or diversify the economy and reduce dependence. Instead, he intensified all the economic problems and crises of the country" wrote Falola and his coauthor (Falola & Ihonvbere, 1985, p. 94). The December 31, 1983, coup broadcast, announcing the overthrow of Shagari's government, was further indicative of the parlous state of Nigerian economy under Shagari.

> Our economy has been hopelessly mismanaged. We have become a debtor and beggar nation. There is inadequacy of food at reasonable prices for our people who are now fed up with endless announcements of importation of foodstuffs. Health services are in shambles as our hospitals are reduced to mere consulting clinics without drugs, water and equipment. Our educational system is deteriorating at an alarming rate. Unemployment figures including the graduates have reached embarrassing and unacceptable proportions. In some states, workers are being owed salary arrears of eight to twelve months, and in others there are threats of salary cuts. Yet our leaders revel in squandermania, corruption, and indiscipline, and continue to proliferate public appointments in complete disregard for our stark economic realities. (Quoted in Shehu Othman, 1984)

The above was in spite of the fact that, in 1979, then president Shagari inherited huge net foreign reserves of ₦5.5 billion from the Obasanjo administration (*New African*, 1986, pp. 8–10). By the time Shagari was toppled in 1983, the administration had nearly squandered all the reserves and was in a serious debt, domestic and foreign. As confirmed by Osaghae (1998, p. 156), in fact, by 1983 the reserves were almost depleted (less than $1 billion remained), and external debts rose to over US$12 billion, up about 200% in four years (Ekwe-Ekwe, 1985, p. 613). Industrial production suffered because of the difficulty of businesses to access foreign exchange to import raw materials and spare parts, food prices rose by over 500% between 1979 and 1981 as agricultural output declined in spite of the enormous expenditure of about $2.4 billion which the Shagari administration devoted to his ill-fated Green Revolution program (Ekwe-Ekwe, 1985, p. 613).

In 1982, for example, Nigeria's monthly imports bill jumped to ₦2 billion (including food, up by 100%), and inflation increased to 55%; foreign debts rose from ₦5 billion to ₦24 billion between 1979 and 1983 (in spite of the collection of ₦42 billion in four years), unemployment rose alarmingly, and corruption became even more rampant (Ihonvbere, 1991, pp. 606–607).

> In fact, in September 1983 alone, Nigeria imported 49,291 tons of rice from Thailand at a cost of ₦10.1 million; in August 1983, Nigeria spent ₦11.4 million on Thai rice alone while between January and September, a total of ₦66.8 million was spent on rice imports from Thailand (Falola & Ihonvbere, 1985, p. 89).

Additionally, Nigeria's Fourth National Development Plan (1981–1985) launched by President Shagari in March 1981 as the economic blueprint to improve the economy by "according priority status to all sectors of the economy" was deemed as "extremely optimistic projections" with "completely misplaced expectations" (Falola & Ihonvbere, 1985). Meanwhile, while the economy suffered, corporate profits soared, indicating favorable "benefits from Shagari's profligate fiscal program, especially business tax breaks" (Ekwe-Ekwe, 1985, p. 614). Shagari's corporate tax breaks benefited transnational corporations as well, especially Anglo-American companies which still dominate the Nigerian economy (Ekwe-Ekwe, 1985, p. 614). These foreign conglomerates reported huge profits while they steadily paid less tax further constraining the economy (Ekwe-Ekwe, 1985, p. 614).

To combat the economic crisis, President Shagari "attempted a feeble reform" (Jega, 2000, p. 18) with the help of the National Assembly through the instrumentality of the austere Economic Stabilization (Temporary Provisions) Act of 1982. The Economic Stabilization Act was aimed to

> reduce public expenditures and curtail imports using import restrictions, monetary controls, financial instruments, and conserve foreign exchange. Import duties were imposed on items that had previously escaped tariffs, all new capital projects were suspended, interest rates were increased across the board by two percentage points, all unused import licenses were recalled, the public investment expenditure was cut 40 percent, and tariffs and gasoline prices were raised. (Herbst & Olukoshi, 1994, p. 462)

The foregoing "had some effects" (Herbst & Olukoshi, 1994, p. 462), however, "because of the core nature of the economic and financial disequilibriums, the government found that austerity measures without structural adjustment constituted an inadequate response to the economic crisis" (Iyoha,

2008, p. 21). At the same time, the government did not appear to take actions that matched with its pronouncements (Iyoha, 2008, p. 21). For example, the Central Bank of Nigeria (CBN) reviewed the continued economic deterioration during 1982–1983, and concluded, "although laudable policies had been adopted to address these [economic] problems, implementation has been faulty and particularly disappointing" (Central Bank of Nigeria, 1984, p. 12). "At the same time our manufacturing sector which is unhappily import-oriented, continues to weaken. . . . To provide and stabilize the economy on a long-term basis, it is imperative that the country now begins the structural re-adjustment process required for renewed economic buoyancy" (President Shagari, Twenty-Third Independence and Inaugural Address to the Nation, October 1, 1983. Quoted in Falola & Ihonvbere, 1985, p. 118).

Babangida and the Economy

According to Jega (2000, p. 18) "by the time Babangida regime came into power, the economic crisis had become acute in all its ramifications. International pressure had been mounted by the Bretton Woods institutions, and domestic demand for a resolution of the crisis had also heightened." Also the World Bank noted, "Nigeria's economy was already on the verge of crisis" (World Bank, 1994, p. vii) following the world oil market glut in 1985; furthermore, General Ibrahim Babangida explained, in September 1985, shortly after assuming power:

> The last twenty months have not witnessed any significant changes in the national economy. Contrary to expectations we have so far been subjected to a steady deterioration in the general standard of living and intolerable suffering by the ordinary Nigerians has risen higher, scarcity of commodities has increased, hospitals still remain mere consulting clinics while educational institutions are on the brink of decay. Unemployment has stretched to critical proportions. (*Newswatch*, September 9, 1985, p. 19. Quoted in Ihonvbere, 1991, p. 609)

In a bid to gauge the mood of Nigerians, the new government invited the citizenry to debate publicly the question of whether the country should agree to an IMF loan and the attendant conditionalities. The regime also declared a 15-month national economic emergency beginning October 1, 1985, that included wage and salary cuts of between 2% and 20% for public and private sector employees. Two authors explained:

> In addition to enabling the government to cope with its worsening fiscal crisis as oil prices declined, the declaration of the emergency sent a signal to Nigerians

> that the economic situation was bad and that, finally, structural measures would have to be taken. The wage freeze also told multilaterals that the new regime was serious about structural adjustment, irrespective of the outcome of the national debate. (Herbst & Olukoshi, 1994, pp. 471 and 473)

The national debate rejected the IMF loan on the grounds of "nationalistic urge to reject reforms imposed from outside" (Herbst & Olukoshi, 1994, p. 474). Upon the rejection of the IMF loan, the linchpin economic policy initiative of President Babangida was the "Structural Adjustment Program (SAP) introduced in 1986 and sponsored by the IMF and the World Bank to stabilize the economy and put it back on a growth path" (Walkenhorst, 2007, p. 3). According to the World Bank (1994, p. 9):

> The aims of SAP were to restructure and diversify the country's productive base in order to increase efficiency and reduce dependence on the oil sector; to achieve fiscal and balance-of-payments viability; to improve the efficiency of public sector investments; and to concentrate government efforts on creating an enabling environment for growth in the private sector. The SAP sought to achieve these aims through: adoption of a market-determined exchange rate (supported by prudent fiscal and monetary policies); liberalization of trade policy and prices and markets; and liberalization of private investment regulations.

However, a policy pronouncement does necessarily translate to policy reality, let alone, policy effectiveness and usefulness. In the Nigerian case on the adoption of Structural Adjustment Program (SAP) as an economic strategy, while arguably sound in conception, SAP left much to be desired. Lewis (1994, p. 437) observed: "Nigeria's persistent economic stagnation is attributable to a mutually reinforcing political dynamic, comprising a weak developmental state and pervasive rent-seeking within the private sector. This syndrome was a source of Nigeria's initial economic crisis in the early 1980s, and it continues to impede structural adjustment initiatives."

Furthermore, Babangida's presidential term (1985–1993) not only bequeathed a sad economic legacy and political turmoil to the nation, but it also escalated the economic misfortune as well (Nugent, 2012; Jega, 2000; Maier, 2009). Like President Shagari before him, President Babangida made no serious efforts to use Nigeria's huge oil revenues, especially the Gulf War windfall[7] to improve the economy and strengthen infrastructure (Agbiboa, 2012a; Agbiboa, 2012b; Fagbadebo, 2007; Osoba, 1996; *The Economist*, June 8, 1996, p. 46; *Tell*, December 20, 1993, p. 17; *Financial Times* of London, January 2, 1995, p. 3). Instead, "Babangida fomented economic adversities" (Lewis, 1996, p. 80) to the extent that on Babangida's watch, "budget deficit was a whopping 10% of the GDP; debt service gulped a quarter of export earnings; annual inflation rate was estimated at 70–100% in June 1993; and real per capita income was ten times less than what it was when he took office 8 years prior" (*The Economist*, Survey of Nigeria, August 21, 1993).

Under Presidents Shagari and Babangida, the Nigerian economy suffered so severely that real per capita Gross National Product (GNP) declined at annualized rate of 0.3% from 1980 through 1989 (Schnitzer, 1994, p. 337). GNP fell from $99 billion in 1980 to $34 billion in 1991 (World Bank Atlas, 1992, p. 19).

Table 1.17 presents that between 1980 and 1989, of the selected countries, except for Côte d'Ivoire, Nigeria is the only one that registered negative GDP growth, and struggled in the 1990–1999 span, compared to Egypt, Botswana, Mali, and Kenya. In the 1980–1989 period particularly, Nigeria's aggregate GDP declined by a massive 31% compared to growth for Uganda at 324%; Botswana, 191%; Egypt, 83%; Mali, 24%; South Africa, 19%; Ghana, 18%. Kenya and Namibia edged up 14% and 5%, respectively. Thailand gained 123% and Indonesia rose 30%.

During this period, Nigeria's foreign economic performance, especially external trade and balance-of-payments' position, left much to be desired. Aggregate exports of goods, services, and income slumped to $9.88 billion in 1995, down 64% from $27.76 billion in 1980 (World Bank, *World Development Report* 1997). Export value of major commodities particularly cocoa, palm kernel, rubber made no gains and at the same time lost grounds by more than half from ₦536.2 million in 1983 to ₦300 million in 1985 (*New African*, October 1986, p. 12). In contrast, import bills skyrocketed to ₦50.43 billion in 1995, up 129% from ₦22 billion in 1980 (World Bank, *World Development Report 1997*). Also, current account balance declined to negative $510 million in 1995, from positive $5.2 billion in 1980; gross international reserves fell to $1.7 billion in 1995, down 84% from $10.6 billion in 1980 (World Bank, *World Development Report 1997*). (Per the World Bank, current account balance is the sum of net exports of goods and services, net primary income, and net secondary income.)

During this period, FDI inflows into Nigeria also suffered (table 1.18). Contemporary Asian countries of Malaysia ($50.9 billion), Indonesia ($24.8 billion), Singapore ($108.8 billion), and Thailand ($36.5 billion) attracted more FDI than Nigeria ($12.4 billion). Even among fellow African countries, Nigeria failed to take a commanding lead and also performed below expectations, placed second to Egypt ($16.1 billion), and when bounced against little known and less populous African countries, the decline gets more pronounced for Nigeria given that Namibia ($547) and Botswana ($488) attracted more FDI per capita than Nigeria ($104). (South Africa most certainly could have attracted more FDI than Nigeria during this period were it not for the intense international antiapartheid campaign against her that

Table 1.17 Nigeria's GDP versus Selected Countries, 1980–2019 ($m)

Country	*GDP 1980*	*GDP 1989*	*GDP 1999*	*GDP 2009*	*GDP 2019*	*GDP Growth 1980–1989 (%)**	*GDP Growth 1990–1999 (%)**	*GDP Growth 2000–2009 (%)**	*GDP Growth 2010–2019 (%)**
Botswana	$1,061	$3,084	$5,484	$10,267	$18,340	191	78	87	79
CD	10,176	9,757	12,377	24,375	58,539	(4)	27	97	140
Egypt	21,670	39,756	90,711	189,147	303,092	83	128	109	60
Ghana	4,445	5,252	7,719	26,048	66,984	18	47	237	157
Kenya	7,265	8,283	12,896	37,022	95,503	14	56	187	158
Mali	1,760	2,182	3,439	10,191	17,280	24	58	196	70
Namibia	2,422	2,532	3,819	8,825	12,367	5	51	131	40
Nigeria	64,202	44,003	59,373	291,880	448,120	(31)	35	392	54
SA	82,980	99,031	136,632	295,936	351,432	19	38	117	19
Uganda	1,245	5,276	5,999	25,020	35,165	324	14	317	41
Indonesia	72,482	94,451	140,001	539,580	1,119,191	30	48	285	107
Thailand	32,353	72,251	126,669	281,710	543,549	123	75	122	93

CD = Côte d'Ivoire.
SA = South Africa.
*Author calculation.
Source: World Bank.

Table 1.18 Foreign Direct Investment Selected Countries, 1980–2019

Country	*FDI 1980–1999*	*1999 Population*	*FDI Per Capita**	*FDI 2000–2019*	*2019 Population*	*FDI Per Capita**
Botswana	$785,428,707	1,610,264	$488	$5,804,237,045	2,303,697	$2,520
Cameroon	1,226,278,984	15,112,592	81	8,865,611,002	25,876,380	343
Egypt	16,057,317,536	67,515,591	238	102,947,300,000	100,388,073	1,025
Ghana	1,221,863,752	18,812,359	65	38,576,211,618	30,417,856	1,268
Kenya	831,075,813	31,098,757	27	11,644,972,397	52,573,973	221
Namibia	964,712,498	1,763,859	547	9,117,593,418	2,494,530	3,655
Nigeria	12,450,597,407	119,260,063	104	88,073,456,852	200,963,599	438
Senegal	678,878,404	9,568,722	71	6,850,744,295	16,296,364	420
SA	8,633,729,422	44,338,543	195	83,948,140,745	58,558,270	1,434
Uganda	913,250,000	22,952,410	40	13,506,122,005	44,269,594	305
Malaysia	50,960,888,260	22,661,298	2,249	145,448,923,906	31,949,777	4,552
Indonesia	24,838,579,037	208,615,169	119	226,989,694,521	270,625,568	839
Singapore	108,859,255,958	3,958,723	27,499	935,063,797,435	5,703,569	163,944
Thailand	36,537,417,344	62,298,571	586	150,574,267,424	69,625,582	2,163

*Author calculation.
SA = South Africa.
Source: World Bank.

forced business divestments and discouraged FDI inflows into the country.) Aside executive mismanagement, other strains of economic problems that afflicted Nigeria during the period under review are discussed, all linked mainly to bad leadership.

Weak Currency, SAP, and Predatory Exchange Rate

Also, in the 1980s and 1990s, the Nigerian naira took a serious beating. It saw its value plunge drastically, especially, with the introduction of World Bank prescribed SAP in 1986 as a remedial measure to cushion the effects of crash in oil prices, and the cumulative effects of years of mismanagement and lack of regenerative investments (World Bank, 1994). The basic thrusts of the World Bank's SAP were shrink spending, devalue the currency, remove subsidies, free prices, liberalize trade, and sell off state companies (*The Economist*, May 1, 1994, p. 44).

However, SAP unleashed more economic hardship especially on the middle class and the poor than it relieved, evidenced by industry and civil-service layoffs, fall in real per capita income, rising inflation, and export compression (see, for example, Marshall, 1994; UNCTAD, 1998). It also increased poverty to a degree that led to a descending spiral of dissatisfaction, dissent, tremendous human cost, and if not destruction of human dignity (*West Africa*, January 23–29, 1995, p. 94). Argued former head of state, General Muhammadu Buhari (now President Buhari) in 1998:

> With the introduction of SAP, the government pauperized the majority of the people of this country. Instead of a graduated 60 percent devaluation of the naira, the national currency experienced its greatest humiliation. In a way, the devaluation of the naira occasioned by SAP has contributed more than any single measure in destroying the moral fiber of Nigerians. The new value of the naira is unrealistic, indefensible, and the result of utter lack of patriotism and perhaps the most painful and most enduring act of official recklessness and lack of regard for the economic well-being of Nigerians. (*Post Express*, May 18, 1998)

Moreover, SAP placed too much emphasis on macroeconomic policies and too little on investments in infrastructure and human development (Wilson, 1990, pp. 5–16). Adebayo Adedeji, former executive secretary to the United Nations Economic Commission for Africa (ECA) had this to say: "Any economic policy program that is anti-people will never succeed. And structural adjustment programs with excessive concentration on macroeconomic aggregate to the neglect of people will not succeed. Well, I am not surprised it [SAP] has not succeeded" (*West Africa*, March 11–17, 1996, p. 381). Jeffrey

Sachs, former director of the Harvard Institute for International Development, added:

> The structural adjustment programs remain deeply flawed. The IMF is so obsessed with price stability it doesn't think very hard about anything else. The World Bank, on the other hand, has hundreds of good ideas but no priorities. World Bank programs call on weak, debt-ridden governments to introduce value-added taxes, new customs administration, civil-service reform, privatization of infrastructure, decentralized public administration and many other wonderful things often within months. (*The Economist*, June 29, 1996, p. 19)

And in the most eloquent testimony of all that SAP was a flop, former World Bank economist, William Easterly, in his 2005 seminal article, "What Did Structural Adjustment Adjust" remarkably concluded:

> The big stylized facts of adjustment lending suggest that structural adjustment did not succeed in adjusting macroeconomic policy and growth outcomes very much. Structural adjustment loans were repeated many times to the same country, which itself is suggestive of limited effect of the earlier adjustment loans. There were some successes, but also some big disasters. (Easterly, 2005, p. 20)

The debris of the economic tornado that hit Nigeria in the 1980s and 1990s continued in the twenty-first century.

NIGERIA: ENTER THE TWENTY-FIRST CENTURY

Over the past several years, as an expert underscored, the Nigerian leadership has "muddled through" (Lindblom, 1959, p. 79) and has taken the nation in the wrong direction on the economy. And the Nigerian people have paid a terrible price for it as the economy has continued to be mired in a business cycle laced with recession, rising business failures, unemployment, and dwindling FDIs. Corruption still dictates and dominates in the place of fair competition, and patronage contracts awarded to cronies determine success in the private sector. The middle class and the working poor have been hardest hit.

By nearly every algorithm of measurement, the middle class has almost disappeared as an effective economic force in Nigeria. Nigeria's economic profile is that of squandered riches, missed opportunities, borrowing, and debt (Ogunyemi, 2011; Pinto, 1987, Lewis, 1996; Sala-i-Martin & Subramanian, 2003). There is nothing fundamentally wrong with the Nigerian economy. Rather, the major problem is that Nigerian leaders have not been smart enough to utilize Nigeria's mammoth resources and enormous pool of human talent to promote economic growth and eradicate poverty.

Pius Okigbo, economist and a former Federal economic adviser, has said that Nigerian economy has been repeatedly managed by "economic sorcerers and astrologers, who try to resolve Nigeria's most serious economic problems on the uneducated guesswork rather than by rational calculations, by intuition rather than by study and knowledge on the basis of data and facts" (Okigbo, 1986). Consequently, the economic psychics have denied Nigeria a deserved economic breakthrough and concurrently inflicted economic kwashiorkor and widening inequality on the people. While Nigeria's contemporaries in Asia have achieved "economic miracle" anchored in high technology and robust finance capital, Nigeria blundered and became economic basket case. Worse, Nigerian people have barely benefited from their oil wealth (Shaxson, 2007; Polgreen, 2006; Akinwotu & Olukoya, 2017; Peck & Chayes, 2015). In the most recent data available 10 years (2009–2018) alone, for example, Nigeria earned a whopping $598 billion in petroleum exports (table 1.19), average of $60 billion per year, sixth highest earner in OPEC, after Saudi Arabia, United Arab Emirates, Kuwait, Iraq, and Iran.

Instead of Nigeria pulling its weight on the stimulus of the staggering sum that the country has earned in oil sales since independence to improve lives, sustain growth, beef up prosperity, and upgrade the country, Nigeria remains economically vulnerable and socially lag as successive Nigerian leaderships mismanaged and frittered away this huge fortune and left the economy prostate and the people poor. The *Economist* recently wrote:

> Nigeria is a country full of poor people. Despite pumping roughly 2m barrels of oil per day, most of its population lives in abject poverty. Much of the blame for that falls on elected politicians, who have spent years lining their pockets with the booty. Billions disappear from the accounts of the opaque state-owned oil company. A rainy-day savings account was depleted even when prices were high. Even worse, government members are accused of involvement in industrial-scale theft, which plunders 100,000 barrels of black gold a day. Workings of the country's electric power network is little better than in the days of military junta, millions of children are out of school, and healthcare is a disgrace. (*The Economist*, April 6, 2015)

What does this mean? In obtuse discomfiture, as the American economist, John Kenneth Galbraith, argued in his influential book *The Affluent Society* (Galbraith, 1958), which depicted America's poverty and inequality amid affluence, Nigeria's petrodollar wealth is anachronism to the squalor and poverty encumbering and degrading the Nigerian people. The economic challenges and meltdown have continued into the fourth republic.

Table 1.19 OPEC Petroleum Exports Revenues, 2009–2018 ($b)

Rank	*Country*	*2009*	*2010*	*2011*	*2012*	*2013*	*2014*	*2015*	*2016*	*2017*	*2018*	*Total*
1	Saudi Arabia	$157	$196	$318	$336	$322	$285	$158	$134	$160	$194	$2,262
2	UAE	59	74	105	118	126	108	52	46	66	75	828
3	Kuwait	47	62	97	113	108	98	49	41	51	58	723
4	Iraq	42	51	83	94	89	84	54	44	60	68	670
5	Iran	56	72	115	101	62	54	27	41	53	60	640
6	Nigeria	26	62	86	95	89	77	42	28	39	55	598
7	Venezuela	54	62	88	94	86	78	36	25	31	35	589
8	Angola	39	47	64	72	68	58	32	26	32	36	473
9	Qatar	27	29	45	116	63	57	28	23	35		423
10	Algeria	31	38	51	48	44	41	22	19	22	26	342
11	Libya	31	42	12	60	40	15	5	9	15	17	247
12	Ecuador	7	10	14	14	14	11	7	5	7	10	99
13	Indonesia			19	16	15	13	6				69
14	EG					12	11	6	4	5	5	43
15	Gabon				9	8	8	5	4	4	4	42
16	Congo						8	4	3	4	4	24
	OPEC	576	745	1,097	1,287	1,147	1,004	533	453	582	649	8,073

UAE = United Arab Emirates.
EG = Equatorial Guinea.
Source: Organization of the Petroleum Exporting Countries.

The Fourth Republic

In an address to the National Assembly on June 6, 1999, shortly after assuming office on May 29, 1999, then president Obasanjo indicated that in the "first quarter of 1999 Nigeria posted a budget deficit of ₦256 billion ($2.56 billion), ₦93 billion more than the total deficit forecast for 1999." Foreign reserves also plunged 47% to "$3.75 billion from $7.1 billion during the same time period and, were expected to drop further to $246 million by the end of the year if the current rate of depletion continues." Also, in a January 13, 2000, press conference, then vice-president, Atiku Abubakar, declared:

> In fact the economy had declined in real terms by about 13.5% in 1998 and virtually all indicators of the economy had signaled serious deterioration in the country's economic performance by the second quarter of 1999. . . . The budget deficit went out of hand rising up to about 8% of the GDP. Poverty and squalor were on the increase pushing Nigeria to slide unjustifiably downwards on the scale of human development.

More than 20 years after the comments by Obasanjo and Abubakar, the economy is still in bad shape, and Nigerians are seriously hurting.

By any calculations, Nigeria's economic performance, since the return to civil rule in 1999, has been dismal and lackluster. A key economic indicator, manufacture industry value-added attests to this (table 1.20). (Per the World Bank, "industry value added is the net output of a sector after adding up all outputs and subtracting intermediate inputs.") In the most recent data available, 10 years (2010–2019), with a population of over 200 million people in 2019 (base year), Nigeria could only boast of an average of 25% manufacture industry value added, behind Egypt's robust 36% with a little over 100 million people, half of Nigeria's. It is the same pattern of underperformance when compared to Zambia, 34%; Botswana, 31%; Namibia, 28%; Ghana, 29%; and Namibia, 28%—all with less populations. The inference is that not only that more people are working and producing in these other countries, Nigerian economy is weak, not employing and producing as it ought to, and remains very much comatose.

Another illustrative key economic indicator of Nigeria's economic headwinds is the volume of exports of goods and services (table 1.21). (Per the World Bank, "exports of goods, services and primary income are the sum of goods exports, service exports and primary income receipts.") During the 2010–2019 ten-year period (most recent data available), total exports of goods and services from Nigeria was $742 billion with a population of over 200 million (2019 base year), trailing South Africa's $1,082 billion with

Table 1.20 Industry Value Added Selected Countries % GDP, 2000–2019

Country	Value Added 2000–2009 (%)*	2009 Population	Value Added 2010–2019 (%)*	2019 Population
Botswana	40.6	1,953,498	31.1	2,303,697
Cameroon	28.0	19,789,919	26.4	25,876,380
Côte d'Ivoire	22.6	20,059,147	22.5	25,716,544
Egypt	33.9	81,134,798	36.4	100,388,073
Ghana	22.8	24,170,940	29.2	30,417,856
Mali	23.0	14,581,429	19.4	19,658,031
Namibia	28.1	2,081,044	27.5	2,494,530
Nigeria	26.4	154,324,933	24.5	200,963,599
Senegal	21.5	12,335,084	23.3	16,296,364
South Africa	27.9	50,477,011	26.5	58,558,270
Uganda	23.0	31,411,096	25.7	44,269,594
Zambia	27.1	13,215,139	33.9	17,861,030
Zimbabwe	27.7	12,526,968	22.4	14,645,468
Indonesia	46.2	238,620,563	41.2	270,625,568
Malaysia	45.8	27,735,040	39.0	31,949,777
Singapore	30.0	4,987,573	24.5	5,703,569

*Author calculation.
Source: World Bank.

Table 1.21 Goods and Services Exports by Selected Countries, 2000–2019

Country	Exports of Goods and Services 2000–2009	2009 Population	Per Capita Exports of Goods and Services 2000–2009*	Exports of Goods and Services 2010–2019	2019 Population	Per Capita Exports of Goods and Services 2010–2019*
Libya	$278,442,300,000	6,133,984	$45,393	$262,329,900,000	6,777,452	$38,706
Malawi	7,216,022,849	14,128,155	511	13,026,685,637	18,628,747	699
Mali	14,784,819,968	14,581,429	1,014	29,145,110,814	19,658,031	1,483
Namibia	24,727,898,744	2,081,044	11,882	45,124,476,925	2,494,530	18,089
Nigeria	454,421,974,651	154,324,933	2,945	741,975,494,267	200,963,599	3,692
Senegal	22,517,546,141	12,335,084	1,825	37,480,674,308	16,296,364	2,300
S. Africa	643,205,342,465	50,477,011	12,743	1,081,658,539,340	58,558,270	18,471
Togo	7,715,996,117	6,250,835	1,234	14,932,479,248	8,082,366	1,848
Uganda	16,126,512,595	31,411,096	513	48,960,244,620	44,269,594	1,106
Zambia	29,493,144,787	13,215,139	2,232	93,623,022,975	17,861,030	5,242
Indonesia	943,252,598,914	238,620,563	3,953	1,939,896,173,786	270,625,568	7,168
Malaysia	1,551,216,721,691	27,735,040	55,930	2,100,178,584,633	31,949,777	65,734
Singapore	2,785,075,440,473	4,987,573	558,403	5,795,521,568,484	5,703,569	1,016,122

* Author calculation.
Source: World Bank.

58 million people (more than three times less of Nigeria's). Libya with 6.7 million people (more than 30 times less of Nigeria's) netted more than $262 billion in goods and services exports during the time period. Malaysia with a population of 32 million people (more than six times less of Nigeria's population) fetched a whopping $2,100 billion, and Singapore with only 5.7 million people (35 times less than Nigeria's) earned mega $5,795 billion in exports of goods and services during the period under review. It is all the same experience of decline in terms of per capita basis (Singapore $1,016,157; Malaysia $65,734; Libya $38,706; South Africa $18,471; Namibia $18,089; Zambia $5,242; Nigeria $3,692). Edge in export volumes could be attributable to quality products, cutting-edge processes and procedures, better trained and motivated workers, friendly business environment, enabling bureaucracy, harmonious regulation, reduced business risks, reliable infrastructure, better facilities, all of which Nigeria is found wanting.

Furthermore, Nigeria continues to fail to take advantage of its large population as a leverage for market potential to attract FDI. Nigeria's FDI performance comparatively remains poor both in sum and in per capita (table 1.22). During the 2010–2019 ten-year review period (most recent data available), Nigeria with a population of over 200 million (2019 base year) attracted less than $50 billion ($48.5 billion actually) in FDI, trailing Singapore's more than $727 billion with 5.7 million people. Thailand, with nearly 70 million people (close to three times less than Nigeria's population) netted more than $90 billion in FDI during the time period. Malaysia with just over 31 million people fetched over $106 billion. It is the same pattern of FDI retrogression for Nigeria on a per capita basis: Namibia ($2,026), Botswana ($1,052), Ghana ($1,016), South Africa ($725), and Egypt ($569), all out performed Nigeria at $241. Edge in FDI inflows could be attributable to leadership perception, incidence of corruption, risks concerns in the destination country, and Nigeria has high rate of corruption and at the same time grappling with both infrastructure and security challenges.

"Democratic Dividend" or Dead End

From the foregoing data, the much-vaunted "democratic dividend"[8] of Nigeria remains a mirage, and the hopes for a bright future has increasingly turned into disillusionment as instead of economic turnaround Nigerians get economic runaround, in place of economic bubble-up, Nigerians experience economic "trickle-down" that rewards only the rich, well connected, and shortchanges the rest of the citizenry.

The concept of democratic dividend needs to be fleshed out, since in essence, it can mean more than just economic growth and better economic

Table 1.22 Foreign Direct Investment Selected Countries, 2000–2019

Country	*Total FDI 2000–2009*	*2009 Population*	*FDI Per Capita 2000–2009**	*Total FDI 2010–2019*	*2019 Population*	*FDI Per Capita 2010–2019**
Botswana	$3,436,798,518	1,953,498	$1,759	$2,424,609,840	2,303,697	$1,052
Cameroon	2,315,746,439	19,789,919	117	6,709,572,569	25,876,380	259
Egypt	47,085,200,000	81,134,798	580	57,097,100,000	100,388,073	569
Ghana	7,841,785,274	24,170,940	324	30,900,326,345	30,417,856	1,016
Namibia	4,260,607,374	2,081,044	2,047	5,053,336,808	2,494,530	2,026
Nigeria	40,707,242,619	154,324,933	264	48,506,381,789	200,963,599	241
Senegal	2,029,960,090	12,335,084	165	4,902,427,895	16,296,364	301
S. Africa	42,445,212,474	50,477,011	841	42,471,759,627	58,558,270	725
Uganda	4,381,261,608	31,411,096	139	9,285,560,397	44,269,594	210
Zimbabwe	433,700,000	12,526,968	35	3,676,625,418	14,645,468	251
Malaysia	43,503,538,266	27,735,040	1,569	105,733,017,218	31,949,777	3,309
Singapore	222,938,684,542	4,987,573	44,699	727,640,408,076	5,703,569	127,576
Thailand	63,607,323,517	66,866,839	951	90,332,931,490	69,625,582	1,297

*Author calculation.
Source: World Bank.

opportunities. Some perspectives will be in order. Aside from anticipated better economic opportunities, Udo (2014, p. 46) argued that the

> measures of democratic dividend in Nigeria must also include the extent to which power is being exercised by the people, through their ability to elect those that will govern them, and their ability to affect the different programs and polices of government through their active involvement in binding decision making . . . people's control of their leaders, their actions and the ability to contribute in the process of governance.

Okeshola and Igba (2013, p. 551) also postulated: "The dividend of democracy means the benefits and the advantages of democracy. These include rule of law (supremacy of the law, equality before the law and fundamental human rights), legitimacy of the state, improved standard of living for the majority of the populace, improved atmosphere of peace and stability etc." In a similar vein, Olatubosun and Ayooluwa (2017, p. 6) noted: "democratization does not solely depend on the creation of the basic institutions of democracy but to a large extent on the creation of the right environment for the institutions to function." Aristotle (*Politics*, Book IV, Chap 4, p. 178) echoed (Udo, 2914; Okeshola & Igba, 2013; Olatubosun & Ayooluwa, 2017) words, may be in not similar terms: "for liberty and equality, as is thought by some, are chiefly to be found in democracy, they will be best attained when all persons alike share in the government to the utmost."

Lacking proper grasp of the workings of the twenty-first century knowledge based and interconnected global economy, successive Nigerian administrations have resorted to patronage, collect and share, earn and squander, borrow and spend, and outright guesswork to grow the economy. In fact, the economic policy of the government perhaps can be said to suffer from what Arrow and Capron (1959, p. 292) described as "a misunderstanding of economic theory as well as from exaggeration of the empirical evidence." The continuing economic decline is not only a clear indication that the administrations' approach is not working, but it also demonstrates that the leadership has not figured out smart ways to harness Nigeria's abundant resources including regular huge oil revenues and windfalls into working models of development and growth. (Nigeria, for example, has accrued $5.9 billion, $13.4 billion, $17 billion, $12.4 billion, $7.9 billion, $2.2 billion, $5.2 billion, $11.5 billion in excess crude oil sales in 2004, 2005, 2006, 2007, 2008, 2010, 2011, and 2012, respectively; generated $2.28 billion in oil block sales between 2003 and 2007) (Central Bank of Nigeria, *Annual Reports*; *This Day*, August 31, 2007). Cumulatively, in the 15-year period, 2004–2018, according to published reports, Nigeria earned a humongous $109.37 billion in excess crude money under Presidents Obasanjo ($33.74 billion), Yar'Adua ($27.36 billion), Jonathan ($44.56 billion), and Buhari ($2.49 billion) (Olufemi & Akintunde, 2019). These four presidential administrations have been called "Nigeria's four seasons of lavishness," because out of the $109 billion accrued excess oil earnings, the government spent $104.7 billion (96%), virtually without savings for a rainy day. Worse, the "lavish" expenditures did not translate into "lasting or productive capital through the development of infrastructure, institutions, or citizens," further confirming that "Nigeria's failure to effectively manage her oil and gas revenues has delayed the country's transition from a developing economy to an advanced one" (Olufemi & Akintunde, 2019).

While some progress (e.g., privatization of state industries, deregulations, telecom growth) has been made, however, it has barely scratched the surface of Nigeria's deep economic problems. The economy is still in the ditch and struggling, poverty is ferocious, and social improvement remains tenuous. Heavy government spending, borrowing, and import dependency further shape and hamper the economy (World Bank, 2003; Akinwunmi & Adekoya, 2018). At the same time, there is acute unemployment problem and the frustration gap, especially, among the young is widening. According to Agu and Evoh (2011, p. v) in an International Labor Organization (ILO) paper:

> The Nigeria economy has experienced robust GDP growth rates over the reform period 2000 to 2010. However, these high levels of economic growth have not translated to the expected increase in employment opportunities for a rapidly

> growing young population. [Research] noted increased unemployment in the reform years as well as increased rate of joblessness and vulnerability during the global crisis period, demonstrating a clear mismatch between the goals of macroeconomic policies and the goal of achieving productive employment and poverty reduction as a key priority of the Nigeria vision and development framework 20:2020.

The unemployment problem in Nigeria is not letting up. According to a report by Nigeria's National Bureau of Statistics (NBS) in March 2021, more than half of Nigeria's labor force (ages 15–64) are unemployed or underemployed. Nigeria's unemployment rate surged to 33.3% in the fourth quarter through December 2020, up from 27.1% in the second quarter of 2020. The unemployment problem direr among young people. During the period under review, unemployment for people aged 15–24 stood at 53.4% (NBS, 2021, p. 13), and at 37.2% for people aged 25–34 (NBS, 2021, p. 14). By international comparison, except for Bosnia and Herzegovina (33.7%), oil-rich Nigeria (33.3%) is scandalously among the top five countries in the world with the highest unemployment rate, Namibia (33.4%), South Africa (32.5%), Angola (30.6%), Mozambique (25.0%) (NBS, 2021, p. 43).

Nigeria can prosper through such key economic reform programs as well as business incentives and industrial policies of the government as the National Economic Empowerment and Development Strategy, Youth Enterprise with Innovation in Nigeria, Public Works and Women/Youth Employment, Subsidy Reinvestment and Empowerment Program, Small and Medium Scale Enterprises, Small and Medium Enterprises Development Agency, Export Expansion Grant Scheme, import duty waivers and exemptions (Nigeria has a situation, for example, whereby "75% duty waivers favor palm oil importers" (*This Day*, December 15, 2014)), National Enterprise Development Program (NEDP), Nigerian Industrial Revolution Plan (NIRP). However, these programs have proven to be largely unproductive and corruption ridden (Page & Okeke, 2019). Also, they are anything but the economic revolution that the people, especially, the middle class and the poor had hoped for and expected upon the return of civil rule, to usher them into a new era of economic opportunities, prosperity, and endless possibilities.

Waivers and Concessions

It must be useful to examine briefly the import duty waivers and exemptions program of the erstwhile Jonathan administration. This is because it was peddled as a major component of government stimulus package by the administration, and also as a way to revive Nigeria's sagged economy and boost economic development. Also, it has come to generate controversy to the increasing displeasure of many Nigerians, including the National Assembly, as to the use and effectiveness of the program. In fact, the misuse and abuse in the waiver regime got so bad that in 2014, the House of Representatives Committee on Customs and Excise "ordered then Finance and Coordinating Minister of the Economy, Ngozi Okonjo-Iweala, to suspend the issuance of waivers, exemption and concessionary permits to importers, pending the outcome of its ongoing probe on the matter" (*Guardian*, February 1, 2014). The House went a step further and reminded the Honorable Minister that the waiver and concession program is in clear violation of section 59 (1) (b) of the 1999 Constitution. The House, inter alia, elaborated:

> We also make bold to add that no authority, including the President, has the constitutional powers to impose or increase tax, duty or fees or any reduction, or withdrawal or cancellation thereof without first introducing a Bill before the National Assembly as clearly stipulated in section 59 (1)(b) of the 1999 Constitution as amended. . . . The net implication of the section of the Constitution we have referred you to is that the current practice of indiscriminate granting of waivers, exemptions and concessions by government is, to say the least, patently and manifestly unconstitutional to the extent that no Bill was introduced before the National Assembly for such purposes.

From January to May 2014, for example, the Nigerian government granted almost ₦26 billion in import duties exemptions and waivers. Ceteris paribus, and holding ₦26 billion constant for say the second half of the year, that would amount to ₦52 billion, equivalent to 1.12% of the 2014 budget (₦4.6 trillion), or the combined total allocations to the Police Service Commission (₦1.8 billion), Federal Character Commission (₦2.2 billion), Public Complaints Commission (₦2.9 billion), Independent National Electoral Commission (INEC, ₦45 billion). Or, if we keep strictly to the ₦26 billion, it is approximately equivalent to the combined Ministry of Environment's ₦21.7 billion and the Independent Corrupt Practices Commission's (ICPC) ₦4.7 billion operating budget for 2014.

Imports duty waivers and exemptions are tested business incentives tools to boost economic growth and enhance job creation around the world (Investment Consulting Group, 2013; United Nations Development Program [UNDP], 2016; PWC, 2015; Gari, 2011, IMF, 2018). They are meant to help investors, businesses, employers, and manufacturers to acquire and purchase critical but not locally available equipment, raw materials, and spare parts tax free (*Punch*, January 28, 2014). However, in Nigeria, for all practical purposes, this program has been misused, abused, and manipulated to near defeat of the purpose to the extent that it "benefits totally undeserving firms and individuals" (*Punch*, January 28, 2014) at immense costs to the economy and the Nigerian people. It has been reported that

> waivers were granted to the Gombe Central Mosque in 2011 to import 13 cartons of the Koran and carpets, and waiver to the Catholic Church, Makurdi to import children's Bibles. In 2012, the Akwa Ibom State Government got a waiver of ₦271.2 million for a private aircraft, while Taraba got ₦13.06 million for a helicopter. In 2013, Rivers State got waivers worth ₦2.18 billion for a Bombardier aircraft and two Bell 412 helicopters . . . ₦450.7 million waivers to massage the First Lady's [Mrs. Jonathan] ego to host the African Women Peace Mission . . . ₦141.2 million to the Delta State Government in 2013 for furniture . . . ₦5.9 million to the Maiduguri Central Mosque in 2012 and ₦14 million for the Watchtower Society of Jehovah's Witnesses to import building materials and cabinet parts for kitchen door drawers. (*Punch*, January 28, 2014)

Another report disclosed that "65% of the 500 beneficiary companies received waivers/concessions for goods not officially approved, which ordinarily should be limited to raw materials, machinery and spare parts" (*Punch*, January 28, 2014). At the same time, some of the companies engaged in "round tripping," prohibited practice of using one waiver permit for multiple transactions and unapproved goods. In 2013, for example, then customs deputy comptroller, Garba Makarfi, stated before the Nigerian Senate: "We lost 7 percent to Export Expansion Grant, which is non-negotiable; this amounted to about ₦37.2 billion. The grant was given to export oriented companies and local manufacturers to export raw materials, but instead, these local manufacturers sell their certificates to dealers who then use them to import cars into the country" (*Punch*, November 25, 2013).

Apart from the misuse and benefiting unintended targets, the import duty waivers program is allegedly replete with corruption. The program has allegedly been described as "corruption-drenched," "instruments of massive corruption," "economic rip-off" (*Punch*, January 28, 2014). Page (2018, p. 5) called it "a lucrative form of patronage." Nigerian *Guardian* editorial (February 19, 2016) called it "disservice to Nigeria . . . odious regime of economic impunity that has lasted so long . . . loophole that benefits only a few . . . a regime of favors for economic cartels and selfish barons." Modebe et al. (2014, p. 3) described it as "an increasingly popular but disturbing method of misappropriating government revenue in Nigeria." Some examples will be appropriate. Between 2003 and 2008, Nigeria reportedly lost ₦1.06 trillion to waivers and exemptions, concessions (Nkwazema, 2008). Further details show that Nigeria allegedly lost ₦12.4 billion, ₦55 billion, ₦71.24 billion, ₦54.59 billion, and ₦9.51 billion to alleged "dubious waivers" in 2003, 2004,

2005, 2007, and 2008 (first three months), respectively (*Punch*, November 25, 2013). In November 2013, Abdullahi Dikko, then the director-general of Nigerian Customs Service, informed the Nigerian Senate that in the first nine months of 2013 alone, the nation allegedly lost ₦603 billion to import duty waivers, exemptions on levies, concessions, and import substitution schemes (*Punch*, November 18, 2013).

Between 2011 and 2013 Nigeria allegedly lost more than ₦1.4 trillion to waivers—₦480 billion in 2011, ₦480 billion in 2012, ₦474 billion in 2012 (*Guardian*, February 1, 2014). Between January and May 2014, Nigeria lost ₦25.8 billion to import waivers. Put together, between November 2000 and May 2014, Nigeria incurred more than ₦2.31 trillion losses to waivers and exemptions, equivalent to 50% of the nation's ₦4.6 trillion budget for 2014. While not been redundant the *Guardian* (February 19, 2016) wrote:

> Statistics showed that in 2007, the 1,843 beneficiaries of waivers caused about ₦165 billion loss to the economy. The highest amount of ₦42.598 billion was recorded in 2007; in 2006, waivers stood at ₦19.379 billion; ₦41.650 billion (2005), and so on. In 2014, former finance minister and coordinator of the economy reportedly declared a loss to import waivers and tax holiday concessions of ₦797.8 billion between 2011 and May 2014, ₦25.814 billion of it in the first five months of 2014 alone. Figures attributed to the then Comptroller-General of the Nigeria Customs Service (NCS) quoted ₦276.9 billion loss between 2000 and 2008. . . . Official claims of ₦585 billion lost to waivers between 2011 and 2015 are only indicative of a mindless regime of profligacy and corruption. That sharp progression is instructive.

Table 1.23 presents cumulative import duties Waivers and Exemptions granted by the Nigerian government by sector and amount via the Federal Ministry of Finance in the 2011–2014 (2014 through May) instance.

From table 1.23, we can deduce a continuing pattern of misuse and abuse of the waivers incentive program. First, it is oil and gas industry favored, to the disadvantage of other sectors, especially the essential power sector. Out of the more than ₦201 billion in waiver concessions during the period, the oil and gas industry received the lion's share of nearly ₦74 billion or 36.6%, indicating muted diversification of the economy. Other and agriculture sectors were distant second and third with almost ₦54 billion (26.7%), ₦27 billion (13.5%), respectively. In 2014, Indorama Eleme Ltd received the highest concession of almost ₦11 billion (56% of ₦19 billion oil and gas sector total), followed by Chevron Nigeria Ltd with close to ₦5 billion or 26% (not shown in the table). Overall, in 2014, nearly three-quarter or 73.1% in waivers went to the oil and gas sector, out of a total ₦26 billion, more than double from four years earlier.

Table 1.23 Waivers and Exemptions by Sector, 2011–2014 (₦ Million)

Sector	*2011*	*2012*	*2013*	*2014**	*Total*	*% Total*
Oil & Gas	18,164	18,139	18,495	18,881	73,679	36.6
Other	2,947	24,281	22,670	3,858	53,756	26.7
Agriculture	21,092	1,377	3,459	1,152	27,081	13.5
Health	4,620	5,968	12,380	790	23,759	11.8
Mines & Steel	9,142	12	595	353	10,101	5.0
Power		3,052	4,403	780	8,236	4.1
Aviation		1,581	2,454		4,035	2.0
Water Resources		96	457		554	0.3
Total	**55,965**	**54,506**	**64,914**	**25,815**	**201,200**	**100.0**

Source: Federal Ministry of Finance, Budget Office of the Federation.
* through May 2014

Second, there is total lack of support to the critical manufacturing sector. The importance of manufacturing to the economy cannot be overemphasized, especially for oil-dependent economy such as Nigeria that urgently needs to diversify her economy away from nonrenewable natural resources. These six salient points about manufacturing from Jon Ryn are apt: manufacturing has been the path to development; foundation of global "Great Power"; most important cause of economic growth; global trade is based on goods, not services; services are dependent on manufactured goods; manufacturing creates jobs (Rynn, 2011). The manufacturing imperative was also harped on by Erik Reinert in his 2008 thought-provoking book, *Why Rich Countries Stay Rich and Why Poor Countries Stay Poor*, arguing mainly that "welfare and economic growth in rich nations were influenced by conscious and deliberate industrialization policy" (Reinert, 2008) which over time buoyed prosperity.

Third, it is difficult to categorize the "Other" item which attracted the second highest concessions amount of almost ₦54 billion, or 28%, further stoking the persistent allegations of lack of transparency in the waivers program and the disconnection between policy intentions and outcomes. The Nigeria House of Representatives has confirmed allegations of impropriety in the waivers program; the House, in a 2014 investigation, disclosed:

> The inclusion by the Finance Ministry of "other goods" in the categories eligible for concessions, according to the Customs, enabled finished goods that add no economic value to the country to be imported. These goods include fish, bulletproof vehicles, kola nut, palm oil and others. Customs records show that concessions in 2011 and 2013 were granted mostly to fuel dealers, with Conoil being the biggest beneficiary in 2013, with ₦53 billion. Oando was next with ₦22 billion, followed by NIPCO Plc (₦19 billion), Sahara Energy (₦14 billion) and Folawiyo Energy (₦12billion). In 2011, the oil firm that benefited most was still Oando with ₦83 billion, followed by Capital Oil and Gas (₦47 billion), Integrated Oil and Gas (₦20 billion), Folawiyo Energy (₦18 billion) and Sahara

> Energy (₦14 billion). The documents show that in 2012, the Nigerian National Petroleum Corporation (NNPC) was the biggest beneficiary, getting ₦80 billion in concessions, and Sopon Nigeria Ltd was the highest non-oil beneficiary in 2011, netting about ₦33 billion. (*Guardian*, February 1, 2014)

Continuing, the House report disclosed:

> Coscharis Motors, which supplied Aviation Minister Stella Oduah's controversial bullet proof cars and supplied 200 cars to the African First Ladies summit in 2012, received waivers of ₦400 million in 2011 and ₦698 million in 2013. Other beneficiaries of import tax concessions include companies in the Dangote Group, the African First Ladies Peace Mission (AFLPM), Inspector General of Police, Chief of Army Staff, Central Bank of Nigeria, Bayelsa State Government, Minister of Police Affairs, Nigerian Police Force, Sokoto State Government, Akwa Ibom State Government and the Watchtower Society. (*Guardian*, February 1, 2014)

From the foregoing narrative, it is clear that the waivers and exemptions program has not lived up to expectations. The economic stimulus the waiver program was supposed to deliver has not arrived. The tendency is starkly worrying, especially, for a country listed by the World Bank in 2014 as "extremely poor" and "the worst place to be born in 2013" by the EIU, the research and analysis arm of the *Economist* of London. This chapter will be incomplete without discussion of the all-important informal sector of Nigerian economy.

NIGERIA'S INFORMAL ECONOMY SECTOR

First, let us resolve the issue of the definition of the informal sector. Benjamin et al. (2014, p. 8) of the World Bank rightfully said, "a central question in the study of the informal sector is its definition: what is informal and what is not?" They are not alone. According to the ILO, "there are no internationally agreed guidelines for the definition of informal jobs [sector]" (ILO, 2002, p. 122). However, from ILO's standpoint, "an informal firm is an unregistered firm where the owner is an individual or a household whose capital is not separable from that of the firm and for which there is not reliable accounting that could permit retracing the operations of the firm" (ILO 2002, p. 126; Benjamin et al., 2012, p. 8). OECD's (2009, 2019) informal employment refers primarily to employment in enterprises that lack registration and a complete set of accounts, not well-recognized and valued, lack social security coverage and legal protection for their employees. IMF (2018, p. 4) stated: "The shadow [informal] economy includes all economic activities which are hidden from official authorities for monetary, regulatory, and institutional reasons." Andrae and Beckman (2013) added, "informality," as implied here, involves small-scale self-employed artisans and entrepreneurs (e.g., tailors, carpenters, mechanics, electricians, masons, fitters, welders, beauticians, barbershops, street trading, agriculture, transporters, eating and drinking places) with small capital investment and limited formal training. As distinguished from the large-scale industry employing wage labor, these establishments mainly ignore labor laws, and in fact, this disregard can be seen as a main criterion of their informality (Andrae & Beckman, 2013, p. 194). Now back to the discussion of Nigeria's informal economy.

The importance of the informal sector to Nigerian economy cannot be overemphasized, especially, in the face of massive unemployment, wrought by the near collapse of Nigeria's formal economy, worsened by decades of poor economic performance manifested by high unemployment rate of 33.3% (NBS, 2021, p. 3), rising poverty incidence of 40.1% (NBS, 2019, p. 5), and growing inequality of up to 35.13 Gini coefficient (NBS, 2019, p. 17). NBS is not alone in pinpointing the worsening of Nigeria's economic crisis, vis-à-vis the parlous sate of the formal economy. Earlier Okonjo-Iweala and Osafo-Kwaako (2007, p. 6) noted,

> Nigeria is the most populous country in Africa, with a GDP second only to South Africa's. Yet, following several years of military rule and poor economic management, Nigeria experienced a prolonged period of economic stagnation, rising poverty levels, and the decline of its public institutions . . . widespread corruption undermined the effectiveness of various public expenditure programs. Moreover, the lack of public investments in previous decades meant that there were severe infrastructural problems that hindered private sector activities. In particular, the poor condition of the power sector prior to economic reforms illustrated the severity of Nigeria's infrastructure deficit.

The anemic Nigerian formal economy has forced many Nigerians out of work and into poverty, as up to 40% of Nigerians live on less than $1.90 per day according to the World Bank, further illustrating the financial vulnerability of many Nigerians, especially to buy food and other necessities. Reports indicate that food is increasingly hard to come by for Nigerian families, as escalating food prices put more pressure on already tight family budgets, made worse by pernicious price inflation rate of 17.23% as reported by NBS recently (NBS, 2021, p. 5). A new "Food Prices Watch" report by NBS is vivid, for example, year-on-year average price increase for 1 dozen eggs 15.62%, 1 kilogram of rice 21.02%, 1 kilogram of yam tuber 29.11%, 1 loaf of bread 7.77%, 1 kilogram of chicken 10.24%, milk 14.49%, garri 62.92%, just to name a few items (NBS, 2021).

According to a recent report by NBS, except for Bosnia and Herzegovina, Nigeria (33.3%) is among the top five countries in the world with the highest unemployment rate. At the same time, the disappearance of manufacturing employment, especially in large towns, has a made a bad situation worse, forcing many Nigerians to eke out a living in the "informal economy," as traders, craftsmen, service providers, occasional wage workers, and apprentices (Andrae & Beckman, 2013, p. 193). In addition, the negative impacts of globalization, particularly loss of jobs and poverty escalation, have had disproportionate impact on Africa including Nigeria. The informal economy sector has come to the rescue to fill the yawning gap left by the struggling formal Nigerian economy (Meagher, 2003, 2006, 2010, 2011, 2014, 2016; Hoffmann & Melly, 2015; CBN, 2016; NBS, 2016; Akande & Akerele, 2008; NISER & World Bank, 2009).

The informal sector provides the livelihood and employment for a critical segment of the Nigerian population, as Nigeria's formal employment sector can no more keep pace with the number of entrants into the labor market (Nigerian Institute of Social and Economic Research (NISER) & World Bank, 2009). The informal sector contributes immensely to employment and output in Nigeria. Meagher (2011, p. 47) called Nigeria's informal sector as "livelihood networks . . . networks of accumulation and survival." Leena Hoffmann and Paul Melly, scholars at Chatham House, London-based international affairs think thank, called Nigeria's informal sector "a pragmatic response to today's realities" (Hoffmann & Melly, 2015, p. vii) and report that informal economic activity accounts for up to 64% of Nigeria's GDP. Majority of the informal sector enterprises in Nigeria employ less than three people, with about 82% of the businesses by individual ownership (Onwe, 2013, p. 70). Studies show that up to 75% of Nigeria's labor force is engaged in informal sector activities (Akande & Akerele, 2008; NISER & World Bank, 2009). While it might be difficult to have accurate statistics on informal sector employment in Nigeria, a recent CBN report is revealing. According to the Central Bank, in the first half of 2015, the informal sector added 416,306 new jobs to the Nigerian economy compared to 182,011 new jobs created in the formal sector, representing nearly 70% of the total new jobs created in Nigeria during the review period (CBN, 2015, p. 99). The CBN is not alone.

A cluster analysis case study research by Kate Meagher (2011) in two different regions of Nigeria, Aba (Eastern Nigeria) and Ilorin (Western Nigeria), further demonstrates the efficacy of Nigeria's informal economy in the alleviation of unemployment in Nigeria. Aba involved shoe and garment cluster, while Ilorin involved weaving cluster. According to Meagher, Aba and Ilorin were chosen because "both cities constitute regional commercial centers with populations of around one million inhabitants, and the two study clusters are noted for their economic dynamism, involving rapid expansion, innovation, and globalization" (Meagher, 2011, p. 49). "As such," according to Meagher, "both cities represent 'best case' scenarios of popular governance, in which social networks and informal institutions have empowered dynamic livelihood strategies and strong, socially embedded popular associations" (Meagher, 2011, p. 49). Meagher's study found that the Aba shoe and garment clusters generated more than 58,000 jobs, with a combined annual turnover of over $200 million (Meagher, 2011, p. 55). With respect to Ilorin weaving cluster, it employed more than 10,000 people with annual turnover of over $12 million (Meagher, 2011, p. 55). The Aba and Ilorin informal manufacturing clusters supported 13,920 and 529 manufacturing firms, respectively, for a total of 14,449 firms (Meagher, 2011, p. 55). The contribution of the informal sector to Nigeria's GDP is no less significant.

A report by the NBS indicated that the share of the informal sector of Nigeria's GDP to be more than 40%, representing almost ₦40 billion (NBS, 2016, p. 1). Whereas Ogbulafor and Malaolu (2013, p. 100) found that since 1970, the size of Nigeria's informal economy has oscillated between 53.6 and 77.2% of the GDP, accounting for 75% of Nigeria's GDP in 2010 proper. Informal cross-border trade (ICBT) also boosts Nigerian economy in a big way.

According to the CBN (2016, p. iv), "informal cross border trade (ICBT) segment of the informal economy sector constitutes a significant proportion of the informal sector activities and remains a source of employment with enormous impact on food security in Nigeria." On the same vein, "ICBT accounts for about 4.0 percent of Nigeria's total trade as well as 7.0 and 3.0 percent of imports and exports, respectively. Similarly, ICBT represents about 10.0 percent of total non-oil imports of Nigeria" (IMF, 2021). A landmark survey conducted by the CBN pursuant to monitor and estimate ICBT across Nigerian international land borders, conducted for 12 calendar months, between June 2013 and May 2014 (CBN, 2016) is revealing.

The findings of the study showed that the total informal trade across the selected borders during the study interval stood at ₦1,090,890.58 billion ($6,912.96 million). Put another way, a zoom in on the $6,912.96 million across the border trade flows amount represents about 20% of Nigeria's total budget of $35 billion (₦10.59 trillion) for 2020. Further breakdown shows that the $6,912.96 million trade transaction amount was nearly 25% more than the combined total of $4,668 million "key sectoral allocations" to education ($1,792 million/₦687 billion), health ($1,150 million/₦441 billion), power ($352 million/₦135 billion), work and housing ($897 million/₦344 billion), agriculture ($477 million/₦183 billion) in the 2020 budget. (For "key sectoral allocations" data, see BudgIT "2020 Budget.") Key across the border trade commodities and corresponding value and percentage were vegetable products ₦618, 271.34 million (56.7%), animal and animal products ₦137, 907.53 million (12.6%), transportation equipment ₦93, 322.01 million (8.6%), and foodstuff ₦69, 560.58 million (6.4%).

In addition, aside the fact that the survey for the first time in Nigeria provided hard data on the "magnitude of cross-border trade between Nigeria and neighboring countries" (CBN, 2016, p. iv), the study also went a long way to "improve compilation of balance of payments statistics (BOP) data that were prior not captured in official customs record, pertinent to bridge the gap between external trade statistics and policy" (IMF, 2021) in Nigeria. The informal sector also helps business start-ups and entrepreneurs to access and raise capital, especially, in a situation of lack of credit history and loan collateral by vast majority of Nigerians, compounded by "rigid and dysfunctional foreign exchange and banking regulations that hamstrung payments for imports and supplies" (Hoffmann & Melly, 2015, p. viii) and purchase of needed but not locally available equipment and spare parts from overseas. The informal sector clusters also engender "intercommunal credit system and trading networks" (Meagher, 2011, p. 54) for the good of the Nigerian economy.

"With little or no support from governments that is expected to protect their interests" according to Osaghae (1999, p. 85), this "self-governing exit from the formal economic system" (Osaghae, 1999) entrepreneurs are forced to rely on self-help economic networks they organize to fill the void created by state failure. Concomitantly, they "have given rise to credit unions, cooperatives, and savings and loans associations" (Osaghae, 1999, p. 86). And have in the process create business capital by "funding startup ventures or supporting small companies that wish to expand but do not have access to capital and equities markets" (Ganti, 2020), further contributing to economic growth and poverty alleviation, and "improvising livelihoods and collective services" (Meagher, 2016, p. 1) in Nigeria. In step, as Meagher (2014, p. 52) argued, as "informal collective organization" (Meagher, 2014, p. 419), the "informal clusters have used" (Meagher, 2011, p. 52) the possibilities of "informalization and casualization" (Meagher, 2014, p. 419) "to generate expanding employment, enterprise development, and globalizing production and distribution networks in the face of state neglect and crumbling infrastructure" (Meagher, 2011, p. 52) in Nigeria.

The Economic Challenge and the Way Forward

The modernization theory of economic growth and development thesis articulated by Samuel Huntington (1968) is helpful to analyze and better understand the policy gaps and missing links inherent in the developmental, leadership, globalization, and modernization challenges facing Nigeria (Nwagbara, 2019). This is because "the function of scientific concepts," argued Kaplan (1964, p. 52), "is to mark the categories which will tell us more about our subject matter than any other categorical sets" (quoted in Tipps, 1973, p. 199). In addition, the analytical trajectory of modernization theory is not only a powerful tool to understand the historical and contemporary economic challenges, but it is also consistent with traditional societies and the quest of developing countries, such as Nigeria to experience modernization and consolidate political order (Nwagbara, 2019, p. 20).

Also, the seminal contribution of Huntington had enormous influence and enduring legacy on how people think of development in "changing" or "transitioning societies," and have helped to spawn a large body of empirical studies and literature on the subject (e.g., Lipset, 1959; Cardoso & Enzo, 1979; O'Donnell, 1973; Inglehart & Welzel, 2005; Arat, 1973; Diamond, 1992; Tipps, 1973), in the process facilitated the "absorption" of modernization theory "into the main corpus of economic theory" (Arrow, 1962, p. 156) and leadership scholarship. Furthermore, the work of Huntington appeared during the period when most colonized countries in Africa gained political autonomy, with "great aspirations to modernize and catch up" (African Union Commission, 2015; Frankema & Waijenburg, 2018; Kinyanjui, 1993; Lundvall & Lema, 2015; Mazrui, 1968; Oyelaran-Oyeyinka, 2014; Sampath, 2014; World Bank, 2009) and in the process they launched what Jorgenson (1961, p. 310) called "frontal attack on the gap between theories of growth and theories of development by presenting a theory of development of a dual economy (advanced and traditional economies)."

Huntington (1968, p. xii) argued that well-managed modernization is good for economic development, which would improve education and ultimately lead to value change, which would in turn promote good political order, in a virtuous circle of interconnectedness. On the other hand, when modernity is mismanaged, dysfunctional, and corrupted, people feel frustrated and alienated, or feel that the "game is rigged," a negative situation Huntington referred to as "praetorianism" could result with concomitant backlash including coups, insurgencies, protests, violence, weak and unstable governments. To counter the threat of praetorianism in transitioning societies, Huntington advocated "modernizing authoritarian leader," who while abridge civil liberties and curtail political participation, achieve rapid economic growth and social progress, exemplified by the likes of Park Chung-Hee in South Korea, Chiang Ching-Kuo in Taiwan, Lee Kwan Yew in Singapore, Suharto in Indonesia, and Mahathir Mohamad in Malaysia who led and brought the "Asian Miracle" growth phenomena.

In a 2006 foreword to Huntington's 1968 book, *Political Order in Changing Societies*, the scholar Francis Fukuyama noted, among other details, "for poor countries, political order and competent institutions are a precondition for economic growth. Sub-Saharan Africa's [Nigeria] internal conflicts and weak governments are powerful inhibitors of the other dimensions of development" (Huntington, 2006 [1968], p. xv). In other words, according to Huntington, "to cope successfully with modernization, a political system must be able, first, to improve policy, that is, to promote social and economic reform by state action" (Huntington, 1968, p. 140). To Huntington, "the most important political distinction among countries concerns not their form of government but their degree of government [political order and leadership]" (Huntington, 1968, p. 1).

In that sense, Huntington preponderantly argued that for traditional societies or developing countries to achieve "modernization" (Huntington, 1965, 1971) and economic growth they must first establish stable political order and avoid "political decay" (Huntington, 1965) manifested in revolutions, insurgencies, coups, protests, civil wars, weak and failing states, and corruption, all of which are inimical to economic growth and development. Huntington's "political decay" thesis has implications especially for Africa [Nigeria], which has had horrendous experiences of instability and crisis of leadership, and consequent poverty, economic decline, stunted growth, and arrested development (Mbaku, 1988, 2014; Fosu, 2002, 2004), part of the experiences that Peter Bauer (1981) termed . . . "third world economic delusion." Thus, the "relevant issue here" according to Zalanga (2016, pp. 74–75), "for postcolonial African societies [including Nigeria] is that they are living in a world that is going through a rapid process of change, but the fundamental question is whether African societies have developed the capacity to absorb and effectively handle the changes taking place in the world."

It is also important to mention that two other influential thinkers on the theory of modernization were Daniel Lerner and Whitman W. Rostow. The remarkable relevance of their pioneering efforts and thought-provoking insights on the challenges on the road to modernization pertinent to economic development, growth, and political order in the developing countries is enduring. Moreover, their works share kindred spirit with this book, since all deal with understanding and explaining the causes, consequences, processes, attitudes, development and leadership challenges, and changes in transitioning and modernizing societies including Nigeria (Inkeles, 1969; Inkeles & Smith, 1970; Gusfield, 1967, 1968; Germont-Duret, 2016). Daniel Lerner, in his memorable work *The Passing of Traditional Society* (1958), identified the interdependence of "urbanization, education (literacy), media participation, political participation" (Lerner, 1958, p. 63) as prerequisite "determinant" factors in the transition process from traditional to modern society before the "take-off" of "modernization." Lerner called the linkages of the "determinant" factors the "critical optimum" (Lerner, 1958, p. 63) of modernization infused into "a rationalist and positivist spirit" (Lerner, 1958, p. 45) of development.

Rostow in his seminal work, titled *The Stages of Economic Growth* (1960), formulated five stages of economic growth through which all countries must undergo to become developed, namely: (1) Traditional Society; (2) Preconditions for Take-off; (3) Take-off; (4) Drive to Maturity; (5) Age of High Mass Consumption. According to Rostow, the five stages of economic growth are "rooted in certain dynamic propositions about supply, demand, and the pattern of production" (Rostow, 1959, p. 1). Also Rostow's work suggests that the "uniqueness of each nation's experience" is an "important determinant of long-term economic development and those historical events can be an important determinant of the evolution of society" (Nunn, 2009, p. 67) and stages of development. In addition, Acemoglu (1995, p. 17) alluded that "[experiences] of past generations as well as expectations of the future influence current rewards," as such study of past stages of development provides examples for the present and roadmap for the future.

Nigeria faces enormous economic challenges aggravated by growing unemployment, productivity decline, out-of-control spending, mounting debt, volatile oil price, spiraling cost of living, and widening inequality (Akinbobola & Saibu, 2004; Zenith Bank, 2016; UNDP, 2017). Without delay, Nigerian leaders must pursue alternative economic plan to the current dispensation of collect and share, earn and squander, borrow and spend, patronage-laden economic policy of the past 20 years. The vision is to bequeath to Nigerian children a richer, better, and stronger nation than the current status quo.

Since the country is in a deep economic crisis, there is need for patriotism and real vision. Sadly, there is no magic wand to turn Nigeria around unless Nigerians instill responsibility and accountability beginning at the top. And that means living up to the highest standards of public service always (Emmanuel & Reed, 2006). Above all, it means doing right by the future by making honest, good faith effort to solve the nation's problems (Emmanuel & Reed, 2006).

Nigerians need an economic agenda that will spur growth, eradicate poverty, reduce insecurity and hardship, and provide broadly shared prosperity. To turn the Nigerian economy around, Nigeria needs a bold agenda that can be counted off on one hand. This discourse proposes five liberating ideas: foster effective leadership, ensure fiscal discipline, improve education and workforce skills, provide infrastructure, and support accountable government.

1. Foster Effective Leadership and Better Economic Management

Effective leadership has eluded Nigeria since independence. And this is mainly why nothing works. The economy is no exception. Nigeria needs leaders who have the vision and passion to move the nation forward and this has been the missing link in the nation's march to greatness. Since the inception of the civil administration in 1999, the most striking fault line of the past 20 years is the absence of leadership accountability and transparency for enhancing Nigeria's ability to compete and win under the new rules of global economic competition. It is time for a new direction that ensures economic growth that lifts the standard of living, the opportunities, and hopes of all Nigerians: opportunities for all, special privileges for none.

What Must Be Done

Leadership must act quickly to jumpstart the economy, especially job creation particularly through construction of public works including roads, bridges, dams, schools, parks, airports, seaports, rails, power grids, and so on; grow the middle class through improved access to credit and financial reforms to ease lending and borrowing; improve the cooperation between the government and private sector to boost productivity; revive agriculture to its past glory as a suitable source of employment, source of food and raw materials, and export earner; offer stimulus in the areas of business incentives, tax breaks, R&D, job training, fighting corruption, infrastructure; investment in better schools, encouragement of science, and harnessing of other critical technologies; citizens must partner with the government in good governance, development, and public administration, support transparency and information access to improve public policy.

2. Restore Fiscal Discipline

Government costs too much and delivers very little in Nigeria (Ejuvbekpokpo, 2012; Adewole & Osabuohien, 2007; World Bank, 2015, 2017). In fact, "government remains the biggest business in Nigeria." Table 1.24 shows Nigeria's revenue and spending for the 21-year period, 1999–2019 since the return to civil rule. Except for 2000 and 2004–2007, the government has run deficit spending (excess crude oil earnings inflow of $33.74 billion during 2004–2006 (Olufemi & Akintunde, 2019) cushioned otherwise deficit spending during this period). In 2019 proper, out of the ₦10.15 trillion that government collected, it spent ₦15.62 trillion, resulting in a deficit of nearly ₦5.5 trillion (more than 50% of revenue collected). In other words, more

Table 1.24 Nigerian Government Budget, 1999–2019 (₦ Billion)

Year	Total Revenue	Total Spending	Surplus/Deficit	Deficit %GDP
1999	₦1,011	₦1,119	−108	
2000	1,987	1,707	280	
2001	2,248	2,510	−262	
2002	2,053	2,290	−238	
2003	2,795	2,890	−95	
2004	4,124	3,389	735	
2005	2,657	1,822	835	
2006	5,965	4,122	1,843	
2007*	4,221	2,242	1,979	
2008	7,461	7,632	−172	31.5
2009	6,263	7,258	−995	29.4
2010	7,136	8,371	−1,235	28.4
2011	8,487	9,774	−1,288	27.6
2012	8,929	10,097	−1,168	24.9
2013	9,590	11,104	−1,513	13.7
2014	8,964	10,184	−1,220	11.3
2015	7,547	9,704	−2,158	10.2
2016	6,688	9,673	−2,986	10.0
2017	8,885	11,938	−3,053	10.4
2018	9,574	13,967	−4,393	10.8
2019	10,147	15,617	−5,471	10.7

*Through October 2007.
Source: Central Bank of Nigeria, Annual Report, Various Years.
Revenue and spending data for 1999–2004 are from International Monetary Fund (IMF)—"Nigeria: Selected Issues and Statistical Appendix," August 6, 2004 (Table 11 and 12).
International Monetary Fund (IMF)—"Nigeria: Selected Issues and Statistical Appendix," August, 2005 (Table 11 and 12).

than 50 kobo of every naira that the government spent in 2019 was borrowed. Over the past 21 years through 2019, Federal spending grew nearly 1,300% or 62% per year. During the same course of time, Federal deficit has ballooned to 4,970%, from ₦108 billion in 1999 to ₦5.5 trillion in 2019. Inextricably linked to reckless spending are the constellation menace of fraud, waste, and abuse.

According to the Economic and Financial Crimes Commission (EFCC), Nigeria lost more than $380 billion to waste and corruption between 1960 and 1999 (*BBC News* Online, October 20, 2006). In addition, per a 2011 report by Global Financial Integrity (a U.S.-based illicit financial flows monitoring group) authored by Dev Kar, a former IMF economist, Nigeria lost $130 billion to corruption between 2000 and 2008. The economic impact of those losses has been enormous, as funds that could have been used to boost economic development and create jobs have been squandered or embezzled, further putting Nigeria's economic health in jeopardy. If you go shopping, below is what $380 billion can buy for you:

- 225 space shuttles
- 795,115 Rolls Royce Phantoms
- 400 million personal computers
- 32 million primary school rooms
- 3,800 kg rice for each Nigerian

Government's fiscal train wreck is exacerbated by the problem of rising debt burden. According to the Debt Management Office (DMO) latest annual report, as at December 31, 2018, Nigeria's Total Public Debt Stock rose by 12.25% to ₦24,387,071.74 million ($79,436.72 million) or 19.09% of the GDP, compared to ₦21,725,773.03 million ($70,999.26 million) as at December 31, 2017 (DMO, *2018 Annual Report*, p. 4). In terms of the composition of the Debt Portfolio, the External Debt Stock as at December 31, 2018, was $25,274.36 million or 31.82% of the Total Public Debt Stock, while the total Domestic Debt Stock was $54,162.35 million or 68.27% of the total Public Debt Stock (DMO, *2018 Annual Report*, p. 4). The national outstanding external debt of $25 billion in 2018 is more than 12 times the $1.997 billion FDI that Nigeria attracted in 2018 (World Bank, 2020).

Linked to the outstanding debt problem is the rising amount devoted to debt service payments at the detriment of other developmental needs. As a percentage of total public debt service in 2017, external and domestic debts were 8.77% and 91.23%, respectively (DMO, *2017 Annual Report*, p. 19). Total debt service rose 20.9% to $5,288.30 million as at December 31, 2017, compared to US$4,381.82 million in 2016 (DMO, *2017 Annual Report*, p. 19). Specifically, external debt service amounted to $464.05 million, while domestic debt service stood at $4,824.25 million (DMO, *2017 Annual Report*, p. 20). The DMO projects that over 10 years (2018 and 2027) Nigeria's external debt service payments would amount to $18,269.33 million (DMO, *2017 Annual Report*, p. 39).

What Must Be Done

Nigeria must put the era of runaway spending, fiscal mismanagement, and debt accumulation behind it. It will be in order to implement the following measures immediately: make public all budget execution reports; require state and local governments to make public budget reports; improve availability of information on public investment projects; strengthen tax collection system so as to "assess all who ought to pay and collect from all who are assessed to pay"; plug loopholes, check the pervasive influence of corruption through better reporting, monitoring, and ongoing reforms (Human Rights Watch, 2007).

3. Improve Education and Workforce Skills

If the Nigerian economy is to prosper and compete in the global market place, it must innovate its work processes, educate, and train its workers in the skills that will be needed for that to occur (Dike, 2015; Brende, 2015; OECD, 2012; UNESCO, 2000; World Bank, 2013; U. S. National Science Foundation, 2018). However, that is not occurring, especially in higher education in Nigeria, in spite of the fact of the enormous benefits of higher education as attested to by many bodies including the World Bank (2017): "Higher education is instrumental in fostering growth, reducing poverty and boosting shared prosperity."

In 2001, the World Bank reported that the "quality and relevance of university education in Nigeria is considered inadequate by public and private employers of university graduates, and by the Government itself. . . . The Federal universities are excessively homogenous institutions and generally have not developed to international standards the academic disciplines that will be vital for future economic growth and development" (World Bank, 2001, pp. 1–2). The World Bank is not alone. Several government and independent reports have highlighted the condition of Nigerian universities as "deplorable," "rotten, and dilapidated" (e.g., Ejiogu Panel, 2004; *Vanguard*, September 2, 2004; Taiwo, 2004); Yakubu Panel 2012 (Oyekanmi, 2012; Awoyinfa et al., 2012; *West Africa*, September 12, 1983). Consequently, Nigerian university graduates are adjudged to be "half-baked and unfit for employment" (Fanimo, 2005).

This trend must be reversed because, argued Lester Thurow, influential economist at the Massachusetts Institute of Technology, USA: "Without a well-educated labor force, enough engineers, and strong science education in our school systems, none of us is going to have a successful economy in the high technology era we are in. To work, modern economies need a mass well-educated labor force. Educated elite will not suffice. Illiteracy hurts the literate" (Thurow, 1985, p. 187; see also Reich, 1991). Emphasized Joseph Stiglitz, economics Nobel laureate, in his remarkable book, *Making Globalization Work*: "Countries that want to participate in the new world of high-tech globalization need technologies, computers, and other equipment in order to connect with the rest of the world. Individuals who want to compete in this global economy have to have the skills and resources to do so" (Stiglitz, 2006).

What Must Be Done

Nigerian leadership must make education a top priority, especially in this era of knowledge intensive global economy; Nigeria's primary and secondary education must continue to be universal and ought to be totally cost free for tuition, books, and supplies; Nigerian teachers must receive adequate training, preparation, and be regularly paid; establish and pilot model programs, such as teacher-residency programs, master-teacher corps of the most highly effective teachers (Partee, 2014); invest in educational technology, computer in the classrooms, establish eminent standards in math and science in K-12 education; Nigerian classrooms must also be connected to the Internet so that students will have access to the best sources of research information and databases in the world; provide access to continuing education opportunities to all citizens (North Carolina Progress Board, 2001); support expanded education access by involving private proprietors through tax breaks and other entrepreneurial incentives.

4. Provide Infrastructure

The importance of infrastructure to economic growth cannot be overemphasized (World Bank, 2010). A January 2015 report by the *Commission on Inclusive Prosperity* at the Center for American Progress (a think tank) cochaired by Lawrence Summers, former U.S. secretary of the treasury and Ed Balls, British Member of Parliament (MP), and Shadow Chancellor of the Exchequer in the British Parliament noted:

> An economy can only grow as fast as its infrastructure systems can move information, people, and goods. Infrastructure investments provide strong jobs and productive assets that serve as the foundation for long-term economic competitiveness, increased prosperity, and a high quality of life. By comparison, failing to invest leads to deteriorating facilities, unpredictable service disruptions, congestion, and higher costs to businesses and households. (Center for American Progress, 2015)

Summers and Balls are not alone. Dukakis and Kantor (1988) were also of the view that infrastructures are the "bricks and mortar and steel and asphalt" of a modern economic development.

Nigeria's current infrastructure base, including roads, bridges, railways, airports, seaports, electricity, telecommunications, water supply, are inadequate and progressively deteriorating, and "suffer diversion of funds"[9] (*Guardian*, October 15, 2008; *Guardian*, July 31, 2012). It fails the business community and frustrates the Nigerian people. And this is seriously hurting economic growth and productivity. In a recent statement, the World Bank declared the following about Nigeria:

> Nigeria's infrastructure needs remain acute. The country needs more railways, roads, and ports to get products to market; electricity for homes, schools and

> businesses; water and sanitation to keep its people healthy and to support crops; and modern communications services for everyone. . . . It's time to get this right, as demand for infrastructure is growing at an unprecedented rate. The link between economic growth and infrastructure is well-established. (*Punch*, September 25, 2017)

Nowhere is Nigeria's infrastructure deficiency and obsoleteness more acute than in road networks and electricity supply.

A. Roads

The importance of transportation infrastructure cannot be overemphasized. According to Carew and Mandel, economists at the Progressive Policy Institute:

> Transportation infrastructure is a critical foundation for sustainable economic growth, attracting business investment, facilitating basic trade and commerce, and allowing for the transport of goods locally, nationally, and worldwide. . . . The condition of state and local transportation infrastructure can be a key determinant of that region's relative competitiveness. (Carew & Mandel, 2014)

Road transportation is the major mode of transportation in Nigeria. However, Nigerian roads are grossly inadequate and dilapidated. Hence, *Newswatch* magazine described Nigerian highways as "roads to hell" (*Newswatch*, December 20, 2009). Also, the restrictive nature of the waterways, coupled with the near collapse of the rail system, and high cost of air travels have further exerted a lot of pressure on the road as over 70% of the total movement in the country are made by road (Nigeria Federal Road Safety Corps, *2011 Annual Report*, p. 54).

Furthermore, Nigeria's deplorable road condition comes at a big cost to the country. A 2003 Central Bank report indicated that Nigeria loses ₦133.8 billion value yearly due to bad roads (₦80 billion economic cost and ₦53.8 billion vehicle repair costs) (*Punch*, November 20, 2011). Also, a 2007 report by the African Development Bank (ADB) showed that inadequate road investment and maintenance would lead to estimated additional costs of $570 million in vehicle operating costs and road accidents in Nigeria annually (Aderinokun, 2007). The Federal Road Safety Corps (FRSC) has stated that Nigeria loses over 3% of her GDP annually due to road traffic crashes, sum equivalent to $10 billion (Dada, 2015). In addition, partly to blame on Nigeria's bad road networks, traffic accident related deaths and injuries on Nigeria's highways are alarming. Nigeria ranks second (191 out of 192 countries in the world with unsafe roads with 162 death rates per 100,000 population from car crashes) in global road traffic accidents (*Daily*

Sun, May 19, 2011). According to WHO estimates, road traffic fatalities kill 21 out of every 100,000 people in Nigeria (WHO, n.d.). According to the FRSC latest report, Nigeria recorded a total of 5,483 traffic deaths in 2019, Kaduna State recorded the highest number of traffic deaths with 484 deaths, followed by Ogun (364), Bauchi (349), Niger (303), Oyo (276), FCT (262), Kano (255), while Bayelsa State recorded the lowest with six deaths (Federal Road Safety Corps, *2019 Annual Report*, p. 82). However, recently Nigeria has taken steps to improve road safety and address road crashes by joining the key United Nations road safety conventions[10] (UNICEF, 2018). But, in spite of the huge expenditures on road construction, rehabilitation, (see bullet points) maintenance, and recent steps to enhance road safety, Nigerian roads are still considered as "death traps" (*This Day*, August 5, 2005) and "roads to misery" (*Guardian*, August 10, 2007):

- "FG Approves ₦60 billion for Roads Projects," *The Tide*, September 20, 2005.
- "FG Awards ₦9.2 billion Road Contracts in Niger Delta Region," *Daily Independent* October 7, 2005.
- "FEC Approves ₦2.7b for Ecological, Infrastructure Projects," *This Day*, November 17, 2005.
- "FG Approves ₦31 billion for Roads Repairs," *This Day*, November 9, 2005.
- "FG Invests ₦400 billion on Roads Since 1999," *This Day*, March 7, 2006.
- The *African Economic Outlook 2005/2006* report released by the OECD and the ADB described the Nigerian transportation system as "inadequate and in deplorable condition."
- "FEC Approves ₦7.4 billion for Road Repairs," *The Tide*, December 1, 2006.
- "85% of Nigerian roads are un-tarred. The railway system is still operating with the same narrow gauge lines built during the colonial era and recent accidents involving domestic airlines attest to the serious deficiencies of the Nigerian air transportation system," *African Economic Outlook 2005/2006 Report, Punch*, May 30, 2006.
- "Federal Government Spends ₦275 billion on Roads," *Daily Independent*, January 11, 2007.
- "Road Construction Gulps ₦299 billion," *Business Day*, April 5, 2007.
- "Senate Probes N1tn Roads Projects," *Punch*, July 6, 2007.
- "FERMA: Only ₦60bn of N650bn Was Spent on Road Maintenance," *Punch*, August 2, 2007.
- "Govt Spends ₦500b to Rehabilitate Roads," *The Guardian*, September 12, 2007.

- “Bad Roads: Nigerians Spend ₦450bn on Vehicles,” *Vanguard*, February 1, 2008.
- “Road Repairs: Obasanjo’s Regime Spent ₦500bn in 8 Years,” *Punch*, February 5, 2008.
- “Senate Begins Probe of $8.7bn Rail Modernization Project,” *This Day*, February 20, 2008.
- “House to Probe ₦1.38 trillion Roads Fund,” *The Guardian*, April 28, 2008.
- “80% of Roads in Bad shape, Says Govt,” *The Guardian*, April 21, 2008.
- “FG Releases ₦78bn for Roads projects,” *Business Day*, June 10, 2008.
- “₦967b Spent on Transport Sector in 8 Years,” *The Guardian*, June 24, 2008.
- “We Got ₦253b for Roads, Says Anenih, Ogunlewe,” *The Guardian*, June 26, 2008.
- “₦124.9bn spent on Rail Projects from 1999–2008,” *Punch*, July 15, 2008.
- “Nigeria Loses ₦450bn Yearly to Bad Roads,” *This Day*, December 4, 2008.
- “FEC Okays ₦116.5bn for 26 Roads,” *Punch*, April 30, 2009.
- “FG Signs ₦70.9bn Road Contracts,” *This Day*, December 12, 2009.
- “FEC Approves ₦10bn Contracts for Transport, Other,” *This Day*, September 22, 2010.
- “FG to Spend ₦700bn on Road Construction, Rehabilitation,” *Punch*, May 2, 2011.
- “FG to Spend ₦2.2tn on Road, Railway Projects,” *Punch*, June 14, 2011.
- “85% Nigerian roads are bad—RAMP,” *Punch*, August 11, 2011.
- “₦1.4trn Appropriated for Roads in Years—Reps,” *Vanguard*, December 11, 2012.
- “On November 22, 2012 the FEC approved ₦176 billion road contracts awards: dualization of the Lokoja-Okene-Auchi-Benin Road; the Gasua-Bayamari Road linking Yobe and Borno states; and the Suleija-Abuja Road. The Kano-Maiduguri Road contract, awarded six years ago but not executed, was reviewed and augmented from ₦172 billion to ₦285 billion, while the Calabar-Ugep, Ogoja-Katsina Ala Road contract was also augmented and approved, among others. Also, dualization of the East-West Road, was first awarded in 2006 for ₦204 billion, it has now been reportedly augmented to ₦349.8 billion, with the completion date fixed for December 2014,” *Punch*, November 30, 2012.
- “FEC approves ₦47.8bRoad Projects,” *The Guardian*, March 27, 2013.
- “FG Seeks ₦921.4bn to Complete 195 Road Projects,” *Punch*, April 25, 2013.
- “FEC Okays N29.7bn for Road, Water Projects,” *Punch*, September 25, 2013.
- “FEC Approved ₦1.3tn Contracts in 2013—BPP,” *Punch*, March 18, 2014.

- "FG Expends Over ₦250bn on Construction of East-West Roads," *Nigerian Tribune*, March 26, 2014.
- "FG Needs ₦300bn to Complete East-West Road—Minister," *Punch*, April 8, 2014.
- "FG Spends ₦1.47tn on 183 Road Projects," *Punch*, November 14, 2014.
- "FEC Okays ₦430.5b for Road Projects," *The Guardian*, December 3, 2014.
- "East-West Road Gulped ₦286bn without Completion—FG," *Vanguard*, February 2, 2016.
- "FG Approves ₦80bn for Construction of 12 Roads," *The Guardian*, March 22, 2017.
- "FG Approves ₦54bn for Reconstruction of Dilapidated Odukpani-Ikot Ekpene Road," *This Day*, May 4, 2017.
- "Across the nooks and crannies of the country, the critical inter-state link roads . . . are in very deplorable conditions. They include the Enugu-Onitsha Road; Odukpani-Itu Road; Oyo-Ogbomoso-Ilorin Road; Ilorin-Jebba-Mokwa Road; Benin-Sapele-Warri Road; Enugu-Port Harcourt Road and Benin-Auchi-Okene Road. These roads have become death traps and reasons for many fatal accidents," *Punch*, October 9, 2019.
- "Bad Roads: FG releases ₦650bn for capital projects," *Punch*, November 14, 2019.

B. Electricity

The record on power supply in Nigeria is either abysmal or unsatisfactory. "A critical constraint to economic growth in Nigeria," argued the United States Agency for International Development (USAID) "has been the lack of reliable electrical power" (USAID, 2015, p. 7). USAID is not alone. Nigeria's unreliable electricity supply is one of the "biggest obstacle to doing business in the country" and a "major hindrance to economic growth" (Olowosejeje, 2019). Olowosejeje, Leahy, and Morrison (2019, p. 149) stated that Nigeria's "limited power supply, have restricted the nation's socioeconomic development." World Bank (2020) stated: "the lack of reliable power has stifled economic activity and private investment and job creation, which is ultimately what is needed to lift 100 million Nigerians out of poverty."

To put the electrical power problem into perspective, South Africa has one-fourth the population of Nigeria but produces 10 times more electricity than Nigeria (USAID, 2015, p. 7; World Bank, November 2019; International Energy Agency & OECD, 2014).[11,12] Nigeria has been called the "house of darkness" because of her notoriously unreliable electricity supply. The *Punch* (November 3, 2019) reported "darkness pervades Nigeria," "Nigerian power sector is in a complete mess" (*Punch*, April 1, 2020). These sentiments are widely shared as report after report indicates (e.g., PricewaterhouseCoopers (PWC), 2013, 2016; NOI Polls, 2014, 2015; Thompson et al., 2017; Nkordeh et al., 2017; Ohajianya et al., 2014; Emodi & Yusuf, 2015). While power failures and outages have been part of Nigerian history, its severity has been on the rise without respite.

The helplessness and quagmire of the power situation is forcefully manifested by colossal financial investments (see bullet points) without commensurate results. It has been reported that between 1999 and 2007, the Obasanjo administration spent more than $13 billion, some say "$16 billion" to improve power supply. Aghast, in 2007, the House of Representatives Committee on Power declared: "It is sad that in the past eight years (1999–2007), over ₦1 trillion was appropriated and approved for the power sector, yet load shedding remains a constant refrain in the distribution of electricity in Nigeria" (*Punch*, November 14, 2007). Unfortunately, the spending bonanza continues without appreciable results. According to the former minister of power, Chinedu Nebo, after spending $35 billion in the 10 years, 2005–2014, on electricity infrastructure, power generation which was put at 3,463.40 megawatts (MW) as of March 20, 2014, dropped 963 MW to 2,500 MW by March 24, 2014. Meanwhile, Nigeria's "average daily electricity supply of 3,800 MW in 2018 dropped to 3,775 MW in 2019" (*Energy Mix Report*, January 31, 2021), further escalating the power unreliability problem.

While power outages are common in Nigeria, the power problem reached the highest nadir on November 29, 2020, when Nigeria suffered a total collapse of the national electricity grid system (*Reuters*, November 29, 2020), further making the country's precarious power supply worse, and hurting Nigeria's struggling economy more. Nigeria's unreliable power supply costs the economy estimated $28 billion annually, equivalent to 2% of the country's GDP (World Bank, 2020). In addition, in spite of the serious health and environmental hazards associated with toxic gas emissions from alternative sources of energy, especially generators, according to ADB, Nigeria spends a staggering $14 billion of foreign exchange annually to import generators, because of the unstable and poor power supply situation in the country (Olalekan, 2020).

- "Federal government expended $4.2 billion on the power sector in 2006," *Nigerian Tribune*, January 9, 2007.
- "Government to Spend ₦280 billion on Power in 2007,"*Vanguard*, January 9, 2007.
- "Power Projects to Cost ₦104b," *Daily Independent*, January 26, 2007.
- "FG Invests $2 billion on Power Project," *This Day*, February 7, 2007.
- "Energy: W/Bank Grants to Nigeria Hit $2.3bn," *This Day*, March 2, 2007.

- "Government Awards ₦445bn Contract to Ease Power Failure," *Business Day*, March 20, 2007.
- "Govt Approves ₦132bn for Power Sector," *New Nigerian*, April 5, 2007.
- "FG Spent ₦7.169trn on Power, Roads, Railways in 7 Years—Minister," *Vanguard*, April 26, 2007.
- "World Bank Invests $272m in Power," *This Day*, May 2, 2007.
- "₦17bn Spent on Power in 2006—Nenadi," *This Day*, May 9, 2007.
- "FG Spent ₦521bn on Power Sector in 8 years—PHCN," *Vanguard*, July 11, 2007.
- "$10b Wasted on Energy," *The Guardian*, January 29, 2008.
- "Power Sector: Obasanjo Spent $16bn, not $10bn—Bankole," *This Day*, February 7, 2008.
- "Nigerian Deals 'Wasted Billions'—Some $2.2bn Energy Contracts Awarded without a Bidding Process by former President and his Energy Minister," *BBC News*, March 14, 2008.
- "Reps Power C'ttee: 34 Ghost Firms Paid ₦6.2bn—Elumelu," *New Nigerian*, March 18, 2008.
- "Power: Reps Uncover Other ₦10bn Inflated Contracts," *Punch*, March 19, 2008.
- "$482m Power Funds Spent as Loans," *The Guardian*, March 21, 2008.
- "Power Probe: Contractor Collects ₦4.5bn, Disappears," *Punch*, April 1, 2008.
- "Reps Panel Discovers ₦58b Stalled Power Projects in Rivers," *The Guardian*, April 3, 2008.
- "Uncompleted ₦9.3b Power Project Commissioned in Bayelsa, Says Panel," *The Guardian*, April 4, 2008.
- "Power Probe: ₦30bn Egbema Power Project Abandoned," *This Day*, April 8, 2008.
- "Power Probe: Reps Uncover 800% Contract Inflation in Zamfara," *Punch*, April 23, 2008.
- "Power Probe: ₦1.9bn projects Missing in Kwara," *Punch*, May 5, 2008.
- "60 million Nigerian Now Own Power Generators," *Vanguard*, January 26, 2009.
- "Power: NEC Approves ₦303.23bn for Projects," *This Day*, February 24, 2009.
- "Govt to Spend ₦323 Billion on Power," *The Guardian*, March 15, 2009.
- "FG to Inject Fresh ₦40bn into Power Sector," *This Day*, March 30, 2009.
- "FG to Spend ₦130bn on Gurara Power Plant," *This Day*, March 31, 2009.
- "NIPP Approves ₦15bn for Power projects," *Nigerian Tribune*, April 15, 2009.
- "₦5bn REA Scam: Projects Inserted in Amended 2008 Budget," *Punch*, May 14, 2009.

- "5bn Scam: Elumelu, Others Awarded 156 Contracts in One Month—EFCC," *Punch*, May 15, 2009.
- "Govt Okays N25b for Power Projects," *The Guardian*, June 4, 2009.
- "Federal Government Disburses $4.6 billion for Power Projects," *This Day*, October 15, 2009.
- "CBN to Fund Power Projects with ₦500 billion Loan," *Daily Trust*, March 3, 2010.
- "Federal Government Approves ₦31 billion for Nine Power Projects," *Vanguard*, November 4, 2010.
- "Federal Executive Council Awards ₦1.8 billion Power Contracts," *The Guardian*, January 20, 2011.
- "Telecoms Operators Spend ₦3.63bn on Fuel Generators Monthly—Investigation," *Punch*, June 27, 2011.
- "FG to Spend ₦881bn on Power Sector in Three Years," *Punch*, July 25, 2011.
- "Electricity: FG Releases $3.7bn, Targets 20,000MW," *Punch*, May 6, 2013.
- "Power Supply: FG to Take $170m French Loan," *Punch*, March 16, 2014.
- "Five Power Firms Get ₦18.26bn Loan," *Punch*, February 3, 2015.
- "Electricity Firms Get Additional ₦39.5b Intervention Fund to Boost Supply," *The Guardian*, February 11, 2014.
- "NIPPS (National Integrated Power Projects) Gulp $8.62bn, Says Jonathan," *Vanguard*, February 21, 2015.
- "FG Spends ₦2.7tn on Power in 16 Years," *Punch*, September 9, 2015.

Nigerian electricity problem extends to the industrial sector. Nigerian firms complain about the high cost of manufacturing, especially from poor public electricity source. According to a World Bank study, 94% of firms report that infrastructure is a major problem (2.5 more worrisome than finance), and 95% of firms own generators, costing 2.42 more than would have been paid with reliable public power provision (Tyler, 2002). The industrial electricity problem was further demonstrated by another survey on power supply by the Power Holding Company of Nigeria (PHCN) to industries carried out by MAN, average power outages increased from 13.3 hours to 14.5 hours per day (*Guardian*, June 6, 2006; *Punch*, October 5, 2006), resulting in 70% added production costs (about three times more than PHCN tariff) in alternative energy supply (*Vanguard*, January 4, 2007) which in turn is passed on to the consumer in the form of higher prices. It is estimated that the Nigerian economy loses $130 billion annually due to power failures (*This Day*, October 20, 2010). (See also Ugwu et al., 2012; Edomah & Nwaubani, 2014.)

What Must Be Done

- Repair and expand existing road network to improve highway access to move people, goods, and services more efficiently and quickly.
- Revive the moribund railway system to augment road transport including the repeal or amendment of the tenuous 1955 Railway Act that prohibits private sector involvement in the rail sector.
- Build new power plants and at the same time repair and maintain existing facilities to ensure affordable and uninterrupted energy supply, including electricity and natural gas. Speed up the liberalization of the power sector to further encourage private sector participation and investment including solar and wind energy.
- Provide safe and cost-effective water, wastewater, erosion control, and waste management systems.
- Encourage public-private partnership (P3) in the provision of infrastructure, especially in the face of increasing public-sector funding gaps and budget cuts (Zhang & Chen, 2013; Hodge & Greve, 2016; Mallet, 2017; World Bank, 2017; DeGood, 2014). Some sources of financing include tolls, bonds, user fees, levies, rent/lease charges, grants, and banks. Closely linked to private capital investment for public projects is the idea of infrastructure banks.
- Establish National Infrastructure Bank to augment strained government infrastructure funding sources. Brookings Institution scholars, William Galston and Korin Davis, pointed out the importance of a national infrastructure bank: "done right, it will increase aggregate infrastructure investment, reduce the influence of politics on project selection, enhance incentives for private capital participation, and facilitate projects that span multiple State and local jurisdictions or include different modes of transportation" (Galston & Davis, 2012).

5. Support for Accountable Government

Effective leadership, fiscal discipline, outstanding education and quality workforce, and superb infrastructure are the four cornerstones of successful economic growth strategy (Iyoha, 2010; Brady & Spence, 2010; Mkapa, 2010; Ying, Eng, & Robinson, 2010; Kigabo, 2010; Cardoso & Graeff, 2010). A fifth cornerstone is accountable government (Clark, 1975; Welch, Hinnant, & Moon, 2005; Isham, Kaufmann, & Pritchett, 1997; Odugbemi & Lee, 2011). Even if development policy helps nations to enhance resources and open up new opportunities, development will still suffer if the resources are not utilized well and there is poor governance epitomized by corruption. The endemic problem of corruption and betrayal of public trust remains the chief albatross on the way to Nigeria's march to greatness (see, for example, Achebe, 1983; Vogl, 2012; Agbiboa, 2012; Brownsberger, 1983; Enweremadu, 2013). Corruption is not only antithetical to good governance, but it also erodes confidence in the system and, too often, stifles growth by diverting collective resources to personal gains or special interests at the detriment of the larger society.

Nigerians must demand accountability from officials at all times because without it, sustainable economic growth and improved social conditions will suffer. There should be political activism on the part of the citizens including demonstrations, sit-ins, and marches urging for change, the Arab Spring provides a good model to effect changes. Accountable government is effective, efficient, and responsive (see, for example, Bovens, 2007; Vigoda, 2003; Bryson, Crosby, & Bloomberg, 2014). It addresses the changing needs of the country and its citizens in an efficient, appropriate, and equitable manner (North Carolina Progress Board, 2001). It demonstrates sound planning and fiscal management. It encourages its citizens to be informed participants in civic affairs and actively involved in the governing process (North Carolina Progress Board, 2001).

Knowledgeable, informed citizens actively participate in their governments and hold their governments accountable for the resources they receive. Citizens are empowered and actively engaged in government. As the owners of government, they have a vested interest in governance, demanding accountability, effective and appropriate services, and responsiveness (North Carolina Progress Board, 2001). The problem of corruption and lack of accountability in Nigerian government must be tackled before it takes the nation to a point of no return.

What Must Be Done

- Build informed electorate; strong local governments; a just and accessible legal system; respect for human rights; a civil society based on tolerance and the rule of law; institutionalized checks and balances (Atwood, 1994).
- Institute government performance measure such as financial accountability, government effectiveness and efficiency, and training for public officials (North Carolina Progress Board, 2001).
- Nurture grassroots citizen participation in public affairs including community service, civic education, and global awareness. This is not only imperative for nurturing democracy, but also such involvement is essential to the full development of human capacities (Dye & Zeigler, 1972, p. 8). John Dewey (1859–1952), an American philosopher and educator, said, "the hallmark of democracy as a way of life may be expressed as the necessity for the participation of people in formation of the values that regulate the coexistence of people" (Dewey, 1937).

- Uphold freedom of speech and of the press, freedom to dissent, and freedom to hold divergent views to insure meaningful individual participation and survival of democracy. The sunshine Freedom of Information law is laudable and must be made to work. English philosopher, John S. Mill (1806–1873), in his 1861 classic *Considerations on Representative Government*, argued, "Man [people] can know the truth only by discovering it himself [themselves]."
- Support respect for and protection of rights and liberties. John Locke (1632–1704), English thinker and philosopher, in his 1689 illustrious book *The Second Treatise of Government*, postulated, "Even in a state of nature (situation without governments), citizens possess inalienable rights to life, liberty, and property." Locke was of the opinion that these rights "were antecedent to government and the State may not legitimately take them away from citizens." Thereby, citizens form a "social contract" (Rousseau, 1762) with each other in establishing a "limited government" to help protect their rights. In return they agree to submit to public authority to better protect life, liberty, and property.

CONCLUSION

This chapter examined the Nigerian economy and its failure to improve the lives of Nigerians, especially the middle class and the poor, in spite of the country's huge oil wealth and talented human capital or resources. It also discussed the role of the informal sector in Nigerian economy. Using Pan-African post-independence political economy analysis, looped into the impact of colonialism, political instability, leadership crisis, mismanagement, corruption, commodity shocks, resource curse, and globalization, it revealed the magnitude and severity of Nigeria's economic problems. Furthermore, it offered pathways to economic rejuvenation and growth.

Nigeria is at a crossroads faced with unprecedented economic crisis. Indeed, the economic crisis of Nigeria is real, alarming, and enduring. Sadly, the country's middle class is no longer an effective economic force in Nigeria. Also, Nigerians are economically worse-off today than they were at independence. The economic decline is protracted, stemming largely from rogue leadership, mismanagement, deficit spending, warped neglect of agriculture and manufacturing in favor of quick cash but nonrenewable and volatile oil and gas economy, and most of all the woeful failure of the Nigerian leadership to utilize Nigeria's abundant resources to improve the economic fortunes of Nigerians, especially the middle class and the poor.

The economic retrogression has been systematic and complex, affecting the entire economy hook, line, and sinker from season to season, from sector to sector, invariably consigning the Nigerian economy to what Shapiro and Ross (1993, p. 7) called "substandard equilibrium." The failure of Nigerian leadership to enable Nigerian businesses and workers to adequately adjust, compete, and win in the global economy, especially, through dedicated governance, investment in good education, attraction of private investment, trade promotion, infrastructure development, job training, improved security, and transparent institutions has been the most devastating to the economy. Nigeria's current productivity gains, net investments, employment availability, income gains, and general economic growth lag pre-independence levels with increasing severity. The choice is clear: Nigeria must change or be damned.

In this initial chapter, I feel morally obligated to air my views on this vital issue of the state of the Nigerian economy, not only as a professional but, more importantly, as a concerned citizen, who wants the best for Nigeria. Also, the timing could not be better because Nigeria has been an uninterrupted democracy for more than 20 years after a long period of repressive military dictatorships and political instability. The new democratic era offers Nigerians a unique opportunity for informed, candid, diverse, and dispassionate discussion on burning national issues without the menacing shadow of an overbearing and callous military dictatorship. Furthermore, for Nigeria's nascent democracy to survive and continue to resonate with the Nigerian people, it must be nourished with strong and sustained economic growth for the benefit of all. Huntington (1991, p. 33), in fact, argued very persuasively when he wrote that "the two most decisive factors affecting the future consolidation and expansion of democracy will be economic development [economic growth] and political leadership [effective leadership]." The mismanagement of the economy is directly related to high cost of governance as Nigeria deals with issues of corruption and out-of-control spending by the government.

NOTES

1. The World Bank defined social protection as "the set of systems that help individuals and families especially the poor and vulnerable cope with crises and shocks, find jobs, invest in the health and education of their children, and protect the aging population." *Social Protection.* Retrieved from https://www.worldbank.org/en/topic/socialprotection.

2. The Commission for Africa was set up in 2004 by the then British prime minister, Tony Blair, to address governance and developmental challenges in Africa. The

Commission published its report "Our Common Interest" in 2005. It acknowledged that everyone would be better-off and has a role to play in creating a strong and prosperous Africa. It put forward a coherent package of measures to achieve this goal. Commission for Africa. *About*. Retrieved from http://www.commissionforafrica.info/about.

3. The concept of "dialectical materialism" was originally used by Karl Marx and Friedrich Engels in the 1860s to explain their theory of "surplus value" under capitalism predicated on the philosophical context of "historical materialism." According to Marx, "surplus value is plainly described as that part of the agricultural worker's labor which the landowner appropriates to himself without giving any equivalent in return, and the product of which therefore he sells though he has not bought." (Karl Marx, *Theories of Surplus Value*. p. 62. A selection from the volumes published between 1905 and 1910 as *Theorien uber den Mehrwert*, edited by Karl Kautsky, taken from Karl Marx's preliminary manuscript for the projected Fourth Volume of *Capital*. Translated from the German edition by G. A. Bonner and Emile Burns. London: Lawrence and Wishart, 1951.) *See* also Karl Marx (1867). *Capital: A Critique of Political Economy*. Volume 1. Book One: The Process of Production of Capital. Friedrich Engels (Ed). Translated from fourth German edition by Samuel Moore and Edward Aveling, transcribed by Hinrich K. Zodiac et al., proofed by Andy Blunden and Chris Clayton (2008), Mark Harris (2010), Dave Allinson (2015). Moscow: Progress Publishers. Karl Marx and Friedrich Engels (1984). See also *Marx & Engels Collected Works Vol 19: Marx and Engels: 1861–1864*. London: Lawrence & Wishart. Retrieved from https://muse.jhu.edu/book/33021.

4. For example, of "illuminating systemic weaknesses in international aid efforts to support development" (Brookings, 2010) *see* William Easterly (2007). *The White Man's Burden: Why the West's Efforts to Aid the Rest Have Done So Much Ill and So Little Good*. Penguin Books; Dambisa Moyo (2009). *Dead Aid: Why Aid Makes Things Worse and How There Is Another Way for Africa*. London: Penguin Books; Sebastian Edwards (2014). *Toxic Aid: Economic Collapse and Recovery in Tanzania*. Oxford: Oxford University Press; Sebastian Edwards (2014). "Economic Development and the Effectiveness of Foreign Aid: A Historical Perspective," NBER Working Paper No. 20685; Brookings Institution (2010). "Making Development Aid More Effective," Washington, DC. Retrieved from https://www.brookings.edu/wp-content/uploads/2016/06/09_development_aid.pdf;

Blessing Chiripanhura and Miguel Nino-Zarazua (2015). "Aid, Political Business Cycles and Growth in Africa," *Journal of International Development*, 27, 1387–1421. Retrieved from https://eds-a-ebscohost-com.subr.idm.oclc.org/eds/pdfviewer/pdfviewer?vid=8&sid=34dd735b-c9b0-4755-bce3-5995f1a7c2e0%40sessionmgr4007.

5. A 2006 film reminiscent of the Sierra Leone Civil War in 1991–2002. The title of the film refers to blood diamonds, "which are diamonds mined in war zones and sold to finance conflicts, and thereby profit warlords and diamond companies across the world."

6. Purchasing power parity measures the total amount of goods and services that a single unit of a country's currency can buy in another country. World Bank (n.d.).

Fundamentals of Purchasing Power Parities. Retrieved from http://pubdocs.worldbank.org/en/332341517441011666/PPP-brochure-2017-webformat-rev.pdf.

7. Over $2.3 billion realized from windfall in oil price during the Gulf War in 1991 was squandered (*Tell*, December 20, 1993, p. 17). The *Financial Times* of London (January 2, 1995, p. 3) also reported that the "Okigbo Panel for the reorganization of the Central Bank of Nigeria" has concluded that the "$12.4 billion recorded in the Oil Revenue Dedicated Accounts between September 1988 and June 1994, was spent in less than six years by President Babangida and the Governor of Central Bank on what could neither be judged high priority nor regenerative investment, while the country was openly reeling with a crushing debt overhang." In another instance, the Dedicated Account "lost $600 million" without a trace (*The Economist*, June 8, 1996, p. 46).

8. Economic growth potential and windows of opportunities that can result from transition to democracy in the process of development, especially, for a country like Nigeria that has experienced long period of military rule.

9. In October 2008, a Senate hearing found that ₦229.9 billion aviation funds were misused by aviation agencies including Federal Airports Authority of Nigeria and Nigeria Civil Aviation Authority (NCAA), *The Guardian*, October 15, 2008. In June 2012, then aviation minister, Stella Oduah, informed a Senate hearing that ₦300 billion aviation intervention fund provided by the Federal Government has been diverted. *The Guardian*, July 31, 2012. Retrieved from http://www.ngrguardiannews.com/index.php?option=com_content&id=93976:the-n300b-aviation-intervention-fund-&Itemid=612.

10. On October 18, 2018, Nigeria acceded to the following agreements (UNICEF, November 1, 2018):

- 1968 Convention on Road Traffic (enters into force 18 October 2019);
- 1958 Agreement concerning the Adoption of Harmonized Technical United Nations Regulations for Wheeled Vehicles, Equipment and Parts which can be Fitted and/or be Used on Wheeled Vehicles and the Conditions for Reciprocal Recognition of Approvals Granted on the Basis of these United Nations Regulations (enters into force 17 December 2018);
- 1997 Agreement concerning the Adoption of Uniform Conditions for Periodical Technical Inspections of Wheeled Vehicles (enters into force 17 December 2018);
- 1998 Agreement concerning the Establishing of Global Technical Regulations for Wheeled Vehicles, Equipment and Parts (enters into force 17 December 2018);
- 1957 Agreement concerning the International Carriage of Dangerous Goods by Road (ADR) (enters into force 18 November 2018). Retrieved from http://www.unece.org/info/media/presscurrent-press-h/transport/2018/nigeria-steps-up-road-safety-efforts-by-joining-the-key-united-nations-road-safety-conventions/doc.html):

11. Annual per capita electricity consumption in Nigeria is one of the poorest in the world—145 kilowatt hours compared to 351 kW hours in Ghana; 229 kW hours

in Senegal; 275 kW hours in Cote d'Ivoire; 164 kW hours in Kenya; 1,653 kW hours in Namibia; 312 kW hours in Angola; 609 kW hours in Zimbabwe; 1,816 kW hours in Botswana; 4,198 kW hours in South Africa; 717 kW hours in Zambia; 4,652 kW hours in Malaysia; 812 kW hours in Indonesia; 8,845 kW hours in Singapore; 5,130 kW hours in the United Kingdom; and 12,994 kW hours in the United States of America. World Bank (November 2019), *Electric Power Consumption (kWh per capita)*. Retrieved from https://data.worldbank.org/indicator/EG.USE.ELEC.KH.PC.

12. Electric power consumption measures the production of power plants, less transmission, distribution, transformation, and energy use costs by power plants. International Energy Agency (IEA) Statistics. Organization for Economic Cooperation and Development/IEA 2014. Retrieved from http://www.iea.org/stats/index.asp, subject to https://www.iea.org/t&c/termsandconditions/.

Chapter 2

High Cost of Governance

"The Nigerian Factor"

Essentially, chapter 2 of the book deals with the problem associated with the high cost of governance in the oil-rich West African nation of Nigeria (Khemani, 2001; Bach, 1989; Ekpo, 1994; Ehwarieme, 1999). It is the opinion of several Nigerians that there is a widespread abuse of the payment for public goods and services, which has had adverse impact on Nigerian people (Martini, 2014; Hoffmann & Patel 2017; Oxfam, 2017). To many of the Nigerian citizenry, the government of the day serves some very useful purposes and, as a result, will continue to perform such important functions as needed by the society and the people. Most certainly, the lives of citizens are variedly impacted daily by "executive, legislative, and judicial activities at all levels of government and [by] diverse policy areas" (*Congressional Quarterly Reporter*, 2008, p. xiii). In fact, the public policy scholar, Thomas Dye, puts it best (Dye, 1998, p. 2) when, inter alia, he wrote: "Governments do many things. They regulate conflict within society; they organize society to carry on conflict with other societies; they distribute a great variety of symbolic rewards and material services to members of the society; and they extract money from society; most often in the form of taxes."

Without the shadow of a doubt, other scholars and researchers have corroborated Dye's viewpoint. For example, Anthony Downs, in his book, *Inside Bureaucracy*, argued: "Bureaucracy not only provide employment for a very significant fraction of the world's population; but they also make critical decisions that shape the economic, educational, political, social, moral, and even religious lives of nearly everyone on earth" (Downs, 1976, p. 1). James Q. Wilson, the bureaucracy theorist, contended:

> The power of the bureaucracy should be measured not by the number of employees, but rather by the extent to which appointed officials [bureaucrats]

> have discretionary authority—that is, their ability to choose courses of action and to make policies that are not spelled out in advance by law. By this test the power of the Federal bureaucracy has grown enormously. . . . Delegated authority now permits appointed officials to decide, within rather broad limits, who may own a television station, what safety features automobiles must have, what kinds of scientific research shall be especially encouraged, what drugs shall appear on the market, which dissident groups shall be investigated, what fumes an industrial smokestack may emit, which corporate mergers shall be allowed, what use shall be made of national forests, and what price farmers shall receive for their products. (Wilson, 2000, pp. 259–260)

It does not end there because the government, for example, protects stock market investors and consumers against fraud and adulterated drugs through the Securities and Exchange Commission as well as the National Agency for Food and Drug Administration and Control, respectively. Furthermore, the government of the day protects workers and their families from exploitation from employers by seeking and enforcing labor standards that make the industrial system more humane and the work place safe for all and sundry (Grossman, n.d.; Schlesinger, 1960).

For security and other purposes, the government maintains Armed Forces, which is charged with defending the citizenry against both foreign and domestic enemies as well as to safeguard the sovereignty of the nation. Trade laws are enacted to prohibit unfair acts of competition and deceptive practices. The government monitors the financial and credit system against abuse and unethical practices through the Central Bank and other banking regulatory mechanisms. It is also a fact that if we rely on businesses and industries to behave well and to regulate themselves in the public interest, they will eventually cut corners and the environment as well as food, water supply, the air, and consumer products would not be as clean, safe, and qualitative as we would like them to be, hence the essence of the Federal Environmental Protection Agency, Consumer Protection Council, and Standards Organization of Nigeria.

In essence, the government provides public safety "by upholding and enforcing the laws, administering regulatory programs, managing records, educating the public and managing emergencies, both directly and through interaction with other agencies" (Louisiana Department of Public Safety and Corrections, n.d.), hence the Nigerian society has police, courts, prisons, fire departments, National Emergency Management Agency. Public health departments provide disease control and prevention, vaccinations, food safety inspections, sanitarian services, licensing and certification of health care facilities, and so on. Government works to reduce the number of highway crashes, fatalities, and injuries by promoting road, driving, and vehicle safety through the Federal Road Safety Commission. These services cost money to provide, both in administrative and program expenditures. However, there is no doubt that government costs too much in Nigeria, and government spending has steadily increased without corresponding benefits in a meaningful way to the Nigerian people, especially the middle class and the poor.

COST DISEASE THEORY AND GOVERNANCE EXPENDITURE IN NIGERIA

The "cost disease" theory, which was advanced by the economist William Baumol (Baumol & Bowen, 1965; Baumol, 1967, 2012), is to be used to explain the high cost of governance in Nigeria. With his colleague (William Bowen in the early 1960s), Baumol proposed the cost disease concept, as the idea, for example, of such services as musical performances, medical care, education, and garbage collection, which consistently increases in cost year after year and faster than inflation (Langer, 2017; Baumol & Bowen, 1965).

The underlying premise of Baumol's theory is that innovation enables workers to produce more output in different sectors of the economy, such as in agriculture and in manufacturing, which pushes up wages nationwide (Atkinson, 2016; *The Economist*, September 29, 2012; World Bank, 2007). However, other such sectors, as the performing arts, cannot reduce labor with ease in the face of rising wages because the quantity of labor required to produce these services is hard to reduce (Wallace, 2012). For instance, a string quartet required the same number of musicians in 1800 as it does today (Cooper, 2017). In view of the foregoing, Frank (2012) succinctly explained: "While productivity gains have made it possible to assemble cars with only a tiny fraction of the labor that was once required, it still takes four musicians nine minutes to perform Beethoven's String Quartet in C minor, just as it did in the 19th century" (quoted in Bowen, 2012, p. 4). However, an arts institution that pays musicians 1800's wages in a 2000's economy risks high employee turnover, as workers leave to take other better-paying jobs.

Consequently, to be viable, the arts institution has to raise wages in order to attract and retain the best musicians (Lee, 2017). At the same time, the music outfit must raise ticket prices to cover the extra labor costs. Baumol and Bowen (1965, pp. 499–500) provided an explanation, where productivity was concerned:

> However, in the sector where productivity is stable, there is no offsetting improvement in output per manhour, and so every increase in money wages is translated automatically into equivalent increase in unit labor cost. . . . The faster the general pace of technological advance, the greater will be the increase in the

> overall wage and the greater the upward pressure on costs in those industries which do not enjoy increase productivity.

In the Nigerian example, the factor that pushes up the price of the metaphoric "music ticket," in this instance the cost of governance, is not innovation in the governmental process or better service delivery, but rather it is as a result of the impact of deep-rooted systematic cost disease problem known as the "Nigerian factor," particularly the abuse of office and official position for personal gain. According to Omotoso (2014, p. 129):

> The national attribute—the "Nigerian factor"—is the major disease affecting service delivery in the country. This term refers to an inelegant or improper way of doing things, which puts sectional interest, political considerations, elite interest, pecuniary considerations, and wealth accumulation over and above public service. This factor is hampering the effectiveness and efficiency of public institutions.

Ameh (2017, p. 678) offered a corroboration of this phenomenon: "Nigerian factor is a corrupt value system and mind-set which are learnt either consciously or unconsciously, which propels an individual to seek for self-gratification against the collective interest and growth of the nation." Omotoso and Ameh are not alone. A number of studies support the existence of and provide excellent analysis of the menace of the Nigerian factor (Udoh, 2003; Smith, 2007; Jibril, 2003).

The concept of state capture can also be used to explain and add value to discussions about the high cost of government in Nigeria. It has been argued that state capture is a "severe form of corruption" (Chipkin, 2017), and it is "a form of meta-corruption with mercenary motivation" (Meirotti, 2018, pp. 3–4). Also, Lodge (2018, p. 14) argued that state capture "harness" the state "to a very particular and especially narrow set of private interests." This situation has been commonplace in oil-dependent Nigeria, where "cabals" in the oil sector become involved in the political space to ensure the election of a government that favors their interests (Meirotti, 2018, p. 7). According to Mbaku (2017, p. 772) "state capture involves the appropriation of state institutions, organs, and functions by individuals or groups." Mbaku adds: "By doing so, these individuals and groups can have control over or influence the design and adoption of new laws, rules, and regulations, as well as the amendment or modification of existing ones" (Mbaku, 2017, p. 772). Chipkin (2017) also argued that "state capture occurs when state institutions, potentially including the executive, state ministries, agencies, the judiciary and the legislature, regulate their businesses to favor private interests."

In the foregoing manner, as Chipkin (2017) "noted, 'state capture' is different from traditional 'corruption' in that many of its activities may be legal; nonetheless, it is regarded as a form of corruption because private influence is exercised illicitly in public affairs, subverting and even replacing transparent and legitimate forms of intermediation." This clarification is important because, as Meirotti (2018, p. 3) observed, the "current definition of corruption seems, in some cases, to fall short of describing the means and motives of misappropriation of state resources in African states."

High cost of governance in Nigeria is particularly fueled by the headwinds of fraud, waste, abuse, corruption, and theft. Some examples will be in order.

A 2014 report by the House of Representatives Committee on Public Accounts indicated that the Federal government incurred illegal expenditures of ₦4.17 trillion between 2004 and 2012 under the bogey of Service Wide Vote (SWV—earmarks for emergencies not covered in the Appropriations Act) (*Punch*, January 24, 2014). In addition, the report showed that the Office of the Head of Service of the Federation could not account for ₦35 billion it collected from the SWV during the same period (Ameh, 2014). The abuse of SWV extends to special funds (earmarks created by law to address special problems and economic emergencies). In Nigeria these statutory funds have been turned into "pocket money for public officials or to be 'borrowed' by our fiscally reckless governments" (*Punch*, April 15, 2013). The amounts involved and magnitude of abuses are gravely unnerving. In 2013, among other discoveries, the Senate Public Accounts Committee uncovered abuses in the utilization of Stabilization Fund, Natural Resources Development Account (NRDA), Derivation Fund and Ecology Fund, where ₦873 billion was allegedly diverted for unrelated projects (*Punch*, April 15, 2013).

Meanwhile, the Nigerian Senate further alleged that ₦191.78 billion of the total special funds receipts between 2002 and 2012 were abused by the presidency and the Finance Ministry largely through dubious "loans" granted to agencies unrelated to the missions of the funds (it is uncertain that the "loans" were repaid) (*Punch*, April 15, 2013). For example, ₦16.26 billion was allegedly granted to the Directorate of Pilgrims Affairs between 2003 and 2005; ₦2 billion "loan" was reportedly given to a construction firm from the NRDA; and ₦10.9 billion "loan" taken from the Derivation and Ecology funds to the Consolidated Revenue Fund, allegedly, to help fund the 2009 budget (*Punch*, April 15, 2013).

In May 2014, Femi Falana, human rights lawyer and a delegate to the 2014 National Conference, called on the Nigerian government to institute a probe into the disbursement of over ₦3 trillion in "security votes" between 2010 and 2014 (Babalola, 2014) ("Security votes" is the governmental practice in Nigeria of "setting aside a huge sum of money, ostensibly for disbursement on security matters in a state, but for which no accountability is demanded or given") (*Punch*, October 2, 2012). In July 2014, the NEITI (oil industry watchdog) audit for the years 2007–2011 disclosed the abuse of ₦994 billion of special funds, saying the funds were either not remitted as required by law, or applied for the purpose for which they were set up (*Punch*, July 14, 2014). No wonder, Obiageli Ezekwesili, former minister and World Bank vice president, said "I Pray for Our Oil to Dry Up in Nigeria" (*Vanguard*, November 4, 2012).

"THE NIGERIAN FACTOR": THIEVERY AND THE STOLEN

"If you see the cost of governance in Nigeria you will feel very sad. Nigeria is a place where you vote a person in and six months later, he buys five cars, has houses and suddenly he is doing a thanksgiving in church and people will be celebrating such a man who should be handed over to police" (*Nigerian Tribune*, February 21, 2013). The foregoing very striking observation was made by then Anambra state governor Peter Obi in February 2013. Earlier, a similar observation was made by a famous singer, the late Fela Kuti, who in the 1970s, made a song titled "Authority Stealing." Kuti was not only an entertainer, but he was also a social critic, who used his music to expose the ills of society, especially the misconduct and malfeasance of public officials in high places. He, in fact, made "Authority Stealing" because he was particularly upset by the scandal of alleged missing billions of naira (Nigerian currency) in oil funds from the coffers of NNPC as well as the failed multimillion naira telephone lines installation and maintenance contract awarded to International Telephone and Telegraph of Africa Ltd headed by a prominent businessman, the late Moshood Abiola.

Nowhere has the lyrics of Kuti's song found more expression than in the graft practiced in governance in Nigeria by the ruling and political elite, who are influential and privileged Nigerians who ought to know better, who instead allegedly chose to use their high official authority to steal from Nigerian taxpayers with galling impunity and unparalleled audacity. Ladan (2017, p. 187) disclosed the following:

> Available statistics from Central Bank of Nigeria Statistical Bulletin (2009) have shown that both, Nigeria's capital and recurrent expenditure has maintained a risen trend over the past five decades. For instance, with a government expenditure of ₦163.90 million in 1961, the expenditure steadily increased to ₦755.96 million in 1969 representing an increase of 461% (or an annual increase of 46.1%). Similarly, the country's expenditure steadily increased from ₦997.20 million in 1971 to ₦7,406.70 million in 1979 which represents an annual increase

> of 83% and by 1980, the expenditure has more than doubled to ₦14,968.50 million. With the return of the country to democratic rule in 1999, the country's expenditure witnessed a phenomenal risen trend. For instance, from ₦947,690.00 million in 1999, the government expenditure grew steadily to ₦3,456,925.40 million in 2009 representing an increase of 365.77%. (CBN, 2009)

By some estimates, Nigeria spends 60–70% of its revenue on recurrent expenditure, leaving a minuscule one-third of national budget for capital development (*Guardian*, February 1, 2011; Ladan, 2017; Ukwueze, 2015). Analysis of government expenditures and budget priorities bears this out. In the first 12 years of the civilian administration (1999–2011), for example, the three tiers of Nigerian government spent a combined total of ₦94,151 billion and ₦69,562 billion on recurrent and capital obligations, respectively (table 2.1). This shakes out to an average of 62% for recurrent and 38% for capital expenditures during this period. The worrying trend of rising recurrent costs to the disadvantage of capital improvements is stark, up from a low of 53% in the 1999–2004 intervals to a peak of 71% in 2011. Conversely, capital expenditures trended down sharply by more than half, from a high of 47% in the 1999–2004 period to 29% in 2011.

The abuses and costs to the Nigerian taxpayer are enormous (Eme & Andrew, 2013; Awomuse, Olorunleke, & Alimi, 2013). The *Guardian* also disclosed:

> Ever since Nigeria adopted American style democracy, the nation's rulers have gone on a spending spree and over time they have become adept at inventing sinecure positions or sometimes non-existent offices that are draining the nation's resources with reckless abandon. It is democracy without any checks and balances. (*Guardian*, January 26, 2012)

Further analysis of government spending priorities during the 1999–2011 period (table 2.2) shows deepening neglect and outright miss-prioritization of fiscal allocations, especially in the critical sectors of education and health in favor of overhead spending. Federal personnel (salaries) and overhead costs (stationeries, fuel, etc.) alone gulped astounding ₦25.44 trillion, almost four times more (average 79%) compared to just ₦6.30 trillion (average 21%) for health and education recurrent and capital expenditures. Also, in the education and health subset, recurrent costs at ₦5.06 trillion are heavily skewed against capital improvements of ₦1.24 trillion (nearly five times less).

ANTECEDENT

The large Nigeria governmental structure costs too much and delivers very little. This has been well documented in many reports and analyses

Table 2.1 Government Recurrent and Capital Expenditures, 1999–2011(₦ Billion)

	Entity	*1999–2004*	*2005*	*2006*	*2007*	*2008*	*2009*	*2010*	*2011*	*Total*
Recurrent Expenditure	Federal	23,969	1,321	1,390	1,589	2,117	2,128	3,109	3,315	38,939
	State	21,205	7,891	8,943	1,217	1,506	1,426	1,648	2,056	45,893
	Local	4,337	375	398	684	819	705	824	1,179	9,320
	Total	49,510	9,587	10,732	3,490	4,442	4,259	5,582	6,550	94,152
	% Grand Total	53	62	62	67	60	60	66	71	58
Capital Expenditure	Federal	15,569	520	552	759	961	1,153	884	919	21,316
	State	26,220	5,147	5,840	855	1,456	1,284	1,522	1,375	43,699
	Local	2,041	214	268	144	563	363	533	422	4,547
	Total	43,830	5,880	6,660	1,758	2,979	2,800	2,939	2,716	69,562
	% Grand Total	47	38	38	33	40	40	34	29	42
	Grand Total	93,340	15,467	17,392	5,248	7,422	7,059	8,521	9,265	163,714

Source: Central Bank of Nigeria, Annual Report, Various Years.

Table 2.2 Selected Federal Expenditures, 1999–2011 (₦ Billion)

	Item	*1999-2004*	*2005*	*2006*	*2007*	*2008*	*2009*	*2010*	*2011*	*Total*
	Personnel Cost	11,353	443	528	761	943	953	1,381	1,722	18,084
	Overhead Cost	3,847	203	259	368	457	564	982	673	7,354
	Total	15,200	647	787	1,129	1,400	1,517	2,363	2,396	25,438
	% Grand Total	80	77	76	75	77	82	86	79	80
Recurrent	Education	2,163	83	119	151	164	137	171	336	3,324
	Health	1,022	56	62	82	98	90	99	232	1,741
Capital	Education	505	32	33	47	49	43	88	35	832
	Health	29	22	32	97	97	53	35	40	405
	Total	3,720	192	246	376	408	323	393	643	6,301
	% Grand Total	20	23	24	25	23	18	14	21	20
	Grand Total	18,920	839	1,033	1,506	1,808	1,840	2,756	3,038	31,739

Source: Central Bank of Nigeria, Annual Report, Various Years.

(Campbell, 2018a, 2018b; Adewole & Osabuohien, 2007). Sadly, it has been confirmed that corruption remains the chief driver of high cost of government in the country (Page, 2018; Transparency International, 2018). A hard look at the Nigerian budget, over a long period of time (i.e., 1960–1986), is very revealing. According to Pius Okigbo, an indigenous economist and scholar:

> Between 1960 and 1966, overall administration consumed 41% of the budget, general administration accounted for 22%, while defense and security had 20%. In 1971–75, the combined ratio fell to 30.5% and general administration dropped to 7%, defense and security gulped 23%. Further savings were realized in the Mohammed/Obasanjo Administration, which brought the aggregate ratio down to 21% for general administration, defense and security accounting for 6.6% and 14.4%, respectively. The Shagari Administration (1979–83) not only failed to build on these savings, but also reversed the combined ratio back to the 41% mark, escalated expenditures for general administration to 19.5% and defense and security to 22%. (Okigbo, 1983)

Statistically, the Buhari/Babangida Administrations' combined ratio was 35.4%, general administration and defense and security pegged at 61% and 20%, respectively. Comparatively, the relative cost of government in 1979–1983 was very similar to 1960–1966, but the Obasanjo military administration (1976–1979) was the most effective in fiscal discipline, while the successor governments from President Shagari to Babangida failed to rein in spending (Okigbo, 1986).

Also, a further evaluation of Babangida's fiscal management style, especially with the Gulf War's oil windfall of 1990, showed massive overspending and cost overruns on his watch; for example, this scenario took place: "In February 1992, $50 million was allocated to purchase 3,000 Peugeot cars for the private use of captains and majors in the Nigerian army" (Herbst & Olukoshi, 1994, p. 498).

> Subsequently, it funded the military intervention in Liberia as well as the purchase of new military equipment estimated at a cost of $250 million to $500 million. . . . Failed to curb spending on the Ajaokuta Steel Plant at an initial price of $1.4 billion and a final price estimated at $4 billion. . . . Continued the commitment to a dubious $2.4 billion aluminum smelter and sponsoring the 1990 OAU Summit at $150 million. (Keeling, 1991, p. 4)

In addition, a 1991 World Bank report also indicated that there was "a breakdown in fiscal and monetary discipline in 1990 . . . not characterized by additional spending and monetary expansion but also by a major surge in expenditures bypassing budgetary mechanisms for expenditure authorization and control" (Holman, 1994, p. 14). This trend of reckless spending, during military governance, has got progressively worse since the return to civil or democratic rule more than 20 years ago.

GOVERNMENT REMAINS A BIG BUSINESS

Given contemporary high magnitudes of government spending (e.g., annual average of 80% gulped on recurrent costs in the 1999–2011 interval (table 2.2)), it will be proper to briefly review historical trends, relate them to the present, and ponder their implications for the future. Table 2.3 shows that in 1959/1960, it cost £81.225 million to run Federal and Regional Governments and Statutory Authorities combined. Administration and General Services portion of the funds was just £8.806 million (10.8%). For the 1955–1962 period or stretch, administrative cost was under 11% of the total budget.

In 1960, three Regions' government structure (Eastern, Northern, and Western), general administration expenditures' situation is not entirely different from the Federal picture. In fact, it mimicked the Federal pattern. Table 2.4 presents combined Regional governments' expenditures (current and capital) in 1960/1961. In 1960, recurrent and capital expenditures amounted to £77.1 million, with education having the largest share of £23.7 million (30.7% of total spending). Expenditure on general administration came to £11.4 million (including security and law enforcement) or 14.8%. Expenditure on roads and waterways amounted to £8.03 million (10.4%), health £6.9 million (8.9%), fire protection and water supply £3.2 million (4.1%). Thus, more than half (£41.7 million or 54.1%) of total expenditures of £77.1 million was devoted to strictly four non-administrative (education, roads, health, fire protection) purposes. Fast forward to the present, the 1960/1961 expenditures contrast sharply to 2017 where general administration (personnel and overhead costs) single-handedly consumed 70% (₦5.06 trillion) of total Federal outlays (₦7.3 trillion). In the 1960/1961 bracket, expenditures on economic services especially agriculture and the development of non-mineral resources was £5.4 million (6.9%); manufacturing and construction £2.9 million (3.7%).

In 2021, the approved Federal budget is ₦13.6 trillion ($35.66 billion). While the nation's needs had increased with growing population, however, increased public spending has not translated into economic and social gains for the Nigerian people, especially the middle class and the poor. In other words, spending and welfare had been inversely related. Nigeria is Africa's major oil producer, but majority of its population of 200 million people live in poverty. In January 2011, a government appointed Presidential Advisory Council (PAC) expressed concern over the high cost of governance and

Table 2.3 Federal and Regional Governments and Statutory Authorities Expenditures, 1955–1962 (£m)

Category	*Actual Expenditure 1955–1959*	*Actual Expenditure 1959/1960*	*Actual Expenditure 1962*	*Total 1955–1962*	*% Total*
Adm and General Services	19,767	8,806	6,912	35,485	10.7
Defense	3,479	1,271	1,305	6,055	1.8
Justice, Police, Prisons	2,992	1,076	1,063	5,131	1.6
Roads	25,679	13,439	14,586	53,704	16.3
Waterways and Harbors	7,733	6,538	5,408	19,679	6.0
Water Supplies	6,992	4,651	6,887	18,530	5.6
Education	12,763	4,954	6,196	23,913	7.2
Medical*	17,140	6,560	10,162	33,862	10.3
Agriculture**	7,746	2,912	5,192	15,850	4.8
Mining and Geology	498	105	81	684	0.2
Electricity	8,107	4,322	5,200	17,629	5.3
Industries	2,775	4,885	2,702	10,362	3.1
Public Works	4,308	1,155	1,847	7,301	2.2
Railways	22,038	7,811	14,883	44,732	13.5
Aviation	1,035	326	939	2,300	0.7
P&T and Broadcasting	7,781	4,809	2,032	14,622	4.4
Survey	520	288	1,557	2,365	0.7
Cooperatives	53	91	82	226	0.1
Grants and Loans	1,292	1,015	335	2,642	0.8
Loans Unclassified	5,250	4,808	5,027	15,085	4.6
Sub Total	157,948	79,822	92,396	330,157	100
Southern Cameroons	4,871	1,403	2,684	8,958	
Total	162,819	81,225	95,080	339,115	

Source: National Economic Council, *Economic Survey of Nigeria 1959*, p. 128.
*Medical and Health (including Chemistry)
** Including Department of Marketing and Exports

Table 2.4 Combined Regional Governments Expenditures, 1960/1961 (£000)

Category	*Amount*	*% Total*
Administration and General Services	10,444	13.6
Justice and police	968	1.3
Roads and waterways	8,025	10.4
Fire protection, water supply	3,161	4.1
Education	23,650	30.7
Health	6,851	8.9
Agriculture and non-mineral services	5,355	6.9
Fuel and power	834	1.1
Other mineral, mfg, construction, etc	2,867	3.7
Transportation and Communication	173	0.2
Other	4,813	6.2
Unallocable expenditure	9,920	12.9
Total	77,061	100.0

Source: Pius Okigbo, 1965.

advised President Jonathan to reduce the number of MDAs. The issues raised by PAC were not new.

The Ayida Panel on Public Service Reform (1995), Anya Expenditure Review Committee (2009), and most recently Oronsaye Presidential Committee on the Rationalization and Restructuring of Federal Government Parastatals, Commissions and Agencies (2012) had all alerted the nation of the waste and crushing public service cost bill. What is more, Emeka Anyaoku, former commonwealth secretary general, had declared severally:

> Our present cost of administration impacts very adversely on the resources available for our national development. We must free the resources spent on government and deploy them on development, which will palpably benefit our toiling and unemployed masses. In this way, we would give our people a greater stake in the democratic dispensation. (*Guardian*, October 27, 2004) (See also Bevan, Collier, & Gunning, 1999; Loubser & Steenekamp, 2017)

On the economic front, for example, the fact that we have 36 federating units means we spend up to 80% of our revenue just on administration. No country has developed on the basis of allocating up to 80% of its revenue to just administration (*Vanguard*, October 16, 2017) (see also Smith, 1981; World Bank, 2015). The *Guardian* (October 29, 2004) argued: "We are unimpressed but will not be distracted by government's list of vacuous achievements which are measured by the level of expenditure without any concrete and functional projects or appreciable improvements to show" (see also Anyadike, 2013; IMF, 2017; UNDP, 2016).

While PAC, *Guardian*, Anyaoku, Anya Committee, and sister Government Panels lament bloated government spending, a review of public service spending in the first 10 years of civil rule (1999–2010) is very instructive, and it offers a living proof of the depth of fiscal recklessness and squander in the public sector. According to reports, during the period under review, the three tiers of government (Federal, State, and Local) spent over ₦15.6 trillion on public servants, representing 30% of the ₦52.103 trillion spent by collective government during the period or 50% of the estimated ₦31.26 trillion recurrent budgets (Ndujihe & Idonor, 2011). Further breakdown showed that the public servants expenditures shares of the Federal, State, And Local to be ₦200 billion, ₦420 billion, and ₦690 billion, respectively (Ndujihe & Idonor, 2011). (The makeup of Nigeria's public servants is as follows: Federal Executive, 472; Federal Lawmakers, 469; State Executives, 2,664; State Lawmakers, 1,152; Local Council Executives, 3,096; Council Lawmakers 8,692; Federal/State Judiciary, 934 giving a total of 17,497) (Ndujihe & Idonor, 2011.)

JUMBO PAY

"Feel like you're not paid enough? Worry about losing your job? Wish you had better benefits? Ever think of quitting? If you answered yes to these questions, one thing is certain: You don't work for the [Nigeria] government" (Sherk, 2010). Nigeria's top public functionaries, according to experts, are the highest paid in the world, even with the country being among the poorest in terms of per capita income, security, social provision, and living standards (Campbell, 2018; Werlin, 2003; Khan & Cheri, 2016; Chiahemen, 2007). In fact, it is a fiscal tsunami and barn burner. To reflect on public expenditure concerns, it was asserted:

> Indeed, with the biggest slice of the nation's resources devoted to the consumption and sumptuous lifestyles of the top personnel, the huge cost of governance has not only become a central question in the truncated growth of Nigeria but also a parameter by which the pace of the nation's decline is measured by the international community and its institutions. . . . Ensconced in their comfort, fed fat on the citizens' sweat and their pockets busting with unearned income, they [top officials] could not be bothered by issues of national development. . . . The profligacy in government and the lavish life-style of state actors amount to a drain on the common wealth and a desecration of the state as well as a betrayal of the people's trust. (*Punch*, May 15, 2012)

In a country where the monthly minimum wage is a paltry ₦18,000, and more than 70% of the population live on less than $2 per day, nowhere is this prodigality more evident than in the salaries and fringe benefits of Nigeria's

National Assembly (Campbell, 2018; Onuigbo et al., 2017; Kazeem, 2015). The situation in the Nigeria's legislature fully qualifies to be described as scandalous; Nigeria pays her legislators salaries and allowances unheard of anywhere else on earth (National Assembly gulps "25%" of Federal overhead budget).

Public figures and institutions have also expressed deep concerns and spoken out against Nigeria's extravagant parliamentary compensation in various forums. Accordingly, Campbell (2018a) made the following comment:

> Not only is parliamentary compensation in Nigeria massive compared to the overall wealth of the country, but it is largely unregulated and subject to abuse. Levels of parliamentary compensation in Nigeria are so high that there is an understanding that service in the National Assembly is an aspect of patronage/clientage relationships and should be rotated between ethnic group, local region, and religion. This is one reason why, following each national election, more than sixty percent of parliamentarians are new.

Bemoaned by the high salaries and lavish benefits of the National Assembly, Atedo Peterside, then chairman of the Technical Committee of the NCP (National Council on Privatization) and a delegate to the 2014 National Conference, decried that "Federal legislators each pay themselves more than President Obama and conspire to avoid disclosing exactly how much they each collect from the Federal Treasury under various guises," and asked "who will save the nation from this unholy coalition of kleptomaniacs?" (Peterside, 2014). The *Punch* called the legislators "overpaid and over-pampered lawmakers" (*Punch*, July 28, 2015) and "virtually useless" (*Punch*, January 25, 2016), who "by their greed, corruption, opaqueness, insensitivity and monumental incompetence, parliamentarians, since 1999, have stunted the entrenchment of democracy and atrophied development. . . . Nigerians have a duty to themselves and to future generations to put an end to the travesty currently playing out at the National Assembly in the name of lawmaking" (*Punch*, February 1, 2016). The *Guardian* (July 13, 2016) wrote:

> Many years ago, Nigerians thought the Senate would be the reflective chamber of the National Assembly and a seminal platform for the growth of Nigeria's wobbly democracy. But now it tends to be saturated by garrulous individuals with no modicum of the required personality excellence the hallowed chamber deserves. . . . The full time status of National Assembly members encourages the infiltration of the legislature with indolent persons, and such others who are not fit to lead. The man-hours spent, and the outputs of work done at the National Assembly are inconsistent with the perquisites they desire to covet.

According to the journalist Ijeoma Nwaogwugwu, "some sobering statistics would awaken us to the enormity of the problem of high cost of governance in Nigeria" (Nwaogwugwu, 2011). According to one estimate, a Nigerian senator takes home at least $1.40 million (₦220.5 million) annually in regular salaries and allowances. Compare this to America (Nigeria copied American presidential system) Congressional pay (Senator/Representative) is $174,000 yearly (except for the Speaker of the House, $223,500); President pro tempore of the Senate and the majority and minority leaders in the House and Senate, $193,400 (Brudnick, 2016).

Members of United States Congress are eligible for a pension at the age of 62 if they have completed at least five years of service (Isaacs, 2017). Members are eligible for a pension at age 50 if they have completed 20 years of service, or at any age after completing 25 years of service (Isaacs, 2017). "The amount of the pension depends on years of service and the average of the highest three years of salary. . . . Congressional pensions, like those of other Federal employees, are financed through a combination of employee and employer contributions" (Isaacs, 2017). United States president Joseph Biden earns $400,000 per year. A British MP earns £64,738 ($98,745) per year, while the Prime Minister Boris Johnson makes £142,500 ($217,355) annually (United Kingdom Parliament, n.d.). This means that a Nigerian senator earns at least eight times more than American senator and as much as three times the American president. Also, it translates that Nigerian Federal legislators earn 15 times higher than the British MP and as much as six times more than the British prime minister per year (table 2.5). Excessive and mismanaged spending is not limited to the Federal level, it extends to the States as well.

Governors in particular are too easy with taxpayer's money and continue to gamble with public funds. The result is that they live above the law, operate in out-of-control manner, and plunge their States into avoidable financial crisis. The full drama played out in July 2015 when President Buhari approved a bailout of more than ₦805 billion ($2 billion) to help State governments resolve accumulated unpaid workers (including Federal employees) salaries. But it should not be that way, especially given the substantial statutory allocations that flow into the States every month. Also, aside regular allocations (for instance, Nigerian 36 States governors received ₦1,598 billion in 2015 proper), according to the Federal Ministry of Finance, ₦3 trillion in additional revenues was distributed to the States and Local governments councils from the excess crude savings account between 2011 and 2015. If these funds (regular allocations and excess crude savings) were properly managed and rightfully applied, the States would have no business being broke in the first place, let alone defaulting on workers' pay.

Instructively, in a different geography but similar political structure, States in America (Nigeria mimics American presidential system) produce goods

Table 2.5 Annual Pay of Selected Heads of Government

Country	*Name*	*Position*	*Salary*
Britain	Boris Johnson	Prime Minister	£142,000*
Canada	Justin Trudeau	Prime Minister	£203,303
France	Emmanuel Macron	President	£210,268
Germany	Angela Merkel	Chancellor	£219,350
Ghana	Nana Akufo-Addo	President	$76,284
Ireland	Leo Varadkar	Prime Minister	£190,246
Nigeria	Muhammadu Buhari	President	₦11.6m**
Nigeria	National Assembly	Senator	₦182.2m***
South Africa	Cyril Ramaphosa	President	$R2.6m
United States	Joseph Biden	President	$400,000
United States	Congress	Senator/Rep	$174,000

Source:
United Kingdom Parliament. (n.d.).
http://www.parliament.uk/about/faqs/house-of-commons-faqs/members-faq-page2/.
Winterman, D., and Lane, M. (2010, June 2). *BBC News* Magazine.
http://news.bbc.co.uk/2/hi/uk_news/magazine/8715505.stm.
United States Congressional Research Service. (n.d.).
Revenue Mobilization Allocation and Fiscal Commission. (n.d.). *Remuneration Package for Political and Judicial Office Holders*, Effective Date July 1, 2009.
http://rmafc.gov.ng/LEGISLATIVE%20ARM3.dpf.
Ghana President. (n.d.).
http://www.bbc.co.uk/news/world-africa-20188452.
South Africa President. (n.d.).
http://www.citypress.co.za/politics/zuma-is-fivetimes-more-expensive-than-obama-20120729/.
* entitled to £193,000.
**₦3.5 million basic salary ($22,293), ₦8.1 million allowances ($51,407), total $73,700.
***₦182.2 million in basic salary and allowances ($1.15 million).
Note: Currency conversion equivalence may vary due to exchange rate fluctuation.

and services, captured in gross State product (State counterpart of the nation's GDP) and raise their own budget revenues without necessarily depending on Uncle Sam (nickname of American Federal government), thereby providing value added and at the same time contributing to overall U.S. economic growth. (According to the U.S. BEA, "GDP by State is comprehensive measure of the economies of each State and the District of Columbia. GDP estimates the value of the goods and services produced in a State" (U.S. BEA, GDP by State, n.d.)). United States GDP (current dollars) by State for 2019 (latest annual data) showed that contributions from the State of California led the way with about $3.13 trillion (14.6% USGDP), followed by Texas with $1.84 trillion (8.8% USGDP), and New York third with $1.77 trillion (8.1% USGDP) (U.S. BEA, October 2, 2020). And if California were to be a country in 2019, it would have the fifth largest economy in the world, after Germany's GDP of $3.86 trillion (*Forbes*, 2019; Hughes, 2020). According to the World Bank, for 2019 (latest data), United States is the largest economy in the world with $21 trillion GDP (24.4%), followed by China with $14 trillion (16.3%), and Japan third with $5 trillion (5.8%) (World Bank, 2021) (% represent country's share of the global economy). The fiscal cliff and precarious economy of the States (vis-à-vis the nation) has made former commonwealth secretary general, Emeka Anyaoku, to refer to them as "36 federating non-viable States" (Adeniji, 2015). The *Guardian* (February 10, 2016) also astutely noted:

> Today's 36 States are parasitic appendages of an all-powerful center, begging for hand-outs and barely able to pay the salaries of their workers. . . . The unjust centralization of Nigeria not only robs everyone and helps no one; it has continued to fuel corruption and perpetuate injustice against all.

Closely linked to high and ballistic spending is the perversion of unwieldy expansion of public offices and political appointees which further drives up the costs of government.

BLOATED WORKFORCE

The number of the Federal Cabinet has gone up, while accountability has gone down to the extent that senior Nigerian officials are derisively called "very important personalities of waste (VIPW)." The Independence Government of October 1, 1960 (table 2.6) comprised of 23 Federal Ministers—16 Cabinet ranks and 7 Non-Cabinet ranks (Sklar, 1963, pp. 508–509).

By 1997, there were 24 Federal Ministers of Cabinet rank and 10 Non-Cabinet rank, excluding plethora of Special Presidential Advisers (*Europa Yearbook*, 1997). These numbers also excluded the 27 members of the ruling Military Council. Upon the return of civil rule in 1999, six additional Federal Ministries were created (Culture and Tourism; Environment; Water Resources; Intergovernmental Affairs and Special Duties; Cooperation and Integration in Africa; Housing). Also, in 2011, the government created two new Ministries: Ministry of Information Technology and Ministry of Trade and Investment, making present total of 32 Cabinet ranks. The practice of creating more Ministries has become a revolving culture of waste and invariably as a way to "guarantee ethnic and religious inclusiveness" in government posts. (Nigerian Constitution provides for "Federal Character Principle"—ethnic balancing measure, requiring for each State to be represented on the Federal Cabinet) (1999 Nigerian Constitution—Chapter VI Section 147(3).)

In all, under former president Jonathan, Nigeria (population about 200 million) had a jumbo Cabinet of 41 Ministers, excluding horde of appointees and consultants not subject to Senate confirmation. (Contrast with the United States, population of about 330 million, has 14 Cabinet Departments or Federal Ministries). Also, there were a slew of Presidential Aides including Special Advisers, Senior Special Assistants, Special Assistants, Chief of Staff

Table 2.6 Nigerian Independence Government, October 1, 1960

No.	Name	Ministry	Party Affiliation	Home Division/ Province
1	Abubakar T. Balewa*	Prime Minister	NPC	Bauchi
2	Muhammadu Ribadu	Defense	NPC	Adamawa
3	Festus Okotie-Eboh	Finance	NCNC	Warri
4	Raymond A. Njoku	Transport and Aviation	NCNC	Owerri
5	Muhammadu I. Wada	Works and Survey	NPC	Kano
6	Joseph M. Johnson	Labor	NCNC	Lagos
7	Zanna B. Dipcharima	Commerce and Industry	NPC	Borno
8	Aja Nwachukwu	Education	NCNC	Afikpo
9	Shehu Shagari	Pensions	NPC	Sokoto
10	Usman Sarki	Internal Affairs	NPC	Bida
11	Maitama Sule	Mines and Power	NPC	Kano
12	T.O. S. Benson	Information	NCNC	Lagos
13	Waziri Ibrahim	Health	NPC	Borno
14	Olu Akinfosile	Communications	NCNC	Okitipupa
15	Musa Yar'Adua	Lagos Affairs	NPC	Katsina
16	Jaja A. Wachukwu	Economic Development	NCNC	Aba
17	Taslim O. Elias	Attorney General	NCNC	Lagos
18	Matthew T. Mbu	M.S. Defense—Navy	NCNC	Ogoja
19	Moses Majekodunmi	M.S. Defense—Army		
20	E. A. Esin**	M.S. Foreign Affairs	NCNC	Calabar
21	Nuhu Bamali**	M.S. Foreign Affairs	NPC	Zaria
22	M.A.O. Olarewaju	M.S. Prime Minister's Office	NPC	Ilorin
23	J. C. Obande	M.S. Prime Minister's Office	NPC	Idoma
24	H. Omo Osagie	M.S. Finance	NCNC	Benin

*Prime Minister and Minister for Foreign Affairs and Commonwealth Relations.
**Minister of State in the Ministry of Foreign Affairs and Commonwealth Relations.
M.S. = Minister of State.
NPC = Northern Peoples' Congress.
NCNC = National Council of Nigeria and Cameroons.
Source: Richard L. Sklar, 1963, pp. 508–509.

to the President, Secretary to the Federal Government, and Head of Service of the Federation. (Vignette: At a Aso Rock meeting of religious affairs advisers in November 2014, the Sultan of Sokoto, Saad Abubakar III, astounded by the large number of Presidential aides in attendance, humorously flayed the issue in his protocol remarks: "The Special Adviser to the President on Political Affairs, the Senior Special Assistant to the President on Christian Matters, the Senior Special Assistant to the President on Muslim Matters, the Special Adviser to the President on Gender Issues, and Special Advisers on Several Issues" (Adetayo, 2014)). Reportedly Jonathan had about 133 aides (Amaefule, Okolor, & Adesomoju, 2015). In a push to reduce both the size and cost of government, President Buhari appointed and inaugurated 36 Ministers in November 2015 as against Jonathan's 41 (*Vanguard*, November

11, 2015). Bloated workforce issue especially large number of political appointees is not restricted to Abuja, it extends to the States.

In October 2016, Cross River governor Ben Ayade appointed over 1,000 (1,106 to be exact) people into various political positions, including 28 commissioners, 65 special advisers, over 100 special assistants, personal assistants, and community relations officers. In March 2014, Taraba acting governor Garba Umar terminated 24 special advisers to the State government and appointed 23 new ones (*Punch*, March 17, 2014). Running up to the 2011 elections, then governor Theodore Orji of Abia appointed 457 new aides (special advisers, senior special assistants, and personal assistants) (Udeaja, 2011). Governor Isa Yuguda of Bauchi at one time had over 1,000 aides including 23 special advisers, 41 senior special assistants, 265 special assistants, 582 personal assistants (he fired all of them immediately after the 2011 elections) (Garba, 2009; Orude, 2011). (On April 29, 2015, barely one month to the end of his tenure, Governor Yuguda reportedly fired 2,000 political aides) (Bakam, 2015). In July 2012, then governor Rochas Okorocha of Imo appointed 78 new aides, including 25 special assistants, 15 senior special assistants, 29 special assistants, seven executive assistants, and two personal assistants (Ogugbuaja & Garba, 2012). In November 2008, then Osun governor Olagunsoye Oyinlola appointed 750 executive assistants into the State's 30 Local councils (25 per Local council), with per capita monthly salary of ₦50,000 (total of ₦37.5 million per month, ₦450 million per year) (Abimboye, 2010). Ghost worker fraud also drives up the cost of government (for the benefit of space, discussion of ghost worker fraud will be restricted to the Federal level only).

In June 2016, it was reported that the Federal Government and 10 States lost over ₦538 billion to ghost worker fraud in five years. (Of the amount, the Federal portion was ₦220 billion paid to 103,000 ghost workers between September 2013 and May 2015. The remaining ₦318.3 billion was paid by 10 States: Katsina, ₦30bn; Kano, ₦17bn; Rivers, ₦60bn; Benue, ₦10.2bn; Oyo, ₦18bn; Abia, ₦26.5bn; Adamawa, ₦20.4bn; Akwa-Ibom, ₦15bn; Bayelsa, ₦120bn; and Ekiti, ₦1.2bn.)

In April 2016, the EFCC announced that it has detected 37,395 ghost workers on the Federal civil service payroll (*Vanguard*, April 19, 2016). Three years earlier in 2013, a similar audit of MDAs uncovered 45,000 ghost workers, which costs tax payers ₦100 billion in wasteful expenditures annually (Agande, 2013). Another report by the Federal Civil Service Commission (FCSC) indicated that ghost workers and pensioners fraud cost the nation ₦12 billion yearly (*Daily Independent*, January 12, 2011). Similarly, the FCSC admitted that it identified over 30% ghost workers on its payroll (*The Sun*, February 27, 2013). Also, the Federal Ministry of Finance discovered that ₦1.5 billion in fraudulent ghost worker payments was made to the Police

Pension program yearly (*Guardian*, December 15, 2011). Partly to blame on ghost worker fraud, according to the Budget Office, in less than four years ending in 2011, public service wage bill increased from ₦800 billion to almost ₦1.7 trillion, and in 2012 proper, of the 72% allocation for recurrent personnel cost, MDAs absorbed 35% excluding the Judiciary and Legislature (*Guardian*, December 15, 2011). In 2011, the National Identity Management Commission uncovered 4,000 or 39% ghost workers (out of 10,300 workers) on its payroll (Oketola, 2011). Also in 2011, the Pension Task Team discovered that over 71,658 fake pensioners nationwide have been on the Federal payroll since 1975 and this discovery reportedly saved the public ₦76 billion in excess pension payment arrears (*The Sun*, February 27, 2013).

In 2010, Nigerian Police reported 100,000 (33%) ghost workers in the organization, out of the officially registered 300,000 policemen and women (Leba, 2013). In 2009, a House of Representatives probe uncovered 10,000 ghost workers in the Customs Service (*This Day*, May 18, 2009). In 2008, it was reported that PHCN had 14,885 ghost workers, by 2012 it has risen to 17,000 (*Vanguard*, July 18, 2011). In 2003, the Ministry of Defense discovered 24,000 ghost workers in a pension program audit (*This Day*, August 30, 2003).

In 2004, government initiated audit of Federal Public Service personnel indicated the presence of "42,000 ghost workers, with the Ministry of Federal Capital Territory (MFCT) having 3,000 ghost workers (costing about '₦63 million monthly') out of 25,000 total staff" (*Punch*, May 5, 2004). Prior in 2003, the same MFCT "lost more than ₦765 million to ghost workers fraud" (*Daily Independent*, October 28, 2004). Bloated workforce and ghost worker fraud are inextricably linked to the waste and fraud in statutory corporations (Federal government owned companies).

STATUTORY CORPORATIONS—PUBLIC LOSS, PUBLIC PAIN

Nigerian public enterprises are characterized by waste, inefficiency, and corruption. The *Economist* of London has described Nigerian State enterprises as "triumphs of towering inefficiency" (*The Economist*, August 21, 1993). For example, reports indicate "a whopping ₦13 trillion spent by the Federal Government to establish and operate 590 state-owned-enterprises (SOEs) between 1978 and 1999 were wasted funds and Nigerians sadly got a rotten public sector in return for this huge investment" (Nsa, 2007). Despite this colossal investment, SOEs employed less than 5,000 workers, had over 5,000 board members, owed workers huge pension liabilities of about ₦2 trillion, consumed over ₦384 billion yearly in subventions and subsidies, and contributed substantial portion of nonperforming debts owed the London and Paris Clubs (Bassey, 2007). Also, the enterprises failed to remit taxes deducted at source from their staff, including Pay-As-You-Earn, Value-Added-Tax, and corporate taxes, thereby failing to yield dividends or service (Bassey, 2007).

Worse, the enterprises drowned in debt. Debt profile of some public enterprises during the period, for instance, showed that NAFCON had liabilities of ₦15 billion; Anambra Motor Manufacturing Company (ANAMMCO), ₦1 billion; Volkswagen of Nigeria, ₦645 million; Steyr Nigeria Limited, ₦2.3 billion; Nigeria Sugar Company, ₦14.7 billion; Nigerian Paper Mill, Jebba, ₦12 billion; Nigeria Newsprint Manufacturing Company, ₦16.8 billion; Iwopin Pulp & Paper Company, ₦3.4 billion; Federal Superphosphate Fertilizer Company, Kaduna, ₦4.9 billion; Nigeria Machine Tools, Oshogbo, ₦2 billion; Jos Steel Rolling Mill, ₦1.3 billion; Oshogbo Steel Rolling Mill, ₦997 million; National Iron Ore Mining Company, ₦708 million; Eleme Petro-Chemical Company, $632 million; Nigeria Ports Authority, ₦6.6 billion; Nigeria Railway Corporation, ₦18.2 billion; and Nigeria Airways, ₦3.9 billion (Bassey, 2007).

Too often in Nigeria executives and officers of nonperforming state companies enjoy tenure. They are rarely dismissed or disciplined for poor performance and mismanagement, let alone, reprimanded for misappropriating public resources or engaging in corruption. Worse, at times, they are bestowed national merit honors and awarded sumptuous retirement. In his memorable 1968 book, *The People's Republic*, Obafemi Awolowo (1909–1987), one of Nigeria's founding fathers, wrote (p. 306):

> With very few exceptions, Nigeria's public corporations are veritable hotbeds of criminal waste of natural and human resources. This is due mainly to fraud, corruption, and unspeakable inefficiency on the part of Nigerians and, sometimes, non-Nigerians, who manage these corporations. Most of the Nigerian executives, in charge of these heavily capitalized public concerns, have been appointed out of sheer favoritism and nepotism, and are without any special merits or qualifications for their onerous assignments, with the result that most of Nigeria's public owned companies are grave and almost unbearable public liabilities, and constitute a permanent drain on the country's coffers.

Awolowo is not alone in his observation, as the situation is not getting any better more than 30 years later going into the return to civil rule in 1999. Inaugurating the NCP in July 1999, for example, then president Obasanjo stated inter alia:

> State enterprises suffer from fundamental problems of defective capital structure, excessive bureaucratic control or intervention, inappropriate technology, gross incompetence and mismanagement, blatant corruption and crippling

> complacency which monopoly engenders. Inevitably, these shortcomings take a heavy toll on the national economy.

In November 29, 2011, editorial, the *Punch* newspaper also offered this perspective:

> Public enterprises have become a conduit for massive looting by public officials and a break on economic growth. Between 1973 and 1995, the Federal Government spent over $100 billion to establish public enterprises. But their returns, at the best of times, were a paltry 0.5 per cent per annum, according to a former BPE head, Nasir el-Rufai. During the period, it was estimated that enterprises were costing the government about ₦265 billion annually to run. Largely moribund, NITEL's debt was put at ₦300 billion as at July 2011. It was estimated that the Federal Government spent over $826.6 million without results on railway contracts between 1999 and 2007. As at 2004, about $300 million had been spent on Turn Around Maintenance of the nation's four refineries without any result. At a time, one NNPC Group Managing Director allegedly ran up a bill of approximately ₦240 million at a luxurious hotel in Abuja. The story is unremittingly bleak.

It would be recalled that Nigeria has spent about $25 billion in turnaround maintenance (TAM) of refineries in the past 25 years (Daka, Jeremiah, & Abu, 2021). On top of that, latest report, according to the *Punch* newspaper, is that the refinery TAM program continues to be a "cesspool of corruption" and "serial fraud" on which in "2019 the NNPC spent ₦218.18 billion on ailing refineries with barely anything to show for it" (*Punch*, April 3, 2020). Regardless of previous rehabilitation's expenditures on the refineries, in March 2021, the Nigerian government approved a fresh round of $1.5 billion for Port Harcourt refinery maintenance. Additionally, notwithstanding prior rehabilitations, a 2020 NNPC report indicated that Warri Refinery, Port Harcourt Refinery, and Kaduna Refinery, from March 2019 to March 2020 period, the three refineries without associated crude plus freight cost and no production, incurred operational expenses of ₦10.88 billion and sustained operating deficit of ₦10.30 billion (NNPC, March 2020, p. 20).

CONCLUSION

This chapter has focused on the high cost of governance in Nigeria. It analyzed the causes and effects of big government spending in the country. The "cost disease" theory propagated by the economist William Baumol was used to explain the high cost of governance in Nigeria. In this case, the cost disease theory was repackaged to mean "Nigerian factor" cost disease issue, particularly the abuse of office and official position for personal gain. Also, it suggested ways to check Nigeria's runaway government spending pattern. Nigerian government costs too much and delivers little. It must be emphasized that the high cost of government in Nigeria is first and foremost as a consequence of the Federal system of government Nigeria is operating, which she can ill afford, let alone sustain, and is fiscally irresponsible and unwise. According to the *Guardian* (January 26, 2012), "it [Nigerian government] is large and obtuse . . . it drains the nation's resources with reckless abandon." Nigeria operates the American style executive presidential system of three-tier government: Federal, State, and Local governments. At the Federal level are the presidency and National Assembly (Senate and House of Representatives), at the State level are 36 governors and respective legislatures, at the Local level are 774 Local government chairpersons and accompanying council members.

By some estimates, Nigeria spends more than 70% of its revenue on recurrent expenditure, leaving a minuscule one-third of national budget for capital improvement. The *Economist* (March 3, 2012) stated: "74% Nigeria official revenues are spent on maintaining the government." Reports indicate that Nigeria's top public functionaries are the highest paid in the world, even with the country being among the poorest in terms of per capita income, security, social protection, and living standards. In a country where the monthly minimum wage is a measly ₦18,000 (about $50), more than 70% of the population lives on less than $2.0 per day, and 2,300 under-five year olds and 145 women of childbearing age die every day from preventable or treatable infectious diseases including malaria and measles, nowhere is this prodigal spending more evident than in the jumbo salaries and fringe benefits of Nigeria's National Assembly.

The National Assembly "gulps 25% of the Federal budget overhead" it has been reported. According to one estimate, a Nigerian senator takes home at least $1.40 million (₦220.5 million) annually in regular salaries and allowances. As previously indicated, compare this to America (Nigeria copied American presidential system) Congressional pay (Senator/Representative) is $174,000 yearly (except for the Speaker of the House, $223,500); President pro tempore of the Senate and the majority and minority leaders in the House and Senate, $193,400. United States president earns $400,000 per year. British MP earns £64,738 ($98,745) per year, while the prime minister makes £142,500 ($217,355) annually.

Another driver or cause of high cost of government in Nigeria is the monster of corruption, euphemistically called "the Nigerian factor," particularly the abuse of office and official position for personal gain, including stealing, fraud, misappropriation, and diversion of state resources and funds. While the nation's expenditures have increased with growing population and other emergent needs and exigencies, however, increased public spending has not translated into economic and social gains for the Nigerian people, especially the middle class and the poor. In other words, spending and improved standards of living have been inversely related. The high cost of governance in Nigeria is unsustainable and risky. It reflects an urgent fiscal crisis that requires changes in the ways and manner government procures and pays for goods and services. But the fiscal pain with the associated extravagance, fraud, and corruption that go with it will not go away until Nigeria's budget and spending processes are radically changed and focused on cleaning the rot that has become of Nigeria's fiscal administration. Nigeria's approach must insist on "results rather than adding to last year spending programs, consolidation, competition, customer choice, fighting corruption, and relentless effort to garner savings while improving public service" (Osborne & Hutchinson, 2006).

Excessive spending and debt are growing to catastrophic levels, with the total public national debt (external and domestic) pegged at $83.883 billion (₦25,701.646 billion) as at the end of June 2019, according to the DMO (DMO, 2019), up $10.675 billion or nearly 15% from $73.208 billion (₦22,379.666 billion) recorded a year prior (DMO, 2018), representing about 16.1% of the GDP, according to ceicdata.com an online data platform (Ceic.com, n.d.). Going down the memory lane, in essence, Nigeria's $83 billion debt burden in 2019 is what it was 14 years ago in 2005–2006 when she benefited from Paris Club debt relief. For the Nigerian leadership to have squandered the debt reduction windfall in just 14 years and have no tangible economic progress to show for it is beyond disappointing (Brannon, 2017).

At the same time, the deficit is also growing out of control. According to the DMO, for example, 84% of the nearly ₦2 trillion (₦1.95 trillion to be exact) or ₦1.643 trillion deficit projected in the 2018 Fiscal Appropriation Act was to be financed through borrowing (DMO, 2018, p. 18, inadvertently numbered p. 3 in the report).

It is time for Nigerian leaders, especially the President and members of the National Assembly, to get government spending and debt under control. Nigerian government can pursue debt limit policy as a mechanism to lessen the debt burden (i.e., debt ceiling) and reduce the cost of government of the country. Debt ceiling policy works by setting targets and limiting government growth by applying effective fiscal restraint rules. In Sweden and Switzerland, for example, the legislature approves annual borrowing authority limited to purpose instead of by amount (Institute for Spending Reform, 2019). (Institute for Spending Reform is a U.S.-based organization devoted to promoting solutions to America's spending and debt problems.) The National

Assembly can impose such a rule where the [Federal Ministry of Finance] can be allowed to borrow only for interest on publicly held debt and payment to [pensions or retirements] (Institute for Spending Reform, 2019), and other entitlement and social welfare programs. (Nigeria rolled out its first national social welfare plan in 2017 with ₦500 billion ($2 billion) startup money and anticipated $500 million loan grant from the World Bank (Malingha, 2017).) (Also, as a poverty alleviation measure, the government announced that for 2017, one million Nigerians will receive ₦5,000 ($16) monthly in income support, and the number of beneficiaries is expected to reach 5 million by 2021 (*Punch*, January 26, 2017).)

Also, the Nigerian government can adopt the Merrifield-Poulson Fiscal Responsibility Rule, as empirical evidences in the literature suggest that some countries have been able to significantly reduce government spending as a share of GDP and in some cases also to reduce tax burdens (OECD, 2011, 2012, 2014; Lienert, 2010; Trapp, Lienert, & Wehner, 2016). The Merrifield-Poulson Fiscal Responsibility Rule "requires agreement on a budget constraint at the outset of the budget process" (Merrifield & Poulson, 2016, p. 252), in addition to "mandatory structural balance aimed at preventing the accumulation of debt over the business cycle, while providing exceptions for extraordinary or emergency expenditure" (Merrifield & Poulson, 2016, p. 251). Schakel, Wu, and Jeurissen (2018, p. 1), for example, found that the presence of fiscal rule on average is associated with a 3% decrease of public health care expenditure in OECD countries between 1985 and 2014. Sadly, high cost of governance is aided and abetted by massive corruption.

Chapter 3

Corruption

This chapter discusses several aspects of the monstrous and endemic corruption in Nigeria. The Caribbean-born scholar Richard Joseph, in his 2009 study, described corruption as "Nigeria's mighty problem." To Nigerians, however, the mighty problem is the failure to create a modern nation that, in the words of the *Guardian* newspaper, to a significant extent "serves the public good. What we [Nigerians] are entitled have instead been captured by individuals and groups, who fasten on the rents from mineral exports or foreign aid and maintain their privileged access to state resources via a cornucopia of corrupt practices" (*Guardian*, April 26, 2012). The *Guardian* added:

> Corruption reports have become a daily feature, of mind-boggling proportions, in newspapers. Here is a monster that has defied successive administrations' soulless cures, thereby threatening to consume the country. Government officials, including civil servants, accumulate wealth and property illegally and with reckless abandon; unmoved by any sanction attached to their conduct. Federal legislators are derisively now referred to as "legislooters"; for helping themselves to loads of unmerited perks, unjustly, and at the expense of the poor citizens. Hardly do any of them condemn corruption openly. Many too have been justifiably accused of having no vision for the country. That should worry any patriotic lawmaker. (*Guardian*, April 26, 2012)

Based on the facts being unearthed about corruption and financial malfeasance, former American president Bill Clinton is correct that, indeed, "Nigeria have not done well with her oil money" (Coffie-Gyamfi, 2013).

Corruption, to some Nigerians, is endemic in all governments (Nye, 1967, p. 417; Friedrich, 1963, p. 167). UNODC and NBS (2017, p. 1) stated: "the problem of corruption is arguably one of the most significant global issues in the contemporary world." Nigeria's ICPC could not agree any less, as it pointed out: "Corruption . . . undermines democratic institutions, retards economic development and contributes to government instability. Corruption attacks the foundation of democratic institutions by distorting electoral processes, perverting the rule of law, and creating bureaucratic quagmires whose only reason for existence is the soliciting of bribes" (ICPC, n.d.). As such, in the view of the EFCC, "corruption is Nigeria's biggest challenge" (*Punch*, February 4, 2020).

Corruption exists in both rich countries and in poor countries, but the nature, extent, and overall dynamics of corruption are, respectively, very different (Graycar, 2015, p. 87). However, what is corruption? The terminology, corruption, can be a flux, meaning different things to different people. No wonder that Heidenheimer et al. (1990, p. 3) noted: "Any attempt to analyze the concept of corruption must contend with the fact that in English and other languages, the word 'corruption' has a history of vastly different meanings and connotations" (quoted in Agbiboa, 2012, p. 327). In addition, "unfortunately, corruption is often difficult to observe because acts of corruption do not typically take place in broad daylight" (Tanzi, 1998, p. 564). As such, Brownsberger (1983, p. 215) pointed out "corruption is a relative concept." On the same spectrum, Klaveren (1970) suggested that "corruption is, of necessity, a furtive affair," thereby making a documentation of it nearly impossible. Hence, corrupt practices can be systemic, pervasive, and routine or they can be petty, sporadic, trivial, and rare (Agbiboa, 2012, p. 327).

Meanwhile, corruption has been defined in several ways. Transparency International (TI) (the anticorruption watchdog) defined governmental or official corruption as "the abuse of entrusted power for private gain." Rose-Ackerman and Palifka (2016, p. 6) described the canker in the following terms: "Corruption is a particularly obvious pathology." Bayley (1966, p. 720), however, argued that "corruption, while being tied particularly to the act of bribery, is a general term covering misuse of authority as a result of considerations of personal gain, which need not be monetary."

In the estimation of Fatile and Okewale, corruption connotes inappropriate act of people economically, politically, socially, and culturally (Fatile & Okewale, 2013, p. 141). Kalu (1991) conceives or regards corruption as the conscious and well-planned act by a person or group of persons to appropriate, by unlawful means, the wealth of another person or group of persons. Corruption can also be seen as diversion of resources from the betterment of the community to the gain of individuals at the expense of the community (Fatile & Okewale, 2013, p. 142). Golden (2012, p. 76) agrees that "political corruption causes misallocations of economic resources and it provides unfair political advantages to those who participate in corrupt activities." Odey (2002) conceptualizes corruption in "Nigeria as the air, which every living person breathes in and out." According to him, "nobody makes any effort to breathe in the air, it comes naturally. Corruption in Nigeria has become so naturalized that many people simply become corrupt unconsciously."

In the 2015 study, Efobi (2015, p. 790) did see "corruption, especially public sector corruption, as the misuse of public office for private gain" and "government pathology" (Aidt, 2003, p. F632). In this case, corruption includes occurrences like unilateral abuse of power by government officials, embezzlement and nepotism, and other practices involving exchange of economic benefits, such as bribery, extortion, and fraud (Efobi, 2015, p. 790).

Conversely, "corruption is thus a description of activities emanating from and related to officialdom" (Eker, 1981, p. 173). Balogun (2003, p. 129) stated, inter alia, that there is corruption when "approved codes or rules have been ignored to attain personal ends or manipulated to frustrate public intentions." On his part, Andreski (1970, p. 346), in the 1970 study, perceived corruption as "the practice of using the power of office for making private gain in breach of laws and regulations nominally in force."

Meanwhile, McMullan (1970, p. 319), in his 1970 publication, defined corruption as "public official is corrupt if he accepts money . . . for doing something that he is under duty to do anyway, that he is under duty not to do, or to exercise a legitimate discretion for improper reasons." "When corruption is the norm," according to the World Bank (2015, p. 60),

> Corruption is the use of public office for private gain, it exists in many forms. Bribery, fraud, extortion, influence peddling, kickbacks, cronyism, nepotism, patronage, embezzlement, vote buying, and election rigging are all examples of actions that fit under that umbrella term. . . . Corruption in the social sense is a common belief that using public office to benefit oneself and one's family and friends is widespread, expected, and tolerated. In other words, corruption can be a social norm.

To sum up, words of Nye (1967, p. 419), within the cauldron of deviancy, referred to corruption as

> behavior which deviates from the formal duties of a public role because of private-regarding (personal, close family, private clique) pecuniary or status gains; or violates rules against the exercise of certain types of private-regarding influence. This includes such behavior as bribery (use of a reward to pervert the judgment of a person in a position of trust); nepotism (bestowal of patronage by reason of ascriptive relationship rather than merit); and misappropriation (illegal appropriation of public resources for private-regarding uses).

The common thread that runs through the various definitions of corruption is the unholy alliance between public and private interests. As in many countries, Nigeria has reprehensible history of official corruption (Andreski, 1968; Huntington, 1968; Eker, 1981; Nye, 1967; Wraith & Simpkins, 1970; Leys, 1970; Bayley, 1966). Therefore, in this book, the terms official as well as governmental and public corruption will be used interchangeably.

ORIGINS OF CORRUPTION IN NIGERIA

The history of Nigeria since independence has been the accounts of misappropriation of funds, embezzlement or looting of treasury, prebendalism, and "settlements" through grafts and contracts (Awoshakin, 2006 quoted in Folarin, 2009; Rose-Ackerman & Palifka, 2016). Or, as stated by the *Guardian* newspaper in 2020: "in our clime [Nigeria], to be in office is open sesame to instant wealth from stolen funds. . . . In the States and at the Federal level, looting the treasury is a national pastime" (*Guardian*, March 26, 2020). One of the reasons why the First Republic was overthrown by the military in 1966 was alleged crass materialism among ministers and "corruption in high places" (Nzeogwu, 1966). Accordingly, Chukwuma Nzeogwu, a major in the Nigerian Army and one of the architects of the coup d'état, said the "enemies" were those "corrupt ministers, VIPs . . . in high places . . . the ten percenters (from fat contracts) . . . who have turned development back by several years . . . and who have made Nigeria big for nothing in international circles" (paraphrased) (quoted in Folarin, 2009 and in Obasanjo, 1987). The problem of official corruption and "its deleterious and corrosive consequences on politics, governance, security and socio-economic development" (Ayee, 2016, p. 5) in Nigeria has earlier beginnings prior to 1960.

The three authors (Njoku, 2011; Oyovbaire, 1985; Onyiloha, 2015) have argued that the emergence of Nigeria, as a British colony, was through the amalgamation of Northern and Southern Protectorates in 1914, and later as a republic, and that the whole exercise was a political "fusion" of various ethnic groups. Perhaps, that development has resulted to such misconduct as corruption, lawlessness, inequality, misrule, and militancy (Onyiloha, 2015). Furthermore, Cayford (1996, p. 183) expatiated on the factors, as he added the following: "In retrospect, it was perhaps unrealistic to hope that a political system largely inherited from the British colonialists under the direction of political class adapted to that system could become anything but corrupt."

While many formerly colonized nations have transcended their colonial past and done well, there is no doubt that their colonial legacy cannot be divorced from some of the ills that have befallen these countries both in the distant and recent past, especially with reference to corruption, or what Eker

(1981) referred to as "irregular incentives." "In the case of Nigeria," according to Brownsberger (1983, p. 215), "I argue that, at least, the roots of corruption go deeper, to a materialism and political fragmentation that are the products of a moment in development." In his own words, Tignor (1993, pp. 179–180) did offer proof about corruption in the following words:

> In the classical era of colonialism, the British were loath to call attention to administrative abuses. . . . In Northern Nigeria, especially between I900 and 1920, the British removed those Fulani office holders whom they regarded as the most venal. They tended, however, to tolerate the corruption of day-to-day administration. . . . Among the Ibo [Nigeria] and Kikuyu [Kenya] a group of aggressive collaborating chiefs arose, indispensable in procuring whatever labor levies were demanded. They carried out these tasks by surrounding themselves with a retinue of followers who were financed by exacting resources from the rest of the population, beyond that allowed by colonial law and theory. Occasionally, the rottenness of colonial administration became so egregious that it could no longer be concealed. . . . Only major colonial outbursts, like the Ibo women's riots in southeastern Nigeria when protesting against the introduction of taxation into their locale, brought the full light of publicity onto colonial misrule and highlighted the venality of local government. The ensuing commission of inquiry revealed much misuse of authority by warrant chiefs, who had no traditional legitimacy in their communities. (Note: To know more of Igbo women riots of 1929 and abuses of warrant chiefs, see in reference Margery Perham (1937, pp. 206–220), Harry A. Gailey (1970), and Adiele E. Afigbo (1972, pp. 249–295), respectively.)

Perhaps no country in Africa has devoted more attention and energy to continuing allegations of corruption than Nigeria (Tignor, 1993, p. 175). In fact, from the late colonial period up until the present, critics of those in power have lamented the level of venality, and numerous published reports have documented a wide range of transgressions and called for reform (Tignor, 1993, p. 175). Corruption was turned into a public issue for the first time in Nigerian history in 1953 when the British colonial government established a commission to investigate the activities of Lagos Town Council (Tignor, 1993, p. 185). The Commission's report contained the first public discussion of widespread corrupt administrative practices in Nigeria, and it very much helps to explain how the British moved the problem of corruption from official secret and confidential correspondence to formal exposure (Tignor, 1993, p. 185). In a revealing background, Tignor (1993, pp. 185–186) elucidated in the following words:

> The introduction of a town council in 1917 had made Lagos the hub of Nigerian political activity. The stakes there rose even higher in 1950 when

> the Lagosian electorate achieved universal adult suffrage. Azikiwe was the dominant political figure in the capital at the time, though often arousing much opposition. In 1950, as many as 18 of the 24 elected Lagos town councilors had campaigned under the auspices of the N.C.N.C. as members of the affiliated Democratic Party. In the next year, following the establishment of the Macpherson constitution, N.C.N.C. won a second convincing electoral victory when Lagos voters returned Azikiwe, Adeleke Adedoyin, Olorun-Nimbe as members of the Federal parliament. The opposition to the N.C.N.C. was stung by its two defeats and sought to unseat its opponents from the Lagos Town Council. Almost immediately after the election results were announced, its leaders claimed that councilors used their powers for self-enrichment and showered favors on their supporters. Their complaints fell on a receptive audience, for British officialdom was by this time certain that corrupt behavior was suffusing the Nigerian political scene. Thus, the wielders of power who, in the classical age of colonial rule might have dealt with a similar problem through suasion and quiet diplomacy, decided that an enquiry should be conducted by Bernard Storey,[1] the town clerk of Norwich. His task in 1953 was not merely to investigate the Lagos Council, but also to issue a formal report, and his 50-page document established a precedent by becoming the first of a series of public airings of Nigerian corruption—the opening salvo in a campaign to publicize bribery, nepotism, and venality as Nigeria's most pressing political ailment.

In a final ringing statement in his report, British-born Bernard Storey, who served as the town clerk of the city of Norwich in the UK, among other details, wrote: "Running like a brightly colored thread through the tangled skein of the Council's administration has been the subject of honesty or the lack of it—of corruption. I could not get away from it at the public inquiry; it was mentioned in connection with almost every matter brought before me" (Storey Report, 1953, p. 49). The Storey Report highly influenced other works dealing with African corruption (Wraith & Simpkins, 1963).

CORRUPTION AS PREBENDAL BEHAVIOR

Although corruption—also referred to as graft—is a major challenge for several other developing countries (Haarhuis, 2005; Nadiz, 2004, both quoted in Enweremadu, 2012), very few countries have been so ravaged by either graft or corruption as the oil-rich West African nation of Nigeria (Enweremadu, 2012, p. 1; UN Office on Drugs and Crime & National Bureau of Statistics, 2017, pp. 5–9). Nigeria's ICPC, in a written statement below, acknowledged the seriousness of corruption in Nigeria:

> Although corruption is a global malaise, the extent of its reach in the country was tragically stupendous. All indicators showed that the spread of this cancer had become frightening. It pervaded private and public institutions and overwhelmed all levels of government. The price of corruption has been extremely high. The economic, political, social and moral bases of the country have been severely eroded and degraded. It has brought Nigeria near the brink and almost rendered it helpless and hopeless. Even religious institutions, the gatekeepers of the nation's moral conscience, were not immune to the ravages of the cancer. (ICPC, *History of ICPC* https://icpc.gov.ng/icpc-history/)

This fact and normative tendency are buttressed by both governmental reports (Office of the Secretary to the Government of the Federation, 2005, quoted in Enweremadu (2012, pp. 183–184)) as well as scholarly studies (Joseph, 1987; Adebanwi, 2012; Agbiboa, 2012; Bamidele, Olaniyan, & Ayodele, 2015) and the designation of Nigeria as the "world's most corrupt nation" by TI. While in the literature, there are several causes of corruption, Maduagwu (1982, p. 1) has provided a neater summary of the causes and sustenance of public service corruption in Nigeria in particular and the culture energizing it generally. According to him:

> Corruption thrives in Nigeria because society sanctions it. No Nigerian official would be ashamed, let alone condemned by his people because he or she is accused of being corrupt. The same applies to outright stealing of government or public money or property. On the contrary, the official will be hailed as being smart. He would be adored as having "made it"; he is a "successful man." And any government official or politician who is in a position to enrich himself corruptly but failed to do so will, in fact, be ostracized by his people upon leaving office. He would be regarded as a fool, or selfish, or both.

To buttress further, according to John Mackintosh: "Some things do shock Nigerians—ingratitude to family, or lack of respect for elders—but not for a man to use his power or position to bring benefits to himself, his family or his village, is quite normal and to be expected" (Mackintosh, 1966, p. 617).

From the above insights by Maduagwu and Mackintosh, the evaluation of public corruption in Nigeria could be better understood in the context of the prevailing societal orientation that influences people's behavior—as explained by Joseph—"socially, economically, politically or culturally." Joseph (1987, p. 55) further explained below:

> The Nigerian state is essentially comparable to the state in most developing countries which are minimally industrialized and in which the majority of the population is tied to agrarian pursuit often of marginal or precarious

> profitability. The state enjoys a pre-eminent position because the nation was created by foreign conquest and domination and not through a gradual process of aggregation or expansion of indigenous societies. The colonial power, and the economic process it fostered, defined the essential elements of the future for the subjugated peoples. Continued foreign penetration and domination of the economy after independence, together with the constraints to peripheral capitalist industrialization in the world economy, meant that access to the state remained disproportionately important in the struggle for resources for upward mobility.

Based on the foregoing quote from Joseph's 1987 book, it is important to explain Nigerian corruption within a theoretical framework. This makes sense because according to social science researchers Chava Nachmias and Frank Nachmias (2008, p. 33) "theories help us explain and predict the phenomenon of interest to us and, in consequence, assist us in making intelligent practical decisions." David Easton (1965) considered theory as the "conceptual framework for analysis." Hill and Hupe (2014, pp. 5–6) stated: "theories give systematic approach to capture the myriads of reality, and in the process impart context in relation to specific policies as particular responses to problems in society."

This book will utilize prebendal theory analysis to interrogate and, in the process, also to discuss several aspects of public corruption in Nigeria. In a nutshell, prebendalism invariably also means the use of official position for personal gain. While other theories such as "development theory and structural functionalism" could be used for our purpose, a major advantage of the "prebendal/clientism mode of analysis has much relevance to the Nigerian case is that it opens up direct line of comparison of the study of corruption in Nigeria with other African as well as non-African countries" (Joseph, 1987, p. 57). The theory of prebendalism as conceptualized by Joseph in his seminal work, *Democracy and Prebendal Politics in Nigeria* (1987), asserts based on "universe of understanding" in Nigeria which sustains prebendal attitude to the commonwealth:

> A prebendal system will be seen not only as one in which the offices of the state are allocated and then exploited as benefices by the office holders, but also as one where such a practice is legitimated by a set of political norms according to which the appropriation of such offices is not just an act of individual greed or ambition but concurrently the satisfaction of the shorter objectives of a subset of the general population. (Joseph, 1987, p. 67)

Consequently, Joseph postulated prebendal politics becomes the norm in Nigeria, whereby politics is seen as life and death struggle and "unremitting and unconstrained struggle for possession and access to state offices, with the chief aim of procuring direct material benefits to oneself and one's acknowledged communal or other sectional group" (Joseph, 1987, p. 75). The theory of prebendalism explains the modus operandi of the competition for and appropriation of public offices for personal gain in the complexity of Nigerian corruption and politics. In effect, prebendal behavior, according to Joseph, is deleterious to both the politics and economy of the country (Joseph, 1987, p. 10):

> Is often wasteful, unproductive and contributes to the increasing affluence of a relative few, paltry gains for a larger number, and misery for the great majority of people. Since it is a self-justifying system, which grants legitimacy to a pattern of persistent conflict, and its modus operandi is to politicize ethnic, regional and linguistic differences, it serves to make the Nigerian polity a simmering cauldron of unresolvable tensions over which a lid must regularly be clamped, and just as regularly removed.

Since the publication of the Storey Report, the problem of official corruption in Nigeria has taken quantum leap. The issue of corruption and its effects on society, according to Afolabi (2010), is probably the most talked-about national malaise in contemporary Nigeria. Both developed and developing countries experience the problem of corruption; however, the level of corruption in a particular country goes a long way to show how that country is perceived by the outside world. Nigerian corruption is alarming. Hence it is a common fact that the bulk of Nigeria's hard currencies are lying in private accounts in London, New York, Paris, Zurich, and Germany (Afolabi, 2010, p. 53). Agbaje (2004) quoted from the work of Achebe (1981) that

> anybody who can say that corruption in Nigeria has not become alarming is either a fool, a crook or else does not live in this country. Corruption in Nigeria has passed the alarming and entered the fatal, and the country will die if we keep pretending that she is only slightly indisposed (p. 88).

Nigeria is one of the most corrupt countries in the world, where graft reigns supreme. Public sector graft, in particular, is graffiti on the face of Nigeria. It has literally defaced Nigeria and consigned the nation to infamy and ridicule. More profound, it impedes honest public service, undermines democracy, and stifles development (Fatile & Okewale, 2013; World Bank, 2012). According to the Gallup Poll, "almost all Nigerians (94%) think that the government is corrupt" (Crabtree, 2012). Such abuses are not new, for example, the Bible has a law disallowing bribery in judicial cases over 3,500 years ago in the Book of Exodus, 23:8. "And you shall take no bribe, for a bribe blinds the discerning and perverts the words of the righteous." The United States

Constitution (Article II, Section 4) made bribery and treason the two explicitly mentioned crimes that could justify the impeachment and removal of an American president. "The President, Vice President and all civil Officers of the United States, shall be removed from Office on Impeachment for, and Conviction of, Treason, Bribery, or other high Crimes and Misdemeanors."

In a 2017 paper, the IMF put the annual cost of global corruption at estimated $2 trillion, accounting for "enormous" 2% of the global GDP (Lagarde, 2017). And according to the IMF paper, "this is just a tip of the icebergs." Corruption involves more than just accepting bribes, and while corruption can exist in any human organization, it seems that corruption in government is the worst according to TI, which expatiates on it below (http://www.transparency.org/layout/set/print/global_priorities/corruption_politics):

> Political corruption affects us all. We elect politicians and political parties expecting them to act in the public interest. By electing them we give them access to public resources and the power to take decisions that impact on our lives. Given this privileged position, immense damage can be inflicted by politicians or parties acting out of greed, or in the service of those who bankroll their ascent to power. It is not surprising that people the world over are demanding absolute probity of their political leaders: citizens in three countries out of four countries polled by TI and Gallup International singled out political parties as the most institution they perceived as most corrupt.

In June 2016, for example, the Nigerian government released an interim report on funds and assets totaling ₦205 billion, $9.2 billion, £6 million, €315,000 (Akinkuotu, 2016) recovered from individuals, who looted the nation's treasury "including monies withheld by past government officials, monies kept in private accounts, monies diverted to private pockets and monies in possession of government officials not disclosed after leaving government" (Kazeem, 2016). The recoveries were made between May 29, 2015, and May 25, 2016. Also, in June 2017 the Presidential Advisory Committee Against Corruption (PACAC) disclosed that, in the short period of "2006–2013, 55 top government functionaries, and businessmen stole ₦1.4 trillion of public funds" (Ujah, 2017). According to the PACAC, the amount of looted funds during the period is much higher when fuel subsidy and arms purchase scams, and NNPC bribe money to influence the 2015 elections are factored in (Ujah, 2017). A 2017 premier national survey report by the United Nations Office on Drugs and Crime (UNODC) and NBS on the "quality and integrity of public services in Nigeria" showed that Nigerians consider corruption to be the third most important problem they face after high cost of living and unemployment (UNODC & NBS, 2017). According to the report, Nigerians spend an estimated ₦400 billion ($4.6 billion) annually to bribe public officials with the police and judiciary in particular receiving the lion's share of nearly 50% and 33%, respectively. There is a link between corruption and underdevelopment in Nigeria, and corruption is largely responsible for the shortcomings and poor performance of Nigerian political economy (Agbiboa, 2012).

CORRUPTION AND UNDERDEVELOPMENT IN NIGERIA

The harmful effects of corruption have been well documented. Some eminent perspectives will be in order. The UNODC, in its "Action against Corruption and Economic Crime," declared as follows:

> Corruption is a complex social, political and economic phenomenon that affects all countries. Corruption undermines democratic institutions, slows economic development and contributes to governmental instability. Corruption attacks the foundation of democratic institutions by distorting electoral processes, perverting the rule of law and creating bureaucratic quagmires whose only reason for existing is the soliciting of bribes. Economic development is stunted because foreign direct investment is discouraged and small businesses within the country often find it impossible to overcome the "start-up costs" required because of corruption.

The UNODC is not alone. Former British prime minister David Cameron averred:

> Corruption is the cancer at the heart of so many of our problems in the world today. It destroys jobs and holds back growth, costing the world economy billions of pounds every year. It traps the poorest in the most desperate poverty as corrupt governments around the world siphon off funds and prevent hard-working people from getting the revenues and benefits of growth that are rightfully theirs. It steals vital resources from our schools and hospitals as corrupt individuals and companies evade the taxes they owe. (Cameron, 2016)

The scholar Francis Fukuyama, discussing corruption and its impact on society, postulated:

> Corruption has in many ways become the defining issue of the 21st century, just as the 20th century was characterized by large ideological struggles between democracy, fascism and communism. . . . Corruption hurts life outcomes in a variety of ways. Economically, it diverts resources away from their most productive uses and acts like a regressive tax that supports the lifestyles of elites at

> the expense of everyone else. Corruption incentivizes the best and the brightest to spend their time gaming the system, rather than innovating or creating new wealth. Politically, corruption undermines the legitimacy of political systems by giving elites alternative ways of holding onto power other than genuine democratic choice. It hurts the prospects of democracy when people perceive authoritarian governments to be performing better than corrupt democratic ones and undermines the reality of democratic choice. (Fukuyama, 2016)

Graycar (2015, p. 87) held the view that "corruption demoralizes government and weakens the whole endeavor of policy formulation and its implementation. It diminishes services and causes fiscal distress but, most of all, it undermines trust and corrodes legitimate community expectations." Also, Gould and Mukendi (2007, p. 427) were of the view that "corruption frustrates good policy intentions and paralyzes management operations." Transparency International (2015) confirmed unabashedly that "corruption and conflict go hand in hand . . . six of the 10 most corrupt countries also rank among the 10 least peaceful places in the world." The above descriptions highlight major aspects of corruption and their negative impacts on the society (Onyiloha, 2015).

Meanwhile, empirical studies indicate that the extent of corruption in a nation is indeed a significant determinant of economic growth (Mauro, 1995). The study of the causes and consequences of corruption has a long history in economics (Mauro, 1996, p. 4), adding that it dated back, at least, to the influential works on rent-seeking literature by Bhagwati (1982), Krueger (1974), Rose-Ackerman (1978), Tullock (1967), and others. Cross-country study, by Mauro (1995, 1996), found that corruption has considerable adverse effects on economic growth, largely by reducing private investment, also through other avenues, including worsening government expenditure on education.

According to Mauro, the negative relationship between corruption and government expenditure on education is "reason for concern since the literature has shown that educational attainment is an important determinant of economic growth" (Mauro, 1996, p. 17). In the Nigerian case proper, Bamidele, Olaniyan, and Ayodele (2015, p. 1) have confirmed:

> In Nigeria, the political class has reduced governance to a veritable mechanism that boosts and consolidates their economic strength and fortune to the detriment of the country's economic growth and development. The annual budgets in Nigeria are proverbial buffets for the rulers, who have turned corruption into a trademark for governance in the country. . . . With high-level corruption, it is impossible to have good governance; without good governance, there will be no development; without development there cannot be peace; and without peace there will be no security.

Ogundiya (2017, p. 281) has pointed out unequivocally that

> corruption has been the bane of legitimacy, democratic stability and socio-economic and political development in Nigeria . . . any attempt to understand the tragedy of development and challenges to democracy in Nigeria must come to grips with the problem of corruption and stupendous wastage of scarce resources.

Most of all, the Nigerian government seems helpless to combat corruption, as "corruption is rarely investigated, and impunity remains widespread at all levels of government" according to the latest Heritage Foundation's *2019 Index of Economic Freedom Report* (p. 327).

The corruption-underdevelopment link is brought to a sharp focus when we survey the Niger Delta region, which bears most of Nigeria's oil and gas reserves. The UNDP has provided an important overview on corruption in its *Niger Delta Human Development Report*; it quotes the following from it:

> Some amazing paradoxes have come from the development of the Niger Delta region. Ordinarily, the Niger Delta should be a gigantic economic reservoir of national and international importance. Its rich endowments of oil and gas resources feed methodically into the international economic system, in exchange for massive revenues that carry the promise of rapid socio-economic transformation within the delta itself. In reality, the Niger Delta is a region suffering from administrative neglect, crumbling social infrastructure and services, high unemployment, social deprivation, abject poverty, filth and squalor, and endemic conflict. (UNDP, 2006, p. 9)

The onset of commercial petroleum production in 1956, discovered in Oloibiri in Bayelsa State, seemed to hold out the promise of rapid development of the hitherto neglected region (Watts, 2004, p. 59). Yet, it was not to be. Instead of development and progress, the Niger Delta has experienced decline and devastation, in addition to what the ICG has referred to as "trail of broken promises" (ICG, 2006). For example, the ex-boss of EFCC, Nuhu Ribadu, has commented that Nigeria was on the wrong path and needed to pursue values, "in which the billions that are being pumped out of the Niger Delta will not end up in the private accounts of those in power, a society in which our conscience will not be shattered when we visit the creeks of the Niger Delta, where over $400 billion in the past 50 years have been erased by unrepentant rogues" (Oyekanmi & Coffie-Gyamfi, 2010). Worse of all, transnational oil companies in joint ventures with the NNPC have presided over enormous environmental pollution and ruination of traditional livelihood (Maiangwa & Agbiboa, 2013; Okonkwo & Etemire, 2017; Ajayi & Adesote,

2013; Okoi, 2019). *Washington Post* (March 18, 2001, p. A22) also noted, "Nigeria's oil exploration leaves the Delta poisoned."

The Niger Delta is Nigeria's mineral-rich colony and chief source of affluence, which the authorities and oil companies have historically neglected, exploited, and abused. According a recent report by the Yar'Adua Foundation,

> in the period spanning 1970 to 2014, Nigeria wasted five oil booms—earning a conservative estimate of $1 trillion in oil revenue but making no significant savings. These earnings have also not translated to lasting or productive capital through human development, infrastructure and institution building. (Ezekwesili et al., 2019, p. 4)

It is a sad paradox, however, that while the Niger Delta—where the oil resources are exploited—remains the epicenter of poverty and despair, the Nigerian State and corporate oil interests are gorging on Delta's mineral riches with reckless abandon. Over the years, oil-producing communities and individual land owners in the Niger Delta area have had serious grievances, which have not been addressed by both the Nigerian Federal Government and oil companies. Their major complaints, as was forcefully articulated by Eghosa Osaghae, the well-known political scientist, are couched in the following words:

> Although the bulk of Nigeria's oil is derived from their lands, they are the most economically backward in the country; government and oil companies invest little to nothing in return for the huge profits they reap from oil exploration; several years of oil exploration and attendant hazards of spillage and gas flaring has polluted their environment and left their communities devastated; farming and fishing, the major occupations of their communities have also suffered enormously; their communities have as well lacked basic amenities, such as, electricity, roads, schools, hospitals, potable water. (Osaghae, 1995)

Indeed, Osaghae is not alone in his observation. Other scholars have provided very useful observations of the situation. They, in fact, include Ebeku (2008, p. 399), who wrote: "Niger Delta oil contributes immensely to the well-being of the Nigerian State; yet the Niger Delta region remains underdeveloped and its indigenous inhabitants are among the poorest in Nigeria." Itse Sagay, legal scholar, also had this to say:

> Although the (1) Oil Pipeline Act 1965, (2) the Petroleum Drilling and Production Regulation Decree 1969, and (3) the Petroleum Decree 1969, allowed for compensation in the event of leakage, spillage, damage to surface rights or their compulsory acquisition thereof, in reality, these communities

> and [private land owners] are left to bargain with oil companies, who exploit their weak economic and legal positions to extort their consent to paltry compensation for lost land and natural resources. (*Vanguard*, April 21, 2005) (The Petroleum Act of 1969 is the main legislation governing the exploration and production of oil matters in Nigeria. The Act vested the entire ownership and control of all petroleum in, under, or upon all land or Nigerian territorial waters in the Nigerian Government.)

Furthermore, the London-based British Broadcasting Corporation (BBC) also had the following to say:

> What irritates the people of the Niger Delta far more than individual leaks is that the oil from their homeland provides the bulk of Nigeria's export earnings and its government income. And yet, they feel they get nothing back. For the most part the oil industry and the people of the Delta exist side by side, their lives hardly touching. A village living next to a well producing oil worth many thousands of dollars a year may have no clean water supply, no passable road, no electricity, and no clinic or school. (Blount, 2008)

Also, the *New York Times* (March 22, 2000) reported that "the Niger Delta sit on billions of dollars in oil reserves but have remained desperately poor."

Consequently, today, there is widespread rage and frustration in the Delta oil-producing communities exemplified by rising tide of discontent, and violent protests, including armed clashes with government forces, attacks on oil platforms, and kidnappings of foreign oil workers as calls for a better share of oil wealth and social justice remain largely ignored by both the Nigerian government and oil companies (Aghedo, 2012; Eke, 2014; Okonofua, 2013, 2016; Aghedo & Osumah, 2014; Schultze-Kraft, 2017; Chinwokwu & Michael, 2019; Nwokolo and Aghedo, 2018). (It is proper to note that based on Nigeria's constitutional stipulation of "Principle of Derivation" 13% of revenues accruing to the Nigerian Government directly from any natural resources shall be allocated to States that produce natural resources such as crude oil and solid minerals. In April 2000, former president Obasanjo commenced implementation of the 13% derivation mandate, and it is ongoing.)

CORRUPTION UNLIMITED

It is very unfortunate to conclude unabashedly that corruption is the chokepoint on the way to greatness by many Nigerians and that it has devastated the country at immense cost and frustration to Nigerian people without remit. Transparency International (2015), for example, pointed out: "Corruption hits hardest at the poor in Nigeria. . . . Corruption is everywhere." Adebanwi (2012, p. 13) pointed out that "so widespread is corruption in Nigeria . . . involving and distorting every fabric of social, economic and political life in Nigeria, that it could as well have been described as the fundamental directive of national policy."

Nigeria's constitutional lawyer, Benjamin Nwabueze, has had this to say about corruption publicly: "Corruption is the foremost factor strangulating the country" (Nwabueze, 2015). Farida Waziri, former chairwoman of the EFCC, enjoined Nwabueze's words: "Corruption has become a living and breathing cancer, which has unfortunately come to be justified by the average man as 'the need to survive'" (CLEEN Foundation, 2010, p. 2). Meanwhile, under a corrupt system, no government that has the interests of the people at heart could flourish because its mission is at odds with the concerns of the people. A government of that nature ignores the worries and anxieties of the people in pursuit of personal gains. This is the Nigerian situation.

The epiphany of Nigerian corruption comes in different flavors, in high and low places. Government contracts are regularly padded to extract kickbacks. People who are doing or did "well" (by abusing their offices and positions) in public office are routinely honored by their communities with chieftaincy tiles or, very often, have streets and public buildings named after them. In Nigerian parlance, "they have arrived." However, foreigners are not spared, as many of the foreign businesses have been defrauded of millions of dollars in goods and cash by Nigerian crime syndicates through counterfeit bank drafts, fake letters of credit, fraudulent money transfer and contract schemes, charity scams, real estate scams, import orders, crude oil scams, corruption of ministries and agencies' letterhead, just to name a few (U.S. Department of State, 1997). Unfortunately, these business scams are not abating even after the Nigerian Government effort to combat these illegal schemes by enacting laws against them (legal code number 419) and issuing advisories in local and foreign media (U.S. Department of State, 1997). The occurrences of such practice are declining as a direct result of the EFCC's dedication to fight these kinds of fraudulent operations (Opara, 2007, p. 84).

Sadly, in the name of security duty assignments police set up checkpoints simply to extort money from motorists, especially bus and truck drivers, and un-cooperating drivers risk the wrath of the police, including suffering shooting deaths—an example of a headline: "Policemen, in Lagos, kill three over ₦20 bribe," *Guardian*, August 18, 2004; "Onitsha boils—As policeman kills bus driver over ₦20 bribe," *Daily Sun*, February 10, 2012; "Policeman kills driver for refusing to give bribe," *Punch*, December 23, 2016; "Policeman shoots teacher over ₦20," *Punch*, June 28, 2010; "Police sale of arms to robbers," *Punch*, December 20, 2016; "Policeman kills Ondo driver over ₦50 bribe," *Punch*, December 3, 2019. One of the most egregious examples of police brutality and corruption in Nigeria was shown to an international audience by the *PBS News Hour* (American TV news program) in December 2015. In the episode, one Godwin Ekpo narrated the ordeal he and his wife suffered at the hands of Lagos police. Ekpo and his wife were shot by the police on the mouth and head, respectively, in front of their children for refusing to give the police ₦2,000 bribe. Mr. Ekpo survived the attack (with scarred face and disfigured mouth), but his wife was not so lucky. Mrs. Ekpo died from the gunshot blast, leaving behind her husband and three young children.

Corruption is pervasive and widespread in Nigeria, and it has permeated all facets of life, and every segment of society is involved (Ogbu, 2008). Lydia Polgreen added "Nigeria's image of rampant corruption touches virtually every aspect of life, from swindling e-mails sent around world to police who routinely set up roadblocks to get bribes" (*New York Times*, November 29, 2005). The giving and accepting of bribes is inculcated into the everyday operation of the country to such an extent that Nigerians seem to accept that it is part of the nation's culture (Opara, 2007, p. 67). The *Economist* (April 7, 2014) added: "Nigeria has a deserved reputation for corruption." The sermon at Abuja!!! It would be recalled that at a church service to mark the 2012 National Democracy Day held at the Ecumenical Center, Abuja, the guest preacher and Ex-Prelate of the Anglican Church of Nigeria, Most Reverend Peter Akinola, challenged his listeners, including then president Jonathan and other high officials to join him in the fight against corruption in the country by committing perpetrators to God (*Premium Times*, May 27, 2012). But there were no takers. The reverend gentleman exclaimed: "There you go! Oh, corruption! So, you are not ready to fight it, because you are all beneficiaries of it. Whether you steal in a small or big way, stealing is stealing." Not only that Reverend Akinola's sentiments are widely shared, Nigeria's corruption pandemic has become so bad that foreigners openly express condemnation and outrage. Here are some evidences:

On a visit to Nigeria in February 2013, Bill Clinton, former American president, as reported earlier, told a gathering of Nigerian leaders: "You haven't done well with your oil money" (Coffie-Gyamfi, 2013). In the run up to the global Anti-Corruption Summit held in May 2016 in London, then British prime minister, David Cameron, in a conversation with the Queen of England, described Nigeria and Afghanistan as two of the most "fantastically corrupt" (*BBC News*, May 10, 2016) countries in the world. While Clinton and Cameron were fancy in their choice of words, however, the poignancy of their comments is clear. And that is, put bluntly, Nigerian leaders are corrupt, unaccountable, and their behaviors have ruined the country.

Also, Walter Carrington, former American ambassador to Nigeria (1993–1997) with "a [55] year-long familiarity with Nigeria" (French, 1997), has described the country as “the underperformer” (Carrington, 2013) because of the “nation’s corrosive cancer of corruption” (Carrington, 2013). At the 29th Convocation of University of Ilorin in October 2013, Carrington declared:

> Corruption is the most terrible monster that confronts Nigeria. . . . I am certain that virtually all the problems associated with governance would be removed if we can all summon the courage to tackle corruption and banish it from our activities. Development doesn’t have a bigger enemy than corruption and the development of Nigeria is hinged on ridding our polity and politics from corruption and corrupt practices. (Carrington, 2013)

Also, Bisa Williams, former deputy assistant secretary, Bureau of African Affairs, United States Department of State, in April 2014 said:

> If you ask me, I would say that corruption is extremely high in this country; there is no other polite way to say this. It is extremely unfortunate, because Nigeria as a country has tremendous intelligent people who do not have to be corrupt, because they have all it takes to be successful. Nigerians are resourceful and they are living in abundance of wealth and to acknowledge the fact that there is corruption in Nigeria is disheartening. (Anyagafu & Sam-Duru, 2014)

Also, in August 2014 interview with a Nigerian newspaper, John Campbell, former U.S. ambassador to Nigeria (2004–2007), said:

> It is mind-boggling how millions of dollars go missing. Take for instance, the serious allegation made by the former Central Bank of Nigeria Governor, Lamido Sanusi. He has claimed that an amount he variously estimated at $10 billion, $20 billion and $50 billion is unaccounted for. The Finance Minister has called for an audit, but I do not believe the results have yet been made public. There are different types of corruption in Nigeria. For example, there is petty corruption. Nigerian police officers are poorly paid. At a checkpoint you hear a police officer saying “Do you have anything for me today?” Because they are poorly paid, it will be difficult for them to keep their families without the “bribes” they levy to let people pass through their checkpoints. Another instance is where a civil servant insists on being paid to perform a service which is supposed to be free of charge. This type of corruption will be very difficult to deal with because it will require a massive restructuring of salaries paid to public servants. But, then there is the corruption where millions of dollars go missing through rigging of contracts, money laundering or oil bunkering.

Furthermore, a United States Department of State *Country Reports on Human Rights Practices* on Nigeria also not only chided the Nigerian government for not doing enough to fight graft, especially official corruption, but also "offered a fresh and undeniable insight into why graft is so deeply entrenched in the Nigerian system" (*Punch*, March 19, 2014). Section 4 of the report titled "Corruption and Lack of Transparency in Government," and it read in part:

> Although the law provides criminal penalties for corruption by officials, the government did not implement the law effectively, and officials frequently engaged in corrupt practices with impunity. Massive, widespread, and pervasive corruption affected all levels of government and security services. . . . The anti-corruption efforts of the ICPC and EFCC remained largely focused on low- and middle level government office holders. Allegations of high-level corruption went unaddressed. (U.S. Department of State, 2014, p. 27)

Even the hugely venal and loathsome, the former Zimbabwe president, Robert Mugabe, took a swipe at Nigeria over corruption. At his 90th birthday luncheon in March 2014, Mugabe said:

> Are we now like Nigeria where you have to reach [inside] your pockets to get anything done. . . . You see we used to go to Nigeria and every time we went there, we had to carry extra cash in our pockets to corruptly pay for everything. You get into a plane in Nigeria and you sit there and the crew keeps dilly-dallying without taking off as they wait for you to pay them to fly the plane. (*Vanguard*, March 16, 2014)

In an April 2015 write-up and interview, Richard Joseph, the prominent Nigerian affairs analyst commented:

> Office holders pilfer public funds with impunity while their people lack clean water, electricity, and gainful employment . . . when governors got their states' allocation, the foreign exchange markets would light up because the money was going straight out. The system of public finance that involves myriad ways of basically stealing money and taking it out of the country, or recycling it into property and other assets, has to be reformed. (Joseph, 2015)

TI always ranks Nigeria near the bottom on its Corruption Perception Index as one of the most corrupt countries in the world. The most moderate estimates suggest that \$4–\$8 billion is stolen from Nigeria's government treasury every year (*The Economist*, December 3, 2011), yet only a handful of politicians are serving a prison sentence for corruption or embezzlement. (According to reports, two former governors: Joshua Dariye (Plateau) and Jolly Nyame (Taraba) are currently serving various prison terms for abuse of office including "corruption, criminal breach of trust, and misappropriation.") On top of that, senior politicians including the president, vice president, governors, and deputy governors still enjoy immunity from prosecution while in office.

There is such widespread corruption in Nigeria, with its corrupt leaders, that some ashamed and very worried citizens of the oil-rich West African nation have called for "psychiatric evaluation" of the transparently corrupt leadership of Nigeria to determine their mental fitness for their high offices. (Former chairwoman of the EFCC, Farida Waziri, famously noted: "The extent of aggrandizement and gluttonous accumulation of wealth that I have observed suggests to me that some people are mentally and psychologically unsuitable for public office," (*Guardian*, October 6, 2009). "We have observed people amassing public wealth to a point suggesting 'madness' or some form of obsessive-compulsive psychiatric disorder," (*Guardian*, February 4, 2014). Indeed, the depth of corruption in the country is breathtaking because it extends to every tentacle of the system from political leadership to the receptionist in the offices one transacts vital business. You don't have to look too far to see the open wounds of corruption in Nigeria: from several unaccountable elected leaders and appointed rogue top executives enjoying government kickbacks, outright bribery, embezzlement of public funds as well as those in conflict of interest situations, while others are benefiting from allocated funds from abandoned projects to inflated contracts, which include idle refineries as well as moribund power plants, unreliable electricity to dry water taps, fuel subsidy scam to pension fund fraud, contracted but unrepaired bad city and rural roads.

For example, in 2004, Joseph Stiglitz, a former World Bank chief economist and former chairman of former president Clinton's Council of Economic Advisers, who was on a visit to Nigeria, revealed that as of the time, Nigerians had stashed away over $100 billion in foreign bank accounts (excluding landed property and other assets) (*Guardian*, February 13, 2013). Also, another visitor to Nigeria in 2008, UN executive director on Drugs and Crime, Antonio Maria Costa, disclosed that between 1960 and 1999, corrupt political rulers had allegedly stolen over $400 billion from the oil-rich Nigerian nation and kept the liquid funds—needed for Nigerian development—in foreign banks (Olukoya, 2008). Furthermore, in the same year (2008), a World Bank report—made public by then bank president Paul Wolfowitz—revealed that Nigeria had lost $300 billion to corruption in the past four decades (Ojiabor, 2008). The bank report also stated that "there is virtual agreement among observers that corruption—political and economic—primarily explains poverty in Nigeria; that corruption has held back economic growth and development and frustrated incentives to align budgetary allocations with development priorities" (Ojiabor, 2008).

In fact, in 2011, then Nigerian attorney general Mohammed Adoki announced publicly that the oil-rich country loses ₦240 trillion ($15.2

billion) annually to corruption (Oyesina, 2011). Very sadly, a lot more unfortunate revelations were to be made, as former external affairs minister Bolaji Akinyemi disclosed that Nigeria had lost ₦75 trillion ($500 billion) to corruption between the nation's independence in 1960 and 2013 (Channels TV, March 15, 2013). Indeed, a subsequent report on illicit financial outflows, released in February 2013 by Global Financial Integrity, a Washington, DC-based research and advocacy organization, revealed that Nigeria lost $129 billion to illegal financial outflows in the 10-year (2001–2010) period (Alawiye, 2013).

As if the foregoing pieces of information about corruption or graft in Nigeria are not enough, at the 2013 G8 Economic Summit in Davos, Switzerland, then British prime minister David Cameron alluded to the fact that "a few years back, a Transparency Initiative exposed a huge black hole in Nigeria's finances, an $800 million discrepancy between companies' payments and government's receipts for oil" (*Vanguard*, January 28, 2013). Also, in January 2013, in a graduation speech at the University of Nigeria, Nsukka, Obiageli Ezekwesili, a former Nigerian government minister and World Bank official alleged that the $67 billion Obasanjo left in foreign reserves and ECA has, allegedly, been misappropriated by succeeding administrations (*Vanguard*, January 28, 2013).

In 2012 alone, according to then Nigeria Central Bank governor Lamido Sanusi, $11 billion dollars was allegedly taken out of the country through Nigerian airports (Nnodim, 2012). During the same year (2012), also EFCC intercepted a total of ₦15.5 billion ($98.5 million) at Nigerian airports (Okolor, 2012). Matters worsened a few years prior because, in August 2009, then American secretary of state, Hillary Clinton, on a visit to Nigeria, declared publicly:

> The lack of transparency and accountability has eroded the legitimacy of the government and contributed to the rise of groups that embrace violence and reject the authority of the state. Without good government, even oil wealth cannot guarantee development. The raw numbers (referring to the 2008 World Bank report which indicated Nigeria has lost $300 billion to corruption in the past four decades) are staggering but they don't tell you how many schools that could have been built; they tell you only how many schools could have been opened, how many more Nigerians could have attended college or how many mothers might have survived childbirth if that money had been spent differently. (Phillips, 2009)

Secretary Clinton did not tell Nigerians what they do not already know about their country; rather, she shone light on the menace of Nigerian corruption, and she was not alone. The *Financial Times* of London also reported the following: "In the quest for a more prosperous and stable Nigeria, there is no more important battle than the battle against corruption. It is not only a moral matter. Future oil supply depends on it. No-one should need reminding of this, least of all Nigeria's head of state" (*Financial Times*, August 11, 2008). The *Guardian* (November 23, 2011) editorial weighed in with the following words editorially:

> The recurrence of corruption as a matter of grave national import has sadly continued unabated, without as much as a reflection of various anti-corruption measures officially adopted in the country. If anything, what is being reflected is a mockery of anti-corruption campaign, depicted in the grandstanding and absence of diligent investigation and prosecution that have trailed the arrest of fliers of high-profile corruption cases. Understandably, Nigerians deride the regular fact that former governors and other notable persons in the country caught in the corruption web need only a few days to stay in the custody of law-enforcement agencies, before they perfect their bail and resume business as usual.

The enormity of Nigerian corruption is beyond the raw monetary figures, it is also a much institutionalized problem.

INSTITUTIONALIZED CORRUPTION

While all the ills of Nigeria cannot be laid at the doorstep of corruption, however, corruption continues to be a major malignant cancer in the body politic of the nation that sends tremor down the spines of Nigerians and serves as an impediment to the nation's progress. By no stretch of imagination, Nigerians are no more venal than other peoples of the world. Actually, Nigeria has a high church population density and religious observances adhered to diligently. According to an analyst, "Nigeria prides itself on being the most religious nation on earth," to the extent that "in 2014, a man was sent to a mental institution for admitting to being an atheist" (Hill, 2020).

Also, churches, prayer houses, chapels, and mosques dot the Nigerian landscape. In schools, prayers are said at the beginning and end of each school day. Even Bible Knowledge is a school taught subject. Godly upbringing is widespread and the norm in many Nigerian homes. Public officials take the oath of office swearing to serve "truthfully, honorably, and so help me God." However, "notwithstanding the panoply of laws deployed over the years against it, corruption is notoriously persistent in Nigeria" (Ocheje, 2018, p. 363). There is corruption and abuse of office everywhere in Nigeria, but it is supposed to be accepted way of life and method of doing business, especially among the leadership. Why? The reasons are as many as the problem is as hydra-headed. For one thing, both the Nigerian public and officials attach little or no stigma to corrupt activities in public office because they view public property and resources as a target for plunder, or the craved "national cake," that everybody must share in. For another, law enforcement is lax and corrupt officials are seldom punished, when they do get sanctioned at all, it is often a slap on the wrist, invariably reinforcing the culture of impunity.

Chidi Odinkalu, former chairman, National Human Rights Commission, further explained in the following words:

> The problem is not that people steal our resources; it is that we allow them to get away with it, even worse, reward them with management of public trust as well as control of the public till, resources and institutions. This does not just happen on an episodic, individualized basis; it has for the most part become generalized as the raison d'être of public office. . . . Simultaneously, we have destroyed the citizen and produced an elite without a coherent articulation of its self-interest who have in turn corrupted politics, politicized anti-corruption and annihilated the institutional capacities of the public space and political processes to exact accountability from it. (CLEEN Foundation, 2010)

Also, the *Punch* newspaper counseled against the prevailing public indifferent attitude to official graft: "To enjoy the benefits of democracy, Nigerians will have to rouse themselves from their insufferable lethargy, shake off their pre-occupation with self, ethnicity and narrow sectarianism, and stop deifying those who, by means fair or foul, occupy public office" (*Punch*, March 9, 2014). To borrow from external scholars, it is very refreshing to quote from Harvard University Cornel West, in his avid 2004 book, *Democracy Matters*; he reminded us of the "dreadful warning" of Benjamin Franklin (one of America's Founding Fathers, 1706–1790) in his closing speech at the Constitutional Convention of 1787, to the effect that a country with "docile citizens could end up as a despotic republic." West further wrote:

> I agree to this constitution with all its faults, if they are such: because I think a general government necessary for us, and there is no form of government but what may be a blessing to the people if well administered; and I believe farther that this is likely to be well administered for a Course of Years and can only end in despotism as other forms have done before it, when the people shall become so corrupted as to need Despotic Government, being incapable of any other. (West, 2004, p. 44)

CORRUPTION AND IMPUNITY

Nigeria's corruption challenge is compounded by the fact that not only that government shows "lack of will" to fight the scourge, but also, she is lax to enforce extant laws to prevent, detect, and punish graft, especially when high-profile cases of elected politicians and appointed public officials are involved. Also, the anti-graft war cases suffer from lack of diligent prosecution in Nigerian courts that often result to bungled cases, stalled trials and mistrials, and worse, outright collapse of prosecution cases, effectively making a mockery of the anti-graft war. The problems and abuses are so flagrant that otherwise reticent public officials openly decry government's "lack of will" to tackle corruption. In 2013, for example, Ekpo Nta, then chairman of ICPC, lamented: "There is no political will to fight corruption in Nigeria. There had been corrupt practices decree, War Against Indiscipline, MAMSA, NOA, Foreign Exchange Decree, Money Laundry Decree, EFCC and ICPC Acts, Fiscal Responsibility Act 2010, etc. We have more than enough laws that will stamp corruption out of our system but the problem is implementation" (Jegede, 2013). Nta is not alone in his observations.

In September 2012, at the induction ceremony of newly selected lawyer Senior Advocates of Nigeria, then Chief Justice of Nigeria (CJN), Justice Aloma Mariam Muktar, did not hide her displeasure and "blamed" then Attorney General of the Federation (AGF), Mohammed Adoke, for the "delays in the prosecution of high-profile corruption cases." Justice Muktar declared:

> The administration of justice is not confined to the courts; it encompasses officers of the law and others whose duties are necessary to ensure that the courts function effectively. . . . It, therefore, follows that the courts cannot on their own prosecute criminal cases, there must be the willingness of all prosecuting agencies to prosecute cases brought before our courts, especially high profile cases of corruption and all others.

In yet another high-profile upbraid, in November 2015, during a meeting with the AGF, Abubakar Malami, Justice Mahmud Mohammed, then CJN, reechoed the "lack of will" syndrome in dealing with corruption cases in Nigeria. The CJN assailed government lawyers for their wanton attitude toward prosecution of "criminal cases especially those involving politically exposed persons or political party family members." He added:

> Experience within the Judiciary shows that there is abject lack of political will to prosecute some of those cases pending before our various courts almost a decade in some instances. . . . It is not because there are no special courts, but mostly for

> reasons of political expedience and other ancillary considerations. . . . I would likewise wish to encourage you (AGF) to display a greater resolve than your predecessors in tackling outstanding cases before the courts. In times past, the Attorney General of the Federation would often lead teams of legal counsel in high profile cases so as to demonstrate the resolve of the government to enshrine the rule of law. . . . Sadly, recent Attorneys-General have become less inclined to do this. I would certainly like to see you, as the Attorney General, appear before us especially in cases of important national purport. (Nnochiri, 2015)

Also, it has been suggested that another apparent impediment to the fight against corruption in Nigeria is "the public attitude towards the judiciary" argued legal scholar, Okechukwu Oko (Oko, 2005, p. 18). In fact, Oko (2005, pp. 18–19) to drive his point home expatiated ruefully thus:

> In Nigeria, there exists a perceptible popular distrust of the judiciary's integrity and its ability to protect civil rights and constrain the excesses of elected officials. For most Nigerians, the judicial process is nothing more than an auction in which justice goes to the highest bidder. Convinced that judges decide cases on the basis of connections and gratification without regard to the legal merits of the case, citizens seek to influence the outcome of cases either by "settling the judge," or intimidating judicial officers. . . . Popular distrust of the judiciary has fueled needless attacks on the integrity and the institution of the judiciary.

And not to mention, who will ever forget the memorable zinger in December 2013, from then Rivers State governor, Chibuike Amaechi: "We [Governors] steal because Nigerians don't stone us" (Akasike, 2013). Translation: crime and no punishment. Considered altogether, in Nigeria's scheme of things, public money and resources are often stolen, misappropriated, squandered, and embezzled without the slightest compunction, especially in high places of government and leadership.

Every regime that has come on board in Nigeria in the past 50 years has cited corruption as a major reason for ousting or succeeding the previous administration, promised to clean up the system, and vow a complete break from the corrupt and vainglorious ways of the preceding administration. Yet the harder they try, the more they fail. After the overthrow of the First Republic in January 1966, the leader of the coup, Major Chukwuma Nzeogwu, said: "Our enemies are the political profiteers, swindlers, the men in high places and low places who seek bribes and demand ten %, those that seek to keep us divided permanently so that they can remain in office as minister and VIPs of waste, the tribalists, the nepotists" (see St. Jorre, 1972, p. 38; Kirk-Green, 1971, p. 71). Also, following the fall of Shagari's government, General Buhari stated:

> While corruption and indiscipline had been associated with our state of underdevelopment, these twin evils in our politics have attained unprecedented height over the past four years. The corrupt, inept and insensitive leadership in the last four years has been the source of immorality and impropriety in our society, since what happens in any society is largely a reflection of the leadership of that country. (Buhari, 1984)

When General Babangida took over power in 1985, he promised to "end the cycle of corruption and instability that had dogged Nigeria since independence" (*The Economist*, August 21, 1993). Yet as soon as the new administration settled into office, they become more corrupt and unaccountable than the previous regimes. Patrick Dele Cole, a historian and former ambassador, noted: "Briefly put—the military in 1966 intervened into politics inter alia, to stop corruption. Every military intervention since then has had this mantra of stopping corruption. Every succeeding Government in Nigeria, it is safe to say, has been more corrupt than its predecessor" (Cole, 2014). No single factor has had a more corrupting influence on Nigeria's public life as oil and gas.

THE CURSE OF OIL

Discussing corruption, in the context of oil curse, the *Economist* (October 3, 2013) provided the following eye-opening overview about how rife corruption happened to be: "The line between legal and illegal oil supplies is easily blurred in a country so rife with corruption. Transactions in Nigeria's oil industry are infamous for their murkiness." Also, *Newswatch* magazine (March 21, 1994, p. 13) added a useful comment about crude oil: "Crude oil term contracts is a good source of kickbacks for government officials, their business associates or relations and NNPC is known to have lost several millions of dollars to such sharp practices." The *Guardian* (February 8, 2005) wrote: "Every expenditure of NNPC is shrouded in some sort of secrecy." Former presidential spokesperson, Reuben Abati, alluded:

> The curse of oil in our context has meant indolence, the emergence of a rentier class, a squandering of riches and the alienation of the poor by the rich. . . . The curse of oil is the source of a national cake mentality that has turned public service into an arena for primate accumulation. It is the root of corruption in Nigeria. (Abati, 2016)

The arrays of opinions are very true. Ever since Nigeria very luckily struck oil for the mineral to become the nation's economic mainstay and chief revenue earner, Nigerian leaders have had trouble separating the public treasury from private pocket. Nigerian leaders see oil as a source of patronage and reward for winning office (*The Economist*, September 27, 2007). One report stated:

> In 1970, oil exports equaled ₦510 million; a decade later they increased to ₦14.2 billion. Since almost all of the oil revenues was funneled through the state, government expenditures increased more than 3,000 percent during the same period. As a result, control of the state became exceptionally valuable, and the explosion of oil revenue fueled the creation of larger and more elaborate patron-client networks. . . . Indeed, the rapid turnover of regime reinforced the tendency of civilian and military holders of public office to raid the state's coffers to buy support. (Herbst & Olukoshi, 1994, p. 456)

No proper metering tracks the output of crude oil, so no one knows exactly how much Nigeria produces or how much is lost in transit (*The Economist*, March 28, 2015; Ibrahim et al., 2017; Amnesty International, 2009). In addition, NEITI reported that the gauges and meters installed at PPMC fuel depots, jetties, tank farms, and pipelines were often "obsolete, defective and in need of repairs and maintenance" (NEITI, 2009–2011 Report). Its 2014 review of NNPC crude oil liftings records also could not account for more than $680 million in the volume of crude oil supposedly lifted that year (NEITI, 2014, p. 63). It is estimated that non-metering of oil wells costs Nigeria $5 billion yearly in lost revenues, representing 10% of total oil revenues from exports (Onuba, 2011). In 2016, the House of Representatives ordered an investigation into undeclared $17 billion oil and gas exports between 2011 and 2014 (Wallace, 2016).

Another window into the magnitude of revenue hemorrhage from oil theft was opened in December 2015 by no less a personality than then Kano Emir, Muhammadu Sanusi II (former governor of the Central Bank). In a television interview, Emir Sanusi told Nick Schifrin of *PBS* (Public Broadcasting Service) *NewsHour* (American daily evening TV news program), how some of the shady oil deals are carried out:

> Basically, all it does is allow a group of people, who themselves don't have any kind of operating background, to pay $50 million for access to the crude oil blocs, valued at over $2 billion and they just take the crude oil, ship it out and don't return the money and there is no trace of where the money has gone. . . . Someone gets a contract to lift crude from the terminals to the refineries and in between that crude is stolen, it is stolen on the high sea. (*PBS NewsHour*, December 2, 2015)

In general government, the Kano monarch disclosed that Nigeria "lost about $1 billion monthly through official theft" (*PBS NewsHour*, December 2,

2015). To cap his renditions to the *PBS NewsHour*, the Emir declared: "In Nigeria, there is no accountability at all and that is why I think Nigeria's corruption is worse than corruption in most parts of the world. It is the worst type of corruption. It's stealing" (*PBS NewsHour*, December 2, 2015). (The interview referred to was part of a *PBS*'s series titled "Nigeria: Pain and Promise" aired on the *PBS* network in the first week of December 2015.)

Meanwhile audits by NEITI have found that accuracy of production figures varies widely depending on the purpose of the report in question (*The Economist*, September 27, 2007). Underpayment of royalty and taxes, non-remittance of oil sales receipts by NNPC, underpayment to NDDC by oil companies, and poor record keeping by NNPC are some of the ways Nigeria loses oil revenues (Eme, Chukwurah, & Iheanacho, 2015; Natural Resources Governance Institute, 2015). Reports by NEITI offer proof of serial abuses, lack of transparency, and corruption in Nigeria's oil industry. In June 2015, NEITI reported:

> Our [NEITI] 2012 audit report discovered that total dividend loans and interest repayment from NLNG paid to the NNPC in 2012 was $2.8 billion. However, in the course of NEITI's audit, NNPC was unable to provide any evidence to show that the funds were remitted to the federation as required by law. . . . The total amount received by NNPC from NLNG under the same circumstances which have not been remitted to the Federation Account stands at $11.6 billion.

In another report issued December 2016 for the 2014 audit year NEITI also disclosed:

> The none remittance of NLNG dividends, interest and loan repayment in the sum of $13.92 Billion in 2013 makes the cumulative amount received from NLNG and not remitted to Federation account by NNPC as at the end of 2014 (including amounts revealed in previous NEITI audit reports) as $14.34 Billion. . . . The recurring non-remittance of NLNG dividends, interest and loan repayments to the Federation Account by NNPC should be investigated. (NEITI, 2016, p. 89)

In yet another report, issued in December 2017 for the 2015 audit year, NEITI disclosed inter alia, for example, under "Summary of Key Findings, Implications and Recommendations":

> Item#1: Unaccounted export sales of $586.011 million for unreconciled export sales receivables in the year under review. . . . There should be proper reconciliation of unexplained/unreconciled difference of previous audit years. . . .
> Item#3: Unaccounted ₦317.476 billion for unreconciled sales receivables in the year under review. This is as a result of unexplained receivables. This imply

> shortfall in amount to be remitted by NNPC as domestic sales proceeds to the federation account. NNPC should account for ₦317.476 billion and remit the said amount to the federation without delay. Item#6: NNPC deducted first line charge of ₦60.997 billion for "Crude and Product Oil losses"; ₦112.818 billion for "Pipeline repairs & maintenance"; and ₦316.721 billion for "Subsidy deduction." Deduction of subsidy as first line charge from domestic crude sales proceeds contradicts the provisions in the Petroleum Support Fund. Also, other deductions are contrary to section 80(1) of the Constitution of the Federal Republic of Nigeria 1999. (NEITI, 2017, pp. 184–202)

NNPC—THE HONEY POT

It has been alleged in Nigeria that the oil oversight department, NNPC, is the poster child of corruption in Nigeria as well as the source of national shame. This characterization is unfortunate, but it seems to be apt in a variety of ways and in words and also in deeds. Sayne, Gillies, and Katsouris (2015, p. 2) had the following to write about the department: "NNPC's approach to oil sales suffers from high corruption risks and fails to maximize returns for the nation. These shortcomings also characterize NNPC as a whole." In April 2014, former governor of old Anambra State, Jim Nwobodo, declared: "Many people do not know what is happening in NNPC, it is a cult" (Umoru & Erinke, 2014). In July 2015, then Senate president, Bukola Saraki, described NNPC as the "engine of corruption" (Aborisade, 2015).

As well, in July 2015, governor of Kaduna State, Nasir el-Rufai called NNPC a "parallel government," arguing that if it is not reformed "it will kill Nigeria" (Nnodim, 2015). Also, in November 2015, the Nigerian historian, Patrick Cole, called "NNPC the Sodom and Gomorrah of corruption" (Cole, 2015). The *Punch* (July 29, 2015) editorialized: "The Nigerian National Petroleum Corporation is an opaque, labyrinthine agency, drunk on corruption and a drain on the country's wealth." Besides, to put all in perspective, back in 1993 the *Economist* (August 21, 1993) reported that NNPC "has no published accounts and international economists had concluded that, given Nigeria's oil production and world oil prices, the difference between what NNPC should have earned and what the authorities reported was about $2.7 billion short. This suggests that almost 10% of GDP disappear each year out of the public treasury."

More than 27 years later, the oil industry vis-à-vis NNPC's financial leakages and fraud instead of abetting have taken a turn for the worse as report after report expose NNPC's scandals and abuses. In June 2017, NEITI reported that it has no proof that NNPC remitted $15.8 billion it received between 2000 and 2014 from the Nigeria Liquefied Natural Gas Company to the Federation Account (Nnodim, 2017). In December 2016, the House of Representatives summoned NNPC and several oil companies operating in Nigeria to appear before it over alleged theft of $17 billion worth of oil and gas through undeclared exports between 2011 and 2014 (Ameh, 2016). In July 2015, then executive secretary of NEITI, Zainab Ahmed, said:

> Between 2009 and 2012, about 160 million barrels of oil valued at $13.7 billion was stolen under the watch of NNPC. . . . Subsidy payments from 2005 to 2012 indicated that $11.63 billion had been paid to NNPC but there is no evidence of the money being remitted to the federation account. . . . Crude oil swap of $866 million was lost from 2009 to 2011 and $824.3 million in 2012. (Isenyo, 2015)

In another 2017 report, NEITI indicated:

> Other sources of revenue losses to the federation, include crude oil theft, as it noted that the total revenue loss to the federation as a result of the problem, as well as deferred production and sabotage between 2011 and 2014 stood at $15.9bn. . . . NPDC failed to remit the sum of $5.5bn and ₦72.4bn comprising of outstanding payments for the Oil Mining Leases divested to it, cash calls paid by the NNPC to the company for already divested assets and legacy liabilities . . . oil swap and offshore processing agreements resulted in the loss of product value equivalent to $518m in 2013 and $198.7m in 2014. (Nnodim, 2017)

In a revealing editorial on August 25, 2014, the *Punch* newspaper appeared to have crystal balled the disturbing findings narrated above by Zainab Ahmed one year later:

> The image Nigerians have of the NNPC is that of a tower of corruption, where the public treasury is looted with reckless abandon. The details are unspeakable: since 2005 its books have not been audited, provoking series of probes into its activities by the parliament. . . . Non-remittance of revenues from crude oil proceeds to the Federation Account, as the 1999 Constitution stipulates, is common with the corporation. . . . When its finances become the subject of endless reconciliations among the Central Bank of Nigeria, the Ministry of Finance and Office of the Accountant-General of the Federation, and also open to forensic examination, it is clear evidence that all is not well.

At a Senate Finance Committee hearing on February 4, 2014, then governor of Central Bank, Lamido Sanusi, charged that NNPC failed to remit $20 billion in oil revenues between January 2012 and July 2013 to the government (Abosisade, 2014). On February 20, 2014, NNPC informed the Senate Finance Committee that $6 billion proceeds from a third-party crude sale arrangement were paid into the account of one of her subsidiaries, Nigerian Petroleum Development Company (NPDC) (Aborisade, 2014). But NPDC denied NNPC's claim, with the former stating: "We did not have the money in NPDC account, we did not receive the $6 billion from the NNPC" (Aborisade, 2014). In a report to Parliament on February 26, 2014, NEITI indicated that NNPC failed to declare $22.8 billion oil proceeds in funding arrangements with her Joint Venture Partners (Ameh, 2014). NEITI further stated that "because NNPC used a different exchange rate from that of the Central Bank in its transactions, the country lost ₦98.3 billion between 2009 and 2011" (Ameh, 2014).

According to a 2013 Report by Chatham House, a Britain-based think tank:

> The Nigerian oil industry has reputation for illegality. . . . The state-run NNPC is widely seen as one of the most politicized and compromised institutions of any oil producing nation. . . . Nigerian crude oil is being stolen on an industrial scale. Some of what is stolen is exported. Proceeds are laundered through world financial centers and used to buy assets in and outside Nigeria. In Nigeria, politicians, military officers, militants, oil industry personnel, oil traders and communities profit, as do organized criminal groups. . . . Nigeria offers a strong enabling environment for large scale theft of crude oil. Corruption and fraud are rampant in the country's oil sector. A dynamic, overcrowded political economy drives competition for looted resources. Poor governance has encouraged violent opportunism around oil and opened doors for organized crime. . . . The estimated annual value of oil stolen from Nigeria is between $3 billion and $8 billion. (Katsouris & Sayne, 2013)

As corroboration from Chatham House's findings above, in November 2013, the House of Representatives disclosed that "NNPC and its subsidiaries have not published their financial details since 2005" (Nwabughiogu & Ovuakporie, 2013). Also, in a recent report, TI found NNPC to be one of the eight most corrupt national oil and gas companies in the world (others are Russia Gazprom, Angola Sonangol, State Oil Company of Azerbaijan, Algerian (SONATRACH), Congo SNPC, National Iranian Oil Company, and Equatorial Guinea (GEPetrol)) (Okafor, 2011; Transparency International, 2011). The TI report also indicated that the eight companies not only scored zero on corruption reporting compliance, but they also declined to disclose relevant information to the evaluation team (Transparency International, 2011).

Another landmark report (Ribadu Report) has further exposed what the *Financial Times* of London described as "the widespread inefficiencies, graft and criminality in Nigeria's petroleum sector" (Wallis, 2012). The Nuhu Ribadu-led Petroleum Revenue Special Task Force was set up in February

2012 by the Nigerian government, after widespread protests that greeted the removal of fuel subsidies by the government. The panel was among others asked to "verify the government's income from oil and gas, and make recommendations to the government" (Ribadu Report, 2012). Covering 2002–2012, the report detailed how the country "lost up to $29 billion in shady deals with oil majors; theft of an alarming 250,000 barrels of crude per day worth about $6.3 billion a year and how $183 million in signature bonuses from seven discretionary oil prospecting licenses issued between 2008 and 2011 were not accounted for" (*Punch*, November 2, 2012). It is important to note in the wake of the protests against the removal of fuel subsidies, a House of Representatives Committee (Farouk Lawan Ad hoc Committee) probe discovered that $6 billion has been defrauded from the fuel subsidy fund between 2009 and 2011 by oil marketers, importers, and officials of the state-owned NNPC (*BBC News* Online, April 24, 2012). The House Committee report was particularly hard on NNPC, charging the following:

> On its part, NNPC was found not to be accountable to anybody or authority. The Corporation, in 2011, processed payment of ₦310.4 Billion as 2009–2011 arrears of subsidy on Kerosene, contrary to a Presidential Directive which removed subsidy on Kerosene in 2009. The Corporation also processed for itself, direct deduction of subsidy payment from amounts it received from other operations such as joint venture before paying the balance to the Federation Account, thereby depleting the shares of States and Local Governments from the distributable pool. Worse still, the direct deduction in 2011 alone, which amounted to ₦847.942 Billion, was effected without any provision in the Appropriation Act. While NNPC feasted on the Federation Account to bloat the subsidy payable, some of the marketers were involved in claiming subsidy on products not supplied. PPPRA laid this foundation by allocating volumes of products each quarter to the marketers which it knew were not in conformity with its own guidelines for participation. (Nigeria House of Representatives. *Report of the Ad-hoc Committee 'To Verify and Determine the Actual Subsidy Requirements and Monitor the Implementation of the Subsidy Regime in Nigeria,'* Resolution No. HR.1/2012, Laid on Wednesday April 18, 2012)

TAMING CORRUPTION

Although "wars" have very often been declared against corruption and headline-grabbing pronouncements made by successive Nigerian governments and their elected top officials, such wars have never worked because the leadership is either directly involved in corrupt practices, or their family members, or cronies are (Ijewereme, 2015; Folarin, 2009). In fact, government anticorruption propositions, upon close scrutiny, turn out to "involve" what Becker (1958, p. 105) referred to as "assumptions of doubtful validity." The endemic problem of betraying public trust, corruption, and conflict of interest must be tackled before it takes Nigeria to a point of no return.

The Center for Advanced Social Sciences (CASS), a think thank in Port Harcourt, agrees in the following words:

> Failure to deal with this problem contributes importantly to theft and waste of public resources, the dissociation of public policy from social needs, the privatization of the State and our inability to develop a national identity. The government which is needed to defeat corruption is the core of the problem in Nigeria. It is in government that corruption thrives most, wasting resources and defeating all prospects of democracy and development. . . . Development has stalled while the enormous oil wealth of the nation has not benefited ordinary Nigerian. . . . The overall effect is not only it is degrading Nigeria morally, but it is also rendering development, the rule of law and democracy impossible. (*Tell*, December 20, 1993, pp. 17–18)

While the CASS lamented of the many consequences of corrupt leadership, the *Economist* offered a living proof of the depth of corruption:

> Corruption in Nigeria is not about a few individuals, who pilfer from the public purse, it is the system. The problem is neither economic nor even political, it is moral. . . . The motto seems to be: "What can I get away with?" In a country where $600 million can be stolen with impunity, the answer is: a lot. . . . Corruption is now so deeply rooted that is doubtful if it can be dug out. (*The Economist*, June 8, 1996, p. 48)

The problem of corruption in Nigeria is grounded on the concept of prebendalism as has been explored and discussed in the book. The prebendalism tendency is premised on the "justifying principle that public offices should be competed for and then utilized for the personal benefit of office-holders as well as of their reference or support group" (Joseph, 1987, p. 8), invariably putting personal benefit over public purpose. No single factor has enabled the political class and the elite in Nigeria more to steal and abuse their offices than the constitutional loophole called the Immunity Clause.

Nigeria is one of those few places in the world where when you see, or, suspect an official abusing their office or stealing stuff you do not stop them or call the police to arrest them, let alone prosecuting them, until four or eight years later. This is as a result of the obnoxious Immunity Clause provision in Nigerian Constitution that shields the president, vice president, governors, and deputy governors from prosecution while they are in office. This clause is the jugular in the high prevalence of corruption among impacted office-holders. The Immunity Clause is found in Section 308 of the 1999 Nigerian Constitution (however, it must be emphasized that the Immunity Clause does not shield the impacted persons from impeachment while in office). It states inter alia:

> Notwithstanding anything to the contrary in this constitution, but subject to the sub section (2) of this section—
>
> (A) No civil or criminal proceedings shall be instituted or continued against a person to whom this section applies during his period of office;
> (B) A person to whom this section applies shall not be arrested or imprisoned during the period, either in pursuance of the process of any court or otherwise ; and
> (C) No process of any court requiring or compelling the appearance of a person to whom this section applies, shall be applied for or issued;
>
> Provided that in ascertaining whether any period of limitation has expired for the purposes of any proceedings against a person to whom this section applies, no account shall be taken of his period of office.

According to the framers of the Nigerian Constitution, the major reason behind the insertion of the Immunity Clause in the Constitution is to avoid distraction of the leadership which could impair government operations (Enweremadu, 2012). However, this argument is flawed because in the First and Second Republics there was no Immunity Clause and there were no distractions and, more importantly, the Republics did not collapse because of lack of immunity, rather, because of the recklessness and greed of the political class. In the opinion of a former CJN, Justice Alfa Belgore, "the immunity clause has become a leeway for looting public treasury by heads of the executive arm of government at the three tiers of government" (*The Street Journal*, December 22, 2012). Justice Belgore's assertion is not without proof. Then chairwoman of the EFCC, Farida Waziri, in 2009 declared: "In just ten years of civil rule, Nigeria has lost ₦285 billion to the political elite—former governors, ministers, members of parliament, and other categories of public servants" (*This Day*, June 15, 2009; Uchegbu, 2009).

WHAT PEOPLE DO WITH CORRUPTION MONEY

Public corruption is widespread, entrenched, and systematic in Nigeria, and has been identified by the World Bank as "the single greatest obstacle to economic and social development . . . a major challenge to its twin goals of ending extreme poverty by 2030 and boosting shared prosperity for the poorest 40 percent of people in developing countries" (World Bank, Brief, December 14, 2020). However, much less attention so far has been paid to what people or governments do with corruption money. Put it more bluntly, what happens to seized, confiscated, and recovered proceeds of corruption by the government? As such, as a "topic of fruitful reflection" (Gooding-Williams, 2017, p. 1), a discussion of what people do with corruption money or proceeds of corruption can add value to the analysis of corruption in the book. For the sake of brevity, the emphasis will be on illicit assets obtained through bribery, patronage, or theft from state budgets (Jimu, 2009).

Proceeds of these forms of corruption are generally transferred from one jurisdiction to another in order to disguise their source (Jimu, 2019). The cross-border flow of the global proceeds from criminal activities, corruption, and tax evasion is estimated at between $1 trillion and $1.6 trillion per year (World Bank, n.d. *Fact Sheet on Stolen Asset Recovery*). Estimates suggest corruption money associated with bribes received by public officials from developing and transition countries results in conservatively estimated $20–$40 billion stolen each year from those jurisdictions (Gray et al. 2014, p. 21; World Bank)—a figure equivalent to 20–40% of flows of official development assistance (World Bank, n.d. *Fact Sheet on Stolen Asset Recovery*). In Africa, an estimated amount over $148 billion or 25% of the GDP of African states is lost to corruption every year (World Bank, n.d. *Fact Sheet on Stolen Asset Recovery*), but the problem is seen in all continents, however.

The discussion of Nigeria's Abacha looted funds as a case in point of what government can do with recovered corruption money, especially funding public infrastructure projects that could bolster economic development, "help improve social indicators, and assist with progress towards the MDGs" (Okonjo-Iweala & Osafo-Kwaako 2008, p. 8) follows. As a force of good of sorts, out of the $505.5 million, for example, of Abacha's loot repatriated from Switzerland between 2005 and 2006, allocations to various pro-poor priority programs were as follows: power ($168.5 million), works ($144.5 million), health ($84.1 million), education ($60.1 million), and water resources ($48.2 million) (Okonjo-Iweala & Osafo-Kwaako 2008, p. 8; Jimu, 2009, p. 7).

While Abacha's case is far from representative of the whole issue of public corruption problem in Nigeria, many Nigerians feel that his government encouraged corruption by stashing away illicit funds in foreign bank accounts, in the amounts and extent unheard off or experienced in the annals of Nigerian history (Nwabughiogu, 2020; World Bank, 2007). It is difficult to know exactly how much Abacha's loot there are; however, the World Bank estimates that Abacha may have looted up to $5 billion of public money while in office (1993–1998), representing 27.1% annual average of Nigeria's GDP over the period Abacha ruled (World Bank, 2007, Table 1, p. 11). Abacha was alleged to have used four methods for plundering public assets: outright theft from the public treasury through the central bank, inflation of the value of public contracts, extortion of bribes from contractors, and fraudulent transactions (World Bank, 2007. p. 18). The ill-got wealth were laundered through a complex web of banks and front companies in several countries and localities, but principally Nigeria, the United Kingdom, Switzerland, Luxembourg, Liechtenstein, Jersey, and the Bahamas (World Bank, 2007, p. 18).

According to reports, successive Nigerian administrations have made the following recoveries of Abacha's loot since his death in 1998: Abdulsalami Abubakar, $750 million; Olusegun Obasanjo, $2 billion; Umaru Musa Yar'Adua, $0; Goodluck Jonathan, $227 million; Muhammadu Buhari, $630 million. According to the Nigerian government, part of these monies has been earmarked to fund three major public works projects across the country: Lagos-Ibadan Expressway (Western Region), Abuja-Kano Road (Northern Region), and Second Niger Bridge (Eastern Region) (*Vanguard*, March 8, 2020. See also World Bank, 2018, p. 20; African Network for Environment and Economic Justice, ANEEJ, 2020).

Abacha's loot rehabilitative application and "paternalistic designs" (Osaghae, 1999, p. 84) are suggestively, perhaps, consistent with what La Porta et al. (1999, p. 224) called "redistributive tendencies" of government. In their study on the "Quality of Government," the scholars found a positive correlation between total government transfers and subsidies (total redistributive activity) and corruption (Graaf & Huberts, 2008). In this instance, "the indicator of performance is government expenditures on transfers, its own consumption, and public sector employment" (La Porta et al., 1999, p. 22), and measures to improve social services (e.g., education, health care), enhance social protection (e.g., income support, affordable housing), and infrastructure improvements (e.g., roads, bridges, transit systems), regardless of whether the sources of funding are corrupt.

Furthermore, corruption money can be used to buy political support and win elections, further justifying "redistributive tendency" of government. Tanzi (1998, p. 564) argued that "sometimes, the abuse of public power [corruption] is not necessarily for one's private benefit but for the benefit of one's party, class, tribe, friends, family, and so on. In fact, in many countries some proceeds of corruption go to finance the activities of the political parties." A good example is use of over the limit campaign donations for "higher motives of officials" (Hodgson & Jiang, 2007, p. 1049) in a democracy. In advanced democracies, for example, Italy, United States, Spain, and Japan, studies suggest that voters might ignore political [public] corruption if it is associated with the delivery of material benefits in the form of pork and patronage (Golden, 2012, p. 81; Tanzi, 1998, p. 564). When this is the case, it is associated with groups of politicians who receive more campaign money contributions for their electoral campaigns expenditures than the law allows. And when they win election, they use their positions and connections to bring "spoils of public office" (Krumholz, 2013, p. 1120) benefits to their constituents (not to themselves) (Golden, 2012), often in the forms of budget deals and legislative pork barrel earmarks for constituency projects, development grants, jobs packages, safety net programs, economic development assistance, business incentives, and so on (e.g., see Citizens Against Government Waste Report (CAGW), 2020). In this way, when politicians win elections through "rule-breaking-behavior," voters are less perturbed because the public officials are seen to have used the otherwise proceeds of corruption to win office, and by extension bring benefits to their constituents through the instrumentality of their office. This tendency echoes the sentiment of what is called "noble cause corruption" (Hodgson & Jiang, 2007; Wahl, 2014; van Halderen & Kolthoff, 2017; Harrison, 1999).

Although these actions are not necessarily for material gain, they remain corrupt because they broke specific rules and undermined the character and moral justification of the officials (Hodgson & Jiang, 2007, p. 1049). In addition, while the "immoral act of corruption may be outweighed by the moral outcomes of the noble cause," provision of expected public goods and services, and promotion of social welfare, "but corruption remains corruption nevertheless" (Hodgson & Jiang, 2007, p. 1049).

WHAT MUST BE DONE IN NIGERIA

Candidates running for and appointees to public office should be thoroughly screened to determine their eligibility, integrity, and good character.

- Such senior government leaders as the president and his or her cabinet, governors, armed and security chiefs, heads of Parastatals must be required to publicly declare all their assets and business interests before taking office, submit annual financial disclosure report while in office, and re-declare all their assets and financial and business interests before leaving office. In 2007, for example, late Nigerian president Umaru Yar'Adua became the first sitting president to publicly declare his assets. In September 2015, President Buhari and Vice President Osinbajo publicly declared their assets as well.
- A "Blind Trust" is another mechanism to guard against conflict of interest. It involves:

> The transfer of such business and other remunerative financial and other interests, which provide financial or other interests to the erstwhile private citizen, to a trust under a different management that can be certified as

> separate and independent of the owner of these interests. Example is where a President owns or is a shareholder in companies, or, a Minister or public office holder is significantly involved in a private enterprise which comes under the regulatory functions of his or her Ministry. (*Tell*, December 20, 1993)

In this regard, it would be proper to allude to President John F. Kennedy. In a special message to the American Congress on Conflict of Interests on April 27, 1961, he said:

> No responsibility of government is more fundamental than the responsibility of maintaining the highest standards of ethical behavior by those who conduct the public business. There can be no dissent from the principle that all officials must act with unwavering integrity, absolute impartiality and complete devotion to the public interest. This principle must be followed not only in reality but also in appearance. For the basis of effective government is public confidence, and that confidence is endangered when ethical standards falter or appear to falter. (Kennedy, 1962, p. 112)

Closely related to checking conflict of interest and abuse of office is to create a permanent independent machinery for the investigation, prosecution, and adjudication of official wrong doing (without statute of limitation), especially of covered high officials. What is suggested here is in the realm of United States Department of Justice Office of Special Counsel (formerly United States Office of the Independent Counsel), "an institution which would insure a prosecutor's independence," especially when it comes to the question: "can the public trust the executive branch of government—the President and his or [her] appointed officials, including the Attorney General to investigate itself fully and fairly?" (Mokhiber, 1998).

The Code of Conduct Bureau (CCB) of Nigeria was, indeed, enshrined in the 1999 Nigerian Constitution to deter official corruption including false declaration of assets. The Fifth Schedule (Part I), Section 11 (1), of the 1999 Constitution makes it compulsory for every public officer, at the beginning and end of his or her tenure, and every four years, to "submit to the Code of Conduct Bureau a written declaration of all his properties, assets" (*Punch*, February 7, 2016). However, the CCB has not lived up to expectations and corruption is rife. In January 2019, for example, Isah Mohammed, chairman of the CCB, indicated of

> flagrant abuse of the CCB law by civil servants and public office holders for non-declaration of their assets at the required regular interval" (*Vanguard*, January 15, 2019). In another instance, in May 2019, Mohammed lamented

> that the "CCB has not been able to perform over the 30 years that it has been in existence . . . vows to prosecute Governors and Ministers that are found to have falsified their assets. (Nnochiri, 2019)

One of the most serious flaws of the CCB, as clearly spelled out, "is that it lacked full proof means to confirm the amount of wealth anybody would have acquired illegally since the CCB depended on individuals to be honest" (*Post Express*, September 9, 1998). Another obstacle is the inability of the National Assembly to do the needful by setting the "terms and conditions" under which people can inspect the assets filed by public officials as the Constitution mandated (*Punch*, February 7, 2016). Also, as BBC's Will Ross alluded, "the CCB which has a pair of handcuffs on its website but has been fairly toothless as the agency which has been checking corrupt practices in the Nigerian public service since 1989" (Ross, 2015). This is not only absurd but it is also a travesty of accountability. No high-ranking public official in Nigeria has been punished for noncompliance to asset declaration request, or, for making false or perjured declarations of the same. (For the first time, in September 2015 the CCB arraigned the then Senate president, Bukola Saraki, for alleged false asset declaration.)

Consequently, it is recommended that the CCB be reformed toward strengthening its enforcement powers and making its duties more specific to cover, among others: independent verification of declaration of assets filed by covered officials; impose censure against public officers who failed to, or intentionally file false and misleading assets and financial information including rejection, withdrawal, or prosecution of such nominees or appointees; maintain periodic and consistent update on information on file; keep a close eye on possible official malfeasance, particularly bribery and corruption and the maintenance of private foreign accounts by serving high officials. To ensure its impartiality the bureau must exercise independence and people of impeccable standing appointed to administer its affairs. Also, citizens can assist in the fight against corruption especially through the vehicle of the Freedom of Information Act and whistleblower program by inspecting filed assets declarations, reporting, and alerting the authorities of possible misdeeds.

In addition, prosecute the perpetrators—there should be no deals like the one in 2014 that dropped charges against the son of late president Sani Abacha, Mohammed Abacha in return for the repatriation of stolen assets to the country (Transparency International, 2015). Pass and implement strong anticorruption legislation—the government must strengthen anticorruption laws and institutions, ensuring that the latter are independent and better resourced (Transparency International, 2015). Furthermore, root out corruption in the Nigerian military. According to TI, "defense sector reforms are urgently needed to reduce the risk of corruption and state fragility in the following issues areas: National Defense policy legislative and public debates, revision of Public Procurement Act, external and public audit of defense expenditures, legislative provision of detailed defense budget and secret spending" (Transparency International, 2015). Nigeria's military establishment scored a very poor "E" grade on a scale from "A" to "F" in Transparency International UK's Government Defense Anti-Corruption Index, which measures corruption risk in defense establishments around the world (Transparency International, 2015). The Defense Anti-Corruption Index placed Nigeria "in one of the highest risk categories for corruption in the defense and security sector in the world" (Transparency International, 2015).

CONCLUSION

This chapter examined government or official corruption in Nigeria. It employed prebendal theory (Joseph, 1987) analysis to examine the problem of public corruption in the oil-rich country. In a nutshell, prebendalism involves the use of official position for personal gain. Corruption commonly defines how Nigeria is viewed on the world stage. Sadly, corruption has destroyed the moral fiber of Nigeria and stunted the nation's development. Nigeria's oil wealth stands in stark contrast to the escalating poverty, inequality, and hopelessness pervading Nigeria. Corruption in Nigeria is neither new nor unusual, but what is special about the Nigerian type of corruption is that it is very resilient and has regrettably become an accepted way of life, in spite of its deleterious impacts.

Meanwhile, many Nigerians have died (and continue to die) from or irreversibly harmed by effects of corruption amid the backdrop of government inspectors allegedly taking bribes and allowing, for example, counterfeit drugs to flow into the country; environmental regulators who, also, allegedly take bribes and let polluters get away with their crimes; substandard buildings and structures that collapse because of alleged compromised inspection processes; deliberately bungled high-profile investigations and adjudications, especially that of politically exposed persons, which perpetuate resources' appropriation, embezzlement, and diversion of public funds, which could otherwise be used to develop the country, just as the USA's ex-president Clinton and others commented on earlier.

Above all, corruption, in its varied forms, also undermines and threatens Nigerian security. The military establishment has been urged "to root out corruption" and "take urgent steps to reduce the risk of corruption as well as to state fragility" per a recent Transparency International of UK's

Government Defense Anti-Corruption Index report. While official corruption is not restricted to Nigeria, the most repulsive aspect of Nigeria's corruption is that, basically, every past and present Nigerian regime, which has ruled the country, has decried corruption and promised to clean up the system. Sadly, to no avail that the efforts never succeeded, hence corruption is not only rampant in Nigeria because of poor pay and poverty, per se, but also Nigerians have increasingly turned a blind eye to the menace because many view public property and resources as targets for plunder, or the craved national cake in which everybody must share. Corruption-deterrent measures can include effective leadership, passing and implementation of strong and better anticorruption laws, strengthening of the CCB, better corruption reporting mechanisms, vigilant citizenry, better funding and the availability of the relevant equipment for law enforcement, international cooperation and sharing of information, and so on. In the end, a serious war must be launched against corruption in its varied forms, including graft.

In what Patrick Daniel Moynihan, a sociologist and former United States senator from New York described as a "tangle of pathologies" (Moynihan, 1965)—from mismanagement of the economy to high cost of governance, and corruption, are all inherently linked to bad leadership.

NOTE

1. The 1953 Bernard Storey *Report of the Commission of Inquiry into the Administration of the Lagos Town Council* was a trailblazing investigative report at the instance of the British colonial administration that looked into the problem of official corruption in Lagos City Council (vis-à-vis Nigeria).

Chapter 4

Leadership

The Missing Link

"WHY NOTHING WORKS"

When it comes to leadership, Nigeria is a nation at risk. The eminent author, Chinua Achebe, has pointed that out; to him, the trouble with Nigeria

> is simply and squarely a failure of leadership" as "there is nothing basically wrong with the Nigerian land or climate. . . . The Nigerian problem is the unwillingness or inability of its leaders to rise to the responsibility, to the challenge of personal example which are the hallmarks of true leadership. (Achebe, 1983)

Achebe is not alone. The journalist and author, Karl Maeir, wrote: "The primary task facing Nigeria's leaders is to convince the majority of their people that the government exists to serve rather than to prey upon them" (Maeir, 2000, p. xxviii). Ray Ekpu, journalist, enjoined the "crisis of Nigerian nationhood is the crisis of leadership failure, that is why nothing works" (*Newswatch*, October 6, 1986). Also, according to the *Guardian* "Nigeria is not working. The leaders, for want of a better word, are the greatest problem" (*Guardian*, March 26, 2020).

In addition, according to Cayford (1996, p. 183): "available political literature on Nigeria is overwhelmingly pessimistic. There are good reasons for that. A history of corrupt politicians, economic mismanagement, ethnic, regional, and religious strife, and a military all too eager to intervene to 'fix the political system' has eroded the bright hopes widely held for this country at independence." No surprise Nigeria has been described as a "crippled giant since independence" (Osaghae, 1998); "predicted Giant that has become a disappointing, even aggravating Lilliput" (Adebanwi & Obadare, 2010,

p. 380), and though still standing, Nigeria is generally assumed as having "fallen" (Maier, 2000). "As a result, together with political uncertainties such as the President's recurrent medical leaves, Nigeria remains unstable" (World Bank, 2017, p. 3). No area in the "crippling" of Nigeria is more dramatized and painful than in the sphere of leadership.

Ojo (2014, p. 67) contends that while the British may have created Nigeria, quite a preponderant of Nigerian leaders cremated it. Nigerian leadership lurches from crisis to crisis and it continues to fail the people and, as a result, to undermine the country. At the same time, good "governance which includes the process by which rulers are selected, monitored, and replaced, and the capacity of governments to effectively formulate and implement sound as well as inclusive policies" (Asefa & Huang, 2015, p. 1) is undermined by the loathsome behavior of Nigerian leaders. Furthermore, the image of Nigerian leaders as "nests of corruption" (Ishiyama, 2015, p. 35) continues to undercut their legitimacy and government effectiveness. While African leaders, including those of Nigeria "have become adept at externalizing blame" (Mills, 2011), for the most part Nigerian leadership failure is not as a result of external conspiracies by "imperialists" and "neocolonialists," a canard that is often invoked every time the leadership runs amok. Instead it is a homegrown problem induced by Nigerian leaders. Nigerian leaders' concept of leadership defies any known rational philosophy in the "history of ideas" (Ebenstein & Ebenstein, 1991).

In the opinion of several Nigerians, their leaders just do not care and have, in fact, continued to play hooky with the serious business of national governance. Furthermore, the leadership is insensitive to ordinary people's hard life conditions and worries about the future (Bang, 2018, p. 275). According to Jerry Rawlings, former Ghanaian president, "the leader has to give a clear signal, sense of direction and the passion to drive change" (Anuforo, 2016). However, in Nigeria, where Nigerian leaders are expected to lead, they instead follow; where they are to act, they react, as well as where they would be required to decisive, they dither; where they would act quickly and promptly, they procrastinate; where they would speak out, they demure; where they would be honest, they cheat; where they would be awake, they fall deeply asleep through the storm; where they would act as adults, they carry on as juveniles; where they would conserve, they splurge; and where they would build, they destroy. Furthermore, where they would stay the course of noble leadership, they follow the senseless and ignoble path of "the imperial presidency" (Schlesinger, 1973[1]).

In fact, the former chairman of Chrysler Motor Corporation, Lee Iacocca, once said something that is very useful at this juncture: "The job of a leader is to accomplish goals that advance the common good. Anyone can take up space. Here's the test of a leader: when he leaves office, we should be better off than when he started" (Iacocca, 2007, p. 3). The *Guardian* agrees with what Mr. Iacocca said: "leadership is not about ethnic domination or selfish power equation; it is rather a disposition of moral strength and sacrifice to genuinely carry out a mission for the common good. It is doing well what leaders have sworn to do for their country" (*Guardian*, January 25, 2016).

Deborah Rhode added to the quality of required leadership: "Leaders must be able to inspire, not just compel or direct those who work under them" (Rhode, 2017, p. 1607). In all, researchers propound the theory that leadership converges around five areas: "Values (such as integrity, honesty, trust, and ethic of service); personal skills (such as self-awareness, self-control, self-direction, persistence, and conscientiousness); interpersonal skills (such as social awareness, empathy, persuasion, and conflict management); vision (such as being forward-looking and inspirational); substantive competence (such as knowledge, preparation, and judgment)" (Rhode, 2017, pp. 1609–1610).

However, Nigerian leaders' approach to leadership is unfortunately at variance with the leadership best practices described in the foregoing quoted statements. For, Nigerian leaders behave as if the principles of good governance are alien to Nigerian cultural practices, as if the values of accountability and transparency are ideas of the West and nowhere else. Nigerian leadership character and profile have been consistently inept, garbage-in and garbage-out, milquetoast, and "ideologically" (Azikiwe, 1980) fuzzy.

It is no surprise, the *Guardian* of London declared, Nigeria suffers from "accumulated deadwood" (Allison, 2015) leadership. Except for the "one brief shining moment" of purposeful and bold leadership of General Murtala Mohammed (July 1975–February 1976), indeed before he was killed tragically in an unsuccessful military coup, since winning independence from Britain, Nigeria has had successive leadership failures as well as abuses, and this is chiefly "why nothing works" in the country. General Mohammed is fondly remembered because he "embarked on a highly popular purge of the public services" (Commonwealth Secretariat, 2007, p. 6). He also announced to return the country to civil rule in October 1979 following the adoption of a new Constitution and holding of general elections (Commonwealth Secretariat, 2007, p. 6). Moreover, the assassinated leader fought corruption by personal example. As Head of State:

> He surrendered to the state his assets acquired by the wrongful use of his office. By this singular and unprecedented act, by his revolutionary ardor to clean up the society of the cankerworm of corruption and, by his sheer zeal and fervor characteristic of one waging a religious war, he was able to create faith in the crusade among the various sectors and levels of the Nigerian society. People were simply propelled to take a cue from him and join the bandwagon of the

> crusade. Within just six months, the mighty edifice of corruption began to crumble. But, alas, he and his awe-inspiring anti-corruption efforts were silenced by the assassin's bullet. With General Mohammed's demise, the eradication of corruption was also eclipsed, not for want of anti-corruption measures, but mainly because the successive rulers, both military and civilian, were not prepared to make example of themselves as corruption-free leaders, as General Mohammed had done. (Nwabueze, 2015)

Consequently, Nigeria reverted or turned to a "corruption friendly nation" status and, in turn, the entire system became the leadership of the corrupt, by the corrupt, and for the corrupt. In a published piece in the U.S.-based *Washington Post*, prior to meeting with President Obama at the White House in the summer of 2015, President Buhari decried Nigeria's leadership morass and vices in the following words:

> There are too few examples in the history of Nigeria since independence where it can be said that good management and governance were instituted at a national level. This lack of a governance framework has allowed many of those in charge, devoid of any real checks and balances, to plunder. The fact that I now seek Obama's assistance in locating and returning $150 billion in funds stolen in the past decade and held in foreign bank accounts on behalf of former, corrupt officials is testament to how badly Nigeria has been run. This way of conducting our affairs cannot continue. (*Washington Post*, July 20, 2015)

All the factors that have impeded Nigeria's progress are tied to and rooted in hooey leadership. This destructive moral crime has taken a serious toll on the country and inflicted incalculable harm on the people. Nigeria is blessed with fertile soil, abundant resources, talented and energetic population, and ought to be Africa's giant. Yet, Nigeria is not only an "underperformer," but she is also in the words of Wole Soyinka "the open sore of a continent [Africa]" (Soyinka, 1997).

Poll after poll agrees with the quotations from Chinua Achebe, Karl Maeir, and Ray Ekpu at the beginning of the chapter. In recent surveys, for example, NOI Polls (a Nigerian opinion survey research agency that partners with the Gallup Poll, USA) reported that an "overwhelming majority (88%) of Nigerians believe that the country is not better off today than it was at independence in 1960, and another 72% do not think that the vision of the founding fathers have been achieved in the first 100 years of Nigerian history" (NOI Polls, 2012, 2013). (In 1914, the British colonial administration unified the Northern and Southern Protectorates of Nigeria to form the single entity of Nigeria.) Concurrently, "the broad masses of Nigerians," argued

Chidi Amuta, a journalist, "hold the government and those who drive it in irredeemable disdain" (Amuta, 2013).

State Failure Theory and the Nigerian Leadership

Samuel Huntington wrote in his remarkable book, *Political Order in Changing Societies*: "The most important political distinction among countries, concerns not their form of government but their degree of government [leadership]" (Huntington, 1968, p. 1). While this say may not be directed at Nigeria per se, it does emphasize the centrality "of a coherent, capable state." The Nigerian leadership crisis will be analyzed from the view of the state failure theory. This is because according to Adebanwi and Obadare (2010, p. 379): "Nigeria offers a magnificent template for examining the chronic schizophrenia that characterizes the African postcolonial state and the resulting social (de)formations that (re)compose, and are, in turn, (re) composed by, the state." In addition, state failure theory is applied to diverse cultures and nations and there is abundant body of empirical data and literature by which it can be tested and analyzed (Peters, 2015; Eriksen, 2011; Le Grand, 1991). Furthermore, it is expected that the Nigerian leadership should work consistently and spare no efforts to satisfy the needs and interests of its citizens based on the constitutional provision that the "security and welfare of the people shall be the primary purpose of government" (Nigerian Constitution 1999, Chapter II, Fundamental Objectives and Directive Principles of State Policy, 14(b)). In other words, suffice it to allude to Aristotle, "the state is the highest form of community and aims at the highest good . . . the ultimate object of the state is the good life" (Aristotle, *Politics*, Book 1, Chap 1, 2, p. 31).

From 1960 to 1999, Nigeria had eight military coups with attendant ills. Topping the list of the factors that have continued to generate feelings of hopelessness and pessimism among the citizenry is the complete failure of leadership in almost all the political and military leaderships, wrapped in the warped legacy of corruption and elite unholy machinations. One common denominator of all the past leaderships has been greed, with Murtala Mohamed exception.

In a June 2015 wide-ranging cover article on Nigeria, the *Economist* (June 20, 2015) posited:

> Various civilian governments elected amid great optimism soon degenerated into instruments of patronage and graft. They, in turn, were overthrown by military dictators promising to root out corruption and restore Nigeria to greatness. Yet the generals, too, soon discovered a taste for the good life and found that greasing the right palms could make it even better.

Consequently, each successive leadership sees public office not only as a means to "chop" (in Nigerian slang) (Human Rights Watch, 2007), but also as a personal calling card charged at tax-payers' expense with reckless abandon.

Above all, it is inexcusable that successive Nigerian leadership has obdurately failed to use the vast resources and oil wealth of the country as a game changer to broaden opportunity, narrow inequality, advance general welfare, generate wealth, innovate the economy, and sustain economic growth and prosperity. And by so callously acting, the leaderships have continued to create persistent poverty. Worse, in spite of rebasing of Nigeria's GDP in 2014 from ₦42.4 trillion to ₦80.2 trillion ($510 billion, to become Africa's largest economy) and 20 years of civil rule that is supposed to bring "democratic dividend" and make people lives better, the World Bank lists Nigeria among the "five severely poor countries in which two-thirds of the world's extremely poor are concentrated" (Udo, 2014). (The other four "severely poor" countries are India, China, Bangladesh, and the DRC) (Famuti, 2014).

Hope Betrayed—Knucklehead as Leaders

In 2010, leaders of Amnesty International, a London-based nongovernmental human rights organization, proclaimed:

> When Nigeria threw off the chains of colonialism, the country was looked to as a beacon of hope and progress in Africa. A country of enormous energy and potential, Nigeria seemed destined to lead the continent to a bright future, one which recognized the inherent dignity and equal and inalienable right for all. Yet, despite some advances, fifty years later it seems the expectations at independence remain largely unfulfilled. (Amnesty International, 2010)

In its October 1, 2019, editorial marking Nigeria's 59th independence anniversary, the *Punch* newspaper wrote: "Nigeria is a truncated dream . . . tottering edifice . . . representing poverty" (*Punch*, October 1, 2019). In December 2019, Theophilus Danjuma, former minister of defense, declared, "the nation is in a big hole" emanating from "governance collapse" (Oyewale, 2019).

Amnesty International, the *Punch*, and Danjuma are not alone in their assessments. In 2015, the *Economist* stated as well:

> Five-and-a-half decades ago, when Nigeria elected its first government at the end of colonial rule, many expected the country to rise quickly to become Africa's leading power. It had people in abundance, the region's best universities and vast natural resources. It exported great pyramids of peanuts, was one of the world's leading sources of cotton and was soon to become Africa's biggest producer of oil. Yet within a few years its hopes were dashed. Nigeria

> suffered the first of many military coups in 1966 and was torn apart by civil war the next year. Corruption spread rapidly, hollowing out institutions and preventing the government from providing even basic services. After decades of theft and misrule, the most populous nation in Africa, and its biggest economy, has come perilously close to fragmentation. (*The Economist*, June 20, 2015)

Also, in a lecture at the University of Benin in October 2015, Walter Carrington, former American ambassador to and a keen observer of the Nigerian scene, lamented the benighted state of Nigeria thus:

> Nigeria has always been portrayed as the country of the future but that future, sadly, never seems to arrive. . . . The oil boom which once lubricated a growing economy turned from a blessing to a curse. Most of the great wealth it provided was embezzled by government officials and their cronies. While the citizens of other oil producing countries prospered, Nigeria became the only member of OPEC to be listed among the world's poorest countries. (Carrington, 2015)

Amnesty International, *Punch*, Danjuma, the *Economist*, and Carrington have, undoubtedly, further confirmed that Nigeria is a nation at risk. On the attainment of independence, Nigerians hoped and the world was full of expectation that this potentially great country and economic powerhouse would be a bellwether and shining example to other African countries. Indeed as a beacon of democracy and responsible leadership. In fact, America's *Time* magazine of December 5, 1960 (p. 20) predicted: "In the long run, the most important and enduring face of Africa might well prove to be that presented by Nigeria." But it was not to be as reality has not matched independence aspirations. Instead of becoming an inspiring model for Africa, Nigeria has become a failed and "perverted state" (Young, 1994, p. ix). ("Perverted state" is a phrase coined by the African expert American scholar, Crawford Young, to describe African countries that went into "disarray and decay" after colonial rule.) (Examples of the "perverted" or "weak" state in the literature include but not limited to Jackson & Rosberg, 1982; Benthuysen, 2015; Reno, 2006; Zartmann, 1995.)

The political leaders, instead of pursuing policies that would make Nigeria great, have adopted a personal survival ruling style and made the accumulation of wealth through corruption and mismanagement the goal of public service. They have aided and abetted political lawlessness and violence as a means of grabbing and retaining power. Nigeria's complex political and constitutional framework started to unravel soon after independence (Commonwealth, 2007). Also, Chinua Achebe pointed out the following:

> Nigeria was rocked by one crisis after another in the years that followed independence. First the Nigerian census crisis of 1963–64 that shook the nation, then the Federal election crisis of 1964, which was followed by the Western Nigeria election crisis of 1965 which threatened to split the country at its seams. (Achebe, 2012, p. 64)

The Nigerian situation got so bad that the military had to intervene to 'restore' order in a coup of January 15, 1966, which was led by Major Chukwuma Nzeogwu. Not only did the coup terminate the First Republic and claimed the lives of leading political figures, including the Federal prime minister, Abubakar Tafawa Balewa; Ahmadu Bello, premier of Northern Region; Samuel Akintola, premier of Western Region, but it also set the stage for the series of harrowing events that would visit the country later. And despite the fact that the ethnic composition of the mutineers and victims led some to suspect that the coup was an attempt to establish Igbo supremacy, but initial reactions favored the new regime, because of the disillusionment with the corruption, favoritism, and disorder associated with the civilian leadership (Nafziger, 1972, p. 224).

In spite of the bitter experience triggered by the mistakes of the First Republic, successive Nigerian leaderships have not learned their lessons. There has been a continuing pattern of one failed leadership after another since that fateful day of January 15, 1966. The regimes of Shehu Shagari, Ibrahim Babangida, and Sani Abacha are illustrative.

Shehu Shagari

General Gowon was forced out of power in 1975 by a coup led by General Murtala Mohammed, which was short lived. Upon the assassination of General Mohammed in 1976, his deputy, General Olusegun Obasanjo, took over and quickly organized a transition to civil rule program, conducted elections, and handed over power to Shehu Shagari in 1979, ushering into power Nigeria's Second Republic (1979–1983). Shagari, who had preferred to be called "the senator from Sokoto State" instead of President, was so overwhelmed by the responsibilities of the presidency that he virtually delegated all responsibilities to his aides, who ran the show. Like Emperor Nero of ancient Rome, President Shagari "slept" while Nigeria burned. *Newswatch* magazine (May 20, 1985 p. 10) wittingly put it in the following words:

> Shagari could not halt the drift. His idea of leadership was simplistic: leave everyone severely alone to do as he wishes and there will be happiness and satisfaction in the land. . . . He left problems alone. Where he should be decisive, he vacillated; where he should be courageous, he weakened; where he should

> act, he appealed. . . . He did not have the intellectual flexibility or the vision of a charismatic leader or the strength of character of a committed visionary to see him through. . . . He did not like the grind, he preferred the grandeur of office. He took the path of least resistance, and molded the presidency in his own image. . . . Shagari, like Pontius Pilate, was afraid of responsibility. Although he was the executive President, he preferred not to be held responsible for anything.

President Shagari's incompetence extended to the management of the economy. On his watch Nigeria's foreign reserves plunged from $8 billion to less than $1 billion, external debt jumped from roughly $4 billion to $15 billion (Diamond, 1984, p. 908). And by the time President Shagari was toppled on December 31, 1983, by General Muhammadu Buhari, it was believed that Nigeria was more than six months and $5 billion in arrears on short-term payments to creditors and suppliers (Diamond, 1984, p. 908).

Ibrahim Babangida

For eight years (1985–1993), General Ibrahim Babaginda ruled Nigeria. While Babangida has denied accusations leveled at him by others, including President Buhari, the *Guardian* (August 2, 2016) wrote that "the world now knows that Nigeria, the largest black nation on earth was nothing more than a toy in the hands of military officers in that era." Instead of reversing the claimed "deep tide of disillusionment and disgust," Babangida worsened the situation and earned himself the unflattering sobriquet, of "evil genius." The regime of General Babangida was allegedly seen as the body that legalized corruption in Nigerian politics (Ijewereme, 2015; Ihonvbere, 1991). There were unprecedented allegations of drug trafficking, bank fraud, advance fee scam (419), state-sponsored violence, including the brutal parcel bomb killing of the journalist, Dele Giwa, "government by settlement" (Peters, 1997) patronage. (The number "419" refers to the article of the Nigerian Criminal Code dealing with fraud. "While the scam is not limited to Nigeria, the nation has become associated with this fraud and it has earned an unenviable reputation for being a center of email scam crimes.")

In addition, Babangida aborted the transition program he had initiated by unceremoniously annulling the June 12, 1993, presidential vote ("cost ₦40 billion, equivalent of ₦2.4 trillion in today's money") (*Vanguard*, November 30, 2014) believed to have been won by Moshood Abiola, which torched off a national political crisis, and he finally exited power ("stepped aside") under controversial circumstances after installing Interim National Government (ING) on August 27, 1993, headed by Ernest Shonekan. Osaghae (1998) called the Babangida transition program "endless" (p. 223) and "tortuous"

(p. 241). Overall, it is believed that Babangida bequeathed a sad legacy on several fronts. He oversaw a budget deficit of 10% of the GDP, an external debt service that gulped a quarter of export earnings, annual inflation rate estimated at 70–100% in June 1993, and real per capita income 10 times less than what it was when he took office (*The Economist*, August 21, 1993). Before Babangida left power, he reportedly pardoned and rehabilitated those found guilty of corruption by both the Mohammed/Obasanjo and Buhari/Idiagbon regimes by restoring the stolen properties that had been confiscated from them (Ihonvbere, 1991, p. 27).

Sani Abacha

The late dictator, General Sani Abacha, ruled Nigeria from 1993 to 1998, which continued the leadership disaster in Nigeria. Abacha was recognized on the world stage for his audacious brutality (Robinson, 2012; Kaufman, 1998; Kalu, 2006; Block, 1998). He did more of stealing than governing. He also epitomized what Jackson and Rosberg (1982) called "personal rule in Black Africa" and his domestic policies were oppressive if not sadistic, while his foreign policy thrust was isolationist and confrontational. His governing style was "repressive, dictatorial, and corrupt" (Agbese, 1999, p. 63). Abacha "brought out the worst in Nigerian politics: repression, intimidation, violence, corruption, betrayals, and the manipulation of primordial loyalties" (Ihonvbere, 1996, p. 193). Analysts have long concluded that Abacha's regime will always "live in infamy" in the annals of Nigerian history (Kraxberger, 2004; Oba, 2004). A 2010 World Bank report stated: "During the military regime of General Sani Abacha from 1993 to 1998, Nigeria reached its nadir. Corruption was rife and most economic and social indicators deteriorated" (World Bank, 2010, p. 12).

General Abacha came to power in November 1993 through a palace coup that replaced Ernest Shonekan's ING. Like others before him, he had promised to make Nigeria better, but only to do the complete opposite. His appetite for misrule, brutality, theft, and corruption was so legendary that he could only have rivaled such former ruthless dictators as Idi Amin of Uganda, Augusto Pinochet of Chile, Ferdinand Marcos of the Philippines, and Mobutu of Zaire (now DRC) (*Newswatch*, October 5, 1998). The taciturn Abacha spared no efforts to use state power to harass, intimidate, silence, and punish his critics (*Newswatch*, October 5, 1998). He oversaw widespread and systematic policy of human rights violations including detention without charge or trial, torture, arbitrary arrests, and persecution on political grounds, especially of the press, opposition figures, and human rights activists considered threat to his regime (*Newswatch*, October 5, 1998). He institutionalized practice of terror, including alleged state-sponsored assassinations and extrajudicial killings of perceived opponents—in 1995, Kudirat Abiola, the wife of presidential claimant, Moshood Abiola, was murdered; Alfred Rewane, democracy advocate killed; attempted murder of Alex Ibru, head of the *Guardian*, an opposition newspaper; attempted assassination of Abraham Adesanya, democracy activist (*Newswatch*, October 5, 1998). All the more reason, no surprise, Wole Soyinka described Abacha as "a murderer and thief of no redeeming quality" and "a man who placed this nation under siege during an unrelenting reign of terror" (Soyinka, 2014).

The case of the playwright and minority rights advocate, Ken Saro-Wiwa, was a classic example of one of the many killings and judicial aberrations engineered by General Abacha. In 1995, Saro-Wiwa and eight of his colleagues in the Movement for the Survival of Ogoni People organization were executed after a show trial for alleged murders over protests of oil exploration related ecological devastation on their Ogoni homeland. In fact, Abacha's regime was totally catastrophic and adversarial to the Nigerian people. *Newswatch* (October 5, 1998) asserted:

> Sani Abacha's administration was perhaps the world's most excellent example of how not to govern. His leadership lacked visibility, articulateness, compassion or sense of duty. . . . To him the welfare of the people meant next to nothing. Gross shortages of essential goods and facilities did not command his supreme attention. Only his security did. And by hindsight, his gargantuan appetite for illegal wealth accumulation.

In Nigeria, corruption is entrenched and political power means access to oil money, and the Abacha regime was no exception. Abacha combined political repression with massive corruption and rapacious greed (Rupert, 1998; Ige, 2002; Enweremadu, 2013; French, 1998). He was Commander-in-Chief as well as Commander-in-Thief. Abacha was alleged to have stolen the equivalent of 2–3% of Nigeria's GDP for each year that he was Head of State (UNODC, 2008).

Although high-level corruption is as Nigeria as *garri* (*garri* is a common Nigerian food made from cassava tubers), General Abacha fundamentally altered the dynamics by reserving the biggest slice of the cake for himself, family members, and his inner circle. While the health of the nation's economy and "essential facilities" deteriorated, Abacha and his surrogates were busy stealing, squandering, and wasting state resources. Summarily, fraud and abuse of public trust were the hallmarks of Abacha's administration. The American *New York Times*, for example, reported that General Abacha "plundered Nigeria with single minded zeal, and may have stashed more than $3 billion in overseas banks in less than five years in office, closely equivalent to the amount that Mobutu of Zaire took decades to accumulate."

In September 1999, after his death in June 1998, the Nigerian Government formally accused Abacha of "systematically plundering the Central Bank and hiding the money in overseas accounts." During a trip to Switzerland in June 2000, then president Obasanjo indicated that "Abacha and his entourage illegally transferred abroad estimated $3 billion of public funds, of which more than $1.8 billion has been traced to and frozen in various European countries, especially in Switzerland." Some specifics have emerged:

In November 1998, the Nigerian Government announced the recovery of more than $600 million from the Abacha family, being part of the money the authorities believed the family acquired illegally (*Vanguard*, November 9, 1998). Also recovered from the Abacha family during this period was another £75 million and ₦252 million in addition to choice properties in Abuja and Lagos as well as holdings in Sierra Leone refineries valued at $420,000 (*Vanguard*, November 9, 1998). In addition, the Nigerian people have nothing to show for the estimated ₦4.1 billion that General Abacha disbursed to the Family Economic Advancement Program, a former pet project of his wife (*Vanguard*, November 10, 1998). In December 1999 and January 2000, Switzerland froze $550 million and $645 million, respectively, in accounts belonging to Abacha (*BBC News*, January 21, 2000). In May 2000, Luxembourg authorities confiscated another $600 million in bank accounts linked to Abacha (*BBC News*, May 9, 2000). In June 2000, Nigeria asked Liechtenstein (located between Germany and Switzerland) to block "more than $150 million in accounts listed for Abacha's family" (*New York Times*, June 20, 2000). On July 5, 2,000 Liechtenstein authorities froze another $500 million in bank deposits owned by General Abacha (*Post Express*, July 7, 2000).

In 2008, Switzerland reportedly announced that it has returned $550.5 million to Nigeria being stolen money stashed away by General Abacha (Oyedele, 2008). Leading up to 2008, Nigeria had recovered $800 million from domestic institutions of the estimated $3–$5 billion Abacha was believed to have stolen during his regime (Oyedele, 2008). In March 2014, the U.S. government announced that it has frozen $458 million stolen by Abacha and his accomplices, laundered through U.S. banks and stashed away in foreign bank accounts (*Punch*, March 6, 2014). The U.S. government charged that "General Abacha was one of the most notorious kleptocrats in memory, who embezzled billions from the people of Nigeria, while millions lived in poverty" (*Punch*, March 6, 2014). In March 2015, Switzerland indicated that she would return $380 million Abacha's loot to Nigeria (Asu, 2015).

Furthermore, General Abacha steered lucrative government contracts, especially fuel importation to benefit him, family, and cronies. In one instance, General Abacha preferred (because of price markup for personal gains) to spend $420 million on imported fuel instead of spending $300 million to keep local refineries in good working condition (*Post Express*, November 19, 1998). Economist and then chairman, National Economic Intelligence Committee, Samuel Aluko, had lamented that "some prominent Nigerians were making more than $100,000 per day per cargo of imported fuel" (*Newswatch*, May 7, 2000).

Analytical Backdrop and Implications of Shagari, Babangida, and Abacha Regimes

From the foregoing discussion, while bad leaderships (except for the "one brief shining moment" of Murtala Mohammed) have been part of Nigerian history since independence, none compares to the leadership incompetence, corruption, "out of control government extravagance" (Herskovits, 1984, p. 171), economic mismanagement, political crisis, and brutality of the regimes of Shagari, Babangida, and Abacha (Diamond, 1984; Rupert, 1998; Othman, 1984; Ekwe-Ekwe, 1985; Ihonvbere, 1987; Herskovits, 1984, Olukoshi & Abdulraheem, 1985; Agbese, 2012; Mahmud, 1993; Momoh, 1996; Nwankwo, 1993; Nnadozie, 1995; Arowosegbe, 2017; Obadare, 1999; Amuwo, 2002; Mimiko, 1995; Agbese, 1999; Enweremadu, 2013; Ogbondah, 2000; Ihonvbere, 1996; Ijomah, 2000). As such, the leaderships deserve to be discussed in this book because, first, to provide more insight and balance into the relationship between leadership and the political economy of underdevelopment in Nigeria, and in the process provide additional analytical framework, which can help to explain and enunciate the worsening Nigerian leadership crisis and development challenges.

Second, the impact of the leadership failures, or, what sociologists William Julius Wilson and Robert Aponte (1985, p. 234) referred to as "fatalistic attitudes" of the referenced administrations on the Nigerian people, is possibly higher than what is currently available in the literature. In light of this, this book will further illuminate on the leadership misadventures of the particular administrations with implications for public policy and constructive debate. Third, as Chabal and Daloz (1999, p. xvii) argued pertinently in their critically acclaimed book, *Africa Works: Disorder as Political Instrument*, there is "need to attempt to explain what is actually happening on the ground in Africa [Nigeria], however unpalatable it may be." In other words, the "Africanization of the study of politics [leadership] on the continent may perhaps be a vital precondition for the understanding of the contemporary African [Nigeria] political scene" (Chazan, 1978, p. 15). Consequently, it is understood that there is a link between the post-colonial African leadership experience and the unparalleled leadership incompetence, political crisis, corruption, abuses, and brutality that trailed the Shagari, Babangida, and Abacha regimes. As such, an examination of the regimes in concert with the broader

African leadership crisis compels the need to understand what "happens on the ground" in Nigeria, and by extension, provides a logical template to further guide and help explain the continuing pattern of leadership crisis, abject poverty, and widespread failures of development in Nigeria, in spite of her abundant resources and oil wealth.

The two premises of Chabal and Daloz's work are: "(1) the present day crisis, or more broadly disorder in Africa [Nigeria] is a crisis of modernity, and (2) this crisis of modernity is rooted in the deep history of the societies in which it is taking place" (Chabal & Daloz, 1999, p. xviii), and invariably they are normal and an integral part of the algorithm of the African leadership process. The authors called their propositions the "political instrumentalization of disorder" (Chabal & Daloz, 1999, p. xviii), meaning, "the process by which political actors in Africa [Nigeria] seek to maximize their returns on the state of confusion, uncertainty, and sometimes even chaos, which characterizes most African politics" (Chabal & Daloz, 1999, p. xviii), and in the process have made "mere survival all but impossible for ordinary people throughout Africa" (Ake, 1993, p. 240).

Additionally, the "political instrumentalization disorder" theory predicates that the realpolitik in Africa vis-à-vis Nigeria is that "what all African States share is a generalized system of patrimonialism and acute degree of apparent disorder, as evidenced by a high level of governmental and administrative inefficiency, a lack of institutionalization, a general disregard for the rules of the formal political and economic sectors, and a universal resort to personalized and vertical solutions to societal problems" (Chabal & Daloz, 1999, p. xix). In essence, the acute misrule, corruption, paternalism, abuses, political turmoil, and brutality that thrived under and was used by the Shagari, Babangida, and Abacha leaderships as a governance strategy to control and perpetuate themselves in power is preordained and acceptable in Africa, and by implication the sine qua non of the political game in Africa, as opposed to the Western "do the right thing" imposed model of governance in Africa influenced by colonialism.

All in all, the major strength of and the overarching contribution of Chabal and Daloz's work to the current literature on African leadership lies in its "empirical analysis on civil society, recycled elites, and corruption, in a succinct" (Dorman, 2001, p. 182) manner. Another "stimulating" strength of the book is that it "challenges the premises underlying Western development assistance to Africa" (Gerhart, 1999). The challenge question is, "why have most African countries failed to develop, despite economic and political reforms tied to new aid infusions" (Gerhart, 1999). In response, the authors wrote, "Africa's informal but durable and culturally rooted 'neopatrimonial' political systems is not dependent on development assistance in the Western sense—and may even be threatened by it" (Gerhart, 1999). Rather, as African leaders navigate the challenges induced by "structural adjustment," globalization, and "eroding law and order, they devise ways to translate social disorder into patronage resources that shore up the loyalty of their client networks" (Gerhart, 1999) and bases of support.

In addition, while "modernization" is occurring (but not of the kind envisaged by the West), the authors contend, "it is an illusion to believe that civil society, opposition parties, or concerns about good governance can undermine the viability of neopatrimonialism" (Gerhart, 1999) in Africa. As a result, in the face of widespread poverty and political disorder, deductively, no matter how inimical neopatrimonialism is to the common good in Africa, neopatrimonialism still works, attracts, and resonates in the African continent, because of its ingrained and broad acceptance by political actors and their loyalists. Put another way, "the political complexion of Africa's predicament and failure to develop has made individuals, communities and societies in Africa to adapt to a situation in which development has not taken place" (Chabal & Daloz, 1999, p. 93).

Chabal and Daloz's core argument that "Africa works" is according to Dorman (2001, p. 181) "both intriguing and probably valid," because it assumes that "if the system did not benefit the elites, it will not last" (Dorman, 2001, p. 181) and Nigeria is no exception. In a sense, despite the assertion that the book articulated "well-focused argument" (Gerhart, 1999), Chabal and Daloz's theory impairs "our understanding of African politics to describe the continent as retarded, dysfunctional, or otherwise inoperative" (Dorman, 2001, p. 181), and in the process reinforces the "brutalist tradition" (Dorman, 2009, p. 10) and "post-colonial governance imbroglio" (Wong, 2012, p. 66) notions of African politics. Furthermore, not only that it perpetuates the "pervasive Afro-pessimism" in the popular culture and media, but also, it is mute on and dismissive of "reformist aspirations" (Dorman, 2001, p. 181) in Africa. In addition, "the normalization of current African politics" inherently reinforces the bleak "preconceptions" about African leadership, as it also "ignores the fact there are many who do not benefit; trickle-down patronage, like trickle-down economics, is not inclusive or equitable" (Dorman, 2001, p. 181). More so, it inherently doubles down on what back in 1968, Lofchie (1968, p. 3) described as a flawed "implicit premise that the survival of civil institutions could be taken for granted in Africa" without risking "decay and breakdown." Moreover, it is contemptuous of the "consent among pan-African scholars that the state in Africa has neither protected the welfare of its citizens, nor delivered what was expected to its people" (Wong, 2012, p. 66). Chabal and Daloz are not alone.

Jean-Francois Bayart's seminal work *The State in Africa: The Politics of the Belly* echoed similar sentiments as Chabal and Daloz's. Bayart's book harped on what he called "the historicity of the African state" (Bayart, 1993,

p. viii), meaning that "modern African politics can only be understood in relation to long-established traditions of government on the continent" (Clapham, 1994, p. 433). By this construct, Chabal (1993, p. 23) inferred that the specific ethos of government and politics in Africa include but not are limited to "ethnicity, kinship, clientelism, witchcraft—which are self-evidently important to understanding politics in Africa." In this scenario, it would be counterintuitive and "deeply unfashionable" (Dorman, 2009, p. 11) to think of governance and how best to understand contemporary African politics without acknowledging these traditions and ethos. Furthermore, the idea is that the attempt to understand contemporary African politics must contend with these provisos because according to Chabal while the

> consensus today is that Africa is in crisis . . . much of what has hitherto passed for an explanation of African politics has often failed meaningfully to account for what has actually happened in Africa since independence. It is necessary because failures of understanding have practical consequences. Where understanding dissolves, prejudice thrives. Where prejudice thrives, the lives of ordinary people become opaque. (Chabal, 1993, p. 3)

The kernel of Bayart's argument rests on the premise of

> entire rejection of externally imposed models of "dependency" and "modernization," "downplaying the influence of colonialism, regarding the African state as the authentic expression of a "governmentality" which are deeply rooted in African historical experience. African states, in short, must be seen in their own terms, as the product of their own societies, and not merely as failed attempts to reproduce some model of government designed elsewhere" (Clapham, 1994, p. 434), or political correctness soundbites imported from the West.

Another pillar of Bayart's "politics of the belly" thesis is that in Africa, for the most part leadership revolves around the use of political power by the ruling elite to "gain access to wealth and control over economic resources" (Clapham, 1994, p. 435), and by implication perpetuate what the philosopher, Karl Marx, called "primitive accumulation," "a process dependent upon the extraction of [resources] from and exploitation of the poor" (Millar, 1978, p. 384) without compunction. Alas, anything to the contrary is deemed antithetical to and a departure from the African political tradition, and therefore unworkable, or, as Chabal and Daloz (1999, p. 95) aptly put it, "a self-evidently reprehensible deviation from a politically legitimate state of affairs" in Africa and Nigeria.

By way of specific illustration, Bayart's "politics of the belly" thesis resonates clearly with the disingenuous philosophy of "stomach infrastructure" politics in Nigeria, which has the attributes of "politics of the belly," manifested intensely in abject poverty, corruption, bad leadership, arrested development, and the "privatization and criminalization of public authority" (Martin, 2000, p. 178) in Nigeria. Since the discussion and analysis of Nigeria's developmental and leadership challenges are at the heart of this book, it would be interesting to briefly discuss the "stomach infrastructure" phenomenon in Nigeria because it will be immensely revealing, and simultaneously bring to sharp focus the real import of "what is actually happening on the ground in Africa [Nigeria]," pertinent to Nigeria's leadership crisis, disorganization, and rampant poverty. In addition, the trouble with Africa is also understood to illustrate the trouble with Nigeria (Pierce, 2006, p. 887), because, with about 20% of the sub-Saharan Africa population (1.107 billion, Nigeria 200,963,599) (World Bank, 2020) Nigeria appears as the representative of Africa.

The central argument of "stomach infrastructure" politics in Nigeria is that "given the patrimonial, and hence corrupt, nature of power, African [Nigerian] politics extends the metaphor of eating and the belly into a solid framework of clientelist vertical relationships—between clients and patrons—that consumes national resources" (Olaopa, 2019). Continuing, Olaopa contended

> "this politics, in history, is defined by the collusion of the legal and the illegal, the amalgam of the public and the private enterprises, the prominence of corruptive behaviors like bribery to facilitate transactions, and the private aggrandizement of public funds and resources. All this speaks to the necessities of surviving a hostile political environment; and using politics as a means to do so" by the Nigerian leadership at the sufferings of the Nigerian people.

Put another way, in dismay, Nigerian leadership has been "reduced to harvesting state resources as payoffs to secure support from societal power brokers" (Lemke, 2003, p. 126) and compradors while the nation drifts.

Overall, Chabal and Daloz and Bayart's works made invaluable contributions to "theory-building" to help address, especially, what Dorman (2009, p. 17) called the "weakness of theory in the political science and political studies of Africa," and in the process provided "a viable theoretical lens" (Wong, 2012, p. 67) for interpretive analytical framework of contemporary African politics grounded in the internal political and cultural logic of Africa. In addition, relevant to what the scholar, Ali Mazrui, referred to as the "African condition" (e.g., poverty, corruption, inefficiency, instability, wars, and strives), they further brought to bear to a wider persuasion the argument that "modern African politics can only be understood in relation to long-established traditions of government on the continent" (Clapham, 1994, p. 433).

The drawbacks to their works lie first and foremost, suggestively, on the cliché that Africa is inherently chaotic, programmed to fail, and that disaster and bad governance are Africa's destiny. In an unfortunate normative sense, "Africa has always been" perceived "and most obviously continues to be" viewed as the "backward or the barbarous continent" (Chabal & Daloz, 1999, p. 141). In essence, inasmuch the politics of the belly is pursued and achieved in Africa, and no matter how precarious the situation is, "Africa's political instability, violent political conflict and protractedly bad governance" (Young, 1999, p. 149) can be condoned as a part of the rubric and repertoire of the African governance orthodoxy including Nigeria's.

In conjunction, in its purest form, their works seem to give tacit approval to the "complete lack of morality" (Clapham, 1994, p. 434), "*Criminalization of the State in Africa*" (Bayart, Ellis, & Hibou, 2009), unabashed greed, and patently impunity and unaccountability by African leaders and governments, insofar as it meets their agenda and serves their purposes. Another weakness of the author's arguments is that they were preoccupied with primordial sentiments of leadership and order in Africa, "process rather than structure, the behavior of individuals rather than the role of institutions" (Clapham, 1994, p. 437), interspersed with their rather contested assertions that anything "foreign" is not only at variance with African "particularities," but also inherently contributes to the African distress and dysfunctionality. Furthermore, while their works are "intensely geared to the idea of continuity" (Clapham, 1994, p. 438), they are value neutral, lack sublimation for modernization, more so they are "peculiarly ill-adapted to the analysis of change, and indeed may readily lead its adherents to overlook that any significant change is even taking place" (Clapham, 1994, p. 438) in Africa. Additionally, Clapham (1994, p. 438) argued the "picture is disconcertingly static, and the features that give the politics of post-colonial Africa its dynamism and much of its tension are almost entirely overlooked." Even as Bayart himself grudgingly acknowledged, the "politics of the belly" has "narrow symbiosis with the grassroots which sustain it" (Bayart, 1993, p. 221), "it leads to an idealization of clientele systems, as providing an effective set of linkages between the mass of the population and the holders of political power, and even to a treatment of bribery in terms of the mechanisms of social solidarity, rather than those of elite exploitation" (Bayart, 1993, pp. 218–219).

1999 to the Present—Another Hope Betrayed; Another Missed Opportunity

In Nigeria the betrayal of the nation and its people extends from the Federal level to the State Houses and, indeed, beyond. First, at the Federal level. Prior to 1999, the Nigerian military has ruled the country for all but 10 years since independence. The author Adebanwi (2012, p. 11) puts the issue succinctly below:

> The unprecedented corruption and gross abuse of power exemplified by General Ibrahim Babangida (1985–1993) and General Sani Abacha (1993–1998) eventually convinced Nigerians, who since independence, regarded military intervention as a semi-messianic means of resolving fundamental contradictions in democratic governance, that there was absolutely nothing redeeming about the Nigerian soldiery in power.

Therefore, when the military under then General Abdulsalami Abubakar decided to cede power and return the country to democracy in 1999, Nigerians heaved a sigh of relief, for not only did it meant a fresh start, but also, there was high hopes and renewed optimism that the incoming civilian leaders must have learned their lessons from the mistakes of the past regimes or their leaders, and that this time around they would act right, and do better for the Nigerian people. Therefore, Oko (2005, p. 11) noted:

> The mood of Nigerian society at the end of military dictatorship was understandably ecstatic. Nigerians based their optimism on the premise that democracy offers opportunities, liberties and freedoms unimaginable in a dictatorship. Citizens hoped that democracy would readily translate into respect for rights and liberties and that they would be able to seek justice unburdened by the restraints and limitations imposed by military dictators.

Oko is not alone in his assessment, as the well-known newspaper, *The Guardian*, also wrote the following:

> With the return to civil rule, expectations of Nigerians were high. Against the background of the impunity of the past, they expected the rule of law, where all are equal before the laws of the land; against a tale of election rigging in the past, they expected that votes would count and those truly chosen by the people would emerge as leaders; against massive human rights violation, they expected the veneration of rights; against a history of assassinations even by the state, they expected to see respect for lives and dignity of man; against a background of poor social services, they expected to see working health centers, well-equipped schools, uninterrupted power supply and well-paved roads. (*Guardian*, May 29, 2013)

Meanwhile, a 2012 report indicated that, annually, Nigeria spends over ₦1 trillion ($6.4 billion) to import four commodities: wheat, ₦635 billion; rice, ₦356 billion; sugar, ₦217 billion; and fish, ₦97 billion (*Punch*, November

28, 2012). (According to the Federal Ministry of Agriculture, "Nigeria is the largest importer of rice in the world, spending ₦356 billion per year importing 2.1 million metric tons of milled rice," *Punch*, April 22, 2013.) Worse, food import bills are increasingly consuming more share of Nigeria's national budget amid growing anxiety over oil price slump. Most recently, a 2015 report attributed that the Federal government spent a total of $4 billion (₦813 billion) in 2013 on items which are currently being produced or could be competitively produced locally, representing one-fifth of the nation's total budget of about ₦4 trillion (*This Day*, July 13, 2015). These six items attracted the most expenditures during the period under review: rice ₦752 billion, sugar ₦464 billion, wheat ₦1.5 billion, fish ₦1.3 billion, textile ₦17.4 billion, and furniture ₦31 (*This Day*, July 13, 2015). At a town hall meeting in August 2016 in Abuja, then minister of agriculture, Audu Ogbeh, lamented: "We became importers of rice, $5m a day; wheat, $6m a day; tomato paste, $400m a year; and $20 billion a year on food" (Amaefule, 2016). (Compare to 1948 total import value under £1 million, £0.2 million for sugar and £0.2 million for wheat flour) (*Economic Survey of Nigeria 1959*, p. 23). At the same time, underinvestment in agriculture and rural development more generally has contributed to widespread chronic malnutrition in Nigeria (USAID, 2015, p. 6). (As of June 2021, according to the Hunger and Nutrition Commitment Index (HANCI), a global hunger tracker, Nigeria ranks 32 ("low commitment to tackling hunger and undernutrition"), tie with Cambodia out of 45 countries measured. The countries behind Nigeria are Myanmar (34), Mauritania (35), Mozambique (36), Afghanistan (37), Cameroon (38), Yemen (39), Liberia (40), Lesotho (41), Sudan (42), Angola (43), Guinea-Bissau (44), and Togo (45). South Africa ranked the best (1) while Togo ranked the worst (45).) (The HANCI ranks governments on their political commitment to tackling hunger and undernutrition. The index was created to provide greater transparency and public accountability by measuring what governments achieve, and where they fail, in addressing hunger and undernutrition.)

Meanwhile, in spite of the apparent dangers of high food import bills, growing population, and malnutrition Nigerian leaders continue to pay lip service to food security as agricultural improvement budgets are routinely slashed. For example, agriculture budget for 2013 and 2014 were ₦39.9 billion (1.7% of total budget) and ₦36.2 billion (1.4% of total budget), respectively (*Vanguard*, March 11, 2014). (Compare ₦40 billion allocated for a new banquet hall for National Assembly in the 2014 budget to agriculture's ₦39.9 billion.) This is at odds with the "Maputo Declaration" (African Union, 2003) (Nigeria is a signatory) which requires parties to allocate 10% of national budget to agriculture (African Union, 2003). (At the Second Ordinary Assembly of the African Union in July 2003 in Maputo (Mozambique), African Heads of State and Governments endorsed the "Maputo Declaration on Agriculture and Food Security in Africa," which among other decisions contained "the commitment to allocate at least 10% of national budget to agriculture and rural development policy implementation within five years.")

Adding to the mix is the inability of farmers to procure seeds and fertilizer because of the pest of corruption. In November 2014, the Federal Ministry of Agriculture indicated that between 1980 and 2010, the government lost over ₦776 billion ($4.8 billion), or an average of ₦26 billion ($162 million) annually to corruption in the seed and fertilizer sector (Egba, 2014). Worse, according to the World Bank, Nigerian households spend disproportionate share of 73% of family budget on food (Indonesia 50%, Vietnam 65%, United States 15%) (Odeh, 2008; Agriculture and Agri-Food Canada, 2010) by implication inhibiting savings and by domino effect perpetuating the cycle of economic insecurity and poverty. In a faith accompli stricture, this concurs with the tendency Arthur Lewis (1950, para. 50) had previously noted: "A poor people spend a very high proportion of its income on food and shelter, and only a small proportion on manufactures [and savings]." Moreover, because of farm neglect, the pivotal role of agriculture in support of industrialization especially "to export more agricultural commodities, develop a self-sufficient economy, emphasizing the home market; or to export manufactures" (Lewis, 1984, p. 122) has been harmed.

As earlier noted, the neglect of agriculture in Nigeria was influenced mainly by the discovery of oil in commercial quantity. Not only has crude oil exports' proceeds doubled down since the mid-1960s, it has remained dominant ever since, accounting for more than 85% of total exports receipts (15.8% of GDP) (Central Bank of Nigeria, 2013, p. 232). Also, oil contributes the lion's share of government revenues. In the 2010–2019 recent decade (table 4.1), oil exports receipts accounted for annual average of nearly 60% (₦4,816 billion) portion of Federal revenues, while the non-oil share averaged 42% (₦3,416 billion) yearly during the same period. And by extension, oil share in total GDP is as influential, more than two times higher compared to the non-oil segment, averaging almost 10% yearly as against non-oil's 4.1%, in the 2010–2019 period (table 4.2). Also, inasmuch oil was virtually no part of the equation of Nigerian economy prior to independence, since the growth of the oil industry in the 1970s, it has generated huge wealth and affluence that if it were properly managed, Nigeria could have been a better and more prosperous country. Instead, according to some observers, "millions of Nigerians survive on ingenuity and doggedness as street vendors, curbside fix-it men, subsistence farmers" (Rupert, 1998, p. A01).

Table 4.1 Federation Account Composition of Revenues, 2010–2019 (₦ Billion)

Composition	*Average 2010–2014*	*2015*	*2016*	*2017*	*2018*	*2019*	*Total Average*
Federally collected revenue	9,781	6,913	5,616	7,318	9,552	10,215	8,232
Oil portion	7,181	3,830	2,694	4,110	5,546	5,537	4,816
% oil portion	73	55	48	56	58	54	58
Non-oil portion	2,600	3,082	2,923	3,208	4,006	4,678	3,416
% non-oil portion	27	45	52	44	42	46	42

Source: Central Bank of Nigeria, Annual Reports, Various Years.
Author calculation.

Table 4.2 Oil and Non-Oil Revenue % GDP, 2010–2019

Year	*Oil*	*Non-Oil*
2010	18.3	6.5
2011	25.1	6.3
2012	19.8	6.5
2013	8.4	3.6
2014	7.6	3.7
2015	4.0	3.2
2016	2.7	2.7
2017	3.6	2.5
2018	4.3	3.0
2019	3.8	3.1
Average	9.8	4.1

Source: Central Bank of Nigeria, Annual Report, Various Years.

Nigeria is also seriously lagging in other key social improvement indicators.

A. Quality of Life Decline

Despite the reported growth in the Nigerian economy and the government's claim that the Buhari administration has created 7 million new jobs since inauguration in 2015 (Tukur, 2017), and the rebasing of the GDP from $454 billion in 2012 to $509 billion in 2013 (making Nigeria the largest economy in Africa and 26 largest in the world) (Ujah et al., 2014), "Nigeria is not one of the African countries recording remarkable improvement in its human development index" according to the UN. In 2019 proper, the UNDP *Human Development Index* (HDI) report, for example, ranked Nigeria 161 out of 189 countries covered and listed it as one of the "low human development index" countries (UNDP, *HDI Report 2020*, p. 243). The report listed and categorized Ghana (138), Kenya (143), Zambia (146), Angola (148), Congo (149), Zimbabwe (150), and Cameroon (153), to name a few, as "medium human development index" countries in Africa that made better HDI improvement than Nigeria. Nigerians die young as well, no surprise, noted Nigerian poet and scholar, Niyi Osundare, has said of Nigeria "as that Hobbesian jungle where life is short and nasty and brutish . . . a country which never fails its citizens in its infliction of untimely 'departures'" (Osundare, 2014). Nigeria's life expectancy at 54 is below Libya 73, Egypt 72, Botswana 69, Gabon 66, Kenya 66, Tanzania 65, and Ghana 64 (table 4.3). And with a per capita income of $5,190, Nigeria falls behind Botswana $17,140, Libya $16,130, Equatorial Guinea $14,640, Gabon $14,350, and South Africa $12,670. Also, betraying her oil wealth, more Nigerians live in poverty. With nearly 40% of Nigerians living on less than $1.90 per day, it is higher compared to less or no resource-rich countries such as Cote d'Ivoire 29.8%, Cameroon 26.0%, and Namibia 13.8%, to name a few (table 4.4).

B. Health Care Crisis

Health care infrastructures are at advanced stage of decay characterized by high maternal and infant mortality (WHO, 2019[2]), resurgence of previously eradicated and contained diseases including polio (Global Polio Eradication

Table 4.3 Selected Quality of Life Indicators, 2019*

Country	*Life Expectancy at Birth*	*Infant Mortality Rate/1,000 Live Births*	*Maternal Mortality Ratio/100,000 Live Births*	*Health care Expenditure Per Capita ($)*	*Health care Expenditure % GDP*	*GNI Per Capita, PPP (current $)*
Botswana	69	32	158	483	5.8	17,140
Egypt	72	17	15	126	4.9	11,840
EG	58	60	380	314	3.0	14,640
Gabon	66	31	368	218	2.7	14,350
Ghana	64	34	334	78	3.5	5,530
Kenya	66	32	377	88	5.2	4,430
Libya	73	10	72	310	6.1	16,130
Nigeria	54	74	1,222	84	3.9	5,190
SA	64	28	78	526	8.3	12,670
Tanzania	65	36	642	37	3.6	2,700
Malaysia	76	7	23	427	3.8	28,830
Indonesia	72	20	282	112	2.9	11,970
Singapore	83	2	4	2,824	4.5	92,270

*2019 or the latest available data.
EG = Equatorial Guinea.
SA = South Africa.
Source: World Bank.

Table 4.4 Percent Population Living on Less Than $1.90 per Day, 2018*

Country	%
Nigeria	39.1
Kenya	37.1
Cote d'Ivoire	29.8
Cameroon	26.0
South Africa	18.7
Botswana	14.5
Namibia	13.8
Ghana	13.0
Sudan	12.2
Egypt	3.8
Malaysia	0.0
Indonesia	3.6

*2018 or latest available data.
Source: World Bank.

Initiative (GPEI), n.d.[3]), tuberculosis (USAID, 2015, p. 6[4]), and HIV AIDS (UNAIDS, 2016–2021 Strategy Report[5]), obsolete equipment, lack of essential drugs, shortage of doctors, flawed health policies and the traumas of service disruptions wrought by government inability to negotiate and prevent avoidable medical staff labor disputes, and worsened by poor funding (Adeloye et al., 2017; Akinyemi & Atilola, 2013). Upon that, the primary health care system which is supposed to be the first line of defense on health issues "has not functioned well in decades" according to a recent UNICEF report. The UNICEF report states,

> The primary health care (PHC) system has not functioned well for decades, with bottlenecks in delivery including a lack of necessary commodities, equipment and skilled and motivated workers; challenges in access in remote areas, including lack of delivery points and a referral system; the cost and perceived poor quality of services; lack of awareness of service availability; and inadequate community mobilization. (UNICEF, 2017, p. 3)

The UNICEF is not alone. The *Guardian* newspaper editorial of October 1, 2017, marking Nigeria's 57th independence anniversary reported:

> The health sector remains a nightmare to Nigerians. Hospitals lack equipment to handle even simple, let alone complex cases. As a nation, therefore millions of hard-earned foreign exchange is spent through visits to foreign hospitals. To know that our Teaching Hospitals once had excellent services and treated visiting patients from Asia and Europe is frustrating. These same hospitals are now

> in a state of anomy, barely carrying out routine services. Where did the rains start beating us? Even the President passed a vote of no confidence in the health sector by his own medical checkups and treatment in the U.K.

Consequently, it is no surprise that Nigerians are not only poorer but also sicker, as health outcomes are influenced by level of poverty and funding for health care. Nigeria, for example, spends $84 per capita on health (table 4.3) and has 40% of the population living in extreme poverty gap of less than $1.90 per day (table 4.4), compared to South Africa which spends $526 per person on health care and has only 19% of the population living in extreme poverty gap of less than $1.90 per day. (World Bank has updated the number of people living in extreme poverty from the previous line of $1.25 per day to $1.90 per day.) It is the same for Botswana, which spends $483 per capita on health care, and has just 15% of the people living on less than $1.90 per day.

As a fact, Section 17 of the 1999 Nigerian Constitution obliges the government to provide for "adequate medical and health facilities for all persons." However, Nigerians are denied this constitutionally guaranteed right to good health care on a daily basis, courtesy of the inexcusable neglect of the health care resources, especially public hospitals that cater to the poor and needy (Umukoro, 2013; Welcome, 2011; Obembe, Osungbade, & Ibrahim, 2017). In a February 15, 2014, editorial, the *Vanguard* newspaper wrote: "Our general hospitals and health centers, the health facilities that are generally available to the people are in worsening states of neglect. Apex medical facilities like the National Hospital, Abuja, is not in a better shape. It is a mere glorified version of the public health centers and hospitals that lack the basic facilities they require to function." Also, the *Guardian* newspaper recently reported: "Indeed, that the nation's health sector is nothing to write home about is evident on so many fronts" (*Guardian*, April 1, 2016). *Vanguard*'s and *Guardian*'s opinions on Nigeria's health care crisis are unimpeachable. Majority of Nigerians are poor and rural dwellers. And in the period before and immediately after independence, they relied on efficient and well-equipped neighborhood public hospitals and rural community primary health centers for their health care needs (Tilley-Gyado et al., 2016). But not anymore. Today, these critical-access and safety-net hospitals are empty shells of their glorious past, as neglect and lack of funding have taken their toll, further widening the health gap between rural and urban Nigeria. The *Guardian* (April 1, 2016) also took notice and documented: "The decay in the public healthcare system today is totally different from what obtained in the good old days when there were cottage hospitals, health centers and dispensaries in communities across the country. The colonialists and missionaries bequeathed an old structure that worked. Unfortunately, all of these have been destroyed."

The National Strategic Health Development Plan for 2010–2015 enunciated by the government is geared toward bolstering health care outcomes for Nigerians (Chukwu, 2011). And Nigerian teaching hospitals are supposed to be the linchpin of this endeavor by integrating cutting-edge medicine, hospital services, medical education, and research. However, the "teaching hospitals have chronic challenges" (Adeyi, 2016, p. 287). According to *Newswatch* magazine, Nigerian teaching hospitals "which were meant to be centers of medical excellence" have become "Centers of Decay" and "tragic tale of failure" (Ajero, 2009). Nigerian teaching hospitals lack basic amenities, equipment, and supplies including running water, electricity, drugs, and so on (Ulasi & Ijoma, 2010; Anochie & Eke, 2003; Onwuchekwa, BellGram, & Asekomeh, 2009). Often patients are asked to bring their own sleeping materials, food, water, bandages, soap, cooling fan, lantern, and so on. Part of the problem is that Nigerian teaching hospitals, like other public health care facilities in the country, suffer from poor administration and mismanagement of resources (Okonta & Okonta, 2018; Ojo & Akinwumi, 2015).

A recent report showed that in the nine years through 2011, Federal Government spent over ₦29 billion to refurbish 14 teaching hospitals in the country (*Guardian*, October 17, 2011[6]). Yet,

> the project is far from satisfactory completion . . . the project has not met its promise of providing state-of-the art medical equipment comparable to others in the world. It has not prevented brain drain, stopped Nigerians from going abroad for medical diagnosis and treatment, and has not improved medical training and research. . . . Other problems are irregular power supply which causes the equipment to breakdown frequently; alleged non-compliance with the terms of the contract by the contractor; and some of the equipment are getting obsolete and do not meet modern technological requirement. (*Guardian*, October 17, 2011)

For another reason, when they do not suffer from fiscal maladministration, Nigerian teaching hospitals and other government hospitals lack or have limited funds to operate with (Kress, Su, and Wang, 2016; Odutolu et al., 2016; Essien, et al., 2014). WHO recommends 15% budgetary allocation to health. Nigeria is noncompliant. Nigeria's public spending on health care amounts to just 3.89% of its $448 billion GDP, according to the latest available data from the World Bank (World Bank, 2021). In 2020, for example, Nigeria allocated a total of ₦441 billion ($1.15 billion) to health (Budget Office and BudgIT, 2020, p. 31), representing less than 5% of the total national budget of ₦10.59 trillion ($34.6 billion). Breakdown of the health budget shows that recurrent expenditures (salaries and overhead) consumed a whopping ₦381 billion (86.4%) of the total health budget, while capital expenditures received only ₦59.9 billion (13.6%). Amid mass poverty (40% of Nigerians live on less than $1.90 per day according to World Bank's latest data) and high unemployment (33.3%, among the highest in the world according to NBS, fourth quarter 2020), perhaps more concerning, according to a report by Nigeria Ministry of Health (2009, p. ix), is that "household out of pocket (HH-OOP) payment continues to be a major source of total health expenditures in Nigeria, accounting for over 70% of total health expenditures, and constitute over 95% of all private health expenditures."

Adding to the problem of inadequate funding is unaccountability and poor financial leadership of allocated and donated funds. In 2008, for example, the Federal government set aside ₦6 billion from the MDG fund to facilitate free medical care for children and pregnant women in six states, namely, Gombe, Niger, Sokoto, Bayelsa, Oyo, and Imo (*This Day*, August 21, 2008). In the same year, Federal government approved ₦12.2 billion ($90 million) from the International Development Association (IDA—World Bank fund for poor countries) for Health Systems Development Projects for 22 states in the country and Federal Ministry of Health (Taiwo, 2008). In 2011, the Federal government announced that it would invest ₦4.1 trillion in health care sector over a five-year period (Chukwu, 2011). Since 2003, Global Fund (Geneva-based charity that offers financial grants to fight AIDS, malaria, and tuberculosis) has invested more than $1.4 billion in Nigeria (Global Fund's largest portfolio) (Global Fund, 2016). However, in May 2016, Global Fund, which has granted Nigeria nearly $331 million between 2010 and 2014 alone, suspended its financial support to the country because of "evidence of systematic embezzlement, theft, collusion, and fraudulent practices in the amount of $3.8 million between 2010 and 2014" (Global Fund, 2016). Nigerian officials embezzled grant funds in varying ways including

> inflating the amounts paid to hotel venues for meeting facilities and rooms; falsifying receipts related to Daily Subsistence Allowance entitlements, transportation expenses to and from venues, fuel and stationery; claiming expenditures for travel not taken, colluding with and receiving kickbacks from hotels and suppliers; and inflating the number of attendees at a meeting or training or its duration. . . . Forgery of supporting documents for items such as airline tickets, boarding passes, hotel invoices, and fuel and stationery receipts. Reimbursements were also made to staff and consultants with little or no supporting documentation. Additionally, the investigators found money transfers between staff members within the program, including payments to the program coordinator. (Global Fund, 2016)

At the same time, there is a growing shortage of skilled health care workers in Nigeria (Adedini et al., 2014; Eriki et al., and WHO, 2015; Uneke, et al., 2007; Okeke, 2016). Also medical brain drain is a challenge. It has been reported that 2,000 medical doctors leave Nigeria annually to practice abroad because of better pay and conditions of service (Muanya & Akpan, 2018). Cumulatively, according to a 2017 report, estimated 35,000 Nigerian doctors are practicing abroad out of the 72,000 registered with the Medical and Dental Council of Nigeria (United Kingdom and the United States are the top destinations of migrant physicians) (Obinna, 2017).

Worse, reliable medical emergency ambulance services are virtually nonexistent in Nigeria. If you need emergency ambulance transportation you are simply out of luck. According to a report by the CLEEN Foundation (Abuja-based nongovernmental organization):

> Every year more and more Nigerians die as a result of failure of emergency response system in coming to the aid of victims of road accidents, gunshot injuries and other trauma cases. Though there are flashes of intervention and reform initiatives at both Federal and state levels, these efforts are often under resourced, uncoordinated, too dispersed and not sustained long enough to provide sufficient care for victims. (CLEEN Foundation, 2010, p. vi)

One case is poignant. Thomas Pickering, one of the American diplomats delegation, who was visiting with presidential claimant Abiola when he suddenly took ill and died in June 1998, described Abiola's last moments, saying, "we all helped to put him in a car, there was no ambulance immediately available" (*BBC News*, July 7, 1998).

Instead of improving local health care situations, Nigerian officials are spending a fortune on foreign medical treatment (see bullet points), while the masses are neglected, invariably inducing capital flight, perpetuating health care inequality, and inhibiting access to care. It was the late human rights activist Gani Fawehinmi who once said: "when the rich get sick they fly out, when the poor get sick they go to the herbalist." Even when Nigerian leaders can receive better medical care at home, according to the *Los Angeles Times*, they "disdain Nigeria's best hospital" in favor of overseas medical treatment including for "routine medical tests" (Dixon, 2017). In June 2016, President Buhari spent two weeks in London to treat an ear infection. According to medical experts, "such a simple ailment" could have been treated at the State House Clinic Abuja, a special presidential hospital reputed to be the best in the country (Dixon, 2017). The hospital provides medical care for the president, vice president, their families and staff, and other entitled public servants (State House, Office of the President). The government upgraded the State House Clinic in 2016 at a cost of $16 million, more than the total capital budget for Nigeria's 16 Federal teaching hospitals (Dixon, 2017).

In spite of the huge budgetary allocations to the State House Clinic over the years ("₦3.94 billion in 2015; ₦3.87 billion in 2016, and ₦3.2 billion in 2017 respectively, for upgrading and provision of necessary drugs and equipment") (Ibemere, 2017), it took the revelations by the First Lady, Aisha Buhari, in October 2017, to indicate that the State House Clinic "has no single syringe" and the "X-ray machine don't work" (*Punch*, October 13, 2017).

- President Yar'Adua left Nigeria on November 23, 2009, and was reported to be hospitalized for heart ailment at Saudi Arabia. He returned home on February 24, 2010, he was not seen in public again, and died May 5, 2010.
- In April 2012, then Senate president, David Mark, "returned to Nigeria from Israel where he underwent a medical treatment" (*Daily Trust*, April 25, 2012).
- In February 2013, contrary to earlier claims that she had gone abroad on vacation, then First Lady, Patience Jonathan, disclosed that she "actually underwent nine medical surgeries in Germany" (*Vanguard*, February 17, 2013).
- In September 2012, then governor Sullivan Chime of Enugu State was flown abroad for medical treatment, he "spent 4 months in hospital abroad before returning" (*Daily Times*, March 3, 2013).
- In August 2013, then Taraba governor, Danbaba Suntai, "returned to Nigeria after 10 months of medical treatment overseas after being involved in a plane crash in October 25, 2012" (*Vanguard*, August 25, 2013).
- On April 20, 2013, then Imo governor, Rochas Okorocha, was "flown abroad for further medical treatment after being involved in car crash the previous day" (*Premium Times*, April 20, 2013).
- In 2013, then Cross River governor, Liyel Imoke, "spent 3 months overseas for medical treatment" (*Channels TV*—Nigeria).
- On January 12, 2014, Senator Magnus Abe (PDP-Rivers) was shot in Rivers and was "flown to London for better medication after first aid treatment in two hospitals in Nigeria" (*Vanguard*, January 13, 2014).
- According to a parliamentary inquiry, "between 2004 and 2012, it cost Nigerian taxpayers ₦1.2 billion to sponsor public officials to overseas medical treatment" (*Punch*, January 24, 2014).
- On September 2, 2015, Senator Godswill Akpabio (former governor of Akwa Ibom) was flown overseas for medical treatment after a car accident the day before (*Punch*, September 2, 2015).
- On January 19, 2017, President Buhari left for London on "medical vacation" and returned to Nigeria on March 10, 2017 (*Punch*, May 13, 2017).
- On May 7, 2017, President Buhari left for London (second time) for medical treatment and returned to Nigeria on August 19, 2017 (*Premium Times*, August 19, 2017).
- On March 29, 2021, the presidency announced, "President Buhari will proceed to London, the United Kingdom, Tuesday March 30, 2021, for a

routine medical check-up. He is due back in the country during the second week of April, 2021" (*Premium Times*, March 29, 2021).

According to the Nigerian Medical Association (NMA) and Federal Ministry of Health, Nigeria spends in excess of $500 million annually on overseas medical treatment with the bulk of the expenditures going to India (Adebayo, 2013; Awoyinfa, 2016). In 2013 proper, Nigeria spent about $350 million on health care in India (Oyedele, 2014). Preference for overseas medical treatment is partly associated with Nigeria outdated and deplorable hospital equipment and facilities (Ulasi & Ijoma, 2010; Anochie & Eke, 2003). The NMA has highlighted this problem: "The equipment are still far from what it should be, we have so many obsolete equipment . . . it is unfortunate that even the newer equipment that are being imported, many of them are not entirely new, they are refurbished but they are presented as new" (Adejoro, 2013). The situation is worse at the National Orthopedic Hospital, Lagos, that is supposed to be the best in the country, the equipment are so old to the point that they are seen as "museum specimens" (Odebode, 2008). Education is dire too, especially the bedrock primary and secondary education.

C. Education's Neglect

A 2016 publication by Brookings Institution's education researchers (Rebecca Winthrop and Eileen McGivney) asserted the following:

> Our current world and the changes coming in the future require education to prepare children for a world of rapid change in technology, increasing interconnectedness, and new forms of employment. No longer is the focus on mastering content knowledge sufficient in the age of Google. Thriving in today's fast changing world requires breadth of skills rooted in academic competencies such as literacy, numeracy and science, but also including such things as teamwork, critical thinking, communication, persistence, and creativity. These skills are in fact interconnected. . . . This interplay of skills is central to both the concept of breadth of skills as well as to the educational strategies needed to help young people cultivate them. (Winthrop & McGivney, 2016)

However, current education delivery in Nigeria falls short to help Nigerian children prepare for and make these critical changes (Antoninis, 2014; Odia & Omofonmwan, 2007; Nwagwu, 1997). In 2007, Obiageli Ezekwesili, then minister of education, warned that if the crisis in the education sector is not addressed, it may lead to Nigerian citizens becoming "weapons of mass destruction" (Onuora, 2007). In 2014, the *Punch* newspaper expressed similar concerns to Ezekwesili's seven years prior, and described the situation in Nigerian schools as "teaching without learning" (*Punch*, March 29, 2014). Several reports by the Federal Ministry of Education (FME) and others bear out Ezekwesili's premonition and *Punch*'s observations (Saint, Hartnett, & Strassner, 2003; World Bank, 2001).

Below is one assessment by the FME: "Our public school system is in a very sorry and pitiful state . . . majority of poor children are trapped in a dilapidated, failing public schools lacking the best of knowledge, skills, and values that assure life success" (*This Day*, February 11, 2007). Another source reported:

> Across the country, primary school pupils sit on the bare floor to receive lessons, while others study under tree shades. Many of their teachers are not better than the taught. At the secondary level, the situation is not better either. At a time, technical equipment imported for the implementation of the 6-3-3-4 system was abandoned at Lagos ports for years. Presently, many secondary schools lack science and mathematics teachers. . . . The situation is further complicated by the conditions of our universities. Routinely, students and teachers go on strike over lack of basic infrastructure for learning—inadequate classrooms, no water and electricity, dry laboratories, non-existent science workshops, and outdated libraries. University administrators with scant regard for academic excellence admit students more than the carrying capacities of their institutions, just as they compete with politicians to abuse funds voted for the running of their schools. (*Punch*, January 21, 2016)

Another survey by the FME sadly revealed that 89% of public secondary schools in Nigeria had no science laboratories, 83% had no science kits, and 95% had no technology workshops which is the fulcrum of education policy today (Okonedo, 2007). In 2008, for example, then chairman of Bauchi State Universal Basic Education Board, Abdullahi Dabo, lamented that 90% of primary and secondary school students in the State receive lessons seated on the bare floor (Egbara, 2008). Also, the deplorable conditions of and incessant labor dispute conflicts and actions (both actual and threatened) by teachers in public schools further undermine education (Okotoni & Okotoni, 2003; Adebayo, 2009). In 2009, for example, teachers' strike in Lagos, Ogun, Oyo, and Kwara States over government's delay in implementing the 27.5% increase on Teachers' Salary Structure disrupted school for several weeks (*This Day*, February 26, 2009).

Also, in 2009, primary and secondary school teachers in Kwara State embarked on indefinite strike for six months to press government to honor its 27.5% salary increment agreement with the teachers' union (*This Day*, May 18, 2009). In April 2013, the Nigerian Union of Teachers (NUT) directed its members in 19 States of the country to commence an indefinite strike action pursuant to the refusal of the impacted States to implement an agreement on the payment of 27.5% Teachers Enhancement Allowance (Okeke, 2013). In April 2014, the NUT called on then governor Gabriel Suswam of Benue to pay the six months' salary arrears owed primary school teachers in the state (*Punch*, April 17, 2014). The menace of unqualified teachers is another big problem (Olatoun, 2010; Amoor, 2010; Ugbe & Agim, 2009).

At the primary school level, for example, then minister for education, Ruqayyah Rufa'i, in 2010 identified 207,818 unqualified teachers nationwide, with the North-East zone having the highest number of 57.7%, followed by North-West 46.8%, North-Central 38%, South-South 19.2%, South-East 16.7%, and South-West 6.7%. In 2008, then Kwara State commissioner for education, Bolaji Abdullahi, said that about 259 teachers who sat for primary four examinations scored zero in the test (Muhammad, 2008). In 2013, Kaduna State commissioner for education, Usman Mohammed, disclosed that out of 1,599 secondary school teachers selected across the State, only one scored above 75% in a Math and literary assessment originally designed for primary four students (*Nigerian Tribune*, March 4, 2013). In August 2013, the news of the discovery by then governor Adams Oshiomhole of Edo State, that a teacher with over 18 years' experience could not read her own age affidavit went viral (*YouTube*, August 15, 2013). In September 2017, it was reported that more than 50% of teachers in Kaduna State failed primary four competency examination, resulting in the termination of 21,000 teachers by Governor Nasir el-Rufai (Ebije, 2017; Isenyo, 2017).

School attendance has also suffered. That can account for part of the reason that Nigeria has low education outcomes with considerable dropout rate of between 12% and 15%, as reported by the World Bank (Subair, 2013). According to the UNICEF, only 1.8 million children are participating in preschool education program in Nigeria, a figure UNICEF described "as very minimal" (Ugwoke, 2006). According to a recent report by UNESCO, more than 10 million Nigerian school age children are not attending school, the highest in the world (the situation has got worse with the insurgency in the Northeast region which has precipitated school closures) (Idoko, 2013). In 2017 proper, the UNICEF reported that over 2,295 teachers have been killed and 19,000 have been displaced, and 1,400 schools destroyed across the Northeast since the Boko Haram insurgency started in 2009 (United Nations, 2017). In Borno State in particular, the worst hit by the Boko Haram menace, about 57% of the schools are closed, leaving estimated 3 million children without education access (United Nations, 2017). In a sad historical sense, this further put Northern Nigeria at educational disadvantage compared to the South, since for example, "no secondary school existed in the North until the founding of Katsina College in 1922, which started as a teacher training college" (Dudley, 1966, p. 72).

Meanwhile, under the guise of improving basic education in particular, huge sums of money are routinely appropriated, much of it end up in private pockets, stolen, or simply disappears. This is believed to be so because there is apparent divergence between allocated funds and fortunes of the education sector. Some examples will be in order. Between 1999 and 2007, Universal Basic Education Commission (UBEC) received more than ₦72 billion as grant from the Consolidated Revenue Fund (CRF) (*The Tide*, October 4, 2007). Between 2005 and 2007, statutory allocations to UBEC from CRF totaled ₦81.255 billion (Chiahemen, 2007). (The 36 states of the federation and Federal Capital Territory contribute an equal amount of matching grant to finance Universal Basic Education (UBE) programs.) Between 2004 and 2008, UBEC disbursed about ₦111 billion to the States as an intervention fund for UBE. Between 2005 and 2008, UBEC disbursed ₦20.4 billion to states as matching grants (*This Day*, January 13, 2009). In 2007, the World Bank approved ₦8 billion ($65 million) IDA credit for Nigeria for the 2007–2011 State Education Sector Project to benefit the "improvement of quality basic education, particularly focusing on girls and the poor in Kaduna, Kano, and Kwara States" (*Business Day*, May 10, 2007). In 2008 alone, the World Bank reported that Nigeria spent about ₦2.4 billion from the country's debt relief fund on the education sector to drive the UBE program:

> ₦702 million on Federal Teachers Scheme (aimed to provide qualified teachers to disadvantaged states), ₦400 million for teachers upgrade program (targeted at grade two teachers through the National Teachers Institute), ₦501.6 million for learning materials and mass literacy campaign, ₦776 million for classroom infrastructure, ₦948 million for UBE program in Abuja, among others. (*This Day*, October 2, 2008)

According to the FME, the Nigerian government invested ₦144.7 billion in basic education (primary and junior secondary schools) between 2009 and 2013 (*Punch*, March 18, 2014). And in March 2014, the presidency announced that it released additional ₦113.75 billion for girl child education between 2006 and 2014 (*Punch*, March 25, 2014). Meanwhile, ₦44 billion in UBE funds that is devoted to basic education remains un-accessed because States have failed to provide counterpart funding while at the same time primary school enrollment has increased more than 10% from 21,857,011 in 2009 to 24,071,559 in 2013 (Abayomi & Areyeka, 2014). Investigatively, in 2008, the ICPC uncovered illegal and unauthorized utilization of funds totaling ₦3.32 billion in the UBEC (Olugbile & Sam, 2008). In 2008 again, Ahmed Modibbo, then executive secretary UBEC, disclosed that officials of State Universal Basic Education Boards (SUBEBs) in Adamawa, Bauchi, Benue, Borno, Cross River, Delta, Ebonyi, Ekiti, Jigawa, Kaduna, Lagos,

Ogun, Ondo, Osun, Oyo, Rivers, and Sokoto indulged in the diversion of funds meant for Federal Teachers' Scheme in their respective States (Nzeshi, 2008). In the foregoing process, Nigerian educational standard has fallen precipitously to the extent that Nigerian university graduates not only fail to get the essential training and critical work force skills they need to work and compete and succeed, but they are also by default adjudged "unemployable" (Fidelis & Iheaka, 2004) with serious implications for the economy and industrial productivity.

D. Industrial Decline

Nigeria previously had a robust industrial evolution due to the then highly industrial training sector that produced required labor. According to Malik and Teal (2008, p. 247), however, "Nigeria's manufacturing sector is weak, uncompetitive and suffers from low capacity utilization. Its contribution to the national economy is both low and declining." From a manufacturing peak of 7.83% in 1982, the contribution of manufacturing as a share of total economic output in Nigeria has generally declined (NBS, 2014, p. 4). Prior to the oil boom of the 1970s, manufacturing contributed approximately 10% to Nigeria's economic output (NBS, 2014, p. 4). Thereafter decline set in, spurred mainly by the increase in oil receipts. A "2014 Nigerian Manufacturing Sector Report" issued by the NBS, among other details stated (NBS, 2014, p. 5), had the following to report:

> Throughout the 1990s and 2000s, Nigeria continued to rely heavily on the export of oil, allowing manufacture to remain in decline. Firms were not export orientated, and lacked efficiency, causing competitive companies to relocate factories abroad. A few key industries, such as beverages, textiles, cement and tobacco kept the sector afloat, but even these operated at under half of their capacity. To this day, production is mainly located in Lagos and its periphery, and to a lesser extent some other commercial towns such as Kano or Kaduna.

Very usefully Nigeria's manufacturing sector represented total GDP of 6.6% in 2010, 9.6% in 2014, 11.5% in 2019, declined by 0.7 percentage points to 8.7% in 2016 (table 4.5). In the 10-year 2010–2019 stretch, manufacturing contributed to an average growth of under 8.8% to the Nigeria's GDP. By historical standards, this growth is poor and unimpressive. In 1956/1957 (table 4.6), manufacturing accounted for more than 7% of Nigeria's GDP and it contributed £58.5 million value (*Economic Survey of Nigeria 1959*, p. 16). That simply means that for more than 60 years (1956/1957–2019), manufacturing share of the GDP has barely bulged. And when it is realized that

Table 4.5 Sectoral Contribution as a Share of GDP (%), 2010–2019

Year	*Agriculture*	*Industry*	*Mfg.*	*Services*
2010	23.9	25.3	6.6	50.8
2011	22.2	28.3	7.2	49.2
2012	21.9	27.1	7.7	50.2
2013	20.8	25.7	8.9	52.4
2014	20.0	24.6	9.6	54.2
2015	20.6	20.2	9.4	58.1
2016	21.0	18.2	8.7	59.8
2017	20.8	22.3	8.7	55.8
2018	21.2	25.7	9.6	52.0
2019	21.9	27.4	11.5	49.7
Average	**21.4**	**24.5**	**8.8**	**53.2**

Source: World Bank.

Table 4.6 Sectoral Contribution as a Share of GDP (%), 1956/1957

Sector	*Amount (£m)*	*%GDP*
Agriculture	501.0	61.8
Transportation and Distribution	119.1	14.5
Construction and Engineering	89.4	11.0
Government	44.9	5.5
Manufactures and Others	58.5	7.3
Total	812.9	100.0

Source: National Economic Council, *Economic Survey of Nigeria 1959*, p. 16.

manufacturing share of GDP was 7.3% in 1956/1957 with a peak of 7.83% in 1982 (uptick of only 0.5 percentage points in 25 years), it makes the manufacturing situation more lugubrious. Growth in the service sector offers a valuable contrast. However, it does not obliterate the fact that manufacturing and industry are in distress, emphasizing the deepening concern that new workers are not entering the labor force, further escalating economic problems.

Indeed, Terence McCulley, former United States ambassador to Nigeria (2010–2013), had an insight that is very instructive, and it is reported here: "Nigeria could inspire billions of dollars of FDI simply by insuring that business contracts are sacrosanct, investment regulations are predictable, and electricity is reliable. Both foreign and Nigerian investors, large and small, will benefit" (*Guardian*, June 26, 2011). But the prospects of a better business environment and economic recovery in Nigeria remain an uphill task "due to a widespread failure on the part of leaders and policy-makers to put in place reforms necessary to underpin competitiveness and bring about much-needed increases in productivity" (World Economic Forum, 2018). The optics are worrisome. In spite of Nigeria's 2017 "new National Action Plan to drive reforms on ease of doing business," according to the World

Economic Forum's "Global Competitiveness Index (GCI) 2017–2018" report, Nigeria ranked 125th (improved only by 2 points from 127th position in 2016–2017) out of 137 countries ranked. The GCI report indicated that "Nigeria has failed to increase its overall score since 2012, and was not among the top 10 ranked countries in Africa" (World Economic Forum, 2018). (The *Global Competiveness Index* measures national competitiveness, defined as the set of institutions, policies, and factors that determine the level of productivity.)

Very importantly, the GCI report identified poor macroeconomic environment, weak institutions, poor infrastructure, substandard health care, and primary education as factors hindering Nigeria's growth (World Economic Forum, 2018). Disappointedly, Nigeria ranked behind less heeled countries such as Ethiopia (108), Ghana (111), Tanzania (113), Uganda (114), Cameroon (116), Zambia (118), Guinea (119), Benin (120), Mali (123), and Zimbabwe (124). The top 10 performing countries in Africa according to the GCI report were Mauritius (45), Rwanda (58), South Africa (61), Botswana (63), Namibia (90), Kenya (91), Senegal (106), Seychelles (107), Ethiopia (108), and Cape Verde (110). Switzerland, United States, and Singapore were the top three global performers, first, second, and third, respectively.

Overseas Nigeria is a byword for corruption, scam, and mounting insecurity with adverse impacts on FDIs. For example, partly because of security risks induced by the Boko Haram insurgency and other militancies that have impacted economic growth negatively (Ewetan & Ese, 2014; Achumba, Ighomereho, & Akpor-Robaro, 2013), FDI net inflow into Nigeria dropped to $1.997 billion in 2018 from $8.132 billion in 2008 (World Bank, 2020). By extension, since security perception is a driver of tourism, insecurity is largely to blame for tourism's low contribution to the Nigerian economy, especially in the Northeast of Nigeria where Boko Haram attacks are predominant (Ezenagu & Enohuean, 2017; Awojobi, 2014). As a result of Boko Haram insurgency (Ezenagu & Enohuean, 2017, p. 4):

> Certain northern destinations of the country were declared unsafe by the Nigerian government. With official declaration of certain states in Nigeria as unsafe tourism destinations, many foreign nations have placed debilitating travelling bans on the country in order to prevent their citizens from visiting and endangering their lives. Despite the fact that tourism is an economic pillar of many nations it cannot thrive in an atmosphere of insurgency such as that created by the Boko Haram terrorist sect. In other words, Boko Haram's wanton destruction of lives and property poses a huge threat to northern Nigeria as a tourism destination and has drastically reduced tourist patronage in the region, witling it down to almost nothing.

In view of this, Okeke (2015) stated, inter alia, that "more than ₦200 billion, which accrued to the Nigerian economy annually prior to Boko Haram when tourists board flights, book hotels, eat and pay for other leisure associated with festival and travels, are lost in the wake of the hostile activities of the violent Boko Haram organization." Also, according to a 2017 report by the United Nations Conference on Trade and Development (UNCTAD), tourism contribution to Nigeria's GDP during the 2011–2014 period was only 4.0% (less than half of Africa's average of 8.5%) compared to South Africa 14.7%, Namibia 14.7%, Botswana 11.3%, Tanzania 11.0%, Kenya 10.9%, Mali 9.4%, Ghana 7.7%, Cameroon 6.6%, Benin 6.0%, to name a few (UNCTAD, 2017). Per the UNCTAD report, the three most tourism driven countries in Africa, measured by contribution to GDP, are all small island developing societies: Seychelles 62%, Cabo Verde 43%, and Mauritius 27% (UNCTAD, 2017). Furthermore, the value chain of tourism and trade strengthens "economic partnerships, delivers prosperity, and enhances competitiveness" (Solis 2016a; Solis 2016b; see also World Economic Forum, 2015), and in spite of the fact that Nigeria is a large regional player with a huge market, her share of world trade is poor. According to the European Commission, Nigeria accounts for a miniscule 0.7% of global exports and 0.4% of regional imports (*This Day*, October 24, 2007). Worse, Nigeria's global export trade ranking compared to her OPEC peers is weaker today than at any other time. WTO data indicate that Nigeria's share (0.3%) in world merchandize trade export falls behind United Arab Emirates (1.5%), Saudi Arabia (1.4%), Indonesia (0.9%), Iraq (0.5%), and Qatar (0.4%), to name a few (WTO, 2020, Table A6, p. 82). By way of corroboration, latest report (March 24, 2021) from the Center for the Study of the Economies of Africa at University of Oxford indicates that "for the fifth consecutive quarter, Nigeria recorded a negative balance of trade with the import component of trade accounting for 65 percent while export component of trade accounted for 35 percent." This development highlights Nigeria's continuing problem of dependence on oil as the cornerstone of the economy as opposed to economic diversification to drive job creation and economic growth. Per the WTO data, China ($2.5 trillion), United States ($1.6 trillion), and Germany ($1.5 trillion) rank first, second, and third, respectively, in global merchandize trade exports, representing 13.2%, 8.7%, and 7.9%, accordingly in world total exports.

A LOOK IN THE MIRROR

While it is attractive to hammer away at the fault lines of Nigerian leadership and its devastating impacts, it must be realized that the leadership problem of the country is a collective and not a selective responsibility. All Nigerians and all segments of the society "have proverbially sinned and have fallen short of the glory" of the motherland and in the process have contributed in one way or another to the problem of leadership in the country. If we have an Emperor of misrule at Aso Rock as president, we also have Dukes of Hazard at the States Houses as governors, as well as barons of calamity at the local council levels as chairperson. Furthermore, if we have roguish civilian political leaders in *agbada*, we also had crooked military leaders in khaki uniform, as well as roguish police leaders in badges. If also we have false prophets in the churches, then we also have derelict imams in the mosques, as well as dubious businesspeople in office suites.

If we have hoodlums, who rob at gunpoint, we also have miscreant state officials, who steal at pen point. If we have corrupt customs officers, we also have bribe taking office clerks, as well as mail rifling postal clerks. If we have corrupt judges on the secular bench, we also have corrupt *alkalis* on the Sharia Court. If we have corrupt university presidents, we also have unscrupulous secondary school principals. If we have government officials who accept kickbacks and approve substandard public works, we also have private entrepreneurs who manufacture and market substandard and adulterated products to the public. If we have university professors who demand sexual favors and financial payoff for grades, we also have electoral officials who accept money and other favors to rig elections. If we have political officials who steal from the public, we also have traditional rulers who cheat their subjects. The problem with Nigeria is not that it is corrupt, because many countries experience corruption, but the depth and scale of corruption in Nigeria is unprecedented and covers all nooks and crannies of the society and the citizenry seem to okay it. Most certainly, the comparison continues infinitely.

The Nigerian situation is a tragedy of the commons, whereby the deadly combination of corruption and ineffective leadership reinforces economic decline, and economic decline in turn retards social progress. Interestingly, at the inauguration of the Constitutional Conference in June 1994, the late General Abacha said: "Our nearly thirty-four years of sovereign existence have been beset with a history of continuous political uncertainty. We have had a crisis of legitimacy, crisis of succession, crisis of authority, and crisis of nationally acceptable leadership."

As observers have indicated, General Abacha merely echoed what his predecessors had said when they took over power. The late Obafemi Awolowo, for example, had much earlier warned of the caveat in the continuing national drift in an open letter to then president Shehu Shagari in July 1981: "It is generally agreed that Nigeria is seriously ill. The economy ails critically, and the body-politic aches in every part of its organism. Everywhere, there is hunger, depression and discontent" (Awolowo, 1981).

Forty years later, the situation instead of improving has worsened. So, what is the missing link? Nigeria is blowing its chance of greatness not for lack of ability and resources, but for lack of leadership. The country earns almost universal scorn in public opinion polls. Emeka Anyaoku, the former commonwealth secretary-general, has this to say:

> The balance sheet of our national performance shows us falling far short of potential on many fronts. The national economic indices show that. The current state of our schools, colleges and universities attest to that. The condition of our hospitals, roads, and of such facilities as water supply, electricity supply and postal and telephone services bring home to the vast majority of our people the point that the country is performing well below its capacity. This in turn has bred among the people obvious disaffection with governance in general. There is a perceptible general feeling among Nigerians that the state is out of tune with the passions of the people. (*West Africa*, January 23–29, 1995, p. 99)

This is a national indictment, but it is necessary. After all, it is also a crisis of confidence that strikes at the very heart of Nigeria's conscience. In fact, it seems that very little is right with the whole system. Against this backdrop, Nigeria must reexamine itself with great urgency because there can be no excuse for any Nigerian to be cheated out of the promise of opportunity that ought to be the center of Nigerian life, especially, given Nigeria's abundant human and natural resources. Additionally, as Africa's most populous country, Nigeria's role in world affairs is very significant. Appearing before the U.S. Senate Foreign Relations Committee in 1995, George E. Moose, then U.S. assistant secretary of state for African Affairs testified about Nigeria in the following words: "Nigeria is too important to ignore. It has Africa's largest population, and it has vast natural resources and economic potential. And, for better or worse, its capacity to influence is significant" (Moose, 1995).

Twenty years later, James Entwistle, then American ambassador to Nigeria, reechoed Moose's sentiments. In a January 2014 interview with Nigerian in the *Guardian* newspaper, Entwistle declared: "In terms why Nigeria is important, you have one of the largest markets in Africa; you are huge; in the Gulf of Guinea, you are a significant oil and gas producer; you are one of the largest democracies in Africa. All of these are things the United States of America deeply cares about and they are parts of the reason we have such a rich partnership with you [Nigeria]" (*Guardian*, January 30, 2014). The United States International Trade Administration reckons:

> Nigeria plays an important leadership role in both West Africa and on the African continent. The headquarters of the Economic Community of West African States (ECOWAS) is in Abuja. Nigeria, which represents roughly 70%

of the 15-country ECOWAS GDP and over half of the ECOWAS region's population, plays an outsized role in ECOWAS. (U.S. International Trade Administration, 2020)

Much earlier in 1977, American scholar, Jean Herskovits, specialist in African history and politics, observed, "Nigeria is a large potential market and provides the opportunity for sizable returns on future U.S. investment, particularly welcome since Nigeria admires American technology and expertize" (Herskovits, 1977, p. 167).

The statements quoted above are unimpeachable. After all, Nigeria occupies a strategic position in Africa and must be encouraged to succeed. Also, her market is big and growing, and American companies are reaping

Table 4.7 U.S. Merchandise Exports to Nigeria, 2016–2019 ($m)

NAICS	*Product*	*2016*	*2017*	*2018*	*2019*	*Total*	*% Total*
930	Used/Second-Hand Merchandise	198	314	560	616	1,688	17
336	Transportation Equipment	264	250	507	496	1,517	15
111	Agricultural Products	297	417	250	504	1,468	15
325	Chemicals	280	286	266	337	1,168	12
333	Machinery; Except Electrical	248	252	260	385	1,145	12
324	Petroleum and Coal Products	132	239	308	218	897	9
334	Computer and Electronic Products	90	88	102	122	403	4
332	Fabricated Metal Products; Nesoi	106	74	80	86	347	3
335	Electrical Equip; App & Computers	71	44	88	69	272	3
311	Food Manufactures	66	68	60	74	268	3
	All Others	142	142	206	292	782	8
	Total	**1,895**	**2,174**	**2,687**	**3,200**	**9,956**	**100**
	Sub-Saharan Africa	13,947	14,115	15,904	15,848	59,814	
	AGOA	12,934	13,616	15,329	15,122	57,001	
	ECOWAS	4,199	4,809	5,621	5,820	20,451	
	% Nigeria to Sub-Saharan Africa	14	15	17	20	17	
	% Nigeria to AGOA	15	16	18	21	17	
	% Nigeria to ECOWAS	45	45	48	55	49	

NAICS = North American Industrial Classification System.
Source: United States Department of Commerce, International Trade Administration/U.S. Census Bureau—Foreign Trade Division.
Author calculation.

increased benefits especially in trade transactions. To illustrate, table 4.7 shows United States total merchandise exports to Nigeria highlighting the top 10 products for the most recent four years, 2016–2019.

In 2019, United States' trade exports to Nigeria surged to $3.2 billion, up by more than $0.5 billion or nearly 20% over the 2018 level, especially in used/second-hand merchandise, transportation equipment, and agricultural products. Also, when compared to the sub-Saharan Africa (SSA) economic region, the African Growth and Opportunity Act (AGOA) trading protocol, and ECOWAS union, Nigeria dominated the SSA, AGOA, and ECOWAS markets for U.S. exporters with a combined absorption of nearly 30% average of all of U.S. exports to SSA, AGOA, and ECOWAS during this period.

WHY LEADERSHIP IS A BIG PROBLEM IN NIGERIA

Leadership is a big problem in Nigeria because since independence (except for the "one brief shining moment" of Murtala Mohammed) Nigerian leaders have practiced what the late Nigerian scholar, Claude Ake, called "cult of personality politics" (Ake, 1966, p. 13) in the name of leadership, with its attendant ills of "cultural fragmentation and bitter intra-elite competition" (Ake, 1966, p. 13), as opposed to pursuing broad based "charismatic legitimation leadership" (Ake, 1966, p. 1). Ake is not alone. Udogu (2014, p. 127) stated: "Nigeria is said to be cursed by the fact that it has been unable to produce sufficient political leaders with national legitimacy." Nnadozie (1995, p. 164) stated that Nigerian leaders "established the state apparatus for self-preservation and praetorian dictatorship." But first, what is charisma? Max Weber defines charisma as "the quality of an individual personality by virtue of which he is set apart from ordinary men and treated as endowed with supernatural, superhuman, or at least specifically exceptional powers or qualities" (Weber, 1947, pp. 358–359). Intuitively, from the foregoing, charisma presupposes effective and exceptional leadership, a "leader who inspires strength and confidence in others" (Emmet, 1958, p. 242). In addition, charisma evokes a "leader perceived as endowed with charisma by enough people to stimulate and condition mass participation" (Ake, 1966, p. 6), "strong and creative person with adaptive ingenuity and strong sense of nationality" (Shils, 1958, p. 1), and by implication, animate the concept of leadership "charismatic legitimization" (Ake, 1966).

The use of the theory of "charisma" as a conceptual tool to explain the problem of leadership in Nigeria accords with the "theory of charismatic legitimation" (Ake, 1966). The theory of charismatic legitimation posits that the recognition of the authority of the state is facilitated if the state's claims are advocated by someone whom the masses respect and trust (Ake, 1966).

In other words, the theory assumes that the masses respect the charismatic leader in a way they do not respect the state and that this personal respect can be used to buttress the state until it wins its own legitimacy (Ake, 1966). In the Nigerian case, as a result of bad leadership experiences, Nigerians are not only cynical about the intentions and actions of their leaders, but also Nigerians are hesitant to "trust and respect" their leaders, and at the same time do not perceive their leaders as a "nucleus of unity and psychological comfort" (Apter, 1963, pp. 15 and 16, quoted in Ake, 1966, p. 3). Put another way, Nigerian leaders "do not arouse devotion to the nation" (Shils, 1958, p. 1), let alone inspire and motivate the people. Hence, Nigerians are lukewarm to gravitate to their leaders, question their legitimacy and acceptance, further stoking ineffective and bankrupt leadership, and national drift.

Effective leadership is the crucial missing link in Nigeria's journey to nationhood, for as it is said, "where there is no leadership, the people suffer," and Nigeria is no exception. Consequently, Nigeria is "viewed to be in virtual pathology threatened by collapse, failure, fragility, weakness, and void of popular legitimacy and administrative capacity" (Hagmann & Peclard, 2010, p. 540). Or, as Brady and Spence said, while not Nigeria specific, Nigerian leadership style do not "keep politicians [leaders] focused on citizens' well-being" (Spence & Brady, 2010, p. 2). Nigerians must hold their leaders responsible for the performance of the country, therefore, the importance of effective leadership cannot be overemphasized. Jones and Olken's (2005, p. 835) study "find robust evidence that leaders matter for growth. . . . Leaders also appear to affect policy outcomes. . . . The results suggest that individual leaders can play crucial roles in shaping the growth of nations." World Bank's 2008 Growth Commission Report noted the importance of "capable, credible, and committed government" (World Bank, 2008, p. 3) leadership in growth and development. Nobel laureate in economics, Michael Spence, and David Brady (2009, p. 3) emphasize, "effective and responsive government are vital to facilitate development."

It is important to state that the book does not suggest that leadership is a personal attribute or charismatic endowment only. Rather, leadership is multifaceted, and leaders can legitimate themselves through institutional, social, cultural, and economic correlates as well. Take for instance, the case of the Asian Tigers. Their leaders though for the most part were "modernizing autocrats" (Fukuyama, 2006, p. 215) and less charismatic; however, they legitimated themselves by delivering economic success. This tendency is akin to what the American political scientist, Samuel Huntington, called "modernizing authoritarian leader" (Huntington, 1965, 1968), who while abridge civil liberties and curtail political participation, achieve rapid economic growth and social progress, exemplified by the likes of Park Chung-Hee in South Korea, Chiang Ching-Kuo in Taiwan, Lee Kwan Yew in Singapore, Suharto in Indonesia, and Mahathir Mohamad in Malaysia who led and brought the "Asian Miracle" growth phenomena (Nwagbara, 2019, p. 21). Diamond (2013) also observed "strong hand . . . authoritarian rulers such as Chiang in Taiwan (r. 1950–75), Park Chung-Hee in South Korea (r. 1961–79), and Lee Kuan Yew in Singapore (r. 1959–90) delivered rapid development."

REINVENTING LEADERSHIP

Frustration over Nigeria's odious leadership, since independence, has forced the citizens to adapt to the tough conditions created by their leadership. However, such adaptation has allowed unpopular and rogue regimes to hold sway, thereby delaying the revolution Nigerian people need to purge itself of corrupt and incompetent leaders. This accommodationist, say nothing, and go about your business and hope the devil would reform itself attitude of Nigerians has inadvertently served the ruling class well, by shielding them from the sufferings, anger, and frustrations of the masses. Unfortunately, Nigerian leadership's cavalier attitude to the pains and sufferings of the middle class and the poor is not only unconscionable but it is also ungodly, if not totally demonizing. And this must change for the better because it behooves on the governing elite to govern right or risk serious social dislocations and possibly upheaval.

The dispossessed majority can no longer afford to wait perpetually on the tranquilizing but spurious government promises that things will get better. They must challenge government's vacillations and broken promises of leadership atonement. To be effective, they must move beyond their self-defeating *siddon de look* (do nothing) servile approach or what Olson (1965) called "collective action problem," organize themselves into a united critical mass toward engaging and nudging the authorities into dialogue and debate, and press for a participatory economy and shared prosperity from the government. Such approach remains the most effective way to get government attention and make sure that Nigeria does not turn into a two society of permanent haves and have-nots. Indian nationalist and former prime minister, Jawaharlal Nehru (1889–1964), once said: "You cannot command success. But success often comes to those who dare and act; it seldom goes to the timid who are afraid of the consequences" (Nehru, 1962, p. 19).

Nigeria must reinvent her leadership because since the founding fathers won independence for Nigeria, the country has suffered serial leadership failures. The leadership has been "defective" and inept. Obafemi Awolowo observed: "A defective leadership and inadequate leadership would only bring curses rather than blessings on the Nigerian peoples. Such a leadership would fail to keep Nigeria harmoniously united, and bestow on the peoples the benefits of an educated, healthy, prosperous, integrated, and happy life"

(Awolowo, 1968, p. xiii). Awolowo's observation is unimpeachable. In the words of James MacGregor Burns, American historian and political scientist, "we need a new compelling leadership that speaks to the real needs of [Nigerians] that will mobilize them behind a drive for deep and enduring change" (Burns, 2006, p. 6). And while there is no such thing as a perfect leadership, there are worthy examples to draw from history. The leadership of the likes of Jesus Christ; Abraham Lincoln, Franklin Roosevelt, John Kennedy, Martin Luther King, and Rosa Park in the United States; Jawaharlal Nehru and Mahatma Gandhi in India; Nelson Mandela in South Africa; Suharto in Indonesia; Lee Kuan Yew in Singapore; and Mustafa Kemal in Turkey have much to recommend to Nigerian leaders. The common thread to these leaders was their desire to make humanity and their countries better places for people better than they found it. These leaders brought hope, inspiration, pride, progress, and honor to the world and their respective countries. This could as well occur in Nigeria, as was the case under the late General Murtala Mohammed. General Mohammed was outstanding for his "courage," which, according to John F. Kennedy, a former United States president, is the "most admirable of human virtues" (Kennedy, 1955).

Also, General Mohammed launched investigations of corruption and purged the civil service. Before he was assassinated in 1976, he announced a precise schedule for a return to constitutional government that culminated in 1979 under General Obasanjo (Ungar, 1989, p. 129). Nigeria could still produce another crop of Murtalas who could lead, manage, and unite the country better. The leader must earn the trust of Nigerians and strive to restore "hope to the forgotten middle class" and the working poor. The leader must work to restore "opportunity for all [Nigerians], responsibility from all [Nigerians], and a sense of community among all [Nigerians]" (Clinton, 1996). The leader must have vision, compassion, charisma, trust, dedication, and moral authority. Above all, the leader must have the courage to make tough decisions and accept responsibility when things go wrong. These leadership qualities are apparently the missing ingredients in the current Nigerian leadership crop.

Solutions to Nigerian leadership crisis must be considered on the backdrop of state failure theory because her post-independence history (except for the short interval of Murtala Mohammed's leadership) shows successive leadership failures. Viewed from the preceding spectrum, state failure theory proposes that Nigeria is a nation at risk, and the "trouble with Nigeria" is bad leadership and poor governance. Clapham (1996, p. 810) lamented Nigeria's leadership failures "induce delusory sense of helplessness" because it does not have to be that way, especially, given Nigeria's enormous pool of human capital and abundant natural resources that ought to be harnessed to improve the country.

There is consensus among pan-African scholars that the state in Africa [Nigeria] has neither protected the welfare of its citizens, nor delivered what was expected to its people (Wong, 2012, p. 67). Adebanwi and Obadare (2016, pp. 2 and 6) described this phenomenon as "the crisis of rule in post-colonial Africa . . . the uneviable history of the African post-colony can be written around the subject of the absence, for the most account, of positive leadership and good governance." Mazrui (1975) identifies the character of the ruling elite that emerged in Africa following independence as the source of instability in the new states of Africa (quoted in Bamgboye, 2014). These ruling elites not only failed to meet the expectations of their citizenry in terms of socioeconomic development of their countries, but also socioeconomic transformation has become illusory as poverty, hunger, disease, insecurity, corruption, and mismanagement of resources prevailed (Bamgboye, 2014, p. 2341).

In the Nigerian case particularly, the weakness of the Nigerian state vis-à-vis the failure of leadership emanates primarily from the incapacity of the state to deliver essential and basic needs to its citizens, and the Nigerian state is inhibited by high-level corruption and bad governance among other ills (Daniel, 2015, p. 633). These challenges have impaired sustainable development, tarnished Nigeria's image, and caused the degrading of Nigeria's prominence both at home and abroad (Daniel, 2015, p. 633). At the same time, failed or acutely failing states pose unique problems for democracy promotion (Diamond, 2006, p. 94). For Nigeria, according to Diamond (2006, p. 95), she "is at severe risk of state failure because of weak or weakening state authority and capacity, high levels of crime and privatized violence, and escalating polarization of domestic politics." Diamond is not alone in his concerns regarding the risks of state failure and leadership crisis in Nigeria. Ebere Onwudiwe and Chloe Berwind-Dart (2010) offered an insight. "Nigerian elections [leadership] have not been about the issues, nor about addressing the many challenges faced by Nigeria's largely struggling citizenry. . . . The failure to address the pressing issues facing ordinary Nigerians is a bleak and irksome reminder that politics [leadership] in Nigeria is not yet by, about, or even for average citizens."

What Must Be Done

- *Demonstrate Effective Leadership*—The president must demonstrate strong leadership and political will to improve the performance of the Federal government. The "bully pulpit" of the presidency must be mobilized to effect desired changes. It is not going to be easy, but the president cannot fail to try for fear of failure. The Italian statesman Niccolo Machiavelli (1469–1527) noted in his popular book, *The Prince*:

> There is no more delicate matter to take in hand, nor more dangerous to conduct, nor more doubtful in its success, than to set up as a leader in the introduction of changes. For he who innovates will have for his enemies all those who are well off under the existing order of things, and only lukewarm supporters in those who might be better off under the new (Machiavelli, [1532] 1992, p. 13).

The crusading and reformist former Ghanaian president, Jerry Rawlings, also enunciated:

> A lot depends on the leader, his sensitivity, his will, his strength and determination. . . . I think that the number one [leader] should be bold enough and identify the right people to take over and move to those institutions in an effective and efficient way. Put your foot down, because those institutions are manned by human beings; and if those human beings lack the character, the strength and the spirit to be able to defy that which is wrong, then we cannot defend freedom and justice. The leader has to give a clear signal, sense of direction and the passion to drive the change. (Anuforo, 2016)

- *Stop the Blame Game*—Nigerian [African] leadership must take responsibility for its actions, assert themselves as responsible for the country's rescue, put its house in order, and refrain from blaming outside influences vis-à-vis "imperialists and neocolonialist" (Nkrumah, 1967) in addition to what Ali Mazrui (1980) referred to as the "African condition" (conspiracy of geography, unfavorable international economic and political order (Sachs, 2003, p. 1)) for its troubles, while at the same time, as Herbst (2014, p. xii) argued "looked without irony, to Western aid to solve their problems." Nigerian leadership cannot continue to plead not guilty of leadership failure by reason of external insanity and "Western hubris" (Herbst, 2014, p. xii). Former president Mandela of South Africa advised:

> Certainly, colonialism and selfish ordering of world affairs, past and present, have undermined Africa's development, but Africa has long traversed a mindset that seeks to heap all blame on the past on others. The era of renaissance we are entering is, and should be, based on our own efforts as Africans to change Africa's conditions for the better. (*The Economist*, May 20, 1995, p. 4)

Benjamin Mkapa, former Tanzanian president, posited:

> [While] a discussion of leadership and governance in Africa will be seriously deficient, if it fails to put previous and current leadership, and the developmental challenges they faced, in their proper historical, cultural, and sociological context, Africa cannot forever hold its history of slavery and colonialism

> responsible for its current poverty levels and economic woes. (Mkapa, 2010, pp. 20–21)

The late Kofi Annan, former secretary general of the UN, added his voice:

> It is time for Africans to hold their leaders and not colonialism responsible for the wars and economic failures that ravage their lives. . . . Where there is insufficient accountability of leaders, lack of transparency of regimes, inadequate checks and balances, non-adherence to the rule of law, absence of peaceful means to change or replace leadership, or lack of respect for human rights, political control becomes excessively important and the stakes become dangerously high. (*News & Observer*, April 17, 1997 p. 15A)

This is exactly the Nigerian situation. It is outrageous that a country endowed with vast natural resources and high rate of literacy could be the icon of abuse and corruption, bastion of incompetence, waste and mismanagement, and consequent pauperization of its citizens. Ipso facto good leadership is apparently lacking in Nigeria, which the Tanzanian founding president, Julius Nyerere, according to Mkapa (2010, pp. 20 and 22) ascribed to constitute of "capacity building, stringent standards of integrity and ethical behavior, supported with effective, efficient, and capable institutions."

- *Demand Accountability*—Meanwhile, it is important for Nigerians to demand accountability and responsible behavior from public officers because without it, political stability, which is the forerunner to sustainable economic growth and improved social conditions, will continue to elude Nigeria. Also, as citizens, they must demand a revolution in government, challenging it to act responsibly and be accountable, starting with the tough and urgent problems of the corruption and economic revival. Nigerian politicians have not conducted themselves very well in playing politics, they have undermined the democratic process and have given the army chances to overthrow the government. Before the collapse of the First Republic in 1966, for example, then president Nnamdi Azikiwe and one of Nigeria's founding fathers (1904–1996), in a 1965 *Foreign Affairs* article, lamented the "crisis rocking Nigeria following independence" (Azikiwe, 1965, p. 447) and had noted with dismay that the reckless conduct of politicians during the "December 1964 Nigeria Parliamentary Elections precipitated a crisis evidenced by flawed electoral machinery, electioneering violence, boycott of elections, carpet-crossing, etc." (Azikiwe, 1965, p. 447).

Very interestingly, in the Second Republic (1979–1983), politicians could not make amends from the mistakes of the First Republic. Larry Diamond, the Hoover Institution's senior fellow at Stanford University, observed:

> What the Nigerian people got from politicians was not performance but arrogance, displays of wealth that were stupidly insensitive to the economic realities of recession, scarcity and suffering. Naira was spread around at social functions and donated to political causes by ministers and legislators in amounts that exceeded and often dwarfed their legitimate annual incomes. Draped in gold and magnificent dress, they assumed the bearing of aristocracy, and became considerably more distant from the people than much of Nigeria's traditional royalty. All of this fed the disillusionment, the steady and perceptible erosion of the legitimacy of the Second Republic. (Diamond, 1984, p. 907)

General Buhari, former head of State and the leader of the military junta that ousted the Second Republic, also observed:

> Unfortunately from my experience, many Nigerian politicians are not bothered about the fundamentals of democracy principally because they are not true democrats: they are democrats of convenience abusing the virtues of democracy when they campaign, rigging the election when they vote, crushing the opposition when they win and betraying the public trust when they rule. (*Post Express*, May 18, 1998)

But this behavior must change for the better. For the Nigerian political class to inspire confidence and elicit public support, it must conduct its business in a civilized political manner. Obafemi Awolowo advised: "If the diverse racial groups in Nigeria considered themselves competent and fit to be self-governing in accordance with civilized standards, they could not, at the same time, turn around to excuse themselves from the generally accepted practice and traditions of representative government" (Awolowo, 1987, p. vii).

- *Build Responsible Citizenship*—Most certainly, Nigerians must challenge themselves to responsible citizenship by giving something back to their country, as the former United States U.S. president, John F. Kennedy, in his presidential inaugural address, urged his fellow Americans: "Don't ask what your country can do for you, ask what you can do for your country" (Kennedy, 1961). Nigerians attitude to the concept of government and public good is pathetic. *Newswatch* magazine (October 6, 1986) noted:

    > Nigerians attitude to public property or the collective good is that of government business is nobody's business. This behavior is characterized by the wanton destruction of public properties. Telephone lines, power cables, road railings and other public utilities are regularly vandalized. Things got so bad enough that Buhari/Idiagbon Administration legislated death for destruction of public property.

This destructive and plundering attitude must change because in the final analysis Nigerians will all rise or fall together. Nigerians must make their country better by restoring long cherished values of family, community, and common purpose.

- *Teach Civics Lessons*—A course in leadership and citizenship must be incorporated into Nigerian educational curriculum, beginning from primary school, showcasing the life and works of Nigeria's founding fathers and others, who have made a difference in Nigerian life. The value system of the citizenry needs to be reoriented and the values of hard work and leadership taught and imbibed in the people using all possible channels such as schools, churches, mosques, homes, and the media.
- *Expand Talent Pool*—The authorities must try to attract quality pool of talent for careers in government. Creating internship programs that bring young bright students for work-study programs in government agencies could do this. Research indicates that a high number of graduates of such programs do settle for career in public service afterward and form the nucleus of a new generation of public managers (Ko & Sidhu, 2012; Clay, 2008; Gerlach & Reinagel, 2016).
- *Support Civil Society*—Nigeria must create a vibrant civil society, to which several professionals have belonged—"that dense network of independent organizations and institutions such as the media, trade unions, religious bodies, that citizens utilize to pursue their agenda" including fighting corruption. While Nigeria's civil society has been hobbled in recent years especially through official propaganda and brinkmanship, however, it still remains a bulwark against bad government, and a critical element to any successful war on corruption and official delinquency.
- *Nudge National Leaders*—Nigeria must adopt measures that produce leaders of national appeal as opposed to leaders of ethnic loyalty. For example, in the Presidential elections, securing 25% of the votes in two-third of Nigeria's 36 States is one of the requirements to win the presidency. This provision has literally forced the presidential candidates to go beyond their respective ethnic base to test their national popularity and agenda.
- *Encourage Broadly Shared Prosperity*—Expansion of the private sector economy will also help to produce good leaders because it is likely to reduce the intensity for the cutthroat pursuit of public office as a means of survival and graft by offering opportunities to those who do not want to seek public office. For example, the economic liberalization policy of the Nigerian Government in the 1970s that was rooted in indigenous participation in the ownership of foreign companies saw Nigeria's value added in manufacturing doubled in real terms between 1970 and 1977, and construction tripled (World Bank, 1980; Chete et al., 2016). The percentage of the

labor force engaged in manufacturing increased from 10 to 17% from 1960 to 1978, services increased from 19 to 27%, while agriculture declined from 71 to 56% (Joseph, 1978).

- *Strengthen Continental Leadership*—Nigeria must aspire to lead Africa. This would help to produce good and capable leaders who will inspire broad confidence among both Nigerians and the international community. This is a formidable task, yet, Nigeria is the only country in black Africa that is large, with the resources to be capable in leading the continent. Nobody else can do it. But that doesn't mean being overzealous or committing Nigerian troops and resources to every conflict. Rather, "it means having tact and foresight and being disciplined enough to accomplish what needs to get done" (Gingrich, 1995). And already Nigeria has a track record of bold leadership role in Africa. For example, Nigeria scored highly in the international scene under General Mohammed, especially, in its support for Angola's independence from Portugal in 1975 under the banner of the Popular Movement for the Liberation of Angola (MPLA), led by the late president Augustino Neto. Nigeria's former external affairs minister, Bolaji Akinyemi, recalled:

> By backing the MPLA at a time when the OAU [AU] could not or would not make up its mind, Nigeria broke with its tradition of basing its position on African issues on OAU positions. The tradition of waiting for consensus to form within the OAU before a public declaration of Nigerian policy was replaced by an early and public declaration of Nigerian policy followed by intensive diplomatic efforts to get OAU to ratify that policy. (Akinyemi, 1978, p. ix)

Also, Nigeria has led peace initiative in Liberia and Sierra Leone, which culminated in the restoration of democracy in those countries; bolstering ECOWAS, and supporting the African Union (AU). Obasanjo forced authoritarian interlopers in Sao Tome and Principe and in Togo to back down in 2003 and 2005 (Joseph & Gillies, 2010, p. 183). The end of the Cold War has brought new realities to international politics and economic cooperation. In the new dispensation, old enemies are talking to each other, frosty alliances are being defrosted, and new friends are being made. Nigeria must also get on the bandwagon, especially, to expand its economic and trade relations beyond the traditional East-West axis. New "alliances for progress" must be built; new markets must be explored especially with some of the newly industrializing Asian Tigers such as China, Korea, Taiwan, Indonesia, Singapore, Malaysia, and Thailand. Nigeria is not significantly behind where these countries were some years ago; they were mainly agrarian with weak manufacturing base. The infusion of development assistance and good management has helped the Asian Tigers to reduce poverty, slow population growth, and increase educational levels (Schnitzer, 1994; Gulati, 1992; Kang, 1995; Henley, 2015). They are not only major players in the world economy today but they are also economic success stories for other developing countries including Nigeria to emulate.

CONCLUSION

This chapter, as hinted from the beginning, analyzed the Nigerian leadership crisis from the perspective of state failure theory. This is because, according to Adebanwi and Obadare (2010, p. 379), "Nigeria offers a magnificent template for examining the chronic schizophrenia that characterizes the African postcolonial state and the resulting social (de)formations that (re)compose, and are, in turn, (re)composed by, the state." Also, state failure theory is applied to diverse cultures and nations and there is abundant empirical data and literature by which it can be tested and analyzed (Peters, 2015; Eriksen, 2011; Le Grand, 1991). State failure theory predicates that lack of effective political leadership is antithetical to development (Huntington, 1968, 1991); incapacity of the state to deliver essential and basic needs to its citizens (Daniel 2015, p. 633); and crisis of rule . . . the absence for the most part, of positive leadership and good governance (Adebanwi & Obadare 2016, pp. 2 and 6).

Bad leadership, as Achebe (1983) and others have written endlessly about, is at the root of the Nigerian crisis. In spite of this harsh reality, Nigerian leaders continue to tread on the perilous and dangerous path of reactive and irresponsible leadership that fail and betray her citizens and undermine their progress, prosperity, and improvement in living standards. At a time of popular discontent, distrust, and cynicism with government, Nigeria needs a new governing philosophy and fresh set of ideas that will move the nation forward. Nigerian leaders must have unimpaired vision and direction, and sound judgment to defeat the terrifying specters of poverty, insecurity, and hopelessness that torment her citizens. Nigeria's great moment of fulfillment and reinvention will only come when she has leaders that have the moral compass to navigate the affairs of the nation better, the passion and vision to rise above self, and do right for the country.

It is, indeed, troubling that a country endowed with vast natural resources and high rate of literacy could be the icon of abuse and corruption, bastion of incompetence, waste and mismanagement, and consequent pauperization of its citizens. Nigeria's discredited and bankrupt leadership since independence must be abandoned. In its place, Nigeria must pursue a new way of managing the affairs of government and the citizens. And this new way must be predicated on a fresh crop of dedicated and progressive leadership, and setting better national agenda to spur the economy to create wealth, prosperity, opportunity, and improved living conditions for all Nigerians. Also, Nigeria must pursue a fundamental shift in the basic canons of conducting public business in Nigeria: rooted in accountability, transparency, results and not rules, efficiency and not expediency, citizen satisfaction and not citizen frustration. But for the revolution to occur and succeed, Nigerians must abandon their current inertia and "collective unconsciousness" and organize themselves into a united critical mass, stand firm and decisive, and demand change to free themselves from unjust, corrupt, and unconscionable leaders.

NOTES

1. This is the title of the 1973 book by the historian, Arthur Schlesinger Jr., that described the excesses of President Richard Nixon, culminating in his resignation of the American presidency over the Watergate scandal. Schlesinger wrote the book out of two concerns: first, that the U.S. presidency was out of control and second, that the presidency had breached its constitutional limits (Schlesinger, 1973, p. x). Arthur Schlesinger Jr. (1973). *The Imperial Presidency.* Boston, Massachusetts: Houghton Mifflin Harcourt.

2. According to a 2019 WHO analysis,

> "nearly 20% of all global maternal death occur in Nigeria. Between 2005 and 2015, it is estimated that over 600, 000 maternal deaths and no less than 900, 000 maternal near-miss cases occurred in the country. In 2015, Nigeria's estimated maternal mortality ratio was over 800 maternal deaths per 100,000 live births, with approximately 58, 000 maternal deaths in that year. By comparison, the total number of maternal deaths in 2015 in the 46 most developed countries (1.3 billion people) was 1,700, resulting in a maternal mortality ratio of 12 maternal deaths per 100, 000 live births. In fact, a Nigerian woman has a 1 in 22 lifetime risk of dying during pregnancy, childbirth or postpartum/post-abortion; whereas in the most developed countries, the lifetime risk is 1 in 4,900." WHO (2019). "Maternal Health in Nigeria: Generating Information for Action." https://www.who.int/reproductivehealth/maternal-health-nigeria/en/.

3. The GPEI, a public-private partnership led by national governments with five partners—WHO, Rotary International, the U.S. Centers for Disease Control and Prevention, UNICEF, and the Bill & Melinda Gates Foundation—has reported: "Nigeria is one of only three countries in the world with ongoing wild poliovirus transmission, alongside Afghanistan and Pakistan." http://polioeradication.org/where-we-work/nigeria/.

4. More than half a million Nigerians contract TB every year. Nigeria has the greatest burden of TB in Africa and is third globally, behind India and China (USAID, 2015, p. 6). https://www.usaid.gov/sites/default/files/documents/1860/Nigeria_CDCS_2015-2020.pdf.

5. Nigeria has the world's second highest HIV burden; 3% of the adult population is HIV-positive and an estimated 3.4 million Nigerians are living with HIV. In 2015, some 260,000 children aged 0–14 years were living with HIV and an estimated 41,000 new infections occurred among children aged 0–14 years, 90% of them

through mother-to-child transmission (UNICEF, 2017, pp. 2–3). file:///C:/Users/Owner/Downloads/UNICEF-Nigeria-country-programme-document-2018-22.pdf.pdf.

According to the United Nations' "UNAIDS 2016–2021 Strategy" Report, Nigeria is among the "five large epidemics and high-prevalence countries" (others are Cameroon, Chad, Cote d'Ivoire, and the DRC) that account for over 78% of the HIV burden and 82% of people newly infected. The report further indicated that "Nigeria accounts for 52% of new infections: priority will be placed on states with a prevalence above 8%: Akwa Ibom, Benue, Cross River, Federal Capital Territory and Nasarawa" (p. 103). https://www.unaids.org/sites/default/files/media_asset/20151027_UNAIDS_PCB37_15_18_EN_rev1.pdf.

6. The Teaching Hospitals are Lagos University Teaching Hospital, University of Ilorin Teaching Hospital, Jos University Teaching Hospital, Obafemi Awolowo University Teaching Hospital, University of Maiduguri Teaching Hospital, Usman Danfodio University Teaching Hospital, Amino Kano University Teaching Hospital, University College Hospital, Ibadan; Ahmadu Bello University Teaching Hospital, University of Port Harcourt Teaching Hospital, University of Nigeria Teaching Hospital, University of Calabar Teaching Hospital, Nnamdi Azikiwe University Teaching Hospital, University of Benin Teaching Hospital.

Chapter 5

Summary and Conclusions

As the summary and conclusions section of the book, chapter 5 drives home that it is very important to conclude this book by reiterating categorically and unequivocally that the overall findings of my analysis are very consistent with the empirical literature that Nigeria has not lived up to expectations since independence. That is particularly so, given the nation's multifarious problems, including crisis of leadership, crisis of values, economic decline, corruption, poverty amid vast oil wealth, weak institutions, resource curse, infrastructural decay, chronic fuel shortages in spite of being a major oil producer, social malaise, insecurity, growing brutal separatist aspirations, elite state capture, political volatility, ethnic tensions, rising crime, and international opprobrium, just to name a few. In fact, in the words of Patrick Utomi, an economist, the "Nigerian promise has been paralyzed and [to] leave the country prostrate" (Utomi, 2007).

In fact, Henley, Tirtosudarmo, and Faudy (2012, p. S49) were also of the view that Nigeria has not lived up to its potential and as visionized by pioneering nationalists, who sacrificed for the nation's decolonization struggle. Among other details, they wrote without equivocation: "Nigeria is a flawed vision that failed to translate its oil wealth into national prosperity . . . policies based on shared growth or the public good." For Peter Lewis, it is to "blame Nigeria's tragic failure to translate its oil wealth into national prosperity on Nigeria's pervasive social, political, and institutional fragmentation" (Lewis, 2007, pp. 77–78).

Yet, another insight from the *British Broadcasting Corporation (BBC)* is captured in the following words: "Nigeria is one of the world's largest oil producers, but few Nigerians, including those in oil-producing areas, have benefited" (*BBC News*, February 18, 2019). On "opportunities for voice through democratic political participation" (Joseph & Herbst, 1997, p. 175) and, in the context of civic discourse since the return to civil rule in 1999, Nobel laureate Wole Soyinka posited: "In Nigeria, the will of the people, which lies at the very heart of democracy, appears to be a conditioned will" (Soyinka, 2019), as "elections become do or die affair for the country" (Lerawaju, 2007) and "Nigerians take the outcomes of the electoral process with accustomed cynicism" (Abati, 2007) worsened by the "brazen disregard of the popular will by electoral commissions" (Utomi, 2007).

Also, in a corollary trenchant observation, Attahiru Jega, former chairman of INEC, observed that democracy, apathy, and cynicism are linked to the "loss of trust and confidence in the electoral process" (Olokor, 2019), a situation that has forcefully been manifested by the continuing pattern of "low voter turnouts (percent of registered voters) in elections since 1999: 52.0% (1999), 69.1% (2003), 57.3% (2007), 55.4% (2011), 44% (2015), 37% (2019)" (Olokor, 2019). Soyinka and Jega are not alone in their brilliant assessments. Inferencing the Commonwealth Observer Group report of the 2007 Nigerian elections, then Commonwealth secretary-general, Don McKinnon, stated inter alia: "the report found serious deficiencies. . . . Nigeria had fallen well short of the democratic standards to which it had committed itself . . . the result of these failings was violence, even death, at the hands of those who sought to subvert democracy" (McKinnon, 2007). Furthermore, the most devastating of all is the failure of Nigerian leadership to use the country's abundant resources to lift Nigerians out of poverty, especially the middle class and the abject poor. The situation is dire to the point that the reticent president Buhari, upon assuming office, was quoted as saying publicly the following: "I felt like absconding after I took office . . . because of the myriad of problems I inherited from past governments. . . . I asked if there was any savings and I was told there was no savings. I asked what they did on agriculture, power, rail and roads. There was nothing" (*Punch*, November 3, 2016). Additionally, the magnitude of the failures of Nigerian leaders and the complicity of their followers was deemed very substantial to the extent that improvement in governance and poverty alleviation measures have subsequently been incorporated into the development agendas and policy actions of such important international organizations as the World Bank, IMF, UN, WHO, UNICEF, the British Commonwealth, ADB, Commission for Africa, and New Partnership for African Development; that was just to name a few of such organizations.

WRITERS' GALORE AS PART OF THE EXAMPLES

Also, as experts concluded, the "Nigerian condition" has influenced works by other experts, scholars, analysts, and writers, including but not limited to Chinua Achebe (*The Trouble with Nigeria*, 1983); Richard Joseph (*Democracy and Prebendal Politics in Nigeria*, 1987); Eghosa Osaghae (*The Crippled Giant: Nigeria Since Independence*, 1998); Karl Maier (*This House Has Fallen: Midnight in Nigeria*, 2000); Peter Lewis (*Growing Apart: Oil, Politics, and Economic Change in Indonesia and Nigeria*, 2007); Wale Adebanwi (*Authority Stealing: Anti-corruption War and Democratic Politics in Post-Military Nigeria*, 2012); Toyin Falola and Julius Ihonvbere (*The Rise and Fall of Nigeria's Second Republic: 1979–1984*, 1985); Wale Adebanwi and Ebenezer Obadare (Eds.) (*Democracy and Prebendalism in Nigeria: Critical Interpretations*, 2013); Joseph-Raji, Aitalohi, and Timmis (World Bank, 2018); Adewale Ademoyega (*Why We Struck: Story of the First Nigerian Coup*, 1982); Alexander Madiebo (*The Nigerian Revolution and the Biafran War*, 1980); and, indeed, Emeka Ojukwu (*Because I Am Involved*, 1989).

Furthermore, there are other credible assessments. Without necessarily rehashing Nigeria's well-known challenges and fault lines, it is very necessary to reemphasize the latest state of affairs in the country, indeed with reference to the *2019 Index of Economic Freedom Report* that was issued by the U.S. based Heritage Foundation, which on the following pages (pp. 326–327) provided the following assessment:

> Nigeria's economic freedom score is 57.3, making its economy the 111th freest in the 2019 Index. Its overall score has decreased by 1.2 points, with a steep drop in fiscal health and lower scores on judicial effectiveness and trade freedom outweighing improvements in government integrity, business freedom, and labor freedom. . . . Although Nigerian governments often pledge to enlarge the private sector through free-market reforms . . . the implementation of such policies has been very slow. State management of scarce resources has empowered political elites who fear that reforms will push up consumer prices, stoke political instability, and antagonize the middle classes, who rely on government-subsidized goods, and private-sector companies that depend on state handouts and protectionist policies. . . . There also have been lethal outbreaks of violence between herders and farmers in the Middle Belt region [including Southeast and Southwest region]. Low global oil prices have battered the petroleum-based economy. Agriculture, telecommunications, and services are contributing to modest economic growth, but more than 60 percent of Nigeria's 170 [200] million people still live in extreme poverty. . . . The judiciary has some independence but is hobbled by political interference, corruption, and a lack of resources. Corruption is rarely investigated or prosecuted, and impunity remains widespread at all levels of government. . . . Despite recent reforms, the structural changes that are needed to develop a more vibrant private sector have not emerged, and the oil sector still dominates overall economic activity. . . .

> Lingering barriers to trade and investment in the form of bureaucratic delays persists.

The "Index of Economic Freedom" measures economic freedom of 186 economies based on four broad categories: rule of law (property rights, government integrity, judicial effectiveness), government size (government spending, tax burden, fiscal health), regulatory efficiency (business freedom, labor freedom, monetary freedom), and open markets (trade freedom, investment freedom, and financial freedom).

The foregoing latest very revealing report further corroborated, in no uncertain terms, the continuing developmental and leadership challenges of the Nigerian nation, indeed as documented and analyzed in my book. Meanwhile, in light of the disclosed travails of Nigeria, with their negative impact on "the aggrieved Nigerian public" (Agbiboa, 2013, p. 244), a special light has been shone on the country's middle class and the poor, coupled with their "deleterious impact on institutional quality" (Sala-i-Martin & Subramanian, 2013, p. 570). Most certainly, it could be a way to rekindle and sustain hope as well as to make up for the lost ground on better economic growth and leadership in Nigeria, both public policy and private sector palliatives should be directed at a variety of variables and cogent Nigerian needs, which is very well identified in the book, with attestation from experts, authors, analysts, researchers, practitioners, civil society, foundations, development partners and, above all, interlocutors.

References

Abati, R. (2016, April 24). Confronting the Curse of Oil. *The Guardian*. Retrieved from http://guardian.ng/opinion/confronting-the-curse-of-oil/.

———. (2007, April 27). Notes on Nigeria's Elections (4). *The Guardian*.

Abimboye, D. (2010, December 5). The Diminishing OBJ. *Newswatch*.

Aborisade, S. (2015, July 24). NNPC, Engine Room of Corruption – Saraki. *Punch*. Retrieved from http://www.punchng.com/news/nnpc-engine-room-of-corruption-saraki.

———. (2014, February 5). NNPC Cannot Account for $20bn, Sanusi insists. *Punch*. Retrieved from http://www.punchng.com/news/nnpc-cannot-account-for-20bn-sanusi-insists.

———. (2014, February 24). Subsidiary Denies Collecting $6bn from NNPC. *Punch*. Retrieved from http://www.punchng.com/business/business-economy/subsidiary-denies-collecting-6bn-from-nnpc.

Aboyade, O. (1966). *Foundations of an African Economy – A Study of Investment and Growth in Nigeria*. New York: Frederick A. Praeger Publishers.

Abayomi, A., & Areyeka, L. (2014, April 3). Why Basic Education Remains a Challenge in Nigeria – Wike. *Vanguard*. Retrieved from http://www.vanguardngr.com/2014/04/basic-education-remains-challenge-nigeria-wike.

Acemoglu, D., Johnson, S., & Robinson, J. A. (2001). The Colonial Origins of Comparative Development: An Empirical Investigation. *American Economic Review*, 91(5), 1369–1401.

———. (2005). Institutions as a Fundamental Cause of Long-run Growth. In P. Aghion & S. N. Durlauf (Eds.), *Handbook of Economic Growth* (Volume 1A, Chapter 6, 385–472). Retrieved from https://economics.mit.edu/files/4469.

———. (2008). *The Role of Institutions in Growth and Development*. Commission on Growth and Development. World Bank. Working Paper No. 10.

———. (2010). The Role of Institutions in Growth and Development. *Review of Economics and Institutions*, 1(2), 1–32. Retrieved from http://www.rei.unipg.it/rei/article/view/14/22.

———. (2017, January 30). The Economic Impact of Colonialism. Retrieved from https://voxeu.org/article/economic-impact-colonialism.

———. (2005). Unbundling Institutions. *Journal of Political Economy*, 113(5), 949–995. Retrieved from https://economics.mit.edu/files/4467.

Acemoglu, D., Verdier, T., & Robinson, J. A. (2004, April-May). Kleptocracy and Divide-and-Rule: A Model of Personal Rule. *Journal of European Economic Association,* 2(2–3), 162–192.

Acemoglu, D., Bautista, M. A., Querubin, P., & Robinson, J. A. (2007). Economic and Political Inequality in Development: The Case of Cundinamarca, Mexico. National Bureau of Economic Research Working Paper No. 13208. Retrieved from https://www.nber.org/papers/w13208.pdf.

Acemoglu, D. (1995). Reward Structures and the Allocation of Talent. *European Economic Review*, 39(1), 17–33.

Achebe, C. (2012). *There Was a Country*. New York: The Penguin Press.

———. (1983). *The Trouble with Nigeria.* Enugu, Nigeria: Fourth Dimension Publishers.

Achiume, E. T. (2019). Migration as Decolonization. *Stanford Law Review*, 71(6), 1509–1574.

Achumba, I. C., Ighomereho, O. S., & Akpor-Robaro, M. O. M. (2013). Security Challenges in Nigeria and the Implications for Business Activities and Sustainable Development. *Journal of Economics and Sustainable Development*, 4(2), 79–99.

Adam, S. [2007] (1776). *An Inquiry into the Nature and Causes of the Wealth of Nations*. S. M. Soares (Ed.). New York: MetaLibiri Digital Library, May 29, 2007. Retrieved from https://www.ibiblio.org/ml/libri/s/SmithA_WealthNations_p.pdf.

Adebanwi, W., & Obadare, E. (2011). When Corruption Fights Back: Democracy and Elite Interest in Nigeria's Anti-corruption War. *The Journal of Modern African Studies*, 49(2), 185–213.

———. (2010). Introducing Nigeria at Fifty: The Nation in Narration. *Journal of Contemporary African Studies*, 28(4), 379–405.

———. (2016). Governance and Unending Search for Leadership in African Politics. In Ebenezer Obadare & Wale Adebanwi (Eds.), *Governance and the Crisis of Rule in Contemporary Africa.* New York: Palgrave Macmillan.

Adebanwi, W. (2012). *Authority Stealing: Anti-corruption War and Democratic Politics in Post-military Nigeria*. Durham, NC: Carolina Academic Press.

Adebayo, F. A. (2009). Parents' Preference for Private Secondary Schools in Nigeria. *International Journal of Educational Sciences*, 1(1), 1–6. Retrieved from https://www.tandfonline.com/doi/abs/10.1080/09751122.2009.11889969.

Adebayo, B. (2013, February 20). Foreign Medical Trip: How Nigeria Loses ₦78bn Annually. *Punch.*

Adedini, S. A., Odimegwu, C., Bamiwuye, O., Fadeyibi, O., & De Wet, N. (2014). Barriers to Accessing Health Care in Nigeria: Implications for Child Survival. Global health Action, 7, 1–10. Retrieved from https://www.ncbi.nlm.nih.gov/pmc/articles/PMC3957799/pdf/GHA-7-23499.pdf.

Adejoro, L. (2013, December 11). Primary Health Care System in Nigeria Comatose. *Daily Times.* Retrieved from http://www.dailytimes.com.ng/article/primary-health-care-system-nigeria-comatose.

Adeloye, D. et al. (2017). Health Workforce and Governance: The Crisis in Nigeria. *Human Resources for Health*, 15(3), 1–8. Retrieved from https://www.ncbi.nlm.nih.gov/pmc/articles/PMC5427605/pdf/12960_2017_Article_205.pdf.

Adeniji, G. (2015, October 23). Anyaoku, Fayemi Bemoan Nigeria's Leadership Crisis. *Punch.* Retrieved from http://www.punchng.com/?p=201919.

Aderinokun, K. (2007, March 23). Nigeria Loses ₦80bn to Deplorable Transport Infrastructure, say ADB. *This Day.*

Adesola, A. O. (1991). The Nigerian University System: Meeting the Challenges of Growth in a Depressed Economy. *Higher Education*, 21, 121–133.

Adetayo, O. (2014, November 29). *Punch.* Retrieved from http://www.punchng.com/columnists/aso-rock-lens-columnists/sultan-and-jonathans-numerous-aides.

Adeyi, O. (2016). Health System in Nigeria: From Underperformance to Measured Optimism. *Health Systems & Reform*, 2(4), 285–289. Retrieved from https://www.tandfonline.com/doi/pdf/10.1080/23288604.2016.1224023?needAccess=true.

Adewole, A. M., & Osabuohien, E. S. C. (2007). Analysis of Cost of Governance and Options for Its Reduction in Nigeria. *Nigerian Journal of Economic and Social Studies*, 49(1), 137–159. Retrieved from http://eprints.covenantuniversity.edu.ng/106/1/Analysis__of_Cost_of_Governance_%26_Options_4its_Reduction_in_Nig.pdf.

Afigbo, A. E. (1972). *The Warrant Chiefs: Indirect Rule in Southeastern Nigeria, 1891–1929.* London: Longman.

———. (2009). Africa and the Abolition of the Slave Trade. *The William and Mary Quarterly*, 66(4), 705–714.

Afolabi, G. K. (2010). Corruption in Contemporary Nigeria. *DLSU Business & Economic Review*, 19(2), 53–61.

African Union Commission. (2015). Agenda 2063 – The Africa We Want. Retrieved from https://www.un.org/en/africa/osaa/pdf/au/agenda2063.pdf.

African Network for Environment and Economic Justice (ANEEJ). (2020). The Disbursement of the Recovered $322.5 Million Abacha Loot in Nigeria.

Agande, B. (2013, February 13). FG Uncovers 45,000 Ghost Workers, Saves ₦100b. *Vanguard.* Retrieved from https://www.vanguardngr.com/2013/02/fg-uncovers-45000-ghost-workers/.

Agbaje, E. B. A. (2004). Corruption, Accountability and Good Governance: Reflection on Governance in Nigeria's Fourth Republic 1999–2003. *Journal of International Politics and Development*, 2(1), 77–99.

Agbese, P. O. (1992). With Fingers on the Trigger: The Military as Custodian of Democracy in Nigeria. *Journal of Third World Studies*, 9(2), 220–253.

———. (1999). Party Registration and the Subversion of Democracy in Nigeria. *Issue: A Journal of Opinion*, 27(1), 63–65.

Agbese, D. (2012). *Ibrahim Babangida: The Military, Politics, and Power in Nigeria.* London: Adonis and Abbey Publishers.

Agbiboa, D. E. (2012a). Serving the Few, Starving the Many: How Corruption Underdevelops Nigeria and How There Is an Alternative Perspective to Corruption Cleanups. *Africa Today*, 58(4), 111–132.

———. (2012b). Between Corruption and Development: The Political Economy of State Robbery in Nigeria. *Journal of Business Ethics*, 108(3), 325–345.

———. (2013). Protectors or Predators? The Embedded Problem of Police Corruption and Deviance in Nigeria. *Administration & Society*, 47(3), 244–281.

Aghedo, I. (2012). Winning the War, Losing the Peace: Amnesty and the Challenges of Post-conflict Peace-building in the Niger Delta, Nigeria. *Journal of Asian and African Studies*, 48(3), 267–280. Retrieved from https://journals.sagepub.com/doi/10.1177/0021909612453987?icid=int.sj-challenge-page.similar-articles.2.

Aghedo, I., & Osumah, O. (2014). Insurgency in Nigeria: A Comparative Study of Niger Delta and Boko Haram Uprisings. *Journal of Asian and African Studies*, 50(2), 208–222. Retrieved from https://journals.sagepub.com/doi/10.1177/0021909614520726?icid=int.sj-challenge-page.similar-articles.3.

Agriculture and Agri-Food Canada. (2010, July). Comparative Consumer Profile – Canada and United States. Retrieved from http://www.ats.agr.gc.ca/info/5645-eng.htm.

Agu, U., & Evoh, C. J. (2011). Macroeconomic Policy for Full and Productive and Decent Employment for All: The Case of Nigeria. Employment Sector Working Paper No. 107. International Labor Organization. Geneva. Retrieved from https://www.ilo.org/public/libdoc/ilo/2011/111B09_338_engl.pdf.

Ahmad, M. H., & Ahmed, Q. S. (2014). Does the Institutional Quality Matter to Attract Foreign Direct Investment? An Empirical Investigation for Pakistan. *South Asia Economic Journal*, 15(1), 55–70. Retrieved from http://journals.sagepub.com/doi/abs/10.1177/1391561414525708.

Aidt, T. S. (2009). Corruption, Institutions and Economic Development. Faculty of Economics, University of Cambridge. United Kingdom. Retrieved from http://www.iig.ox.ac.uk/output/articles/OxREP/iiG-OxREP-Aidt.pdf.

———. (2003). Economic Analysis of Corruption: A Survey. *Economic Journal*, 113(491), F632-F652.

Aiyede, E. R. et al. (2015). The Political Economy of Social Protection Policy Uptake in Nigeria. Partnership for African Social & Governance Research (PASGR). PASGR Working Paper 002.

Ajakaiye, O. (2008). Towards Securing Fiscal Policy Coordination in Nigeria. In P. Collier, C. S. Soludo, & C. Pattillo (Eds.), *Economic Policy Options for a Prosperous Nigeria*. New York: Palgrave Macmillan. Retrieved from https://zodml.org/sites/default/files/%5BPaul_Collier,_Charles_C._Soludo,_Catherine_Pattil_0.pdf.

Ajayi, J. F. A. (1974). The Aftermath of the Collapse of Old Oyo. In J. F. A. Ajayi & M. Crowder (Eds.), *History of West Africa*. London: Longman.

———. (2002). Unfinished Business: Confronting the Legacies of Slavery and Colonialism in Africa. Retrieved from https://www.cssscal.org/pdf/publication/ade_ajayi.pdf.

Ajayi, J. F. A., & Uya, O. (2010). *Slavery and Slave Trade in Nigeria.* In J. F. A. Ajayi & O. Uya (Eds.), *From Earliest Times to the Nineteenth Century.* Safari Books Ltd.

Ajayi, A. I., & Adesote, A. S. (2013). The Gains and Pains of the Amnesty Program in the Niger Delta Region of Nigeria, 2007–2012: A Preliminary Assessment. *Journal of Asian and African Studies,* 48(4), 506–520.

Ajaero, C. (2009, May 17). Centers of Decay. *Newswatch.*

Akachi, Y., & Atun, R. (2011). Effect of Investment in Malaria Control on Child Mortality in Sub-Saharan Africa in 2002–2008. *PLoS One*, 6(6): e21309, 1–12. Retrieved from https://www.ncbi.nlm.nih.gov/pubmed/21738633.

Akande, S. O., & Akerele, W. O. (2008). Employment Generation in the Informal Sector of Nigerian Economy. Nigerian Institute of Social and Economic Research (NISER).

Akasike, C., & Okpi, A. (2013, December 15). We Steal Because Nigerians Don't Stone Us. *Punch.*

Ake, C. (1981). *A Political Economy of Africa.* Lagos, Nigeria: Longman Press, Ltd.

———. (1996). *Democracy and Development in Africa.* Washington, DC: The Brookings Institution.

———. (1985). The State in Contemporary Africa. In *The Political Economy of Nigeria.* Claude Ake (Ed). Lagos, Nigeria: Longman.

———. (n.d.). The Case for Democracy. *In African Governance in the 1990s.*

———. (1993). The Unique Case of African Democracy. *International Affairs*, 69(2), 239–244.

———. (1966). Charismatic Legitimation and Political Integration. *Comparative Studies in Society and History*, 9(1), 1–13.

Akeredolu-Ale, E. O. (1975). *The Underdevelopment of Indigenous Entrepreneurship in Nigeria*. Ibadan, Nigeria: Ibadan University Press.

Akinbobola, T. O., & Saibu, M. O. O. (2004). Income Inequality, Unemployment, and Poverty in Nigeria: A Vector Autoregressive Approach. *The Journal of Policy Reform*, 7(3), 175–183. Retrieved from https://www.tandfonline.com/doi/abs/10.1080/1384128042000261800.

Akinkuotu, E. (2016, June 4). FG Releases List of Recovered Loot. *Punch.* Retrieved from http://punchng.com/fg-releases-list-looters/.

Akinwotu, E., & Olukoya, S. (2017, July 18). 'Shameful' Nigeria: A Country that Doesn't Care about Inequality. *The Guardian* (London). Retrieved from https://www.theguardian.com/inequality/2017/jul/18/shameful-nigeria-doesnt-care-about-inequality-corruption.

Akinwunmi, A. K., & Adekoya, R. B. (2018). Assessment of the Impact of External Borrowing on the Economic Growth of the Developing Countries - Nigerian Experience. *Asian Business Research*, 3(1), 29–40.

Akinyemi, O., & Atilola, O. (2013). Nigerian Resident Doctors on Strike: Insights from and Policy Implications of Job Satisfaction among Resident Doctors in a Nigerian Teaching Hospital. *International Journal of Health Plan Management*, 28(1), e46–61. Retrieved from https://www.ncbi.nlm.nih.gov/pubmed/22961749.

Akinyemi, B. (1978). *Nigeria and the World: Readings in Nigerian Foreign Policy.* Bolaji Akinyemi (Ed.). Ibadan: Oxford University Press.

Akinloye, B. (2014, August 3). I insist Nigeria is Dancing on the Brink – John Campbell. *Punch.* Retrieved from http://www.punchng.com/news/i-insist-nigeria-is-dancing-on-the-brink-john-campbell.

Alawiye, A. (2013, December 13). Nigeria Lost $129bn to Illegal Financial Outflows – Report. *Punch.* Retrieved from http://kaaf.com/2013/01/Nigeria-lost-129bn-to-illegal-financial-outflows--Report-490123.

Alesina, A., & Dollar, D. (2000). Who Gives Foreign Aid to Whom and Why? *Journal of Economic Growth,* 5(1), 33–63. Retrieved from https://link.springer.com/article/10.1023/A:1009874203400.

Alesina, A., & Zhuravskaya, E. (2008). Segregation and the Quality of Government. Retrieved from https://voxeu.org/article/how-ethnic-fragmentation-undermines-good-governance.

Alesina, A., Easterly, W., & Matuszeski, J. (2006). "Artificial States," National Bureau of Economic Research (NBER). Cambridge, MA. NEBR Working Paper No. 12328. Retrieved from https://www.nber.org/papers/w12328.

Allison et al., (2018). Dealing with Oil Spill Scenarios in the Niger Delta: Lessons from the Past. In *The Political Ecology of Oil and Gas Activities in the Nigerian Aquatic Ecosystem.* Prince E. Ndimele (Ed.). Academy Press, pp. 351–368.

Allison, S. (2015, November 12). Nigeria Gets New Cabinet After Six Months Delay. *The Guardian* (London). Retrieved from https://www.theguardian.com/world/2015/nov/12/nigeria-buhari-cabinet-analysis.

Aliyu, Y. (2006). A Presentation to Workshop on Debt, Finance, and Emerging Issues in Finance Integration. Commonwealth Secretariat, London, March 6–7.

Amaefule, E., Okolor, F., & Adesomoju, A. (2015, April 29). Jonathan, Sambo, Others to Get ₦3.24bn Severance Pay. *Punch.* Retrieved from http://www.punchng.com/news/jonathan-sambo-others-to-get-n3-24bn-severance-pay.

Amaefule, E. (2016, August 10). Town Hall Drama: Nigerians Tackle Buhari's Ministers. *Punch.* Retrieved from http://punchng.com/town-hall-drama-nigerians-tackle-buharis-ministers/.

Ameh, O. (2017). Nigerian Factor: A Monster in Nigeria's Wheel of Progress and the Way Out. *Saudi Journal of Humanities and Social Sciences*, 2(8), 677–681.

Ameh, J. (2014). Reps Uncover Fresh Missing ₦35bn. *Punch.* Retrieved from http://www.punchng.com/news/reps-uncover-fresh-missing-n35bn.

———. (2014, February 26). NNPC Fails to Declare $22.8bn Oil Proceeds – NEITI. *Punch.* Retrieved from http://www.punchng.com/news/nnpc-fails-to-declare-22-8bn-oil-proceeds-neiti.

———. (2016, December 8). Reps Summon NNPC, Shell, Others Over $17bn Stolen Crude. *Punch.* Retrieved from http://punchng.com/reps-summon-nnpc-shell-others-17bn-stolen-crude/.

Amnesty International. (2009). Nigeria: Petroleum, Pollution and Poverty in the Niger Delta. Retrieved from https://www.es.amnesty.org/uploads/media/REPORT_Petroleum__Pollution_and_Poverty_in_the_Niger_Delta.pdf.

———. (2010, October). *Nigeria – Fifty Years of Independence: Making Human Rights a Reality.*

Amoor, S. S. (2010). The Need to Improve Teacher Quality in Business Education Program in Nigerian Universities. *International Journal of Educational Research*, 11(1), 2–11.

Amuta, C. (2013, February 19). Can We Abolish the People? *This Day.* Retrieved from http://www.thisdaylive.com/articles/can-we-abolish-the-people-/139899.

Amuwo, A. (2010). Between Elite Protectionism and Popular Resistance: The Political Economy of Nigeria's Fractured State Since Juridical Independence. *Journal of Contemporary African Studies*, 28(4), 423–442.

Amuwo, K. (2001). Introduction: Transition as Democratic Regression. In *Nigeria During the Abacha Years 1993–1998*. Ibadan, Nigeria: Institut français de recherche en Afrique (IFRA Nigeria). Retrieved from https://books.openedition.org/ifra/623.

———. (2002). Between Intellectual Responsibility and Political Commodification of Knowledge: Nigeria's Academic Political Scientists under the Babangida Military Junta, 1985–1993. *African Studies Review*, 45(2), 93–121.

———. (2010). Beyond Prebendal Politics: Class and Political Struggles in Post-Colonial Nigeria. In Wale Adebanwi & Ebenezer Obadare (Eds.), *Democracy and Prebendalism in Nigeria.* New York: Palgrave Macmillan.

Andrae, G., & Beckman, B. (2013). Lagos Tailors, Trade Unions, and Organizations in the Informal Economy. *African Studies Review*, 56(3), 191–208.

Andreski, S. (1970). Kleptocracy as a System of Government in Africa. In Arnold J. Heidenheimer (Ed.), *Political Corruption: Readings in Comparative Analysis.* New York: Holt Rinehart and Winston.

———. (1968). *The African Predicament: A Study in the Pathology of Modernization.* New York: Atherton Press.

Annan, K. (2000, July 12, p. 5). Organization of African Unity (now African Union) Summit. Lome, Togo. *Daily Graphic.* Quoted in George Ayittey (2002). "Why Africa is Poor." Profile Books: London. Retrieved from http://ieas.unideb.hu/admin/file_6845.pdf.

Anochie, I., & Eke, F. (2003). Chronic Renal Failure in Children: A Report from Port Harcourt, Nigeria (1985–2000). *Pediatric Nephrology*, 18(7), 692–695. Retrieved from https://link.springer.com/article/10.1007/s00467-003-1150-0.

Anoruo, E., & Braha, H. (2005). Corruption and Economic Growth: The African Experience. *Journal of Sustainable Development in Africa,* 7(1), 43–55.

Antoninis, M. (2014). Tackling the Largest Global Education Challenge? Secular and Religious Education in Northern Nigeria. *World Development*, 59, 82–92. Retrieved from https://www.sciencedirect.com/science/article/abs/pii/S0305750X14000187.

Anyadike, N. O. (2013). New Revenue Sharing Formula Clamor by the Nigerian State Governors: Propelling Factors and Matters Arising. *Public Policy and Administration Research*, 3(2), 27–36.

Anyagafu, V. S., & Sam-Duru, P. (2014, April 6). US Slams Nigeria: Corruption Extremely High – Dep. Asst. Secretary of State. *Vanguard.* Retrieved from http:

//www.vanguardngr.com/2014/04/us-slams-nigeria-corruption-extremely-high-country-dep-asst-secretary-state.

Apter, D. (1963). *Ghana in Transition*. New York: Atheneum.

Arat, Z. F. (1973). Democracy and Economic Development: Modernization Theory Revisited. *Comparative Politics*, 21(1), 21–36.

Aristotle. *Politics*. Benjamin Jowett (Trans.). New York: The Modern Library. Retrieved from http://www.bard.edu/library/arendt/pdfs/Aristotle-Politics.pdf.

Armadov, A. K. (2013). Oil, Democracy, and Context. *Comparative Political Studies*, 47(9), 1238–1267. Retrieved from http://journals.sagepub.com/doi/abs/10.1177/0010414013495358.

Arrow, K. J. (1962). The Economic Implications of Learning by Doing. *The Review of Economic Studies*, 29(3), 155–173.

Arrow, K. J., & Capron, W. M. (1959). Dynamic Shortages and Price Rises: The Engineers-Scientist Case. *The Quarterly Journal of Economics*, 73(2), 292–308.

Arowosegbe, J. O. (2017). Corruption and Profligacy as Governance Failure in Nigeria. *Journal of the Historical Society of Nigeria*, 26, 122–153.

Aryeetey, E., & Asmah, E. (2011). Africa's New Oil Economies: Managing Expectations. Brookings Institution. Washington, DC. Retrieved from https://www.brookings.edu/wp-content/uploads/2016/06/01_africa_economy_agi.pdf#page=24.

Asefa, S., & Huang, W. C. (2015). Introduction. In *The Political Economy of Good Governance*. W. E. Upjohn Institute for Employment Research. Kalamazoo, Michigan, USA.

Asiyai, R. I. (2015). Improving Quality Higher Education in Nigeria: The Roles of Stakeholders. *International Journal of Higher Education*, 4(1), 61–70. Retrieved from http://www.sciedu.ca/journal/index.php/ijhe/article/view/6062/3624.

Asu, F. (2015, March 18). Switzerland to Return ₦75.2bn Abacha Loot to Nigeria. *Punch*. Retrieved from http://www.punchng.com/news/switzerland-to-return-n75-2bn-abacha-loot-to-nigeria.

Atkinson, R. D. (1998, February). Building New Skills for the New Economy. Progressive Policy Institute. *Backgrounder*.

———. (2013). Prospering through Innovation Economics. In Robert D. Atkinson (Ed.), *The Politics of Growth, Stability and Reform*. Policy Network & Global Progress.

———. (2012). Think Like an Enterprise: Why Nations Need Comprehensive Productivity Strategies. Information Technology & Innovation Foundation.

Atume, F. (2010). Nigeria. In *Engineering: Issues, Challenges and Opportunities for Development*. United Nations Educational, Scientific and Cultural Organization. Retrieved from http://unesdoc.unesco.org/images/0018/001897/189753e.pdf.

Atwood, J. B. (1994, May 4). Administrator, United States Agency for International Development. Statement at White House Press Conference on the South African Initiative, Washington, DC.

Austen, R. A. (1979). The Trans-Saharan Slave Trade: A Tentative Census. In H. A. Gemery & J. S. Hogendorn (Eds.), *The Uncommon Market: Essays in the Economic History of the Atlantic Slave Trade*. New York: Academic Press.

Auty, R. M. (1993). *Sustaining Development in the Mineral Economies: The Resource Curse Thesis*. London: Routledge.

———. (Ed.) (2001). *Resource Abundance and Economic Development*. Oxford University Press.

———. (1994). The Resource Curse Thesis: Minerals in Bolivian Development, 1970–90. *Singapore Journal of Tropical Geography*, 15(2), 95–111. Retrieved from https://www.scribd.com/document/76242025/68-Minerals-in-Bolivian-Development-1970-90-Auty.

———. (2001). Why Resource Endowments Can Undermine Economic Development: Concepts and Case Studies. Paper Prepared for the BP-Amoco Seminar, Lincoln College, Oxford University, United Kingdom.

———. (1994). Industrial Policy Reform in Six Newly Industrializing Countries: The Resource Curse Thesis. *World Development*, 22(1), 11–26. Retrieved from https://www.sciencedirect.com/science/article/pii/0305750X94901651.

———. (2008). Political Economy of African Mineral Revenue Deployment: Angola, Botswana, Nigeria and Zambia Compared. Working Paper.

Auty, R. & Evia, J. L. (2001). A Growth Collapse with Point Resources: Bolivia. In R. Auty (Ed.), *Resource Abundance and Economic Development*. Oxford: Oxford University Press.

Awad, A. B. (2011). Foreword. In Ugochukwu Agwu & Chijioke J. Evoh, *Macroeconomic Policy for Full and Productive and Decent Employment for All: The Case of Nigeria*. Employment Sector Employment Working Paper No. 107. International Labor Organization, Geneva. Retrieved from https://www.ilo.org/wcmsp5/groups/public/---ed_emp/---emp_policy/documents/publication/wcms_169560.pdf.

Awojobi, O. N. (2014). The Socio-Economic Implications of Boko Haram Insurgency in the North-East of Nigeria. *International Journal of Innovation and Scientific Research*, 11(1), 144–150.

Awolowo, O. (1968). *The People's Republic*. Ibadan, Nigeria: Oxford University Press.

———. (1987). *The Travails of Democracy and the Rule of Law*. Ibadan, Nigeria: Evans Brothers Limited.

———. (1981, July). Letter on the State of the Nation to President Shehu Shagari.

Awomuse, B. O., Olorunleke, K., & Alimi, R. S. (2013). The Effect of Federal Government Size on Economic Growth in Nigeria, 1961–2011. *Developing Country Studies*, 3(7), 68–76.

Awoyinfa, S. et al., (2012, April 15). Nigerian Varsities: Saddled with Ageing Infrastructure. *Punch*.

Awoyinfa, S. (2016, January 23). Nigeria Spends $1bn Annually on Medical Tourism – Minister. *Punch*. Retrieved from http://www.punchng.com/nigeria-spends-1bn-annually-on-medical-tourism-minister/.

Ayee, J. A. (2016). The Roots of Corruption: The Ghanaian Enquiry Revisited. The Institute of Economic Affairs (IEA), Ghana.

Ayittey, G. B. N. (2002, August). Why Africa is Poor. In *Sustainable Development: Promoting Progress or Perpetuating Poverty?* Julian Morris (Ed.). Retrieved from http://ieas.unideb.hu/admin/file_6845.pdf.

Ayogu, M. (1997). Empirical Studies of Nigeria's Foreign Exchange Parallel Market II: Speculative Efficiency and Noisy Trading. African Economic Research Consortium, Nairobi. Retrieved from https://aercafrica.org/wp-content/uploads/2018/07/RP69.pdf.

Ayotebi, O. (2015, November 18). Nigerians Shouldn't Be Begging, Says Buhari. *Punch*. Retrieved from http://punchng.com/nigerians-shouldnt-be-begging-says-buhari.

Azikiwe, N. (1980). *Ideology for Nigeria: Capitalism, Socialism, or Welfarism?* Macmillan Publishers.

———. (1965). Essentials for Nigerian Survival. *Foreign Affairs*, 43(3), 447–461.

Azubuike, L. (2005). Privatization and Foreign Investments in Nigeria. *Tulsa Journal of Comparative and International Law*, 13(1), 59–89. Retrieved from https://digitalcommons.law.utulsa.edu/cgi/viewcontent.cgi?article=1273&context=tjcil.

Babalola, A. (2014, May 19). Falana Calls for Probe of ₦3tn Security Budgets. *This Day*.

Babatunde et al., (2018). Bunkering Activities in Nigerian Waters and their Eco-economic Consequences. In Prince E. Ndimele (Ed.), *The Political Ecology of Oil and Gas Activities in the Nigerian Aquatic Ecosystem* (pp. 351–368). Academy Press.

Bach, D. (2005). Inching Towards a Country Without State: Prebendalism, Violence and State Betrayal in Nigeria. In C. Clapham, J. Herbst & G. Mills (Eds.), *Africa's Big States*. Johannesburg, South Africa.

———. Managing a Plural Society: The Boomerang Effects of Nigerian Federalism. *Commonwealth and Comparative Politics* (formerly called *Journal of Commonwealth & Comparative Politics*), 27(2), 218–245.

Bairoch, P. (1993). *Economics and World History: Myths and Paradoxes*. Chicago: University of Chicago Press.

Bakam, A. (2015, April 29). Yuguda Sacks 2,000 Aides. *Punch*. Retrieved from http://www.punchng.com/news/yuguda-sacks-2000-aides.

Balandier, G., & Cunneen, J. E. (1952). The Fact of Colonialism: A Theoretical Approach. *Cross Currents*, 2(4), 10–31.

Baliamoune-Lutz, M., & Ndikumana, L. (2008). Corruption and Growth in African Countries: Exploring the Investment Channel.

Balogun, M. J. (2003). Causative and Enabling Factors in Public Integrity: A Focus on Leadership, Institutions, and Character Formation. *Public Integrity*, 5, 127–147.

Bamidele, O., Olaniyan, A. O., & Ayodele, B. (2015). Seized by Sleaze: The Siege of Corruption and a Search for Workable Options in Nigeria. *International Social Science Review*, 90 (1), Article 3, 1–26.

Bamgboye, P. O. (2014). The Military and Socio-Economic Development in Nigeria (1983 – 1999): A Critical Appraisal. *Mediterranean Journal of Social Sciences*, 5(23), 2340–2344. Retrieved from http://www.mcser.org/journal/index.php/mjss/article/viewFile/4789/4646.

Bang, H. P. (2018). The American Dream: Who Else but the Young Can Revive It? *Policy Studies*, 39(3), 274–291.

Baranson, J. (1969). Role of Science and Technology in Advancing Development of Newly Industrializing States. *Socio-Economic Planning*, 3(4), 351–383.

Bayart, J. F. (1993). *The State in Africa: The Politics of the Belly*. Addison-Wesley Longman Ltd.

Bayart, J. F., Ellis, S., & Hibou, B. (2009). *Criminalization of the State in Africa*. Indiana University Press.

Bayley, D. H. (1966). The Effects of Corruption in a Developing Nation. *The Western Political Quarterly*, 19(4), 719–732.

BBC News. (2011, August 25). Nigeria's EFCC 'Failing to Tackle Corrupt Politicians.' Retrieved from https://www.bbc.com/news/world-africa-14671687.

———. (2015, December 24). Nigeria Boko Haram: Militants 'Technically Defeated' – Buhari. Retrieved from https://www.bbc.com/news/world-africa-35 173618.

———. (2018, February 26). Nigeria Dapchi School Kidnappings: What we Know. Retrieved from https://www.bbc.com/news/world-africa-43197694.

———. (2006, October 20). Nigerian Leaders 'Stole' $380 billion. Retrieved from http://news.bbc.co.uk/2/hi/africa/6069230.stm.

———. (2016, May 10). David Cameron calls Nigeria and Afghanistan 'fantastically corrupt.' Retrieved from http://www.bbc.com/news/uk-politics-36260193.

———. (2000, May 9).

———. (2000, January 21).

———. (2019, February 18). Nigeria Country Profile. Retrieved from https://www .bbc.com/news/world-africa-13949550.

Becker, G. S. (1958). Competition and Democracy. *The Journal of Law & Economics*, 1, 105–109.

Bhagwati, J. (1982). Directly Unproductive, Profit Seeking (DUP) Activities. *Journal of Political Economy*, 90(5), 988–1002.

Bates, R. H. (2008a). *When Things Fell Apart: State Failure in Late-century Africa*. New York: Cambridge University Press.

———. (2008b). The Logic of State Failure: Learning from Late-Century Africa. *Conflict Management and Peace Science*, 25(4), 297–314.

———. Bates, R. H. (2008c). State Failure. *Annual Review of Political Science*, 11, 1–12.

Barro, R. J. (2003). Determinants of Economic Growth in a Panel of Countries. *Annals of Economics and Finance*, 4, 231–274. Retrieved from http://down.aefweb .net/WorkingPapers/w505.pdf.

———. (2013). Education and Economic Growth. *Annals of Economics and Finance*, 14(2), 301–328. Retrieved from ftp://ftp.aefweb.net/WorkingPapers/w571.pdf.

Bassey, D. (2007, April 7). FG Spends ₦384bn Annually on NITEL, PHCN, Others, say Chigbue. *Daily Independent*.

Bauer, P. (1963). *West African Trade: A Study of Competition, Oligopoly and Monopoly in a Changing Economy*. London: Routledge & Kegan Paul Ltd, 1963, p. 195. (First published by Cambridge University Press in 1954).

———. (1984). Remembrance of Studies Past: Retracing First Steps. In G. M. Meier & D. Seers (Eds.), *Pioneers of Development*. World Bank.

———. (1981). *Equality, the Third World and Economic Delusion*. Cambridge, MA: Harvard University Press.

Bauer, A., et al., (2016). *Natural Resource Revenue Sharing*. United Nations Development Program. Retrieved from https://resourcegovernance.org/sites/default/files/documents/nrgi_undp_resource-sharing_web_0.pdf.

Baumol, W. J., & Bowen, W. G. (1965). On the Performing Arts: The Anatomy of Their Economic Problems. *American Economic Review*, 55(1/2), 495–502.

Baumol, W. J. (1967). Macroeconomics of Unbalanced Growth: The Anatomy of Urban Crisis. *American Economic Review*, 57(3), 415–426.

———. (2012). *The Cost Disease: Why Computers Get Cheaper and Health Care Doesn't*. Yale University Press.

Bazilian et al., (2013). Oil, Energy Poverty and Resource Dependence in West Africa. *Journal of Energy & Natural Resources Law*, 31(1), 33–53.

Beck, M. (2007). Der Rentierstaats-Ansatz und das Problem abweichender Fälle. *Zeitschrift für Internationale Beziehungen*, 14(1), 43–70. Retrieved from https://www.nomos-elibrary.de/10.5771/0946-7165-2007-1-43.pdf?download_full_pdf=1.

Becker, G. S. (1960). Underinvestment in College Education. *American Economic Review*, 50, 346–354.

———. (1962). Investment in Human Capital: A Theoretical Analysis. *The Journal of Political Economy*, 70(5), Part 2, 9–49.

Beckman, B. (1982). Whose State? State and Capitalist Development in Nigeria. *Review of African Political Economy*, 23, Scandinavian Perspectives on Africa, 37–51.

Benjamin, N. et al. (2014). Informal Economy and the World Bank. Policy Research Working Paper, WPS 6888. Retrieved from http://documents1.worldbank.org/curated/en/416741468332060156/pdf/WPS6888.pdf.

Benthuysen, J. V. (2015). In-between Anarchy and Interdependence: From State Death to Fragile and Failing States. *Third World Quarterly*, 36(1), 22–39.

Berman, S. (2009, March 12). What to Read on Modernization Theory. *Foreign Affairs*.

Berry, S. (1967). Cocoa in Western Nigeria, 1890–1940: A Study of an Innovation in a Developing Country (Unpublished Ph.D. dissertation). University of Michigan.

Bevan, D., Collier, P., & Gunning, J. W. (1999). Nigeria and Indonesia. In *The Political Economy of Poverty, Equity, and Growth*. World Bank. Retrieved from http://documents.worldbank.org/curated/en/118981468775569456/text/multi-page.txt.

Bhorat, H. (2015). *Inequality in Africa: Implications for the Sustainable Development Goals*. Washington, DC: Brookings Institution.

Blackburn, K., Bose, N., & Haque, E. H. (2004). Endogenous Corruption in Economic Development. The University of Nottingham, Research Paper 2004/16, 1–33. Retrieved from https://pdfs.semanticscholar.org/4bac/8e796bd9484d2ca3020117d5ea13583e859a.pdf.

Blanton, R. et al. (2001). Colonial Style and Post-colonial Ethnic Conflict in Africa. *Journal of Peace Research*, 38(4), 473–491. Retrieved from http://journals.sagepub.com/doi/abs/10.1177/0022343301038004005.

Block, R. (1998, June 9). Sani Abacha, Brutal Dictator of Nigeria, Dies of Heart Attack. *Wall Street Journal*. Retrieved from https://www.wsj.com/articles/SB89731953880222500.

Blount, M. (1998, October 21). *BBC News* Online.

Boone, P. (1995). Politics and the Effectiveness of Foreign Aid. National Bureau of Economic Research (NBER), Working Paper 5308.

Bovens, M. (2007). Analyzing and Assessing Accountability: A Conceptual Framework. *European Law Journal,* 13(4), 447–468. Retrieved from https://onlinelibrary.wiley.com/doi/full/10.1111/j.1468-0386.2007.00378.x.

Bowen, W. G. (2012). The 'Cost Disease' in Higher Education: Is Technology the Answer? Retrieved from http://www.ithaka.org/sites/default/files/files/ITHAKA-TheCostDiseaseinHigherEducation.pdf.

Bradshaw, Y. W., & Tshandu, Z. (1990). Foreign Capital Penetration, State Intervention and Development in Sub-Saharan Africa. *International Studies Quarterly*, 34(2), 229–251.

Brady, D., & Spence, M. (2010). Leadership and Politics: A Perspective from the Commission on Growth and Development. In D. Brady & M. Spence (Eds.), *Leadership and Growth*. Commission on Growth and Development. Washington, DC: World Bank. Retrieved from https://openknowledge.worldbank.org/bitstream/handle/10986/2404/527080PUB0lead101Official0Use0Only1.pdf?sequence=1.

———. (2009). Leadership and Politics: A Perspective from the Growth Commission. *Oxford Review of Economic Policy*, 25(2), 205–218.

Brannon, I. (2019, August 6). Nigeria's Deceptively Large External Debt Could Threaten its Economy. *Forbes*.

Brautigam, D. (1992). Governance, Economy, and Foreign Aid. *Studies in Comparative International Development*, 27(3), 3–25.

Bräutigam, D. A., & Knack, S. (2004). Foreign Aid, Institutions, and Governance in Sub-Saharan Africa. *Economic Development and Cultural Change*, 52(2), 255–285.

Breit, W., & Hirsch, B. T. (2004). (Eds.), *Lives of the Laureates*. 4th Edition. Cambridge, MA: MIT Press.

Brende, B. (2015, July 7). Why Education is the Key to Development. World Economic Forum. Retrieved from https://www.weforum.org/agenda/2015/07/why-education-is-the-key-to-development/.

Brownsberger, W. N. (1983). Development and Governmental Corruption - Materialism and Political Fragmentation in Nigeria. *The Journal of Modern African Studies*, 21(2), 215–233.

Brudnick, I. A. (2016). Congressional Salaries and Allowances. U.S. Congressional Research Service, Report #7-5700. Retrieved from https://fas.org/sgp/crs/misc/RL30064.pdf.

BudgIT. (2017). Ebola: Health Funding in Focus Countries - Guinea, Liberia, Nigeria, Sierra Leone. Retrieved from http://yourbudgit.com/wp-content/uploads/2017/10/Ebola_Health_Budget_Funding.pdf.

———. (2020). Budget. Retrieved from https://yourbudgit.com/wp-content/uploads/2020/03/2020-Budget-Analysis.pdf.

Buhari, M. (2015, July 20). Nigeria Committed to Good Governance and Fighting Terror. *The Washington Post.*

———. (1984, January 1). Major General. New Year Day Broadcast to the Nation.

Burns, A. (1963). *The History of Nigeria.* London: George Allen & Unwin Ltd.

Burns, J. M. (2006). *Running Alone – Presidential Leadership, JFK to Bush II.* New York: Basic Books.

Business Day. (2007, May 10). Nigeria Gets ₦8bn World Bank Education Facility.

Bryson, J. M., Crosby, B. C., & Bloomberg, L. (2014). Public Value Governance: Moving Beyond Traditional Public Administration and the New Public Management. *Public Administration Review*, 74(4), 445–456. Retrieved from https://onlinelibrary.wiley.com/doi/abs/10.1111/puar.12238.

Caddy, J. (2001). Why Citizens Are Central to Good Governance. *OECD Observer*, 229. Retrieved from http://oecdobserver.org/news/archivestory.php/aid/553/Why_citizens_are_central_to_good_governance.html.

Cain, P. J., & Hopkins, A. G. (1980, November). The Political Economy of British Expansion Overseas, 1750–1914. *Economic History Review*, XXXIII(4), 463–490.

Clay, J. A. (2008). MPA Field Experience: Public Service Internships. Retrieved from https://www.memphis.edu/padm/documents/Internship%20handbook.pdf.

Campbell, J. (2018, July 3). Electricity Distribution is Holding Nigeria Back. Council on Foreign Relations. Retrieved from https://www.cfr.org/blog/electricity-distribution-holding-nigeria-back.

Campbell, J. (2018a). Uproar Over Parliamentary Salaries in Nigeria, Again. Council on Foreign Relations. Washington, DC. Retrieved from https://www.cfr.org/blog/uproar-over-parliamentary-salaries-nigeria-again.

———. (2018b). Obasanjo's Costly Failed Third-term Bid. Council on Foreign Relations. Washington, DC. Retrieved from https://www.cfr.org/blog/obasanjos-costly-failed-third-term-bid.

Campbell, J., & Page, M. T. (2018). *Nigeria – What Everyone Needs to Know.* New York: Oxford University Press.

Campbell, J (2014, August 3). Interview by B. Akinloye. I insist Nigeria is Dancing on the Brink. *Punch.* Retrieved from http://www.punchng.com/news/i-insist-nigeria-is-dancing-on-the-brink-john-campbell.

Campbell, A., & Marston, W. A. (1999). *Louisiana: The History of an American State.* Montgomery, Alabama: Clairmont Press.

Cameron, D. (2016). Foreword. In *Against Corruption: A Collection of Essays.* Policy Paper. United Kingdom Government.

Cardoso, F. H., & Graeff, E. (2010). Political Leadership and Economic Reform: The Brazilian Experience in the Context of Latin America. In D. Brady & M. Spence (Eds.), *Leadership and Growth.* Commission on Growth and Development. Washington, DC: World Bank. Retrieved from https://openknowledge.worldbank.org/bitstream/handle/10986/2404/527080PUB0lead101Official0Use0Only1.pdf?sequence=1.

Cardoso, F. H., & Enzo, F. (1979). *Dependency and Development in Latin America*. University of California Press.

Carew, D. G., & Mandel, M. (2014, March). Infrastructure Investment and Economic Growth: Surveying New Post-crisis Evidence. Progressive Policy Institute, Washington, DC.

Carbone, G., & Cassani, A. (2016). Nigeria and Democratic Progress by Elections in Africa. *Africa Spectrum*, 51(3), 33–59. Retrieved from https://journals.sagepub.com/doi/pdf/10.1177/000203971605100302.

Carrington, W. (2015, October 22 and 23). Nigeria and the Future of the Black World. *Punch*. Retrieved from http://www.punchng.com/opinion/nigeria-and-the-future-of-the-black-world.

———. (2013, October 26). Nigeria the Underperformer: The Dangerous Mix of Corruption and Poverty. *Vanguard*. Retrieved from https://www.vanguardngr.com/2013/10/nigeria-underperformer-dangerous-mix-corruption-poverty-walter-carrington/.

Caselli, F., & Michaels, G. (2009). Do Oil Windfalls Improve Living Standards? Evidence from Brazil. *American Economic Journal: Applied Economics*, (51), 208–38. Retrieved from https://www.aeaweb.org/articles?id=10.1257/app.5.1.208.

Cayford, S. (1996). The Ogoni Uprising: Oil, Human Rights, and a Democratic Alternative in Nigeria. *Africa Today*, 43(2), 183–198.

Ceic.com. *Nigeria Government Debt: % of GDP*. Retrieved from https://www.ceicdata.com/en/indicator/nigeria/government-debt--of-nominal-gdp.

Center for American Progress. (2015, January). Report of the Commission on Inclusive Prosperity. Lawrence H. Summers and Ed Balls (co-chairs). Washington, DC. Retrieved from https://cdn.americanprogress.org/wp-content/uploads/2015/01/IPC-PDF-full.pdf.

Center for the Study of the Economies of Africa (CSEA). (2021, March 24). Nigeria Economic Update (11). University of Oxford. Retrieved from http://cseaafrica.org/nigeria-economic-update-issue-11-7/.

Central Bank of Nigeria. Various Years. *Annual Report and Statement of Accounts*. Abuja.

———. (2016). Measuring Informal Cross-Border Trade in Nigeria. Retrieved from https://www.cbn.gov.ng/out/2018/sd/measuring%20informal%20cross-border%20trade%20in%20nigeria.pdf.

———. (2016). *Economic Report for the First Half of 2015*.

———. *Annual Economic Report for 2013*, p. 232.

Cerqueti, R., Coppier, R., & Piga, G. (2008). Corruption, Growth and Ethnic Fractionalization: A Theoretical Model. Retrieved from https://core.ac.uk/download/pdf/294785833.pdf.

Chabal, P., & Daloz, J. P. (1999). *Africa Works: Disorder as Political Instrument*. Bloomington and Indianapolis: Indiana University Press.

Chabal, P. (1993). *Power in Africa: An Essay in Political Interpretation*. Palgrave Macmillan.

Channels Television. (2013, March 15). Retrieved from http://www.channelstv.com/home/2013/03/15/nigeria-lost-n75trillion-to-corruption-since-1960-professor-akinyemi/.

Chazan, N. H. (1978). The Africanization of Political Change: Some Aspects of the Dynamics of Political Cultures in Ghana and Nigeria. *African Studies Review*, 21(2), 15–38.

Chete et al., (2016). Industrial Development and Growth in Nigeria: Lessons and Challenges. Brookings Institution. Washington, DC. Retrieved from https://www.brookings.edu/wp-content/uploads/2016/07/L2C_WP8_Chete-et-al-1.pdf.

Chiahemen, T. (2007, August 6). Nigerian Ministers, Legislators Highest Paid in the World. *The Independent*.

———. (2007, November 14). UBEC Receives ₦81b in Three Years. *Daily Independent*.

Chikwem, F. C. (2016). The Political Economy of Fuel Importation Probes and Development of Refineries in Nigeria. *Insight on Africa,* 8(1), 18–39. Retrieved from https://journals.sagepub.com/doi/10.1177/0975087815612287?icid=int.sj-challenge-page.similar-articles.2.

Chukwu, L. (2011, September 14). Govt to Spend ₦4.1 Trillion in Health Sector. *The Guardian*.

Chinwokwu, E. C., & Michael, C. E. (2019). Militancy and Violence as a Catalyst to Kidnapping in Nigeria. *International Journal of Police Science & Management,* 21(1), 17–35. Retrieved from https://journals.sagepub.com/doi/10.1177/1461355719832619.

Chipkin, I. (2017). Corruption's Other Scene: The Politics of Corruption in South Africa. In J. Murphy & N. Jammulamadaka (Eds.), *Governance, Resistance and the Post-colonial State: Management and State Building.* Retrieved from https://www.taylorfrancis.com/books/e/9781134842124/chapters/10.4324%2F9781315544168-2.

Chiripanhura, B., & Nino-Zarazua, M. (2015). Aid, Political Business Cycles and Growth in Africa. *Journal of International Development*, 27, 1387–1421.

Clapham, C. (1996). Governmentality and Economic Policy in Sub-Saharan Africa. *Third World Quarterly*, 17(4), 809–824.

———. (2012). Globalization, Economic Reforms and Democracy in Nigeria. *Africa Development*, 27(2), 25–61.

———. (n.d.). Neoliberal Reforms and Power Configuration in Contemporary Africa: The Case of Nigeria.

———. (1985). *Third World Politics*. Madison, WI: The University of Wisconsin Press.

———. (1996). *Africa and the International System*. Cambridge University Press.

———. (2018). The Ethiopian Developmental State. *Third World Quarterly*, 39(6), 1151–1165.

———. (1994, July). [Review of the book *The State in Africa: The Politics of the Belly*, by Jean-Francois Bayart]. *African Affairs*, 93(372), 433–439.

Citizens Against Government Waste (CAGW). 2020 Congressional Pig Book Summary. Retrieved from https://www.cagw.org/sites/default/files/pdf/CAGWPigBook2020.pdf.

Clark, E. (1975). Holding Government Accountable: The Amended Freedom of Information Act: An Article in Honor of Fred Rodell. *The Yale Law Journal*, 84(4), 741–769.

CLEEN Foundation. *National Crime Victimization Survey: Summary Report 2012,* Abuja, Nigeria. Retrieved from http://www.cleen.org/crimevictimisationsurvey.html.

———. (2010). *Corruption and Governance in Nigeria.* Conference Proceedings, Monograph Series, No. 7. Retrieved from http://www.cleen.org/Corruption%20and%20Governance%20Challenges%20in%20Nigeria%20-%20Final%20Version.pdf.

———. (2010). Emergency Response to Victims of Gun Violence and Road Accidents, Conference Proceedings, Monograph series, No. 9. Retrieved from http://www.cleen.org/Emergency%20Response%20to%20Victims%20of%20Gun%20Violence%20and%20Road%20Accidents.pdf.

Clinton, W. J. (1996). *Between Hope and History: Meeting America's Challenges for the 21st Century.* New York: Random House Incorporated.

Coffie-Gyamfi, C. (2013, February 26). You Haven't Done Well with Oil Money, Clinton Tells Nigeria. *The Guardian.*

Coghe, S. (2020, November 19). Disease Control and Public Health in Colonial Africa. *Oxford Research Encyclopedia of African History.* Retrieved from https://oxfordre.com/africanhistory/view/10.1093/acrefore/9780190277734.001.0001/acrefore-9780190277734-e-620.

Cole, P. D. (2014, May 12). Political Corruption and the Rise of the Oligarchs. *The Guardian.*

———. (2015, November 18 and 19). The Ijaws: A Nation in Distress. *The Guardian.* Retrieved from http://www.ngrguardiannews.com/2015/11/the-ijaws-a-nation-in-distress

Coleman, J. S. (1960). *Nigeria: Background to Nationalism.* Berkeley and Los Angeles: University of California Press.

Collier, P. (2007). *The Bottom Billion – Why the Poorest Countries Are Failing and What Can Be Done About It.* New York: Oxford University Press.

———. (2010). The Political Economy of Natural Resources. *Social Research*, 77(4), 1105–1132.

Collier, P., & Gunning, J. W. (1999). Why Has Africa Grown Slowly? *Journal of Economic Perspectives*, 13(3), 3–22. Retrieved from https://pubs.aeaweb.org/doi/pdfplus/10.1257/jep.13.3.3.

Collier, P., & Hoeffler, A. (2005). Resource Rents, Governance, and Conflict. *Journal of Conflict Resolution*, 49(4), 625–633. Retrieved from http://journals.sagepub.com/doi/abs/10.1177/0022002705277551.

Commonwealth Secretariat. (2007). *Report of the Commonwealth Observer Group. Nigeria State and Federal Elections, 14 and 21 April 2007.*

Community Leadership Initiative. (2011). The Birth of Nigerian Campus Cult/Gang Groups and Its Consequences. Retrieved from http://www.campuscults.net/index.html.

Congressional Quarterly Researcher. (2008). *Issues for Debate in American Public Policy*. 8th Edition. Washington, DC: CQ Press.

Cooper, P. (2017, May 10). The Exaggerated Role of 'Cost Disease' in Soaring College Tuition. *Forbes*.

Corbacho, A., & Schwartz, G. (2007). Fiscal Responsibility Laws. In M. S. Kumar & Teresa Ter-Minassian (Eds.), *Promoting Fiscal Discipline* (pp. 58–105). International Monetary Fund.

Crabtree, S. (2012, January 16). Almost all Nigerians Say Gov't is Corrupt. Gallup .com. Retrieved from http://www.gallup.com/poll/152057/almost-nigerians-say-gov-corrupt.aspx.

Crossman, A. (2019, September 29). A Brief Guide to Modernization Theory. *ThoughtCo*. Retrieved from https://www.thoughtco.com/modernization-theory-3026419.

Cotter, W, R. (1979). How AID Fails to Aid Africa. *Foreign Policy*, 34, 107–119.

Dada, B. T. (2015, December 16). Nigeria Loses 3% GDP Annually to Road Accidents – FRSC. *Leadership*. Retrieved from http://allafrica.com/stories/201512150143.html.

Daily Independent. (2011, January 12).

———. (2004, October 28).

Daily Sun. (2011, May 19).

Daka, T., Jeremiah, K., & Abuh, A. (2021, March 18). After $25b on Maintenance, FEC Approves New $1.5b for PH Refinery. *The Guardian*.

Daniel, G. H. (2015). Impact of State Weakness on Nigerian Foreign Policy Reputation: A Critical Analysis. *International Journal of Scientific and Research Publications*, 5(12), 633–642.

Daramola, A., Ehui, S., Ukeje, E., & Mcintire, J. (2008). Agricultural Export Potential in Nigeria. Center for the Study of African Economies, University of Oxford, United Kingdom. Retrieved from https://www.csae.ox.ac.uk/materials/data/777/agriculturalexportpotentialinnigeria.pdf.

Davidson, B. (1992). *The Black Man's Burden: Africa and the Curse of the Nation-State*. James Currey.

Decalo, S. (1985). African Personal Dictatorships. The *Journal of Modern African Studies*, 23(2), 209–237.

DeGood, K. (2014, December 8). Public-Private Partnerships. Center for American Progress. Washington, DC. Retrieved from https://www.americanprogress.org/issues/economy/report/2014/12/08/102515/public-private-partnerships.

Desta, M. G., & Hirsch, M. (2012). African Countries in the World Trading System: International Trade, Domestic Institutions and the Role of International Law. *International and Comparative Law Quarterly*, 61, 127–170.

Dewey. J. (1937, April 3). Democracy and Educational Administration. *School and Society*.

Diamond, L. (1984). Nigeria In Search of Democracy. *Foreign Affairs*, 62(4), 905–927.

Retrieved from https://www.foreignaffairs.com/articles/nigeria/1984-03-01/nigeria-search-democracy.

———. (2005). The State of Democratization at the Beginning of the 21st Century. *The Whitehead Journal of Diplomacy and International Relations*, 13–18. Retrieved from http://blogs.shu.edu/journalofdiplomacy/files/archives/04_diamond.pdf.

———. (1992). Economic Development and Democracy Reconsidered. In G. Marks & L. Diamond (Eds.), *Reexamining Democracy: Essays in Honor of Seymour Martin Lipset*. Newbury Park, CA: Sage Publications.

———. (2013). Why Wait for Democracy? *The Wilson Quarterly*, 37(1). Retrieved from https://www.wilsonquarterly.com/quarterly/winter-2013-is-democracy-worth-it/why-wait-for-democracy/.

———. (2006). Promoting Democracy in Post-Conflict and Failed States: Lessons and Challenges. *Taiwan Journal of Democracy*, 2(2), 93–116.

Desta, M. G., & Hirsch, M. (2012). African Countries in the World Trading System: International Trade, Domestic Institutions and the Role of International Law. *International and Comparative Law Quarterly*, 61, 127–170.

Dike, K. O. (1956). *Trade and Politics in the Niger Delta, 1830–1885*. London: Oxford University Press.

Dike, V. E. (2015, October 28). "Why Nations Fail" to Develop. *SAGE Open*. Retrieved from http://journals.sagepub.com/doi/full/10.1177/2158244015611714.

Dixon, R. (2017, February 20). Nigerian President Disdains His Country's Best Hospital for Medical Care in Britain. But What Ails Him? *Los Angeles Times*. Retrieved from http://www.latimes.com/world/africa/la-fg-nigeria-president-health-20170220-story.html.

Dossa, S. (2007). Slicing up 'Development': Colonialism, Political Theory, Ethics. *Third World Quarterly*, 28(5), 887–899.

Dorman, S. R. (2001). [Review of the book *Africa Works: Disorder as Political Instrument,* by Patrick Chabal and Jean-Pascal Daloz]. *Canadian Journal of African Studies / Revue Canadienne des Études Africaines*, 35(1), 181–183.

———. (2009, October). Patrick Chabal: An Appreciation? *Critical African Studies*, 2, 10–18. Retrieved from https://www.tandfonline.com/doi/pdf/10.1080/20407211.2009.10530746.

Downs, A. (1967). *Inside Bureaucracy*. A Rand Corporation Research Study. Boston: Little, Brown and Company.

Drezner, D. W. (2004). The Global Governance of the Internet: Bringing the State Back In. *Political Science Quarterly,* 119(3), 477–498.

DuBois, W. E. B. (1896). *The Suppression of the African Slave Trade to the United States of America, 1638–1870*. New York: Longmans, Green, and Co.

Dudley, B. J. (1966). *Parties and Politics in Northern Nigeria*. London: Frank Cass and Company Limited.

Dukakis, M. S., & Kantor, R. M. (1988). *Creating the Future*. New York: Summit Books.

Dumett, R. E. (1968). The Campaign Against Malaria and the Expansion of Scientific Medical and Sanitary Services in British West Africa, 1898–1910. *African Historical Studies*, 1(2), 153–197.

Dumont, R. (1966). *False Start in Africa*. London: Andre Deutsch.

Dunning, T., & Wirpsa, L. (2004). Oil and the Political Economy of Conflict in Colombia and Beyond: A Linkages Approach. *Geopolitics*, 9(1), 81–108. Retrieved from https://www.tandfonline.com/doi/abs/10.1080/14650040412331307842.

Dunn, K., & Shaw, T. (2001). *Africa's Challenge to International Relations Theory*. Palgrave Macmillan

Dye, T. R. (1998). *Understanding Public Policy*. New Jersey: Prentice Hall.

Dye, T. R., & Zeigler, L. H. (1972). *The Irony of Democracy*. Belmont, CA: Wadsworth Publishing Company Inc.

Easterly, W. (2009). Can the West Save Africa? *Journal of Economic Literature*, 47(2), 373–447. Retrieved from http://www.nber.org/papers/w14363.

———. (2003). Can Foreign Aid Buy Growth? *Journal of Economic Perspectives*, 17(3), 23–48. Retrieved from https://www.aeaweb.org/articles?id=10.1257/089533003769204344.

———. (2005). Can Foreign Aid Save Africa? Clemens Lecture Series. Paper 13. Saint John's University. Retrieved from https://digitalcommons.csbsju.edu/cgi/viewcontent.cgi?article=1006&context=clemens_lectures.

———. (2007). How the Millennium Development Goals are Unfair to Africa. Brookings Global Economy and Development. Working Paper No. 14. Retrieved from https://www.brookings.edu/wp-content/uploads/2016/06/11_poverty_easterly.pdf.

———. (2007). Are Aid Agencies Improving? *Economic Policy*, 22(52), 633–678.

———. (2002). The Cartel of Good Intentions: The Problem of Bureaucracy in Foreign Aid. *Journal of Policy Reform*, 5(4), 223–250.

———. (2005). What Did Structural Adjustment Adjust? The Association of Policies and Growth with Repeated IMF and World Bank Adjustment Loans. *Journal of Development Economics*, 76, 1–22. Retrieved from https://pdfs.semanticscholar.org/97b9/214aae653f821ebfb582c0f6d54c529d5181.pdf.

———. (2005). "Can Foreign Aid Save Africa," Clemens Lecture Series. Paper 13. Saint John's University. Retrieved from https://digitalcommons.csbsju.edu/cgi/viewcontent.cgi?article=1006&context=clemens_lectures.

———. (2014). *The Tyranny of Experts: Economists, Dictators, and the Forgotten Rights of the Poor*. Basic Books.

———. (2007). *The White Man's Burden: Why the West's Efforts to Aid the Rest Have Done So Much Ill and so Little Good*. Penguin Books.

———. (2002). *The Elusive Quest for Growth: Economists' Adventures and Misadventures in the Tropics*. The MIT Press.

———. (2007, March 23). Africa's Poverty Trap. *Economist's View*. Retrieved from https://economistsview.typepad.com/economistsview/2007/03/william_easterl.html.

Easterly, L., & Levine, R. (1997). Africa's Growth Tragedy: Policies and Ethnic Divisions. *The Quarterly Journal of Economics*, 112(4), 1203–1250.

Easterly, W., Levine, R., & Roodman, D. (2004). Aid, Policies, and Growth: Comment. *American Economic Review*, 94(3), 774–780. Retrieved from https://www.aeaweb.org/articles?id=10.1257/0002828041464560.

Ebeku, K. S. A. (2008). Niger Delta Oil, Development of the Niger Delta and the New Development Initiative: Some Reflections from a Socio-legal Perspective. *Journal of Asian and African Studies,* 43(4), 399–425. Retrieved from https://journals.sagepub.com/doi/10.1177/0021909608091974?icid=int.sj-challenge-page.similar-articles.3.

Ebije, N. (2017, September 12). Over 50% Teachers in Kaduna Failed Pry 4 Test – el-Rufai. *The Sun.* Retrieved from http://sunnewsonline.com/over-50-teachers-in-kaduna-failed-pry-4-test-el-rufai/.

Edike, T. (2013, February 17). Nigeria is Becoming a Failed State – Nwabueze. *Vanguard.* Retrieved from http://www.vanguardngr.com/2013/02/nigeria-is-becoming-a-failed-state-nwabueze/.

Edomah, N., & Nwaubani, S. (2014). Energy Security Challenges in Developing African Mega Cities: The Lagos Experience. *Built Environment*, 1–9. Retrieved from https://www.aiu.edu/applications/DocumentLibraryManager/upload/BES_0002%20Full%20Paper%201.pdf.

Edozie, R. K. (2008). New Trends in Democracy and Development: Democratic Capitalism in South Africa, Nigeria and Kenya. *Politikon*, 35(1), 43–67. Retrieved from https://www.tandfonline.com/doi/pdf/10.1080/02589340802113055?needAccess=true.

Edwards, S. (2014). *Toxic Aid: Economic Collapse and Recovery in Tanzania.* Oxford: Oxford University Press.

Efobi, U, (2013). Politicians' Attributes and Institutional Quality in Africa: A Focus on Corruption. *Journal of Economic Issues*, XLIX (3), DOI: 10.1080/00213624.2015.1072393, 787–813.

Egba, T. (2014, November 4). Nigeria Loses ₦776bn to Corruption in Fertilizer Sector – Akinwumi. *The Sun.* Retrieved from http://sunnewsonline.com/new/?p=89294.

Egbara, G. (2008, July 25). 90 Percent of Students Seat on Bare Floor. *Daily Independent.*

Ehwarieme, W. (1999). The Military, Oil and Development: The Political Economy of Fiscal Federalism in Nigeria. In *Fiscal Federalism and Nigeria's Economic Development.* Collected volume of papers presented at the 1999 Annual Conference of the Nigerian Economic Society.

Eicher, C. K. (1967). The Dynamics of Long-term Agricultural Development in Nigeria. *Journal of Farm Economics*, 49(5), 1158–1170.

Eisenhart, M. (1991). Conceptual Frameworks for Research Circa 1991: Ideas from a Cultural Anthropologist; Implications for Mathematics Education Researchers. Paper Presented at the Proceedings of the Thirteenth Annual Meeting North American Paper of the International Group for the Psychology of Mathematics Education, Blacksburg, Virginia, USA.

Ejoh, E. (2015, December 4). Nigeria Earned $293bn Royalty from Oil and Gas Companies in 7 Years. *Vanguard.* Retrieved from http://www.vanguardngr.com/2015/12/nigeria-earned-293bn-royalty-from-oil-and-gas-companies-in-7-yrs-neiti.

Eke, S. J. (2014). No Pay, No Peace: Political Settlement and Post-amnesty Violence in the Niger Delta, Nigeria. *Journal of Asian and African Studies,* 50(6), 750–764.

Retrieved from https://journals.sagepub.com/doi/10.1177/0021909614541085?icid=int.sj-challenge-page.similar-articles.1.

Ekeh, P. P. (1975). Colonialism and the Two Publics in Africa: A Theoretical Statement. *Comparative Studies in Society and History,* 17(1), 91–112.

Ekekwe, E. N. (1985). State and Economic Development in Nigeria. In Claude Ake (Ed.), *Political Economy of Nigeria*. Lagos: Longman.

Ekwe-Ekwe, H. (1985). The Nigerian Plight: Shagari to Buhari. *Third World Quarterly*, 7(3), 610–625. Retrieved from https://www.jstor.org/stable/i382911.

Eker, V. (1981). On the Origins of Corruption: Irregular Incentives in Nigeria. *The Journal of Modern African Studies,* 19(I), 173–182.

Ekpo, A. H. (1994). Fiscal Federalism: Nigeria's Post-independence Experience, 1960–1990. *World Development*, 22(8), 1129–1146.

Ekpu, R. (1986, October 6). *Newswatch.*

Ejuvbekpokpo, S. (2012). Cost of Governance on Economic Development in Nigeria. *Global Journal of Management and Business Research*, 12(13), 1–7.

Emmanuel, R., & Reed, B. (2006, October 18). *The Plan: Big Ideas for America.* Democratic Leadership Council. *Blueprint Magazine*. Progressive Policy Institute. Retrieved from http://www.ppionline.org/.

Eme, O. I., & Andrew, V. O. (2013). Civil Service and Cost of Governance in Nigeria. *International Journal of Accounting Research*, 1(2), 27–48. Retrieved from https://www.omicsonline.org/open-access/civil-service-and-cost-of-governance-in-nigeria-IJAR-1-108.pdf.

Eme, O. E., Chukwurah, D. C., & Iheanacho, E. N. (2015). Addressing Revenue Leakages in Nigeria. *Arabian Journal of Business and Management Review*, 5(4), 1–19. Retrieved from https://www.researchgate.net/publication/304273051_Addressing_Revenue_Leakages_in_Nigeria.

Emerson, R. (1969, January). Colonialism. *Journal of Contemporary History*, 4(1), 3–16.

Emmet, D. (1958). *Function, Purpose and Powers: Some Concepts in the Study of Individuals and Societies*. London: Macmillan.

Emodi, N. V., & Yusuf, S. D. (2015). Improving Electricity Access in Nigeria: Obstacles and the Way Forward. *International Journal of Energy Economics and Policy*, 5(1), 335–351. Retrieved from http://dergipark.gov.tr/download/article-file/361387.

Encyclopedia Britannica. (n.d.). *Social Contract.* Retrieved from https://www.britannica.com/topic/social-contract.

Energy Mix Report. (2021, January 31).

Engerman, S. L., & Sokoloff, K. L. (2005). Colonialism, Inequality, and Long-run Paths of Development. National Bureau of Economic Research (NBER). NBER Working Paper No. 11057. Retrieved from https://www.nber.org/papers/w11057.

Entwistle, J. (2014, January 30). U. S. Ambassador. Interview by the *Guardian.* I Don't See Sign of Nigeria Breaking Up in 2015. Retrieved from http://www.ngrguardiannews.com/index.php/features/policy-a-politics/147642-i-don-t-see-sign-of-nigeria-breaking-up-in-2015-says-u-s-ambassador.

Enright, A. (2018, February 1). Amazon's Profit tops $3 billion as 2017 Revenue Grows 31%. *Internet Retailer.* Retrieved from https://www.digitalcommerce360.com/2018/02/01/amazon-grows-revenue-31-2017-profit-tops-3-billion/.

Enweremadu, D. U. (2013). Nigeria's Quest to Recover Looted Assets: The Abacha Affair. *Africa Spectrum*, 2, 51–70.

———. (2012). Anti-Corruption Campaign in Nigeria (1999–2007): The Politics of a Failed Reform. African Studies Center – French Institute for Research in Africa. Retrieved from https://openaccess.leidenuniv.nl/bitstream/handle/1887/20102/asc-075287668-3254-01.pdf?sequence=2.

Eriki, P. et al. (2015). Surgical Workforce in Nigeria: Stock and Flow of Medical and Dental Practitioners in Nigeria, with Special Focus on Health Workforce Training in Cross River State. World Health Organization. Retrieved from https://www.who.int/workforcealliance/031616NigeriaCaseStudyweb.pdf.

Eriksen, S. S. (2011). 'State Failure' in Theory and Practice: The Idea of the State and the Contradictions of State Formation. *Review of International Studies*, 37(1), 229–247.

Esteban, J., & Ray, D. (2008). On the Salience of Ethnic Conflict. *American Economic Review*, 98(5), 2185–2202.

Ezekwesili, O., Adenikinju, A., Onyeanakwe, A., & Longe, B. (2020). Stabilizing Nigeria's Volatile Economy. Shehu Musa Yar'Adua Foundation. Abuja, Nigeria. Retrieved from https://yaraduafoundation.org/files/Necessity_of_a_Stabilization_Mechanism_for_Nigeria.pdf.

Ezenagu, N., & Enohuean, E. (2017). Public Perception of Boko Haram Insurgency on Destination Image and Tourist Flow in Northern Nigeria. *African Journal of Hospitality, Tourism and Leisure*, 6(4), 1–14.

Fagbadebo, O. (2007). Corruption, Governance and Political Instability in Nigeria. *African Journal of Political Science and International Relations*, 1(2), 28–37. Retrieved from https://academicjournals.org/article/article1381995587_Fagbadebo.pdf?ref=theblueish.com/web.

Falola, T., & Ihonvbere, J. (1985). *The Rise and Fall of Nigeria's Second Republic.* London: Zed Books Ltd.

Famuti, T. (2014, April 8). Too Many Nigerians Living in Poverty – Jonathan. *Punch.* Retrieved from http://www.punchng.com/i-punch/too-many-nigerians-living-in-poverty-jonathan.

Fanimo, D. (2005, July 26). Nigerian Graduates Unfit for Employment, Say Industry Chiefs. *The Guardian.*

Fardmanesh, M. (1991). Dutch Disease Economics and the Oil Syndrome: An Empirical Study. *World Development*, 19(6), 711–717. Retrieved from https://www.sciencedirect.com/science/article/pii/0305750X9190205V.

Fatile, J. O., & Okewale, R. A. (2013). Corruption and Democracy in Nigerian Local Government. *Review of Public Administration and Management*, 1(3), 140–155. Retrieved from http://www.arabianjbmr.com/pdfs/public/3.pdf.

Fearon, J. D. (2004). Why Do Some Civil Wars Last so Much Longer than Others? *Journal of Peace Research*, 41(3), 275–301.

———. (2005). Primary Commodity Exports and Civil War. *The Journal of Conflict Resolution*, 49(4), 483–507.

Fearon, J. D., & Laitin, D. D. (2003). Ethnicity, Insurgency, and Civil War. *American Political Science Review,* 97(1), 75–90.

Federal Ministry of Agriculture and Rural Development. *Agricultural Transformation Agenda – Nigeria.* Retrieved from https://fmard.gov.ng/ata-nigeria/.

Federal Ministry of Health. (Nigeria). (June 2010). National Malaria Control Program. Advocacy, Communication and Social Mobilization Strategic Framework and Implementation Plan. Retrieved from http://www.afro.who.int/sites/default/files/2017-06/nigeria-national-acsm-implementation-plan.pdf.

———. (March 2014). National Malaria Elimination Program.

Federal Republic of Nigeria. (2017). *Economic Recovery & Growth Plan 2017–2020.* Ministry of Budget and National Planning. Retrieved from http://www.budgetoffice.gov.ng/index.php/economic-recovery-growth-plan-2017-2020.

Fidelis, S., & Iheaka, I. (2004, June 28). Nigerian Graduates, Not Employable – Osuji. *Punch.*

Financial Times (London). (1995, January 2, p. 3).

———. (2008, August 11). Nigerian Graft.

Folarin, S. (2009). The Anti-corruption War in Nigeria: A Critical Appraisal of the Role of the ICPC and EFCC. *Nigerian Journal of Economic and Financial Crimes*, 1(2), 14–36. Retrieved from http://eprints.covenantuniversity.edu.ng/8519/1/Untitled%204.pdf.

Foley, D. K. (2008). The Long-period Method and Marx's Theory of Value. Department of Economics. New School for Social Research. New York, NY. Retrieved from http://havenscenter.org/files/foley.marx.lp.method.pdf.

Forbes, (2019). Best States for Business 2019. California. Retrieved from https://www.forbes.com/places/ca/?sh=1bf331583fef.

Forsyth, P. J., & Kay, J. A. (1980). The Economic Implications of North Sea Oil Revenues. *Fiscal Studies,* 1, 1–28. Retrieved from https://onlinelibrary.wiley.com/doi/abs/10.1111/j.1475-5890.1980.tb00556.x.

Fosu, A. K. (2002). Political Instability and Economic Growth: Implications of Coup Events in Sub-Saharan Africa. *American Journal of Economics and Sociology*, 61(1), 331–348.

———. (2004). Mapping Growth into Economic Development. *American Journal of Economics & Sociology*, 63(5), 1173–1192.

———. (2015). Growth, Inequality and Poverty in Sub-Saharan Africa: Recent Progress in a Global Context. *Oxford Development Studies*, 43(1), 44–59. Retrieved from https://www.tandfonline.com/doi/abs/10.1080/13600818.2014.964195.

Frankema, E., & van Waijenburg, M. (2018). Africa Rising? A Historical Perspective. *African Affairs*, 117(469), 543–568. Retrieved from https://academic.oup.com/afraf/article/117/469/543/5038419.

Franklin, J. H. (2010). *From Slavery to Freedom: A History of African Americans.* 9th Edition. McGraw-Hill.

French, H. W. (1998, June 14). The World; West Africa Trembles with Nigeria. *The New York Times*. Retrieved from https://www.nytimes.com/1998/06/14/weekinreview/the-world-west-africa-trembles-with-nigeria.html.

———. (1997, September 26). U.S. Envoy to Nigeria is Given a Stormy Farewell. *The New York Times*. Retrieved from http://www.nytimes.com/1997/09/26/world/us-envoy-to-nigeria-is-given-a-stormy-farewell.html.

French, H. (2014, April 18). Spare the Advice. *The New York Times*, para. 5–6. Retrieved from https://www.nytimes.com/2014/04/20/books/review/the-tyranny-of-experts-by-william-easterly.html.

Friedrich, C. J. (1963). *Man and His Government: Empirical Theory of Politics*. New York: McGraw Hill.

Fukuyama, F. (2016). What is Corruption? In *Against Corruption: A Collection of Essays*. Policy Paper. United Kingdom Government.

———. (2011). *The Origins of Political Order: From Prehuman Times to the French Revolution*. New York: Farrar, Straus and Giroux.

———. (2014). *Political Order and Political Decay: From the Industrial Revolution to the Globalization of Democracy*. New York: Farrar, Straus and Giroux.

———. (2008). What Do We Know About the Relationship Between the Political and Economic Dimensions of Development? In *Governance, Growth, and Development Decision Making*. Washington, DC: World Bank.

———. (2006). *America at the Crossroads*. New Haven and London: Yale University Press.

Gailey, H. A. (1970). *The Road to Aba*. New York: New York University Press.

Galbraith, J. K. (1958). *The Affluent Society*. New York: Mentor Books.

Galston, W. A., & Davis, K. (2012). Setting Priorities, Meeting Needs: The Case for a National Infrastructure Bank. Brookings Institution, Washington, DC. Retrieved from http://www.pwfinance.net/document/research_reports/Brookings%20NIB.pdf.

Gallup, J. L., & Sachs J. D. (2001). The Economic Burden of Malaria. *American Journal of Tropical Medicine and Hygiene*, 64(1, 2), S, 85–96.

Ganti, A. (2020, March 16). Venture Capitalist (VC). *Investopedia*.

Garba, A. (2009, May 29). Yuguda Sacks Commissioner, 911 Aides. *The Guardian*.

Gari, G. (2011). The Use of Free Zones for the Promotion of the Offshore Industry in MERCOSUR Countries: A Reasonable Choice? Inter-American Development Bank. Policy Brief, No. IDB-PB-138.

Gaventa, J., & Runciman, C. (2016). Untangling Economic and Political Inequality: The Case of South Africa. In *World Social Science Report*. United Nations Educational, Scientific and Cultural Organization (UNESCO) and International Social Science Council (ISSC). Paris. Retrieved from http://unesdoc.unesco.org/images/0024/002459/245939e.pdf.

Gerhart, G. M. (1999, November/December). [Review of the book *Africa Works: Disorder as Political Instrument* by Patrick Chabal and Jean-Pascal Daloz]. *Foreign Affairs*. Retrieved from https://www.foreignaffairs.com/reviews/capsule-review/1999-11-01/africa-works-disorder-political-instrument.

Germont-Duret, C. (2016). Tradition and Modernity: An Obsolete Dichotomy? Binary Thinking, Indigenous Peoples and Normalization. *Third World Quarterly*, 37(9), 1537–1558.

Gerlach, J. D., & Reinagel, T. P. (2016). Experiential Learning in MPA Programs: A Case for Complementarity between Internship and Service Learning Requirements. *Political Science & Politics*, 49(1), 132–138.

Gingrich, N. (1995, November). U.S. House of Representatives Speaker. A Blueprint for America: Nine Strategies for a Strong Country. *USA Today*, pp. 18–20.

Global Fund. (2016, May 3). *Investigation in Nigeria*. Retrieved from http://www.theglobalfund.org/en/oig/updates/2016-05-03_Investigation_in_Nigeria/.

———. (2016, May 3). *Global Fund Grants to Nigeria*. Investigative Report, Geneva, Switzerland, 1–27. Retrieved from http://www.theglobalfund.org/en/oig/updates/2016-05-03_Investigation_in_Nigeria/.

Global Polio Eradication Initiative (GPEI) (n.d.). Retrieved from http://polioeradication.org/where-we-work/nigeria/.

Golden, M. A. (2012). Corruption in the Wealthy World. Brown *Journal of World Affairs*, xviii(11), 75–84.

Gosling, J. J., & Eisner, M. A. (2014). *Economics, Politics and American Public Policy*. New York: Routledge.

Gottheil, F. M. (1977). On an Economic Theory of Colonialism. *Journal of Economic Issues*, XI(1), 83–102.

Graaf, G., & Huberts, L. W. J. C. (2008). Portraying the Nature of Corruption Using an Explorative Case Study Design. *Public Administration Review*, 68(4), 640–653.

Grant, C., & Osanloo, A. (2014). Understanding, Selecting, and Integrating a Theoretical Framework in Dissertation Research: Creating the Blueprint for the "House." *Administrative Issues Journal: Connecting Education, Practice, and Research*, 4(2), 12–26. Retrieved from https://files.eric.ed.gov/fulltext/EJ1058505.pdf.

Gray, C. W., & Kaufmann, D. (1998, March). Corruption and Development. *Finance & Development*, 7–10. Retrieved from https://www.imf.org/external/pubs/ft/fandd/1998/03/pdf/gray.pdf.

Gray, L., Hansen, K., Recica-Kirkbride, P., & Mills, L. (2014). Few and Far - The Hard Facts on Stolen Asset Recovery. Stolen Asset Recovery Initiative. World Bank. UNOCD. OECD.

Graycar, A. (2015). Corruption: Classification and Analysis. *Policy and Society*, 34, 87–96.

Greif, A. (1998). Historical and Comparative Institutional Analysis. *American Economic Review*, 88(2), 80–84.

Grossman, J. (n.d.). Fair Labor Standards Act of 1938: Maximum Struggle for a Minimum Wage. United States Department of Labor. Retrieved from http://www.dol.gov/dol/aboutdol/history/flsa1938.htm. This article originally appeared in *Monthly Labor Review* of June 1978.

Gooding-Williams, R. (2017, September). W.E.B. Du Bois. *Stanford Encyclopedia of Philosophy*.

Gould, D. J., & Mukendi, T. B. (2007). Bureaucratic Corruption in Africa: Causes, Consequences and Remedies. *International Journal of Public Administration*, 12(3), 427–457.

Government of Nigeria. (2021, March). National Bureau of Statistics. *Labor Force Statistics: Unemployment and Underemployment Report.* Q4 2020.

Gudrun Østby, G., Nordås, R., & Rod, J. K. (2009). Regional Inequalities and Civil Conflict in Sub-Saharan Africa. *International Studies Quarterly*, 53(2), 301–324. Retrieved from https://academic.oup.com/isq/article-abstract/53/2/301/1852205?redirectedFrom=fulltext.

Guillén, M. F., & Suárez, S. L. (2005). Explaining the Global Digital Divide: Economic, Political and Sociological Drivers of Cross-National Internet Use. Social Forces. *Social Forces*, 84(2), 681–708.

Gulati, U. C. (1992). The Foundations of Rapid Economic Growth: The Case of the Four Tigers. *American Journal of Economics and Sociology*, 15(2), 161–172.

Gusfield, J. R. (1967). Tradition and Modernity: Misplaced Polarities in the Study of Social Change. *American Journal of Sociology*, 72(4), 351–362.

———. Tradition and Modernity: Conflict and Congruence. *Journal of Social Issues*, 24(4), 1–8.

Haggard, S., & Kaufman, R. R. (1995). *The Political Economy of Democratic Transitions*. Princeton: Princeton University Press.

Haarhuis, K. C. (2005), Promoting Anti-corruption Reforms: Evaluating the Implementation of a World Bank Anti-corruption Program in Seven African Countries (1999–2001). Wageningen: Posen and Looijen Printers.

Hagmann, T., & Peclard, D. (2010). Negotiating Statehood: Dynamics of Power and Domination in Africa. *Development and Change*, 41(4), 539–562.

———. (2010). Negotiating Statehood: Dynamics of Power and Domination in Africa. *Development and Change*, 41(4), 539–562.

Hagmann, T., & Hoehne, M. V. (2009). Failures of the State Failure Debate: Evidence from the Somali Territories. *Journal of International Development*, 21, 42–57.

Hall, R. E., & Jones, C. I. (1999). Why Do Some Countries Produce So Much More Output Per Worker Than Others? *The Quarterly Journal of Economics*, 114(1), 83–116.

Hallak, J., & Poisson, M. (2007). Introduction. In *Corrupt Schools, Corrupt Universities: What Can Be Done?* UNESCO. International Institute for Education Planning. Retrieved from http://unesdoc.unesco.org/images/0015/001502/150259e.pdf.

Hammonds, D. H. (1993). Strategic Success in the Global Economy. In W. Marshall & M. Schram (Eds.), *Mandate for Change*. Progressive Policy Institute. New York: Berkley Books.

Harrison, B. (1999, August). Noble Cause Corruption and Police Ethic. *FBI Law Enforcement Bulletin*, 68(8), 1–10. Retrieved from https://www.ojp.gov/ncjrs/virtual-library/abstracts/noble-cause-corruption-and-police-ethic.

Hartnett, T. (2000, November). *Financing Trends and Expenditure Patterns in Nigerian Federal Universities: An Update. Internal Report.* Washington, DC: World Bank.

Helleiner, G. K. (1966). *Peasant Agriculture, Government, and Economic Growth in Nigeria*. Homewood, Illinois: Richard D. Irwin Inc.

Heidenheimer, A. J., Johnston, M., & Le Vine, V. T. (1990). Introduction. In A. J. Heidenheimer, M. Johnston, & V. T. Le Vine (Eds.), *Political Corruption: A Handbook* (pp. 165–171). New Brunswick, NJ: Transaction Publishers.

Heldring, L., & Robinson, J. (2013, January 10). Colonialism and Development in Africa. Retrieved from https://voxeu.org/article/colonialism-and-development-africa.

Henley, D. (2015). *Asia-Africa Development Divergence: A Question of Intent*. London: Zed Books.

Henley, D., Tirtosudarmo, R., & Fuady, A. H. (2012). Flawed Vision: Nigerian Development Policy in the Indonesian Mirror, 1965–90. *Development Policy Review*, 30(S1), S49–S71.

Herbst, J. (2014). *States and Power in Africa: Comparative Lessons in Authority and Control*. 2nd Edition. Princeton: Princeton University Press.

———. (1997). Responding to State Failure in Africa. *International Security*, 27(3), 120–144.

Herbst, J., & Olukoshi, A. (1994). Nigeria: Economic and Political Reforms at Cross Purposes. In S. Haggard & S. B. Webb (Eds.), *Voting for Reform: Democracy, Political Liberalization, and Economic Adjustment*. World Bank. Oxford University Press. Retrieved from http://documents.worldbank.org/curated/en/116811468760536681/pdf/multi0page.pdf.

Herbst, J, & Joseph, R. (1997). Responding to State Failure in Africa. *International Security*, 22(2), 175–184.

Heritage Foundation. (2020). *2019 Index of Economic Freedom Report*. Retrieved from https://www.heritage.org/index/country/nigeria.

Herskovits, J. (1984). Dateline Nigeria: Democracy Down but Not Out. *Foreign Policy*, 54, 171–190.

———. (1977). Dateline Nigeria: A Black Power. *Foreign Policy*, 29, 167–188.

Higbee, J., & Schmid, F. A. (2004). Rule of Law and Economic Growth. *Economic Synopses*, 19. Retrieved from https://files.stlouisfed.org/files/htdocs/publications/es/04/ES0419.pdf.

Hill, S. (2020, January 24–31). Black China: Africa's First Superpower Is Coming Sooner Than You Think. *Newsweek*. Retrieved from https://www.newsweek.com/2020/01/31/nigeria-next-superpower-1481949.html.

Hill, M., & Hupe, P. (2014). *Implementing Public Policy*. 3rd Edition. Thousand Oaks, CA: Sage Publications Inc.

Hino, H., et al. (2000, January). *Nigeria: Statistical Appendix*. International Monetary Fund Staff Country Report No. 00/6. Retrieved from https://www.imf.org/en/Publications/CR/Issues/2016/12/30/Nigeria-Statistical-Appendix-3393.

Hodge, G. A., & Greve, C. (2016). On Public–Private Partnership Performance. *Public Works Management & Policy*, 22(1), 55–78. Retrieved from http://journals.sagepub.com/doi/full/10.1177/1087724X16657830.

———. (2015). Uncovering the Hidden Value of Digital Trade. Lisbon Council and Progressive Policy Institute. Interactive Policy Brief, Issue 19.

Hodgson, G. M., & Jiang, S. (2007). The Economics of Corruption and the Corruption of Economics: An Institutionalist Perspective. *Journal of Economic Issues*, XLI(4), 1043–1061.

Hoffman, A. (1995). Nigeria: The Policy Conundrum. *Foreign Policy*, 101, 146–158.

Hoffmann, L. K., & Patel, R. N. (2017). Collective Action on Corruption in Nigeria: A Social Norms Approach to Connecting Society and Institutions. Chatham House Report. Retrieved from https://www.chathamhouse.org/sites/default/files/publications/research/2017-05-17-corruption-nigeria-hoffmann-patel.pdf.

Hoffmannn, L., & Nolte, I. (2013). The Roots of Neopatrimonialism: Opposition Politics and Popular Consent in Southwest Nigeria. In Wale Adebanwi & Ebenezer Obadare (Eds.), *Democracy and Prebendalism in Nigeria*. Palgrave Macmillan.

Hoffmann, L. K., & Melly, P. (2015, December 7). Nigeria's Booming Borders: The Drivers and Consequences of Unrecorded Trade. Chatham House. London, England. Retrieved from https://www.chathamhouse.org/2015/12/nigerias-booming-borders-drivers-and-consequences-unrecorded-trade.

Hughes, R. (2020, June 27). "If California Were a Country." Bull Oak Capital.

Holman, J. (1992, March 16). Inconsistencies in State Funds. *Financial Times* (London).

Holmes, R. et al., (2011, September). Social Protection in Nigeria: An Overview of Programs and their Effectiveness. Overseas Development Institute. Project Briefing No. 59. Retrieved from https://www.odi.org/sites/odi.org.uk/files/odi-assets/publications-opinion-files/7324.pdf.

Hopkins, A. G. (2005). The New Economic History of Africa. *The Journal of African History*, 50(2), 155–177.

Hull, R. W. (1993). [Review of the book *The Black Man's Burden: Africa and the Curse of the Nation-State]. African Studies Review*, 36(3), 157–159.

Human Rights Watch. (2007, January). "*Chope Fine": The Human Rights Impact of Local Government Corruption and Mismanagement in Rivers State, Nigeria*. 19 (2A). Retrieved from http://hrw.org/reports/2007/nigeria0107/nigeria0107web.pdf.

———. (2011). Corruption on Trial? The Record of Nigeria's Economic and Financial Crimes Commission.

Human Right Watch. (2006, April). "They Do Not Own This Place" – Government Discrimination Against "Non-Indigenes in Nigeria." 18 (3A).

Humphreys, M., Sachs, J. D., & Stiglitz, J. E. (2007). What Is the Problem with Natural Resources Wealth? In M. Humphreys, J. D. Sachs, & J. E. Stiglitz (Eds.), *The Resource Curse*. New York: Columbia University Press.

Hunger and Nutrition Commitment Index (HANCI) (n.d.). Retrieved from http://www.hancindex.org/hanci/.

Huntington, S. P. (1968). *Political Order in Changing Societies*. New Haven: Yale University Press.

———. (1965). Political Development and Political Decay. *World Politics*, 17(3), 386–430.

———. (1971). The Change to Change: Modernization, Development, and Politics. *Comparative Politics*, 3(3), 283–322.

———. (1991). *The Third Wave: Democratization in the Late Twentieth Century*. University of Oklahoma Press.

———. (1991). Democracy's Third Wave. *Journal of Democracy*, 2(2), 12–34. Retrieved from https://www.ned.org/docs/Samuel-P-Huntington-Democracy-Third-Wave.pdf.

Iacocca, L. (2007). *Where Have All the Leaders Gone?* New York: Sribner.

Ibemere, D. (2017, October 12). Reps to Probe ₦11bn State House Clinic Budget. *This Day*. Retrieved from https://www.businessdayonline.com/reps-probe-n11bn-state-house-clinic-budget/.

Ibrahim, S. M., Bills, P., Allport, J., & Racasan, R. (2017). The Impediments to Nigeria Understanding Oil Production Volumes, Losses and Potential Solutions. *International Journal of African and Asian Studies*, 36, 36–44. Retrieved from https://iiste.org/Journals/index.php/JAAS/article/viewFile/37844/38929.

Idang, G. J. (1978). The Nigerian Public Enterprises as Instruments of Socio-economic Policies: A Case Study of a Government Trading Company in the Cross River State of Nigeria. *Indian Journal of Public Administration*, 24(4), 999–1015. Retrieved from https://journals.sagepub.com/doi/abs/10.1177/0019556119780404?journalCode=ipaa.

Idike, A. et. al., (2019). The Practice of Inclusive Representation in Nigeria Bureaucracy: The Federal Character Principle Experience. *Cogent Social Sciences*, 5(1), 1–21. Retrieved from https://www.tandfonline.com/doi/full/10.1080/23311886.2019.1601545?src=recsys.

Idoko, C. (2013, March 14). Nigeria Has Worst Global Education Indicators – UNESCO. *Nigerian Tribune*.

Ige, B. (2002). Abacha and the Bankers: Cracking the Conspiracy. *Crime and Society*, 2(1), 111–117. Retrieved from https://www.unodc.org/documents/treaties/publications/abacha_bankers.pdf.

Ihonvbere, J. O. (1991). Adjustment, Political Transition, and the Organization of Military Power in Nigeria. *Ufahamu – A Journal of African Studies*, 19(1), 22–43. Retrieved from https://escholarship.org/content/qt586678h6/qt586678h6.pdf.

———. (1991). A Critical Evaluation of the Failed 1990 Coup in Nigeria. *The Journal of Modern African Studies*, 29(4), 601–626.

———. (1987). Economic Contraction and Foreign Policy in the Periphery: A Study of Nigeria's Foreign Policy towards Africa in the Second Republic (1979–1983). *Africa Spectrum*, 22(3), 267–284.

———. (1996). Are Things Falling Apart? The Military and the Crisis of Democratization in Nigeria. *The Journal of Modern African Studies*, 34(2), 193–225.

Ihonvbere, J. O., & Ekekwe, E. N. (1988). Dependent Capitalism, Structural Adjustment and Democratic Possibilities in Nigeria's Third Republic. *Africa Spectrum*, 23(3), 273–291.

Ijere, M. O. (1974). Colonial Policy in Nigerian Agriculture and Its Implementation. *Agricultural History*, 48(2), 298–304.

Ijewereme, O. B. (2015). Anatomy of Corruption in the Nigerian Public Sector. *SAGE Open*, 5(2). Retrieved from https://doi.org/10.1177/2158244015581188.

———. (2015). Anatomy of Corruption in the Nigerian Public Sector: Theoretical Perspectives and Some Empirical Explanations. *SAGE Open*, 5(2). Retrieved from https://journals.sagepub.com/doi/full/10.1177/2158244015581188.

Ijomah, B. I. C. (2000). Nigeria's Transition from Military to Civilian Rule: An Overview. *Journal of Political and Military Sociology*, 28, 293–310.

Independent Corrupt Practices Commission (ICPC). (n.d.). ICPC was inaugurated in 2000 by the Nigerian government pursuant to the Corrupt Practices and Other Related Offences Act 2000 (Act 2000) as anti-corruption effort by the government to mainly "receive complaints, investigate and prosecute offenders" and the mandate to "rid Nigeria of corruption through lawful enforcement and preventive measures." Retrieved from https://icpc.gov.ng/icpc-history/. https://icpc.gov.ng/.

Inglehart, R., & Welzel, C. (2005). *Modernization, Cultural Change, and Democracy: The Human Development Sequence.* Cambridge University Press.

Inkeles, A. (1969). Making Men Modern: On the Causes and Consequences of Individual Change in Six Developing Countries. *American Journal of Sociology*, 75(2), 208–225.

Inkeles, A., & Smith, D. H. (1970). The Fate of Personal Adjustment in the Process of Modernization. *International Journal of Comparative Sociology*, 11(2), 81–114.

Inikori, J. E. (2000). Africa and the Trans-Atlantic Slave Trade. In *Africa Volume I: African History before 1885.* North Carolina: Carolina Academic Press.

Isenyo, G. (2015, July 30). Oil Worth $13.7bn Stolen Under NNPC, Says NEITI. *Punch.* Retrieved from http://www.punchng.com/news/oil-worth-13-7bn-stolen-under-nnpc-says-neiti.

———. (2017, December 29). El-Rufai, Kaduna Teachers Disagree over Court Order. *Punch*. Retrieved from http://punchng.com/el-rufai-kaduna-teachers-disagree-over-court-order/.

Institute for Economics & Peace. (2020). *Global Terrorism Index 2020: Measuring the Impact of Terrorism.* Retrieved from https://www.visionofhumanity.org/wp-content/uploads/2020/11/GTI-2020-web-2.pdf.

———. (2015, November). *2015 Global Terrorism Index.* Retrieved from http://www.visionofhumanity.org/sites/default/files/English%20Media%20Release%20GTI%202015.pdf.

Institute for Spending Reform. (n.d.). Retrieved from https://spendingreform.org/about/.

International Crisis Group. (2014, April 3). Curbing Violence in Nigeria (II): The Boko Haram Insurgency. Africa Report No. 216.

———. (2006, July 19). Nigeria: Want in the Midst of Plenty. Africa Report No. 113.

———. (2006, July 19). Nigeria: Want in the Midst of Plenty. Africa Report No. 113.

———. (2016). Nigeria: The Challenge of Military Reform. Retrieved from https://www.crisisgroup.org/africa/west-africa/nigeria/nigeria-challenge-military-reform.

———. (2006). *The Swamps of Insurgency: Nigeria's Delta Unrest.* Africa Report No. 115. Retrieved from https://www.crisisgroup.org/africa/west-africa/nigeria/swamps-insurgency-nigerias-delta-unrest.

International Energy Agency (IEA) Statistics. Organization for Economic Cooperation and Development/IEA 2014. Retrieved from http://www.iea.org/stats/index.asp, subject to https://www.iea.org/t&c/termsandconditions/.

International Labor Organization. (2002, June 20). Decent Work and the Informal Economy: Sixth Item on the Agenda. Report VI, Ninetieth Session of the International Labor Conference, Geneva. Retrieved from https://www.ilo.org/public/english/standards/relm/ilc/ilc90/pdf/rep-vi.pdf.

International Monetary Fund. (2018). Nigeria: Selected Issues. IMF Country Report No. 18/64.

———. International Monetary Fund. (2021). Nigeria: Informal Trade with Neighboring Countries.

———. (2015, January 20). Global Growth Revised Down, Despite Cheaper Oil, Faster U.S. Growth. Retrieved from http://www.imf.org/external/pubs/ft/survey/so/2015/NEW012015A.htm.

———. (2008, May). Globalization: A Brief Overview. Retrieved from https://www.imf.org/external/np/exr/ib/2008/pdf/053008.pdf.

———. (2017). Nigeria: Selected Issues. IMF Country Report No. 17/81.

Investment Consulting Group. (2013). Benchmarking Investment Incentives in CARIFORUM Countries. Report Produced for Caribbean Export Development Agency. Amsterdam, The Netherlands.

Isa, A. A. (2016). The Treasury Single Account (TSA) as an Instrument of Financial Prudence and Management: Prospects and Problems. *Research Journal of Finance and Accounting*, 7(4), 66–70.

Isaacs, K. P. (2017). *Retirement Benefits for Members of Congress*. Congressional Research Service, Report # 7-5700. Retrieved from http://www.fas.org/sgp/crs/misc/RL30631.pdf.

Isham, J., Kaufmann, D., & Pritchett, L. H. (1997). Civil Liberties, Democracy, and the Performance of Government Projects. *The World Bank Economic Review*, 11(2), 219–242. Retrieved from https://academic.oup.com/wber/article-abstract/11/2/219/1666702.

Ishiyama, J. (2015). Political Parties, Democracy, and "Good Governance." In *The Political Economy of Good Governance*. W. E. Upjohn Institute for Employment Research. Kalamazoo, Michigan, USA.

Iyoha, M. A. (2008). Leadership, Policy Making, and Economic Growth in African Countries: The Case of Nigeria. In D. Brady & M. Spence (Eds.), *Leadership and Growth*. Commission on Growth and Development. Washington, DC: World Bank. Retrieved from https://openknowledge.worldbank.org/bitstream/handle/10986/2404/527080PUB0lead101Official0Use0Only1.pdf?sequence=1.

Jack, J. T. C. B. et al., (2016). Dependency and Third World Underdevelopment: Examining Production-Consumption Disarticulation in Nigeria. *African Research Review*, 10(5), 204–223.

Jackson, R. H., & Rosberg, C. G. (1982). Why Africa's Weak States Persist: The Empirical and Juridical in Statehood. *World Politics*, 35(1), 1–24.

———. (1982). *Personal Rule in Black Africa*. Berkeley, Los Angeles, London: University of California Press.

Jalal, K., & Mustapha, M. (2016). Corruption Impacts on Growth and Development of the Moroccan Society. *Journal of Economics and Finance*, 7(1), 20–31. Retrieved from http://www.iosrjournals.org/iosr-jef/papers/Vol7-Issue1/Version-1/C07112031.pdf.

Janssens, P. G. (1980). Comparative Aspects. The Belgian Congo. In E. E. Sabben-Clare, D. J. Bradley, & K. Kirkwood (Eds.), *Health in Tropical Africa During the Colonial Period* (pp. 207–226). Oxford: Clarendon Press.

Janus, T. (2012). Natural Resource Extraction and Civil Conflict. *Journal of Development Economics*, 97(1), 24–31. Retrieved from https://www.sciencedirect.com/science/article/pii/S0304387811000095.

Jeffries, R. (1993). The State, Structural Adjustment and Good Government in Africa. *Journal of Commonwealth & Comparative Politics*, 31(1), 20–35. Retrieved from https://www.tandfonline.com/doi/abs/10.1080/14662049308447646.

Jega, A. (2000). Introduction. In Attahiru Jega (Ed.), *Identity Transformation and Identity Politics Under Structural Adjustment in Nigeria*. Nordiska Afrikainstitutet, Uppsala and Center for Research and Documentation, Kano, Nigeria.

Jegede, J. (2013, February 12). Nigeria Lacks Will to Fight Corruption, Says ICPC Boss. *Premium Times*. Retrieved from http://www.premiumtimesng.com/news/119996-nigeria-lacks-will-to-fight-corruption-says-icpc-boss.html.

Jibril, M. (2003, October 3). The Nigerian Factor and the Nigerian Condition. *The Guardian*, pp. 8 and 10.

Jimu, I. (2009). Managing Proceeds of Asset Recovery: The Case of Nigeria, Peru, the Philippines and Kazakhstan. Basel Institute on Governance.

Johns Hopkins Bloomberg School of Public Health. (2021). Malaria. Retrieved from https://www.malariafreefuture.org/malaria.

Jones, B. F., & Olken, B. A. (2005). Do Leaders Matter? National Leadership and Economic Growth since World War II. *The Quarterly Journal of Economics*, 120(3), 835–864.

Jorgenson, D. W. (1961). The Development of a Dual Economy. *The Economic Journal*, 71(282), 309–334.

Joseph, R. A. (1987). *Democracy and Prebendal Politics in Nigeria: The Rise and Fall of the Second Republic*. Cambridge University Press.

———. (2009, May 21). Economic Transformation and Developmental Governance in Nigeria: The Promise of the Obama Era. Brookings Institution. Washington, DC.

———. (1978). Affluence and Underdevelopment: The Nigerian Experience. *The Journal of Modern African Studies*, 16(2), 221–239.

———. (2013, July 26). Prebendalism and Dysfunctionality in Nigeria. *Africa Plus*. Retrieved from https://africaplus.wordpress.com/2013/07/26/prebendalism-and-dysfunctionality-in-nigeria/#_edn9.

———. (2015, April 21). The Buhari Challenge: Making Nigerian Democracy Work. *Africa Plus*.

———. (April 9, 2015). Interview by Jerome McDonnell of WBEZ/NPR in Chicago. Surprising of Conduct of Nigerian Presidential Elections. Retrieved from https://africaplus.wordpress.com/2015/04/21/the-buhari-challenge-making-nigerian-democracy-work.

Joseph, R. A., & Gillies, A. (2010, May). Nigeria's Season of Uncertainty. *Current History,* 179–185.

Joseph, R., & Herbst, J. (1997). Responding to State Failure in Africa. *International Security*, 22(2), 175–184.

July, R. W. (1983). Toward Cultural Independence in Africa: Some Illustrations from Nigeria and Ghana. *African Studies Review*, 26(3/4), 119–131.

Jütting, J., & de Laiglesia, J. R. (2009). Is informal Normal? Towards More and Better Jobs in Developing Countries. OECD. Retrieved from https://www.oecd-ilibrary.org/development/is-informal-normal_9789264059245-en.

Kalu, U. (Ed.). (1991). *Perspectives on Corruption and Other Economic Crimes in Nigeria.* Lagos: Fabog Nigeria Enterprises.

Kalu, K. A. (2006). The International Dimension of Regime Change: Economic Sanctions and the 1993 Democratic Transition in Nigeria. *African Social Science Review*, 3(3), Article 1. Retrieved from https://digitalcommons.kennesaw.edu/assr.

———. (1996). Political Economy in Nigeria: The Military, Ethnic Politics and Development. *International Journal of Politics, Culture and Society*, 10(2), 229–247.

Kang, D. C. (1995). Governing the Market: Economic Theory and the Role of Government in East Asian Industrialization. *International Organization*, 49(3), 555–587.

Kaplan, A. (1964). *The Conduct of Inquiry*. San Francisco: Chandler Publishing Company.

Karl, T. L. (1997). *The Paradox of Plenty: Oil Booms and Petro-States.* Berkeley, CA: University of California Press.

Katsouris, C., & Sayne, A. (2013, September). Nigeria's Criminal Crude: International Options to Combat the Export of Stolen Oil. Chatham House. Retrieved from http://www.chathamhouse.org/sites/default/files/public/Research/Africa/0913pr_nigeriaoil.pdf.

Katz, M. et al. (2005, August). *Nigeria: Selected Issues and Statistical Appendix.* International Monetary Fund Staff Country Report No. 05/303. Retrieved from https://www.imf.org/external/pubs/ft/scr/2005/cr05303.pdf.

Kaufman, M. T. (1998, June 9). New Chapter in Nigeria: The Obituary, Sani Abacha, 54, a Beacon of Brutality in an Era When Brutality Was Standard. *The New York Times.*

Kazeem, Y. (2015, June 4). Nigeria Has Some of the World's Highest Paid Lawmakers and this Start-up Wants to Slash their Pay. *Quartz Africa.*

Khan, A., & Cheri, L. (2016). An Examination of Poverty as the Foundation of Crisis in Northern Nigeria. *Sage Journals – Insight on Africa*, 8(1), 59–71. Retrieved from http://journals.sagepub.com/doi/abs/10.1177/0975087815612283?journalCode=ioaa.

Khemani, S. (2001, July 24). Fiscal Federalism and Service Delivery in Nigeria: The Role of States and Local Governments. World Bank. Retrieved from http://www1.worldbank.org/publicsector/decentralization/March2003Seminar/FiscalFedReport.pdf.

Keeling, W. (1991). Nigeria May Prove World Bank's Acid Test. *Financial Times* (London).

Kennedy, J. F. (1955). *Profiles in Courage*. New York: Harper & Row Publishers.

———. (1962). *To Turn the Tide*. New York: Harper & Brothers.

———. (1961, January 20). Inaugural Address. Retrieved from http://www.powerfulwords.info/speeches/John_F_Kennedy/5.htm.

Khemani, S. (2001, July 24). Fiscal Federalism and Service Delivery in Nigeria: The Role of States and Local Governments. World Bank. Retrieved from http://www1.worldbank.org/publicsector/decentralization/March2003Seminar/FiscalFedReport.pdf.

Kigabo, T. R. (2010). Leadership, Policy Making, Quality of Economic Policies, and their Inclusiveness: The Case of Rwanda. In D. Brady & M. Spence (Eds.), *Leadership and Growth*. Commission on Growth and Development. Washington, DC: World Bank. Retrieved from https://openknowledge.worldbank.org/bitstream/handle/10986/2404/527080PUB0lead101Official0Use0Only1.pdf?sequence=1.

Kigotho, W. (2013, October 5). Corruption is Eroding Higher Education's Benefits. *University World News*. Retrieved from http://www.universityworldnews.com/article.php?story=20131001160142405.

Kilby, P. (1969). *Industrialization in an Open Economy: Nigeria 1945–1966*. Cambridge: Cambridge University Press.

Kinyanjui, K. (1993). Culture, Technology and Sustainable Development in Africa. *Asian Perspective* 17(2), 269–295.

Ko, K., & Sidhu, D. J. K. (2012). The Impact of Internship in Public Organizations on University Students' Perceptions and Career Choice. *International Review of Administrative Sciences*, 78(4), 710–732. Retrieved from https://journals.sagepub.com/doi/abs/10.1177/0020852312455307.

Kittrell, E. R. (1965). The Development of the Theory of Colonization in English Classical Political Economy. *Southern Economic Journal*, 31(3), 189–206.

Kirk-Green, A. H. M. (1971). *Crisis and Conflict in Nigeria*. Oxford: Oxford University Press.

Kolawole, O. (2020, November 24). Why ASUU, Nigeria's Union of University Academic Staff, is against Government Automated Payment System. *Techpoint .africa*. Retrieved from https://techpoint.africa/2020/11/24/asuu-rejects-ippis-suggests-utas/.

Krause, K. (2002). State Failure, State Collapse, and State Reconstruction: Concepts, Lessons and Strategies. *Development and Change*, 33(5), 753–774.

Kraxbeger, B. (2004). The Geography of Regime Survival: Abacha's Nigeria. *African Affairs*, 103(412), 413–430. Retrieved from https://doi.org/10.1093/afraf/adh005.

Kress, D. H., Su, Y., & Wang, H. (2016). Assessment of Primary Health Care System Performance in Nigeria: Using the Primary Health Care Performance Indicator Conceptual Framework. *Health Systems & Reform*, 2(4), 302–318. Retrieved from https://www.tandfonline.com/doi/pdf/10.1080/23288604.2016.1234861?needAccess=true.

Krishna, K. (2007). Is International Aid the Panacea for Africa's Problems? *World Affairs: The Journal of International Issues,* 11(3), 68–84.

Krueger, A. (1974). The Political Economy of the Rent-seeking Society. *American Economic Review*, 64(3), 291–303.

Krumholz, S. (2013). Campaign Cash and Corruption: Money in Politics, Post-Citizens United. *Social Research,* 80(4), 1119–1134.

Ladan, H. (2017). Public Expenditure and Economic Growth in Nigeria: An Application of Co-integration and Error Correction Modeling. *Journal of Economics and Business Research*, 23(1), 185–208.

Lagarde, C. (2017, September 18). Transparency, Anti-corruption, and Sustainable Development. Brookings Institution, Washington, DC.

Langer, E. (2017, May 5). William Baumol, Economist who found Logic in Rising Healthcare Prices, Dies at 95. *The Washington Post.*

La Porta, R., Lopez-De-Silanes, F., Shleifer, A., & Vishny, R. (1999). The Quality of Government. *Journal of Law, Economics, & Organization*, 15(1), JLEO Bureaucracy Conference, 222–279.

Larewaju, K. (2007, February 11). Nigeria: Obasanjo Explodes – April Polls Do or Die Affair for PDP. *Vanguard.*

Lazarus, N. (1986). Great Expectations and after: The Politics of Post-colonialism in African Fiction. *Social Text*, 13(14), 49–63.

Leba, L. (2013, June 17). Ghost Workers and Indulgent Exorcists. *Vanguard.* Retrieved from http://www.vanguardngr.com/2013/06/ghost-workers-and-indulgent-exorcists.

Le Billon, P. (2001). The Political Ecology of War: Natural Resources and Armed Conflicts. *Political Geography*, 20(5), 561–584. Retrieved from https://www.sciencedirect.com/science/article/pii/S0962629801000154.

Le Grand, J. (1991). The Theory of Government Failure. *British Journal of Political Science*, 21(4), 423–442.

Lee, T. B. (2017, May 4). William Baumol, Whose Famous Economic Theory Explains the Modern World, Has Died. *Vox.* Retrieved from https://www.vox.com/new-money/2017/5/4/15547364/baumol-cost-disease-explained.

Lemke, D. (2003). African Lessons for International Relations Research. *World Politics*, 56(1), 114–138.

Leontief, W. (1941). *The Structure of American Economy, 1919–1929: An Empirical Application of Equilibrium Analysis.* Cambridge, MA: Harvard University Press.

Lere, I. B. (2014). Globalization and Development: The Impact on Africa – a Political Economy Approach. *OIDA International Journal of Sustainable Development*, 7(9), 153–162. Retrieved from https://papers.ssrn.com/sol3/papers.cfm?abstract_id=2560140.

Lerner, D. (1958). *The Passing of Traditional Society.* New York: The Free Press.

Lewis, W. A. (1955). *The Theory of Economic Growth.* London: George Allen & Unwin Ltd.

———. (1984). "Development Economics in the 1950s," In Meier & D. Seers (Eds.), *Pioneers of Development.* G. M. World Bank.

———. (1969). *Aspects of Tropical Trade, 1883–1965*, Wicksell Lectures, Stockholm.

———. (1970). The Export Stimulus. In William A. Lewis (Ed.), *Tropical Development 1880–1913* (pp. 13–45). Evanston: Northwestern University Press.

———. (1950, May). The Industrialization of the West Indies. *Caribbean Economic Review.*

Lewis, P. (2007). *Growing Apart – Oil, Politics, and Economic Change in Indonesia and Nigeria.* Ann Arbor, MI: The University of Michigan Press.

———. (1994). Economic Statism, Private Capital, and the Dilemmas of Accumulation in Nigeria. *World Development*, 22(3), 437–451. Retrieved from https://www.sciencedirect.com/science/article/pii/0305750X94901341.

———. (1996). From Prebendalism to Predation: The Political Economy of Decline in Nigeria. *The Journal of Modern African Studies*, 34(1), 79–103.

Leys, C. (1970). New States and the concept of corruption. In Arnold J. Heidenheimer (Ed.), *Political Corruption: Readings in Comparative Analysis.* New York: Holt Rinehart and Winston.

———. (1965). What is the Problem about Corruption? *The Journal of Modern African Studies*, 3(2), 215–230.

Lienert, I. (2010). Should Advanced Countries Adopt a Fiscal Responsibility Law? International Monetary Fund. IMF Working Paper. WP/10/254. Retrieved from https://www.imf.org/external/pubs/ft/wp/2010/wp10254.pdf.

Lindberg, S. (2006). The Surprising Significance of Elections in Africa. *Journal of Democracy*, 17(1), 140–151.

———. (Ed.) (2009). *Democratization by Elections: A New Mode of Transition.* Baltimore: Johns Hopkins University Press.

Lindblom, C. E. (1959). The Science of "Muddling Through." *Public Administration Review*, 19(2), 79–88. Retrieved from https://faculty.washington.edu/mccurdy/SciencePolicy/Lindblom%20Muddling%20Through.pdf.

Lipset, S. M. (1959). Some Social Requisites of Democracy: Economic Development and Political Legitimacy. *American Political Science Review*, 53(1), 69–105.

Lonsdale, J. (1981). States and *Social* Processes in Africa: A Historiographical Survey. *African Studies Review,* 24(2/3), 139–225.

Locke, J. (1689 [1952]). *The Second Treatise of Government.* Thomas P. Peardon (Ed.). New York: The Bobbs-Merrill Company Inc.

Lodge, T. (2018). State Capture: Conceptual Considerations. In M. Meirotti & G. Masterson (Eds.), *State Capture in Africa: Old Threats, New Packaging.* Retrieved from https://www.eisa.org.za/pdf/sym2017papers.pdf.

Lofchie, M. F. (1968). Political Theory and African Politics. *Journal of Modern African Studies*, 6(1), 3–15.

Loomba, A. (2005). *Colonialism/Postcolonialism (The New Critical Idiom).* 2nd Edition. London and New York: Routledge.

Lorcin, P. M. E. (1999). Imperialism, Colonial Identity, and Race in Algeria, 1830–1870: The Role of French Medical Corps. *Isis,* 90(4), 653–679.

Loubser, R., & Steenekamp, C. (2017). Democracy, Well-being, and Happiness: A 10-nation Study. *Journal of Public Affairs*, 17:e1646, 1–12.

Louisiana Department of Public Safety and Corrections. (n.d.). *Public Safety Services – Mission*. Retrieved from http://dps.louisiana.gov/mission.html.

Lundvall, B. A., & Lema, R. (2015). Growth and Structural Change in Africa: Development Strategies for the Learning Economy. *African Journal of Science, Technology, Innovation and Development*, 6(5), 455–466.

Lynn, K. T. (1997). *The Paradox of Plenty: Oil Boom and Petro-States*. Berkeley: University of California Press.

Macartan Humphreys, Jeffrey D. Sachs, & Joseph E. Stiglitz (2007). In M. Humphreys, J. D. Sachs, & J. E. Stiglitz (Eds.), *Escaping the Resource Curse*. New York: Columbia University Press.

Machiavelli, N. [1532]. (1992). *The Prince*. New York: Dover Publications, Inc.

Mackintosh, J. P. (1966). *Nigerian Government and Politics*. London: George Allen and Unwin Ltd.

Maclean, S. J. (2010). Mugabe at War: The Political Economy of Conflict in Zimbabwe. *Third World Quarterly*, 23(3), 513–528. Retrieved from https://www.tandfonline.com/doi/abs/10.1080/01436590220138402.

Mahler, A. (2010). Nigeria: A Prime Example of the Resource Curse? Revisiting the Oil-Violence Link in the Niger Delta. German Institute for Global and Area Studies (GIGA). Retrieved from https://www.jstor.org/stable/pdf/resrep07605.pdf.

Maiangwa, B., & Agbiboa, D. E. (2013). Oil Multinational Corporations, Environmental Irresponsibility and Turbulent Peace in the Niger Delta. *Africa Spectrum*, 48(2), 71–83. Retrieved from https://journals.sagepub.com/doi/10.1177/000203971304800204?icid=int.sj-abstract.similar-articles.2.

Maier, K. (2000). *The House Has Fallen*. Boulder, CO: Westview Press.

Mailafia, O. (2008). Economic Growth and Policy Choice in Nigeria: Lessons from the Asia Pacific. In P. Collier, C. C. Soludo, & C. Pattillo (Eds.), *Economic Policy Options for a Prosperous Nigeria*. New York: Palgrave Macmillan.

Mallet, W. J. (2017). Public Private Partnerships (P3s) in Transportation. U. S. Congressional Research Service. Washington, DC. Retrieved from https://fas.org/sgp/crs/misc/R45010.pdf.

Malingha, D. (2017, June 21). Nigeria Rolls Out $2 Billion Brazil-Like Social-Welfare Plan. *Bloomberg*. Retrieved from https://www.bloomberg.com/news/articles/2017-06-21/nigeria-rolls-out-2-billion-brazil-like-social-welfare-plan.

Malik, A., & Teal, F. (2008). Towards A More Competitive Manufacturing Sector. In Paul Collier, Chukwuma C. Soludo, and Catherine Pattillo (Eds.), *Economic Policy Options for a Prosperous Nigeria*. New York: Palgrave Macmillan. Retrieved from https://zodml.org/sites/default/files/%5BPaul_Collier,_Charles_C._Soludo,_Catherine_Pattil_0.pdf.

Mahmud, S. (1993). The Failed Transition to Civilian Rule in Nigeria: Its Implications for Democracy and Human Rights. *Africa Today*, 40(4), 87–95.

Manning, P. (1990). *Slavery and African Life*. Cambridge, UK: Cambridge University Press.

Marshall, K. (1994). Foreword. In *Africa's Experience with Structural Adjustment*. Proceedings of the Harare Seminar, May 23–24, 1994. World Bank. Kapil Kapoor

(Ed). Retrieved from http://documents.worldbank.org/curated/en/341501468764060235/pdf/multi0page.pdf.

Martin, G. (1982). Africa and the Ideology of Eurafrica: Neo-Colonialism or Pan-Africanism? *The Journal of Modern African Studies,* 20(2), 221–238.

Martin, G. (2000, Summer-Autumn). [Review of the book *The Criminalization of the State in Africa,* by Jean-François Bayart, Stephen Ellis and Béatrice Hibou: *Africa Works: Disorder as Political Instrument* by Patrick Chabal and Jean-Pascal Daloz], *Africa Today*, 47(3/4), 177–181.

Martini, M. (2014). Nigeria: Evidence of Corruption and the Influence of Social Norms. U4 Expert Answer. Transparency International.

Marx, K., & Engels, F. (1984). *Marx & Engels Collected Works* Vol 19: Marx and Engels: 1861–1864. London: Lawrence & Wishart. Project MUSE database. Retrieved from https://muse.jhu.edu/book/33021.

Marx, K. [1995–1996] (1867). *Capital: A Critique of Political Economy.* Volume 1. Book One: The Process of Production of Capital. Frederick Engels (Ed). Translated from fourth German edition by Samuel Moore and Edward Aveling, transcribed by Hinrich K. Zodiac et al., proofed by Andy Blunden & Chris Clayton (2008), Mark Harris (2010), Dave Allinson (2015). Moscow: Progress Publishers.

———. (1905 and 1910). *Theory of Surplus Value.* A selection from the volumes published between 1905 and 1910 as *Theorien uber den Mehrwert*, by Karl Kautsky (Ed.), taken from Karl Marx's preliminary manuscript for the projected Fourth Volume of *Capital.* Translated from the German edition by G. A. Bonner and Emile Burns. London: Lawrence and Wishart, 1951.

Matti, S. (2010). Resources and Rent Seeking in the Democratic Republic of the Congo. *Third World Quarterly*, 31(3), 401–413. Retrieved from https://www.jstor.org/stable/27867932?seq=1#page_scan_tab_contents.

Mauro, P. (1995). Corruption and Growth. *The Quarterly Journal of Economics*, 110(3), 681–712. Retrieved from http://homepage.ntu.edu.tw/~kslin/macro2009/Mauro%201995.pdf.

———. (1996). The Effects of Corruption on Growth, Investment, and Government Expenditure. International Monetary Fund Working Paper 96/98, 1–28.

May, C. D. (1984, January 5). Nigerian Ruler Tells Diplomats Why He Took Over. *The New York Times*, p. A00009. Retrieved from https://www.nytimes.com/1984/01/05/world/nigerian-ruler-tells-diplomats-why-he-took-over.html.

Mazrui, A. M. (2003). Recolonization or Self-colonization? In A. Mazrui & W. Mutunga (Eds.), *Governance and Leadership: Debating the African Condition.* Trenton, NJ: Africa World Press, Inc.

———. (1975). *Soldiers and Kinsmen in Uganda: The Making of a Military Ethnocracy.* Beverley Hills: Sage Publications.

———. (1968). From Social Darwinism to Current Theories of Modernization: A Tradition of Analysis. *World Politics*, 21(1), 69–83.

———. (1980). *The African Condition.* London: Cambridge University Press.

Mbaku, J. M. (1994). Military Coups as a Rent Seeking Behavior. *Journal of Political and Military Sociology*, 22, 241–284.

———. (2000). Governance, Wealth Creation and Development in Africa: The Challenges and the Prospects. *African Studies Quarterly*, 4(2), 29–47. Retrieved from http://sites.clas.ufl.edu/africa-asq/files/ASQ-Volume-4-Issue-2-Mbaku .pdf.

———. (2018). Rule of Law, State Capture, and Human Development in Africa. *American University International Law Review*, 33(4), 771–836.

———. (2018). Constitutions, Citizenship and the Challenge of National Integration and Nation Building in Africa. *International and Comparative Law Review*, 18(1), 7–50.

———. (1988). Political Instability and Economic Development in Sub-Saharan Africa. *Review of Black Political Economy*, 17(1), 89–111. Retrieved from https://doi.org/10.1007/BF02900956.

———. (2014). The Rule of Law and Poverty Eradication in Africa. *African and Asian Studies*, 13(4), 530–557.

M'baye, B. (2006). The Economic, Political, and Social Impact of the Atlantic Slave Trade on Africa. *The European Legacy*, 11(6), 607–622.

McGowan, P. J., & Smith, D. L. (2009). Economic Dependency in Black Africa: An Analysis of Competing Theories. *International Organization*, 32(1), 179–235.

McKinnon, D. (2007, June 5). What Now for Democracy in Nigeria? *The Guardian*.

McMullan, M. (1970). Corruption in the Public Services of British Colonies and Ex-colonies in West Africa. In Arnold J. Heidenheimer (Ed.), *Political Corruption: Readings in Comparative Analysis*. New York: Holt Rinehart and Winston.

Meagher, K. (2016). The Scramble for Africans: Demography, Globalization and Africa's Informal Labor Markets. *The Journal of Development Studies*, 52(4), 483–497. Retrieved from https://www.tandfonline.com/doi/full/10.1080/00220388 .2015.1126253.

———. (2003). A Back Door to Globalization? Structural Adjustment, Globalization & Transborder Trade in West Africa. *Review of African Political Economy*, 30(95), Africa, Imperialism & New Forms of Accumulation, 57–75.

———. (2010). The Tangled Web of Associational Life: Urban Governance and the Politics of Popular Livelihoods in Nigeria. *Urban Forum*, 21, 299–313.

———. (2011). Informal Economies and Urban Governance in Nigeria: Popular Empowerment or Political Exclusion? *African Studies Review*, 54(2), 47–72.

———. (2014). Disempowerment from Below: Informal Enterprise Networks and the Limits of Political Voice in Nigeria. *Oxford Development Studies*, 42(3), 419–438.

———. (2016). Taxing Times: Taxation, Divided Societies and the Informal Economy in Northern Nigeria. *Journal of Development Studies*, 1–17.

———. (2014). Smuggling Ideologies: From Criminalization to Hybrid Governance in African Clandestine Economies. *African Affairs*, 113(453), 497–517.

———. (2006). Social Capital, Social Liabilities, and Political Capital: Social Networks and Informal Manufacturing in Nigeria. *African Affairs*, 105(421), 553–582.

Mede, N. F. (2016). Ministry of Budget and National Planning. Federal Republic of Nigeria. Nigeria's Experience with Identity Systems and Civil Service Reform. Paper Presented at the ID 4 Africa Annual Meeting, held at Rwanda.

Medina, L., & Schneider, F. (2018). Shadow Economies Around the World: What Did We Learn Over the Last 20 Years? IMF Working Paper, WP /18/17.

Meirotti, M. (2018). Introduction. In M. Meirotti & G. Masterson (Eds.), *State Capture in Africa: Old Threats, New Packaging*. Retrieved from https://www.eisa.org.za/pdf/sym2017papers.pdf.

Meltzer, J. P. (2014, October). The Importance of the Internet and Transatlantic Data Flows for U.S. and EU Trade and Investment. Brookings Institution, Working Paper 79.

Mensah, J. A. (2016). The Valuation of Corruption. *Journal of Mathematical Finance*, 6, 728–746. Retrieved from http://file.scirp.org/pdf/JMF_2016111713570869.pdf.

Merrifield, J., & Poulson, B. (2016). Swedish and Swiss Fiscal-rule Outcomes Contain Key Lessons for the United States. *The Independent Review*, 21(2), 251–274. Retrieved from https://www.independent.org/pdf/tir/tir_21_02_07_merrifield-poulson.pdf.

Merloni, F. (2018). *Corruption and Public Administration: The Italian Case in a Comparative Perspective*. New York: Routledge.

Mikesell, R. (1997). Explaining the Resource Curse, with Special Reference to Mineral-exporting Countries. *Resources Policy*, 23(4), 191–99.

Millar, J. R. (1978, July). A Note on Primitive Accumulation in Marx and Preobrazhensky. *Soviet Studies*, 30(3), 384–393.

Mill, J. S. (1861[1972]). *Considerations on Representative Government*. H.B. Acton (Ed.) London: J.M. Dent & Son Ltd.

Mills, G. (2011). *Why Africa is Poor: And What Africans Can Do About It*. Penguin Global.

Milliken, J. (Ed.) (2003). *State Failure, Collapse & Reconstruction*. Wiley-Blackwell.

Mkandawire, T. (2014). The Spread of Economic Doctrines and Policymaking in Postcolonial Africa. *African Studies Review*, 57(1), 171–198.

Mkapa, B. W. (2010). Leadership for Growth, Development, and Poverty Reduction: An African Viewpoint and Experience. In D. Brady and M. Spence (Eds.), *Leadership and Growth*. Commission on Growth and Development. Washington, DC: World Bank.

Mlambo, A. (2018). African Economic History and Historiography. *Oxford Research Encyclopedia of African History*.

Mimiko, N. O. (1995). Between Yugoslavia and Czechoslovakia: The Abacha Coup, the National Conference, and Prospects for Peace and Democracy in Nigeria. *Social Justice*, 22(3), 129–142.

Ministry of Niger Delta Affairs. Retrieved from http://www.nigerdelta.gov.ng/index.php/the-ministry.

Modebe, N., Okoro, O., Okoyeuzu, C., & Uche, C. (2014). The (ab) Use of Import Duty Waivers in Nigeria. African Studies Center, Leiden. Working Paper No. 113. Retrieved from https://openaccess.leidenuniv.nl/bitstream/handle/1887/23019/ASC-075287668-3416-01.pdf.

Mokhiber, J. (1998, May). A Brief History of the Independent Counsel Law. Retrieved from http://www.pbs.org/wgbh/pages/frontline/shows/counsel/office/history.html.

Momoh, A. (1996). The Structural Adjustment Program and the Transition to Civil Rule in Nigeria (1986–1993). *Africa Development / Afrique et Développement*, 21(1), 19–37.

Morelli, M. (2015). Resource Concentration and Civil Wars. *Journal of Development Economics*, 117, 32–47.

Mosley, P. (1985). The Political Economy of Foreign Aid: A Model of the Market for a Public Good. *Economic Development and Cultural Change*, 33(2), 373–393. Retrieved from https://www.journals.uchicago.edu/doi/abs/10.1086/451466?journalCode=edcc.

Moose, G. E. (1995, July 20). United States Assistant Secretary of State for African Affairs. Testimony before the U.S. Senate Foreign Relations Committee.

Moynihan, D. P. (1965). *The Negro Family: The Case for National Action.* United States Department of Labor, Office of Policy Planning and Research. Retrieved from https://www.dol.gov/oasam/programs/history/webid-meynihan.htm.

Moyo, D. (2009). *Dead Aid: Why Aid is Not Working and How there is a Better Way for Africa.* Penguin Books.

Mozaffar, S. (1989). Democracy and Prebendal Politics in Nigeria: The Rise and Fall of the Second Republic. [Review of the book, *Democracy and Prebendal Politics in Nigeria: The Rise and Fall of the Second Republic*, by Richard A. Joseph]. *The International Journal of African Historical Studies*, 22(3), 500–504.

Muanya, C., & Akpan, A. (2018, April 22). 2,000 Medical Doctors Leave Nigeria Yearly. *The Guardian.* Retrieved from https://guardian.ng/news/2000-medical-doctors-leave-nigeria-yearly/.

Muhammadu Sanusi II. Emir of Kano. (2015, December 2). Interview by Nick Schifrin, PBS *NewsHour*. Nigeria: Pain and Promise. Retrieved from http://www.bing.com/news/search?q=PBS+NewsHour%2c+Nigeria+Pain+And+Promise&qpvt=pbs+newshour%2c+nigeria+pain+and+promise&FORM=NWRFSH.

Muhammad, A. (2008, November 26). 259 Teachers Score Zero in Primary 4 Exams. *New Nigerian.*

Muiu, M. W. (2010). Colonial and Postcolonial State and Development in Africa. *Social Research*, 77(4), 1311–1338.

Myrdal, G. (1968). *Asian Drama: An Inquiry into the Poverty of Nations.* Volume II. Pantheon.

Na, K., Kang, Y. H. & Kim, Y. S. (2018). The Effect of Corporate Governance on the Corruption of Firms in BRICs (Brazil, Russia, India & China). *Social Sciences*, 7(85), 2–16.

Nachmias, C. F., & Nachmias, D. (2008). *Research Methods in the Social Sciences.* 7th Edition. New York: Worth Publishers.

Nadiz, V. R. (2004). The State of Corruption: Indonesia. In V. Bhargava & E. Bolongaita (Eds.), *Challenging Corruption in Asia: Case Studies and a Framework for Action* (pp. 209–235). Washington, DC: World Bank. Retrieved from https://elibrary.worldbank.org/doi/abs/10.1596/0-8213-5683-6.

Nafziger, E. W. (1972, July). The Economic Impacts of the Nigerian Civil War. *The Journal of Modern African Studies*, 10(2), 223–245.

National Bureau of Statistics (Nigeria). (2014, October 14). Nigerian Manufacturing Sector, *Summary Report 2010–2012*.

———. (2021, March). *Labor Force Statistics: Unemployment and Underemployment Report.* (Q42020).

———. (2016). *Formal and Informal Sector Split of Gross Domestic Product 2015.*

———. (2019). *2019 Poverty and Inequality in Nigeria: Executive Summary.*

———. (2021, February). *Selected Food Prices Watch.*

———. (2021, February). *Consumer Price Index February 2021.*

National Economic Council. (1959). *Economic Survey of Nigeria 1959.* Federal Government Printer, Lagos.

National Research Council. (1999). *Harnessing Science and Technology for America's Economic Future: National and Regional Priorities*. Washington, DC. National Academy Press.

Natural Resources Governance Institute. (2015). Inside NNPC Oil Sales: A Case for Reform in Nigeria. Retrieved from https://resourcegovernance.org/sites/default/files/NRGI_InsideNNPCOilSales_AnnexB.pdf.

Nawaz, S., Iqbal, N., & Khan, M. A. The Impact of Institutional Quality on Economic Growth: Panel Evidence. *The Pakistan Development Review*, 53(1), 15–31.

Ndan, J. D. (2013). Fiscal Responsibility and Repositioning of Nigerian Budgetary Process and Outcomes. *ABU Journal of Public Administration*, 2(2), 78–89. Retrieved from https://journals.abu.edu.ng/pdf/28.pdf.

Ndukwe, I. (2017, December 7). Getting Nigeria's Railway Back on the Tracks with China. *BBC News*. Retrieved from https://www.bbc.com/news/world-africa-42172955.

Ndujihe, C., & Idonor, D. (2011, January 21). High Cost of Governance: Your Govt's Too Large, Danjuma Tells Jonathan. *Vanguard.*

Ndulo, M. (2003). The Democratization Process and Structural Adjustment in Africa. *Indiana Journal of Global Legal Studies,* 10(3), 315–368. Retrieved from https://www.repository.law.indiana.edu/cgi/viewcontent.cgi?article=1258&context=ijgls.

Nehru, J. (1962). *India's Freedom.* London: George Allen & Unwin Ltd.

New African. (1986, October). Survey of Nigeria, 8–10.

Newell, S. (2016). Life Writing in the Colonial Archives: The Case of Nnamdi Azikiwe (1904–1996) of Nigeria. *Life Writing,* 13(3), 307–321.

News Agency of Nigeria (NAN). (2019, October 19). ASUU States Reasons why IPPIS Can't be Implemented in Federal Universities. Retrieved from https://www.pulse.ng/news/local/asuu-states-reasons-why-ippis-cant-be-implemented-in-federal-universities/f3wszyl.

News & Observer. (1998, April 17, p. 15A). Raleigh, North Carolina, USA.

Newswatch. (2009, December 20).

———. (1994, March 21, p. 13).

———. (1998, October 5).

———. (2000, May 7).

———. (1986, October 6).

Nigerian Constitution. (1999). Chapter VI Section 147(3).

Nigeria. (2009). Federal Ministry of Health. *National Health Accounts 2006–2009.*

Nigeria Debt Management Office. (2018). *2018 Annual Report and Statement of Accounts.* Retrieved from https://www.dmo.gov.ng/publications/reports/dmo-annual-report-statement-of-accounts/3060-2018-annual-report/file.

———. (2018). *2017 Annual Report and Statement of Accounts.* Retrieved from https://www.dmo.gov.ng/publications/reports/dmo-annual-report-statement-of-accounts/2503-2017-annual-report/file.

———. (2019). *Nigeria's Total Public Debt as at June 30, 2019.* Retrieved from https://www.dmo.gov.ng/debt-profile/total-public-debt/2950-nigeria-s-public-debt-as-at-june-30-2019/file.

Nigeria Extractive Industries Transparency Initiative (NEITI). *Physical and Process Audit Report for the Period 2009 to 2011.* Retrieved from http://neiti.gov.ng/phocadownload/EITI-Physical-And-Process-Final-Audit-Report-2009-2011.pdf.

———. *2014 Oil & Gas Industry Audit Report.* Retrieved from https://eiti.org/sites/default/files/documents/neiti-oil-gas-report-2014-full-report-301216.pdf.

———. *2015 Oil & Gas Industry Audit Report.* Retrieved from https://eiti.org/sites/default/files/documents/neiti-oil-gas-report-2015-full-report-281217.pdf.

Nigeria Federal Road Safety Corps. *2019 Annual Report.*

Nigerian National Petroleum Corporation. (2020, March). Monthly Report. *Financial and Operations Report.*

Nigerian Institute of Social and Economic Research (NISER) (2009). Study of Skills Development for the Informal Sector of the Nigerian Economy.

Nigerian Tribune. (2013, February 21). Governor Obi on Values and Cost of Governance.

———. (2013, March 4). Kaduna's Teaching Crisis. [Editorial].

Nissanke, M., & Sindzingre, A. (2006). Institutional Foundations for Shared Growth in Sub-Saharan Africa. *African Development Review*, 18(3), 353–391.

Nissanke, M., & Thorbecke, E. (2007). Globalization, Growth, and Poverty in Africa. Retrieved from https://www.wider.unu.edu/publication/globalization-growth-and-poverty-africa.

———. (2010, June). The Poor under Globalization in Asia, Latin America and Africa. Retrieved from https://www.wider.unu.edu/publication/poor-under-globalization-asia-latin-america-and-africa.

Nixon, C. R. (1972). Self-Determination: The Nigeria/Biafra Case. *World Politics*, 24(4), 473–497.

Njoku, F. O. (2011). Corruption: The Bane of Nigeria's Development. In E. C. Anowai, *Pope John Paul II Annual Memorial Lecture Series* (pp. 5–44). Awka, Nigeria: Demercury Bright Printing.

Nkordeh, N., Oni, O., Olowononi, F., & Bob-Manuel, I. (2017). Nigeria's Power Generation: Analyzing the Cost Implication of Poor Generation on the Running Cost of Telecom Business in Nigeria. Proceedings of the World Congress on Engineering and Computer Science Volume 1. San Francisco, California, USA.

October 25–27. Retrieved from http://www.iaeng.org/publication/WCECS2017/WCECS2017_pp271-275.pdf.

Nkrumah, K. (1966). *Neo-colonialism: The Last Stage of Imperialism.* New York: International Publishers.

———. (1967). *Challenge of the Congo.* New York: International Publishers.

Nkwazema, S. (2008, June 26). Nigeria Lost ₦1.06tr to Waivers. *This Day.*

Nnadozie, E. (1995). [Review of the book *Nigeria: The Political Transition and Future of Democracy,* by Arthur Agwuncha Nwankwo]. *African Studies Review,* 38(1), 164–166.

Nnamocha, P. N., Obioma, B. K., Igwemma, A. A., & Nwoko, I. A. (2017). Foreign Exchange and Industrial Sector Growth in Nigeria (1981–2015). *Journal of Economics and Sustainable Development,* 8(24), 71–80.

Nnochiri, I. (2015, December 1). No Political Will to Prosecute High-Profile Corruption Cases, Says CJN. *Vanguard.* Retrieved from http://www.vanguardngr.com/2015/12/no-political-will-to-prosecute-high-profile-corruption-cases-says-cjn.

———. (2019, May 2). Assets Declaration: CCB Boss Talks Tough, Vows to Prosecute Govs, Ministers. *Vanguard.* Retrieved from https://www.vanguardngr.com/2019/05/assets-declaration-ccb-boss-talks-tough-vows-to-prosecute-govs-ministers/.

Nnodim, O. (2012, November 16). $11 billion Cash Taken Abroad through Nigerian Airports. *Punch.*

———. (2015, July 14). NNPC Must Die, Says el-Rufai. *Punch.* Retrieved from http://www.punchng.com/news/nnpc-must-die-says-el-rufai.

———. (2017, June 15). No Evidence that NNPC Remitted $15.8bn NLNG Dividend – NEITI. *Punch.* Retrieved from http://punchng.com/no-evidence-that-nnpc-remitted-15-8bn-nlng-dividend-neiti/.

———. (2017, June 15). No Evidence that NNPC Remitted $15.8bn NLNG Dividend – NEITI. *Punch.* Retrieved from http://punchng.com/no-evidence-that-nnpc-remitted-15-8bn-nlng-dividend-neiti/.

Nnoli, O. (1978). *Ethnic Politics in Nigeria.* Enugu, Nigeria: Fourth Dimension Publishers.

———. (1981). A Short History of Nigeria Underdevelopment. In O. Nnoli (Ed.), *Path to Nigeria Development.* Dakar: CODESRIA.

———. (1993). Ethnicity. In Joel Krieger (Ed.), *The Oxford Companion to Politics of the World.* New York: Oxford University Press.

NOI Polls. (2015a, August 4). Nigerians are Spending Almost Three Times the Cost of Electricity on Alternative Sources of Power. Retrieved from http://noi-polls.com/root/index.php?pid=343&parentid=13&ptid=1.

———. (2015b, July 28). Almost 8 in 10 Nigerian Households Rely on Alternative Sources of Power as Erratic Power Supply Persist. Retrieved from http://noi-polls.com/root/index.php?pid=341&parentid=13&ptid=1.

———. (2015c, August 18). Average Cumulative Power Supply Still Deplorable as Nigerians Receive Less than 6 hours Per Day. Retrieved from http://noi-polls.com/root/index.php?pid=346&parentid=13&ptid=1.

———. NOI Polls (Nigeria), 2012 and 2013. Retrieved from http://216.92.121.187/index.php?s_id=3&p_id=222&p_pt=1&parent=13#.UVfIYKK-rXC.

North Carolina Progress Board. (2001). *The Eight Imperatives for the Year 2020.* A Summary of Findings, Facts, Visions, Goals, and Targets. Retrieved from http://www.ncprogress.org/.

North, D. C. (1990). *Institutions, Institutional Change, and Economic Performance.* New York: Cambridge University Press.

———. (1981). *Structure and Change in Economic History.* New York: W. W. Norton.

———. (1991). Institutions. *Journal of Economic Perspectives*, 5(1), 97–112.

———. (1994). Economic Performance through Time. *American Economic Review*, 84(3), 359–368.

Nowell, C. E., Webster, R. A., & Magdoff, H. (2020, December 9). Western Colonialism. *Britannica.* Retrieved from https://www.britannica.com/topic/Western-colonialism/Portugals-seaborne-empire.

Ntuomi, F., Djimde, A. A., Mbacham, W., & Egwang T. (2004). The Importance and Future of Malaria Research in Africa. *American Journal of Tropical Medicine and Hygiene*, 71(2).

Nsa, C. (2007, April 5). Public Enterprises Gulped ₦13 trillion. *New Nigerian.*

Nugent, P. (2012). *Africa Since Independence: A Comparative History.* 2nd Edition. New York: Palgrave Macmillan.

———. (1989). Hobbes in Agbada: Democracy and Civil Order in Nigeria. *Africa*, 59(2), 221–228.

Nunn, N. (2009). The Importance of History for Economic Development. *Annual Review of Economics*, 1, 65–92. Retrieved from https://www.annualreviews.org/doi/pdf/10.1146/annurev.economics.050708.143336.

———. (2007). The Long-term Effects of Africa's Slave Trades. National Bureau of Economic Research (NBER). NBER Working Paper No. 13367, 2–39. Retrieved from https://www.nber.org/papers/w13367.

Nwabueze, B. (2015, August 14). Position of Igbo Leaders of Thought on Corruption Probe. *The Guardian.* Retrieved from http://www.ngrguardiannews.com/2015/08/position-of-igbo-leaders-of-thought-on-corruption-probe-4.

———. (2004). *Constitutional Democracy in Africa* (Vol. 3). Ibadan, Nigeria: Spectrum Books Limited.

———. (2015, August 10). Politics, Governance, and Development. *The Guardian.* Retrieved from http://www.ngrguardiannews.com/2015/08/politics-governance-development-3.

Nwabughiogu, L. (2020, March 8). Revelations on Abacha Loot: How funds were taken out of Nigeria — Al-Mustapha. *Vanguard.* Retrieved from https://www.vanguardngr.com/2020/03/revelations-on-abacha-loot-how-funds-were-taken-out-of-nigeria-al-mustapha/.

Nwabughiogu, L., & Ovuakporie, E. (2013, November 13). Reps Probe NNPC's Alleged $6.8bn Fraud. *Vanguard.* Retrieved www.vanguardngr.com/2013/11/reps-probe-nnpcs-alleged-6-8bn-fraud/.

Nwagbara, U. (2019). *Investigating the Relationship Between Health and Economic Growth in Africa 1960–2015.* (PhD Dissertation). Southern University and A&M College, Baton Rouge, Louisiana, USA.

Nwagbara, U., & Esedo, K. (2017). The Return of Ethno-nationalism in the Globalist Age. Paper Presented at the Annual Conference of the National Association of African American Studies. Dallas, Texas, USA, February 13–18.

Nwagwu, C. C. (1997). The Environment of Crises in the Nigerian Education System. *Comparative Education*, 33(1), 87–96. Retrieved from https://www.tandfonline.com/doi/abs/10.1080/03050069728659.

Nwankwo, A. A. (1993). *The Political Transition and Future of Democracy*. Enugu, Nigeria: Fourth Dimension Publishers.

Nwaogwugwu, I. (2011, June 20). Nigeria: The Cost of Governance. *This Day.*

Nwogu, S. (2013, March 21). Nigeria Sitting on Keg of Gunpowder – Obasanjo. *Punch.* Retrieved from http://www.punchng.com/news/nigeria-sitting-on-keg-of-gun-powder-obasanjo/.

Nwokolo, N., & Aghedo, I. (2018). Consolidating or Corrupting the Peace? The Power Elite and Amnesty Policy in the Niger Delta Region of Nigeria. *Chinese Political Science Review*, 3(3), 322–344. Retrieved from https://link.springer.com/article/10.1007%2Fs41111-018-0098-y.

Nye, J. S. (1967). Corruption and Political Development: A Cost-benefit Analysis. *The American Political Science Review*, 61(2), 417–427. Retrieved from https://www.jstor.org/stable/1953254.

Nzeogwu, C. K. (1966). Interview with British Broadcasting Corporation (BBC) in Kaduna on January16, 1966.

Nzeshi, O. (2008, May 21). UBE Funds: 19 States Face Probe. *This Day.*

Nzongola-Ntalaja. G. (2002). *The Congo from Leopold to Kabila: A People's History*. London: Zed Books Ltd.

Obadare, E. (1999). Democratic Transition and Political Violence in Nigeria. *Africa Development / Afrique et Dévéloppement,* 24(1/2), 199–219.

Obama, B. (2016, October 8). The Way Forward. *The Economist.*

Oba, A. A. (2004). The African Charter on Human and Peoples' Rights and Ouster Clauses Under the Military Regimes in Nigeria: Before and after September 11. *African Human Rights Law Journal*, 4, 275–302. Retrieved from http://www.corteidh.or.cr/tablas/R21563.pdf.

Obasanjo, O. (1987). *Nzeogwu: An Intimate Portrait of Major Chukwuma Kaduna Nzeogwu*. Ibadan, Nigeria: Spectrum.

Obembe, T. A., Osungbade, K. O., & Ibrahim, C. (2017). Appraisal of Primary Health Care Services in Federal Capital Territory, Abuja, Nigeria: How Committed Are the Health Workers? *The Pan African Medical Journal*, 28(134), 1–12. Retrieved from https://www.ncbi.nlm.nih.gov/pmc/articles/PMC5847130/pdf/PAMJ-28-134.pdf.

Obi, C. I. (2014). Oil and Conflict in Nigeria's Niger Delta Region: Between the Barrel and the Trigger. *The Extractive Industries and Society*, 1(2), 147–153.

———. (2010). Oil Extraction, Dispossession, Resistance, and Conflict in Nigeria's Oil-rich Niger Delta. *Canadian Journal of Development Studies*, 30(1–2), 219–236.

Obinna, C. (2017, December 31). 35, 000 Doctors Have Left Nigeria for the UK, US – Report. *Vanguard.* Retrieved from https://www.vanguardngr.com/2017/12/35-000-doctors-left-nigeria-uk-us-report/.

Ocheje, P. D. (2018). Norms, Law and Social Change: Nigeria's Anti-corruption Struggle, 1999–2017. *Crime, Law & Social Change,* 70, 363–381.

O'Connor, K. J., Blanco, L. R., & Nugent, J. B. (2018). Does Oil Really Curse Democracy? A Long-run Time-series Analysis of 127 countries. *Resources Policy*, 57, 264–277.

Odebode, N. (2008, January 9). Foreigners See Our Hospitals Machines as Museum Specimens. *Punch.*

Odeh, O. (2008, April 23). Nigerian Households Spend 73% of Family Budget on Food – World Bank. *Daily Independent.*

Odey, O. J. (2002). *Democracy our Lofty Dreams and Crazy Ambitions*. Enugu: Snap Press Ltd.

Odia, L. O., & Omofonmwan, S. I. (2007). Educational System in Nigeria Problems and Prospects. *Journal of Social Sciences*, 14(1), 81–86. Retrieved from https://www.tandfonline.com/doi/abs/10.1080/09718923.2007.11978347.

O'Donnell, G. A. (1973). *Modernization and Bureaucratic-Authoritarianism.* University of California Press.

OECD. (2019). Tackling Vulnerability in the Informal Economy. Retrieved from http://www.oecd.org/publications/tackling-vulnerability-in-the-informal-economy-939b7bcd-en.htm.

———. (n.d.). Is Informal Normal? Messages, figures and data. Retrieved from https://www.oecd.org/dev/inclusivesocietiesanddevelopment/isinformalnormalmessagesfiguresanddata.htm.

Odugbemi, S., & Lee, T. (2011). *Accountability Through Public Opinion: From Inertia to Public Action*. Washington, DC: World Bank. Retrieved from https://elibrary.worldbank.org/doi/abs/10.1596/978-0-8213-8505-0.

Odutolu, O. et al. (2016). Putting Institutions at the Center of Primary Health Care Reforms: Experience from Implementation in Three States in Nigeria. *Health Systems & Reform*, 2(4), 290–301. Retrieved from https://www.tandfonline.com/doi/pdf/10.1080/23288604.2016.1234863?needAccess=true.

Office of the Secretary to the Government of the Federation. (2005, August). Detailed List of Panels, Commissions and Committees from May, 1999 to May, 2005. Abuja, Nigeria.

Ogbondah, C. W. (2000). Political Repression in Nigeria, 1993–1998: A Critical Examination of One Aspect of the Perils of Military Dictatorship. *Africa Spectrum*, 35(2), 231–242.

Ogbu, O. N. (2008). Combating Corruption in Nigeria: A Critical Appraisal of the Laws, Institutions, and the Political Will. *Annual Survey of International & Comparative Law*, 14(1), Article 6, 2008.

Ogbulafor, J. E., & Malaolu, V. A. (2013). Size and Causes of the Informal Sector of the Nigerian Economy: Evidence from Error Correction Mimic Model. *Journal of Economics and Sustainable Development*, 4(1), 85–103. Retrieved from https://iiste.org/Journals/index.php/JEDS/article/viewFile/4100/4128.

Ogugbuaja, C., & Garba, A. (2012, July 17). Okorocha Appoints 79 Aides, Yuguda Sacks 2,000. *The Guardian.*

Ogundiya, I. S. (2017). Political Corruption in Nigeria: Theoretical Perspectives and Some Explanations. *The Anthropologist*, 11(4), 281–292.

Ogunyemi, A. O. (2011). Rethinking the Origin of Nigeria's Debt Burden: A Historical Reconstruction. *Journal of the Historical Society of Nigeria*, 20, 26–44. Retrieved from https://www.jstor.org/stable/41857173?seq=1#page_scan_tab_contents.

Ohajianya, A. C., Abumere, O. E., Owate, I. O., & Osarolube, E. (2014). Erratic Power Supply in Nigeria: Causes and Solutions. *International Journal of Engineering Science Invention*, 3(7), 51–55. Retrieved from https://www.researchgate.net/publication/318685479_Erratic_Power_Supply_In_Nigeria_Causes_And_Solutions.

Oji, O. G., & Agu, C. (2008). How Competitive and Efficient are Nigerian Ports? In P. Collier, C. C. Soludo, & C. Pattillo (Eds.), *Economic Policy Options for a Prosperous Nigeria*. New York: Palgrave Macmillan. Retrieved from https://zodml.org/sites/default/files/%5BPaul_Collier,_Charles_C._Soludo,_Catherine_Pattil_0.pdf.

Ojiabor, O. (2008, June 3). Corruption Has Ruined Nigeria. *Punch*.

Ojie, A. E., & Ewhrudjakpor, C. (2009). Ethnic Diversity and Public Policies in Nigeria. *The Anthropologist*, 11, 7–14. Retrieved from https://www.tandfonline.com/doi/abs/10.1080/09720073.2009.11891072.

Ojo, T. O., & Akinwumi, A. F. (2015). Doctors as Managers of Healthcare Resources in Nigeria: Evolving Roles and Current Challenges. *Nigerian Medical Journal*, 56(6), 375–380. Retrieved from https://www.ncbi.nlm.nih.gov/pmc/articles/PMC4743284/?report=printable.

Ojo, E. O. (2014). Nigeria, 1914–2014. From Creation to Cremation? *Journal of the Historical Society of Nigeria*, 23, 67–91. Retrieved from https://www.jstor.org/stable/24768942?seq=1.

Okafor, N. I., Abada, I. M., & Omeh, P. H. (2018). Exposing Ghost Workers in Nigeria: An Emerging Ethical Dimension to Get Things Right. *American Based Research Journal*, 7(3), 32–43.

Okafor, C. (2011, March 2). TI: NNPC, Seven Others Most Corrupt Oil Companies. *This Day*.

Okedu, K. E., Kenu, S., Idowu, K., & Uhunmwangho, R. (2018). Impact of the Independent Power Producers and National Integrated Power Projects on the Deregulation of the Nigerian Electricity Sector. *Journal of Sustainable Development in Africa*, 20(1), 147–170.

Okeke, C. (2015, February 20). Insurgency Crippled Heritage Sites, Tourism. *Leadership*. Retrieved from http://leadership.ng/business/412826/insurgency-crippled-heritage-sites-tourism.

Okeke, O. E. (2016). A Descriptive Research on the Causes and Effect of Nursing Shortage on Some Hospitals in Enugu State, Nigeria. *Texila International Journal of Nursing*, 2(2), 1–10. Retrieved from http://www.texilajournal.com/thumbs/article/Nursing_Vol%202_Issue%202_Article_10.pdf.

Okeke, F. (2013, April 22). Nigeria: Teachers Begin Indefinite Strike in 19 States. *Daily Trust*. Retrieved from http://allafrica.com/stories/201304220992.html.

Okeshola, F. B., & Igba, A. (2013). An Assessment of Dividends of Democracy in Bukuru Local Government Area of Benue State Nigeria 1999–2011. *African Journal of Political Science and International Relations*, 4(6), 550–561.

Oketola, D. (2011, July 22). Identity Commission Uncovers 4,000 Ghost Workers. *Punch*.

Okigbo, P. N. C. (1965). *Nigerian Public Finance*. Evanston: Northwestern University Press.

———. (1962). *Nigerian National Accounts 1950–57*. Federal Ministry of Economic Development, Lagos.

———. (1986, November 11). Economic Sorcerers and Astrologers. *New Nigerian*.

———. (1983). Economic Planning in Nigeria Since 1960. In M. O. Kayode & Y. B. Usman (Eds.), *The Economic and Social Development of Nigeria*. Proceedings of the National Conference on Nigeria since Independence, Zaria, March 1983, vol II.

———. (1989). *National Development Planning in Nigeria 1900–92*. Enugu, Nigeria: Fourth Dimension Publishing Company Ltd.

———. (1965). *Nigerian Public Finance*. Evanston: Northwestern University Press.

Oko, O. (2005). Seeking Justice in Transitional Societies: An Analysis of the Problems and Failures of the Judiciary in Nigeria. *Brooklyn Journal of International Law*, 31(1), 9–82. Retrieved from https://brooklynworks.brooklaw.edu/cgi/viewcontent.cgi?article=1278&context=bjil.

Okoi, O. (2019, October). Peace building and Transformational Change in Nigeria's Oil Region. *Conflict Resolution Quarterly*. Retrieved from https://onlinelibrary.wiley.com/doi/abs/10.1002/crq.21270.

Okonjo-Iweala, N., & Osafo-Kwaako, P. (2007). Nigeria's Economic Reforms: Progress and Challenges. Brookings Institution. Retrieved from https://www.brookings.edu/wp-content/uploads/2016/06/20070323okonjo_iweala.pdf.

———. (2008). The Role of Civil Society Organizations in Supporting Fiscal Transparency in African Countries. Background Note for Discussion. University of Oxford. Center for the Study of the Economies of Africa (CSEA). Policy Brief PB/08/001. Retrieved from https://www.r4d.org/wp-content/uploads/Ngozi-CSO_Paper_Revised_Version.pdf.

Okonedo, B. (2007, May 1). Survey Explains Collapse of Education Sector. *Business Day*.

Okonkwo, T., & Etemire, U. (2017). "Oil Injustice" in Nigeria's Niger Delta Region: A Call for Responsive Governance. *Journal of Environmental Protection*, 8, 42–60. Retrieved from http://www.scirp.org/pdf/JEP_2017012215395618.pdf.

Okonofua, B. A. (2013). Triangulation, Emotional Reactivity, and Violence in the Niger Delta. *SAGE Open*, 3(2), 1–14. Retrieved from https://journals.sagepub.com/doi/pdf/10.1177/2158244013483758.

———. (2016). The Niger Delta Amnesty Program: The Challenges of Transitioning from Peace Settlements to Long-term Peace. *SAGE Open*, 6(2), 1–16. Retrieved from https://journals.sagepub.com/doi/pdf/10.1177/2158244016654522.

Okonta, K. E., & Okonta, O. C. (2018). Industrial Crises in a Tertiary Health Institution (THI) in Nigeria: The Perspective of Resident Doctors. *International Journal of Healthcare Management*, 11(4), 269–275. Retrieved from https://www.tandfonline.com/doi/abs/10.1080/20479700.2017.1397323?scroll=top&needAccess=true&journalCode=yjhm20.

Okotoni, O., & Okotoni, A. (2003). Conflict Management in Secondary Schools in Osun State, Nigeria. *Nordic Journal of African Studies* 12(1), 23–38. Retrieved from http://www.njas.helsinki.fi/pdf-files/vol12num1/okotoni.pdf.

Okwe, M. (2017, August 17). TSA Saved Government ₦56.4b Overdraft Charges in One Year, Says AGF. *The Guardian*. Retrieved from http://guardian.ng/news/tsa-saved-government-n56-4b-overdraft-charges-in-one-year-says-agf/.

Oladapo, O. T. et al., (2016). When Getting there is not Enough: A Nationwide Cross-sectional Study of 998 Maternal Deaths and 1451 Near-misses in Public Tertiary Hospitals in a Low-income Country. *BJOG*, 123(6), 928–938. Retrieved from https://obgyn.onlinelibrary.wiley.com/doi/full/10.1111/1471-0528.13450.

Olalekan, F. (2020, March 17). Nigerians Spend $14 billion on Generators, Fuel. *Nairametrics*. Retrieved from https://nairametrics.com/2020/03/17/nigerians-spend-14-billion-on-generators-fuel-as-senators-seek-ban-on-generator-use/.

Olaopa, T. (2019, June 5). Stomach Infrastructure and Nigeria's Emergent Political Culture. *The Guardian*. Retrieved from https://guardian.ng/issue/stomach-infrastructure-and-nigerias-emergent-political-culture/.

———. (n.d.). Seminar on Sharing Success Stories and Challenges in E-Governance/E-Administration. Notes for Ministry of Communication Technology – Nigeria. Retrieved from http://workspace.unpan.org/sites/Internet/Documents/UNPAN92928.pdf.

Olatoun, A. A. (2010). Teachers and Students' Academic Performance in Nigerian Secondary Schools: Implications for Planning. *Florida Journal of Educational Administration & Policy*, 3(2), 86–103. Retrieved from https://eric.ed.gov/?id=EJ903008.

Olatubosun, F. O., & Ayooluwa, A. O. (2017). An Assessment of Democratic Governance in the Nigerian Fourth Republic. *International Journal of Politics and Good Governance*, VIII (8), 976–1195. Retrieved from http://www.onlineresearchjournals.com/ijopagg/art/243.pdf.

Olken, B. A., & Pande, R. (2011). Corruption in Developing Countries. National Bureau of Economic Research (NBER), NBER Working Paper No. 17398. Retrieved from http://www.nber.org/papers/w17398.

Olokor, F. (2012, December 11). EFCC Intercepts ₦15.5bn at Airports in 2012. *Punch*. Retrieved from http://www.punchng.com/news/efcc-intercepts-n15-5bn-at-airports-in-2012.

———. (2019, October 24). Prediction on Nigeria's Break-up May Be Fulfilled – Jega. *Punch*. Retrieved from https://punchng.com/prediction-on-nigerias-break-up-may-be-fulfilled-jega/.

Olson, M. C. (1965). *The Logic of Collective Action: Public Goods and the Theory of Groups*. Harvard University Press.

Olugbile, S., & Sam, V. (2008, March 28). ICPC Uncovers ₦3.32bn Fraud in UBEC. *Punch*.

Olukoya, S. (2008, July 2). Nigeria Makes Progress on Stolen Cash. *BBC News*. Retrieved from Http://news.bbc.co.uk/go/pr/fr/-/2/hi/business/7484022.stm.

Oluwasanmi, H. (1966). *Agriculture and Nigerian Economic Development*. Ibadan, Nigeria: Oxford University Press.

Olowosejeje, S., Leahy, P., & Morrison, A. (2019). The Economic Cost of Unreliable Grid Power in Nigeria. *African Journal of Science, Technology, Innovation and Development*, 11(2), 149–159.

Olowosejeje, S. A. (2019, June 1). Nigeria's Unreliable Electricity Costs its Economy $29 billion a Year—Solar Power Would Save Billions. *Quartz* (USA).

Olufemi, J., & Akintunde, B. (2019, February 13). Special Report: Nigeria's four Seasons of Lavishness with ₦15.46 Trillion Excess Crude Fund. *Premium Times*.

Olukoshi, A. O. (1993). General Introduction: From Crisis to Adjustment in Nigeria. In *The Politics of Structural Adjustment in Nigeria*. London: James Currey.

Olukoshi, A., & Abdulraheem, T. (1985). Nigeria, Crisis Management under the Burhari Administration. *Review of African Political Economy*, 34, 95–101.

Omotoso, F. (2014). Public-service Ethics and Accountability for Effective Service Delivery in Nigeria. *Africa Today*, 60(3), 119–134.

Onimode, B. (1978). Imperialism and Multinational Corporations: A Case Study of Nigeria. *Journal of Black Studies*, 9(2), 207–232.

Onuba, I. (2011, September 8). Nigeria Loses ₦750bn annually to Non-metering of Oil Wells. *Punch*. Retrieved from http://www.nairaland.com/756829/nigeria-loses-n750bn-5bn-annually.

Onuigbo, R. A., Idike, A. N., Eme, O. I., & Anyadike, N. (2017). National Assembly Members and their Jumbo Pay Controversy: Matters Arising. *Specialty Journal of Humanities and Cultural Science*, 2 (1), 46–60. Retrieved from http://sciarena.com/storage/article/file/AC478Article.pdf.

Onuorah, M. (2007, April 2). Stakeholders Okay Education Bill, Sector Emergency. *The Guardian*.

Onwe, O. J. (2013). Role of the Informal Sector in Development of the Nigerian Economy: Output and Employment Approach. *Journal of Economics and Development Studies*, 1(1), 60–74.

Onwuchekwa, A., BellGram, H., & Asekomeh, G. (2009). Stroke at the University of Port Harcourt Teaching Hospital, Rivers State, Nigeria. *Tropical Doctor*, 39(3), 150–152. Retrieved from https://journals.sagepub.com/doi/abs/10.1258/td.2008.080285.

Onwudiwe, E., & Berwind-Dart, C. (2010). Breaking the Cycle of Electoral Violence in Nigeria. United States Institute of Peace. Washington, DC. Retrieved from https://www.usip.org/sites/default/files/SR263-Breaking_the_Cycle_of_Electoral_Violence_in_Nigeria.pdf.

Onyiloha, C. A. (2015). An Ethical Appraisal of Nigerian Policy on Corruption vis-a-vis Global Anti-corruption Practices. Retrieved from https://www.ajol.info/index.php/jrhr/article/viewFile/119643/109103.

Opara, I. (2007). Nigeria Anti-corruption Initiatives. *Journal of International Business & Law*, 6(1), 65–93. Retrieved from https://law.hofstra.edu/pdf/academics/journals/jibl/previousvolumes/jibl_volume_6.pdf.

Organization for Economic Cooperation and Development. (OECD). (2000). Fighting Corruption in the Developing Countries. OECD Observer. Retrieved from http://oecdobserver.org/news/archivestory.php/aid/291/Fighting_corruption_in_the_developing_countries.html.

———. (2012). Research Universities: Networking the Knowledge Economy. Program on Innovation, Higher Education and Research for Development (IHERD). Retrieved from https://www.oecd.org/sti/Session%205_Networking%20the%20Knowledge%20Economy.pdf.

———. (2018). Illicit Financial Flows: The Economy of Illicit Trade in West Africa.

———. (2015). The Future of Productivity. Retrieved from http://www.oecd.org/eco/growth/OECD-2015-The-future-of-productivity-book.pdf.

———. (2012). *Survey on Budgeting Practices and Procedures: Types and Legal Foundation of Fiscal Rules*. Paris: OECD Publishing.

OECD. (2014). *Budgeting Practices and Procedures in OECD Countries*. Paris: OECD Publishing. Retrieved from https://doi.org/10.1787/9789264059696-en.

———. (2011). Restoring Public Finances. Special Issue of the OECD Journal on Budgeting, 2011(2), Paris: OECD Publishing. Retrieved from https://www.oecd.org/governance/budgeting/47558957.pdf.

———. (2014). Growth Prospects and Fiscal Requirements over the Long Term. OECD Economic Outlook, 2014(1). Retrieved from https://www.oecd.org/economy/Long-term-growth-prospects-and-fiscal-requirements.pdf.

Orude, P. (2011, May 11). Yaguda Sacks All Aides. *The Sun*.

Osaghae, E. (2003). Explaining the Changing Patterns of Ethnic Politics in Nigeria. *Nationalism and Ethnic Politics*, 9, 54–73. Retrieved from https://www.tandfonline.com/doi/abs/10.1080/13537110412331301475?src=recsys.

———. (1998). *Crippled Giant: Nigeria Since Independence*. Bloomington: Indiana University Press.

———. (1995). The Ogoni Uprising: Oil, Politics, Minority Agitation and the Future of the Nigerian State. *African Affairs*, 94(376), 325–344.

———. (1999). Exiting from the State in Nigeria. *African Journal of Political Science / Revue Africaine de Science Politique*, 4(1), 83–98.

———. (2006). Colonialism and Civil Society in Africa: The Perspective of Ekeh's Two Publics. *Voluntas,* 17, 233–245.

Osayimwese, I., & Iyare, S. (1991). The Economics of Nigerian Federalism: Selected Issues in Economic Management. *Publius*, 21(4), 89–101.

Osborne, D., & Hutchinson, P. (2006). *The Price of Government: Getting the Results We Need in an Age of Permanent Fiscal Crisis*. New York: Basic Books.

Oshiomole, A. (2013, August 15). YouTube. Retrieved from http://www.youtube.com/watch?v=6OJDt-8i0Mw.

Oslon, M. C. (1965). *The Logic of Collective Action: Public Goods and the Theory of Groups.* Harvard University Press.

Osman, R. H., Alexiou, C., & Tsaliki, P. (2011). The Role of Institutions in Economic Development: Evidence from 27 Sub-Saharan African Countries. *International Journal of Social Economics*, 39(1/2), 142–160. Retrieved from https://www.emeraldinsight.com/doi/pdfplus/10.1108/03068291211188910.

Osoba, S. O. (1996). Corruption in Nigeria: Historical Perspectives. *Review of African Political Economy*, 69, 371–386.

Osundare, N. (2014, April 2). The Orator's Last Bow. *Vanguard.* Retrieved from http://www.vanguardngr.com/2014/04/orators-last-bow.

Otaha, I. J. (2013). Food Insecurity in Nigeria: Way Forward. *African Research Review*, 7(4), 26–35. Retrieved from https://www.ajol.info/index.php/afrrev/article/viewFile/96670/86004.

Othman, S. (1984). Classes, Crises and Coup: The Demise of Shagari's Regime. *African Affairs*, 83(333), 441–461.

———. (1989). [Review of the book *Democracy and Prebendal Politics in Nigeria: The Rise and Fall of the Second Republic*, by Richard A. Joseph]. *Third World Quarterly*, 11(2), 210–212.

Owen, O., & Usman, Z. (2015). Briefing: Why Goodluck Jonathan Lost the Nigerian Presidential Election of 2015. *African Affairs*, 114(456), 455–471.

Oxfam International. (2017). *Inequality in Nigeria: Exploring the Drivers.* Retrieved from https://www.oxfam.org/sites/www.oxfam.org/files/file_attachments/cr-inequality-in-nigeria-170517-en.pdf.

Oxford Business Group. (n.d.). Nigeria Rehabilitating and Expanding Transport Network. Retrieved from https://oxfordbusinessgroup.com/overview/taking-action-rehabilitating-and-expanding-transport-network-key-realising-its-potential. See also *The Report: Nigeria 2016.*

Oyedele, D. (2008, June 5). Switzerland: We've Returned All Abacha Loot. *This Day.*

———. (2014, March 11). Nigerians Spent $350m on Healthcare in India in 2013. *This Day.* Retrieved from http://www.thisdaylive.com/articles/nigerians-spent-350m-on-healthcare-in-india-in-2013/173410.

Oyekanmi, R. L. (2012, November 13). How Graft, Poor Staffing, Others Mar Public Varsities. *The Guardian.*

Oyekanmi, R., & Coffie-Gyamfi, C. (2010, June 7). How Graft Hobbles Nigeria by Ribadu. *The Guardian.* Retrieved from http://www.nigeria70.com/nigerian_news_paper/how_graft_hobbles_nigeria_by_ribadu/228773.

Oyelaran-Oyeyinka, B. (2014). The State and Innovation Policy in Africa. *African Journal of Science, Technology, Innovation and Development*, 6(5), 481–496.

Oyesina, T. (2011, October 18). Nigeria Loses ₦240 trillion Annually to Corruption. *Nigerian Tribune.*

Oyewale, W. (2019, December 20). We're in a Big Hole as a Nation —TY Danjuma. *Punch.* Retrieved from https://punchng.com/we-are-in-a-big-hole-as-a-nation-ty-danjuma/.

Oyovbaire, E. S. (1985). *Federation in Nigeria.* London: Macmillan.

———. (1983). Structural Change and Political Processes in Nigeria. *African Affairs*, 82(326), 3–28.

Packard, R. M. (2009). "Roll Back Malaria, Roll in Development"? Reassessing the Economic Burden of Malaria. *Population and Development Review*, 35(1), 53–87.

———. (2001, September). 'Malaria Blocks Development' Revisited: The Role of Disease in the History of Agricultural Development in the Eastern and Northern Transvaal Lowveld, 1890–1960. *Journal of Southern African Studies,* 27(3), 591–612.

Page, M., & Okeke, C. (2019). Stolen Dreams: How Corruption Negates Government Assistance to Nigeria's Small Businesses. Carnegie Endowment for International Peace.

Page, M. (2018). A New Taxonomy for Corruption in Nigeria. Carnegie Endowment for International Peace. Retrieved from https://carnegieendowment.org/2018/07/17/new-taxonomy-for-corruption-in-nigeria-pub-76811.

Paquette, D. (2020, December 15). Boko Haram Claims Kidnapping of over 300 Boys in Nigeria, Marking an Alarming Move West. *The Washington Post.* Retrieved from https://www.washingtonpost.com/world/africa/boko-haram-nigeria-300-boys-kidnap/2020/12/15/98a4bf32-3eaf-11eb-b58b-1623f6267960_story.html.

Partee, G. L. (2014). Attaining Equitable Distribution of Effective Teachers in Public Schools. Center for American Progress. Washington, DC. Retrieved from http://www.americanprogress.org/wp-content/uploads/2014/04/TeacherDistro.pdf.

Peck, S., & Chayes, S. (2015). The Oil Curse: A Remedial Role for the Oil Industry. Carnegie Endowment for International Peace. Retrieved from http://carnegieendowment.org/2015/09/30/oil-curse-remedial-role-for-oil-industry-pub-61445.

Peel, M. (2006). Nigeria Related Financial Crime and Its Links with Britain. Chatham House. Retrieved from https://www.chathamhouse.org/sites/default/files/public/Research/Africa/nigeria1106.pdf.

Peters, B. G. (2015). State Failure, Governance Failure and Policy Failure: Exploring the Linkages. *Public Policy and Administration*, 30(3–4), 261–276. Retrieved from https://journals.sagepub.com/doi/10.1177/0952076715581540.

Peters, J. (1997). The Nigerian Military and the State. Volume 4, page 214.

Peterside, A. (2014, March 13). Letter to My Countrymen: This National Conference Must Succeed. *This Day.* Retrieved from http://www.thisdaylive.com/articles/letter-to-my-countrymen-this-national-conference-must-succeed/173565.

Perham, M. (1937). *Native Administration in Nigeria.* London: Oxford University Press.

Phillips, A. (2009, August 17). Clinton is Worried About Nigeria. *Newswatch.*

Pickering, T. (1998, July 7). U.S. Undersecretary of State. Interview by *BBC News.* Abiola's Death – an Eyewitness Account. Retrieved from http://news.bbc.co.uk/2/hi/africa/128491.stm.

Pierce, S. (2006, October). Looking like a State: Colonialism and the Discourse of Corruption in Northern Nigeria. *Comparative Studies in Society and History*, 48(4), 887–914.

Pinto, B. (1987). Nigeria During and after the Oil Boom: A Policy Comparison with Indonesia. *World Bank Economic Review*, 1(3), 419–445. Retrieved from http://documents.worldbank.org/curated/en/198091468775789095/pdf/multi-page.pdf.

Polgreen, L. (2006, January 1). Blood Flows with Oil in Poor Nigerian Villages. *The New York Times*. Retrieved from https://www.nytimes.com/2006/01/01/world/africa/blood-flows-with-oil-in-poor-nigerian-villages.html.

———. (November 29, 2005). As Nigeria Tries to Fight Graft, a new Sordid Tale. *The New York Times*.

Polhemus, J. H. (1977). Nigeria and Southern Africa: Interest, Policy, and Means. *Canadian Journal of African Studies / Revue Canadienne des Études Africaines*, 11(1), 43–66.

Popoola, S. I. et al., (2018). Datasets on Demographic Trends in Enrollment into Undergraduate Engineering Programs at Covenant University, Nigeria. *Data in Brief*, 18, 47–59. Retrieved from http://eprints.covenantuniversity.edu.ng/11003/1/Popoola%20et%20al%20demographic%20trend.pdf.

Post Express. (1998, May 18).

———. (1998, September 9).

———. (2000, July 7).

———. (1998, November 19).

Prado, M. M., & Carson, L. (2014). Brazilian Anti-corruption Legislation and Its Enforcement: Potential Lessons for Institutional Design. International Research Initiative on Brazil and Africa (IRIBA). School of Environment, Education and Development, The University of Manchester. United Kingdom.

Premium Times. (2012, May 27). At Democracy Day Church Service, Jonathan, Ministers, Decline to Say "Amen" to Prayer Against Corruption. Retrieved from http://premiumtimesng.com/news/5314-at_democracy_day_church_service_jonathan_ministers_refuse_to_com.html.

Przeworski, A., & Limongi, F. (1997). Modernization: Theories and Facts. *World Politics*, 49(2), 157–158. Retrieved from https://scholar.harvard.edu/files/levitsky/files/przeworski_limogni.pdf.

Price Waterhouse Coopers (PWC). (2015). *Doing Business in Mexico*. Retrieved from https://www.pwc.de/de/internationale-maerkte/assets/doing-business-mexico.pdf.

———. (2018). *Global Economic Crime and Fraud Survey 2018*. Retrieved from https://www.pwc.com/gx/en/economic-crime-survey/pdf/GlobalEconomicCrimeSurvey2016.pdf.

———. (2013, December). *A Privatized Power Sector: The Pain and the Glory*. Retrieved from https://www.pwc.com/ng/en/assets/pdf/pwc-a-privatized-power-sector-the-pain-and-the-glory.pdf.

———. (2016, July). *Powering Nigeria for the Future*. Retrieved from http://www.pwc.com/gx/en/growth-markets-centre/assets/pdf/powering-nigeria-future.pdf.

Prichard, W., Salardi, P., & Segal, P. (2018). Taxation, Non-tax Revenue and Democracy: New Evidence Using New Cross-country Data. *World Development*, 109, 295–312.

Punch. (2014, May 7). Examining Jonathan's Media Chart. [Editorial].

———. (2014, December 15). It's Risky to Dump National Conference Report. [Editorial]. Retrieved from http://www.punchng.com/editorial/its-risky-to-dump-national-conference-report.

———. (2019, December 11). Buhari's Lawlessness: Our Stand. [Editorial]. Retrieved from https://punchng.com/buharis-lawlessness-our-stand/.
———. (2014, January 28). Okonjo-Iweala's TEDxEuston Blunder on Waivers. [Editorial].
———. (2013, November 25). Okonjo-Iweala's Gaffe on Abuse of Waivers.
———. (2013, November 18). Jonathan, Okonjo-Iweala and Waivers.
———. (2017, September 25). Nigeria's Infrastructure Needs Remain Acute – World Bank. Retrieved from http://punchng.com/nigerias-infrastructure-needs-remain-acute-world-bank/.
———. (2011, November 20). Before the Return of Toll Gates. [Editorial].
———. (November 3, 2019).
———. (2020, April 1). Buhari, Resolve Electricity Privatization Crisis. Retrieved from https://punchng.com/buhari-resolve-electricity-privatisation-crisis/.
———. (2007, November 14).
———. (2006, October 5).
———. (2014, January 24). Abuse of ₦4.17 Trillion Service Wide Vote. [Editorial]. Retrieved from http://www.punchng.com/editorial/abuse-of-n4-17-trillion-service-wide-vote.
———. (2013, April 15). Stop Abuse of Special Funds. [Editorial].
———. (2012, October 2). Kwankwaso's Stance on Security Vote. [Editorial].
———. (2014, July 14). Plundering of Special Funds. [Editorial]. Retrieved from http://www.punchng.com/editorial/plundering-of-special-funds.
———. (2015, July 28). ₦400m Cars and Curbing Government Waste. [Editorial]. Retrieved from http://www.punchng.com/editorials/n400m-cars-and-curbing-government-waste.
———. (2016, January 25). How to Deploy Recovered Loot. [Editorial]. Retrieved from http://www.punchng.com/how-to-deploy-recovered-loot/.
———. (2016, February 1). Time to Tame Greedy and Reckless National Assembly. [Editorial]. Retrieved from http://www.punchng.com/time-to-tame-greedy-and-reckless-national-assembly/.
———. (2014, March 17). Taraba Acting Governor Sacks 24 Special Advisers. Retrieved from http://www.punchng.com/news/taraba-acting-gov-sacks-24-special-advisers.
———. (2004, May 5).
———. (2020, April 3). Reps Probing of Refineries' TAM Scam. [Editorial]. Retrieved from https://punchng.com/reps-probing-of-refineries-tam-scam/.
———. (2011, November 29). Reviving Privatization Program. [Editorial].
———. (2017, January 26). Nigeria Deploys Social Welfare Scheme to help the Poor.
———. (2020, February 4). Corruption Nigeria's Biggest Challenge - EFCC. Retrieved from https://punchng.com/corruption-nigerias-biggest-challenge-efcc/.
———. (2014, March 19). Damning US Corruption Report on Nigeria. [Editorial]. Retrieved from http://www.punchng.com/editorial/damning-us-corruption-report-on-nigeria.
———. (2014, March 9). We, the People. [Editorial]. Retrieved from http://www.punchng.com/editorial/we-the-people.

———. (2015, July 29). NNPC Stinks, Kill It Now. [Editorial]. Retrieved from http://www.punchng.com/editorials/nnpc-stinks-kill-it-now.

———. (2014, August 25). NNPC Changes: Diezani Owes Nigerians Explanation. [Editorial]. Retrieved from http://www.punchng.com/editorial/nnpc-changes-diezani-owes-nigerians-explanation.

———. (2012, November 2). Jonathan, Alison-Madueke and the Ribadu Report. [Editorial].

———. (2016, February 7). Anti-graft War: Beyond Asset Declaration. [Editorial]. Retrieved from http://www.punchng.com/anti-graft-war-beyond-asset-declaration/.

———. (2016, February 7). Anti-graft War: Beyond Asset Declaration. Retrieved from http://www.punchng.com/anti-graft-war-beyond-asset-declaration/.

———. (2019, October 1). 59 Years After, Nigeria Represents Poverty. [Editorial]. Retrieved from https://punchng.com/59-years-after-nigeria-represents-poverty/.

———. (2014, March 6). US Seizes $458m Abacha Loot. Retrieved from http://www.punchng.com/news/us-seizes-458m-abacha-loot/.

———. (2012, November 28). Alarming Food Import Bill. [Editorial].

———. (2017, October 13). Embarrassing Condition of State House Clinic. [Editorial]. Retrieved from http://punchng.com/embarrassing-condition-of-state-house-clinic/.

———. (2016, November 3). I Felt Like Absconding After I Took Over – Buhari.

———. Teaching Without Learning in Nigerian Schools. *Punch.* [Editorial]. Retrieved from http://www.punchng.com/editorial/teaching-without-learning-in-nigerian-schools.

———. (2016, January 21). Buhari's Technical Education Program. [Editorial]. Retrieved from http://www.punchng.com/buharis-technical-education-programme/.

———. (2014, March 18). FG Invests ₦144.7b in Basic Education.

———. (2014, March 25). FG Releases ₦113.75bn for Girl Child Education. Retrieved from http://www.punchng.com/news/fg-releases-n113-75bn-for-girl-child-education.

———. (2014, April 17). NUT Urges Benue to Pay Teachers. Retrieved from http://www.punchng.com/news/nut-urges-benue-to-pay-teachers.

Rajan, R. G., & Subramanian, A. (2005). Aid and Growth: What Does the Cross-Country Evidence Really Show? National Bureau of Economic Research (NBER), Working Paper 11513.

Rapley, J. (2007). *Understanding Development: Theory and Practice in the Third World.* 3rd Edition. Boulder, CO: Lynne Rienner Publishers.

Rawlings, J. (2016, July 10). Interview by E. Anuforo. Nigeria Inspires the Rest of Africa to Demand Democratic Change. *The Guardian.* Retrieved from http://guardian.ng/interview/rawling-nigeria-inspires-the-rest-of-africa-to-demand-democratic-change/.

Reich, R. (1991). *The Work of Nations.* New York: Vintage Books.

Reno, W. (2006). Congo: From State Collapse to "Absolutism" to State Failure. *Third World Quarterly*, 27(1), 43–56.

Reinert, E. S. (2008). *How Rich Countries Got Rich and Why Poor Countries Stay Poor.* Public Affairs.

Reuters. (2020, November 29). Electricity Grid Collapses in Nigeria, Africa's Largest Economy.

Reyes, G. E. (2001). Four Main Theories of Development: Modernization, Dependency, World Systems, and Globalization.

Rhode, D. L. (2017, June). Leadership in Law. *Stanford Law Review*, 69, 1603–1666. Retrieved from https://review.law.stanford.edu/wp-content/uploads/sites/3/2017/06/69-Stan.-L.-Rev.-1603.pdf.

Ricardo, D. [1817] (1911). *Principles of Political Economy and Taxation*. London: J. M. Dent & Sons.

Roberts, S. (2015, October 14). Diepreye Alamieyeseigha, Nigerian Notorious for Corruption, Dies at 62. *The New York Times*.

Robinson, J. A., Torvik, R., & Verdier, T. (2006). Political Foundations of the Resource Curse. *Journal of Development Economics*, 79(2), 447–468. Retrieved from https://www.sciencedirect.com/science/article/pii/S0304387806000137.

Robinson, J. (2012, December 8). Swiss to Return Abacha Money – Finally. Retrieved from http://www.jeffreyrobinson.com/blog/?p=223.

Rodney. W. (1973). *How Europe Underdeveloped Africa*. London: Bogle-L'Ouverture Publications.

———. (1985). The Colonial Economy. In A. Adu Boahen (Ed.), *General History of Africa. VII: Africa Under Colonial Domination 1880–1935*. Paris: UNESCO, 332–381.

———. (1970). *A History of the Upper Guinea Coast, 1545–1800*. Oxford: Clarendon Press.

———. (1967). *West Africa and the Atlantic Slave Trade*. Nairobi, Kenya: East African Publishing House.

Rodrik, D. (2008). Thinking About Governance. In *Governance, Growth, and Development Decision Making*. Washington, DC: World Bank. Retrieved from http://siteresources.worldbank.org/EXTPUBLICSECTORANDGOVERNANCE/Resources/governanceandgrowth.pdf.

———. *One Economics, Many Recipes: Globalization, Institutions, and Economic Growth*. Princeton: Princeton University Press.

Rodrik, D., Subramanian, A., & Trebbi, F. (2002). Institutions Rule: The Primacy of Institutions Over Integration and Geography in Economic Development. International Monetary Fund, Working Paper 02/189. Retrieved from https://www.imf.org/external/pubs/ft/wp/2002/wp02189.pdf.

Rodriquez, F., & Sachs, J. D. (1999). Why Do Resource Abundant Economies Grow More Slowly? A New Explanation and Application to Venezuela. *Journal of Economic Growth*, 4(3): 277–303. Retrieved from https://link.springer.com/article/10.1023/A:1009876618968.

Romer, D. (2006). *Advanced Macroeconomics*. 3rd Edition. New York: McGraw Hill/Irwin.

Rose-Ackerman, S. (1978). *Corruption: A Study in Political Economy*. New York: Academic Press.

Rose-Ackerman, S., & Palifka, B. J. (2016). *Corruption and Government – Causes, Consequences, and Reform*. Cambridge University Press.

Rosenberg, N. (2004). Innovation and Economic Growth. Retrieved from https://www.oecd.org/cfe/tourism/34267902.pdf.

Roosevelt, F. D. (1933, March 4). First Inaugural Address. Retrieved from http://www.bartleby.com/124/pres49.html .

Ross, M. (2013). The Politics of the Resource Curse: A Review. In C. Lancaster & N. van de Walle (Eds.), *The Oxford Handbook of the Politics of Development*. Oxford University Press.

———. (2001). Does Oil Hinder Democracy? *World Politics*, 53(3), 325–361. Retrieved from https://scholar.harvard.edu/files/levitsky/files/ross_world_politics.pdf.

———. (1999). The Political Economy of the Resource Curse. *World Politics*, 51(2), 297–322.

———. (2012). *The Oil Curse: How Petroleum Wealth Shapes the Development of Nations*. Princeton and Oxford: Princeton University Press.

———. (2001). *Extractive Sectors and the Poor*. Oxfam America Report. Retrieved from https://www.oxfamamerica.org/static/oa3/files/extractive-sectors-and-the-poor.pdf.

———. (2006). A Closer Look at Oil, Diamonds, and Civil War. *Annual Review of Political Science*, 9(1), 265–300.

———. (2004). How Does Natural Resource Wealth Influence Civil wars? Evidence from Thirteen Cases. *International Organization*, 58, 35–67.

Ross, E. L. et al. (n.d.). The Economic Impacts of Newly Discovered Oil in Uganda, Using a Recursive Dynamic CGE Model. Retrieved from https://www.gtap.agecon.purdue.edu/resources/download/6277.pdf.

Ross, W. (2015, September 4). Nigeria's President Muhammadu Buhari Declares Assets. *BBC News*. Retrieved from http://www.bbc.com/news/world-africa-34150508

Rostow, W. W. (1960). *The Stages of Economic Growth: A Non-Communist Manifesto*. Cambridge: Cambridge University Press.

———. The Take-Off into Self-Sustained Growth. *The Economic Journal*, 66(261), 25–48.

Rothchild, D. (1970). African Federations and the Diplomacy of Decolonization. *The Journal of Developing Areas*, 4(4), 509–524.

Rushefsky, M. (2013). *Public Policy in the United States*. 5the Edition. New York: M. E. Sharpe.

Rousseau, J. (1762). *The Social Contract*.

Rupert, J. (1998, June 9). Corruption Flourished in Abacha's Regime. *The Washington Post*.

Rynn, J. (2011, May 23). Six Reasons Manufacturing is Central to the Economy. Next New Deal. The Blog of the Roosevelt Institute. Retrieved from http://www.nextnewdeal.net/six-reasons-manufacturing-central-economy.

Sachs, J. D. (2003). Institutions Don't Rule: Direct Effects of Geography on Per Capita Income. National Bureau of Economic Research (NBER). NBER Working Paper No. 9490. Retrieved from https://www.nber.org/papers/w9490.

———. (2011). *The Price of Civilization.* New York: Random House.

Sachs, J., & Malaney, P. (2002). The Economic and Social Burden of Malaria. *Nature*, 415, 680–685.

Sachs, J. D., & Warner, A. M. (2001). The Curse of Natural Resources. *European Economic Review*, 45, 827–838. Retrieved from https://www.earth.columbia.edu/sitefiles/file/about/director/pubs/EuroEconReview2001.pdf.

———. (1997). Sources of Slow Growth in African Economies. *Journal of African Economies*, 6 (3), 335–376.

———. (1995). Natural Resource Abundance and Economic Growth. Center for International Development and Harvard Institute for International Development. Harvard University. Cambridge: MA. Retrieved from https://pdfs.semanticscholar.org/7b14/045909f42117197b82a910782ab68330a3e7.pdf.

Saint, W., Hartnett, T. A., & Strassner, E. (2003). Higher Education in Nigeria: A Status Report. *Higher Education Policy*, 16(3), 259–281. Retrieved from https://link.springer.com/article/10.1057/palgrave.hep.8300021.

Sala-i-Martina, X., & Subramanian, A. (2013). Addressing the Natural Resource Curse: An Illustration from Nigeria. *Journal of African Economies*, 22(4), 570–615. Retrieved from https://academic.oup.com/jae/article/22/4/570/744831?login=true.

———. (2003). Addressing the Natural Resource Curse: An Illustration from Nigeria. *Journal of African Economies*, Centre for the Study of African Economies (CSAE), 22(4), 570–615. Retrieved from http://www.nber.org/papers/w9804.

———. (2008). Addressing the Natural Resource Curse: An Illustration from Nigeria. In P. Collier, C. Soludo, & C. Pattillo (Eds.), *Economic Policy Options for a Prosperous Nigeria*. New York: Palgrave Macmillan. Retrieved from https://zodml.org/sites/default/files/%5BPaul_Collier,_Charles_C._Soludo,_Catherine_Pattil_0.pdf.

Sam, K., Coulon, F., & Prpich, G. (2017). Management of Petroleum Hydrocarbon Contaminated Sites in Nigeria: Current Challenges and Future Direction. *Land Use Policy*, 64, 133–144. Retrieved from https://www.sciencedirect.com/science/article/pii/S0264837716302228.

Sampath, P. G. (2014). Industrial Development for Africa: Trade, Technology and the Role of the State. *African Journal of Science, Technology, Innovation and Development*, 6(5), 439–453. Retrieved from https://www.tandfonline.com/doi/pdf/10.1080/20421338.2014.970438?needAccess=true.

Sangmpam, S. N. (1995, 3rd Quarter). Social Theory and the Challenges of Africa's Future. *Africa Today*, 42(3), 39–66.

Santos, T. D. (1970). The Structure of Dependence. *American Economic Review*, 60(2), 231–236. Retrieved from http://web.unair.ac.id/admin/file/f_20003_Dos_Santos_Structure-LAMPIRAN_3.pdf.

Sarter, M. (2006). The Consequences of Atheoretical, Task-driven Experimentation: Theoretical Comment on Paban, Chambon, Jaffard, and Alescio-Lavtier (2005). *Behavior Neuroscience*, 120(2), 493–495. Retrieved from https://www.ncbi.nlm.nih.gov/pubmed/16719713.

Sarraf, M., & Jiwanji, M. (2001). Beating the Resource Curse: The Case of Botswana. The World Bank. Environmental Economics Series, No. 83, 1–36. Retrieved from http://documents.worldbank.org/curated/en/412021468227707937/Beating-the-resource-curse-the-case-of-Botswana.

Saunders, R. J., Warford, J. J., & Wellenius, B. (1994). *Telecommunications & Economic Development*. 2nd Edition. World Bank. Baltimore and London: The John Hopkins University Press. Retrieved from http://documents.worldbank.org/curated/en/244111468763783754/pdf/multi-page.pdf.

Sayne, A., Gillies, A., & Katsouris, C. (2015). Inside NNPC Oil Sales: A Case for Reform in Nigeria. Natural Resource Governance Institute. Retrieved from https://resourcegovernance.org/sites/default/files/NRGI_InsideNNPCOilSales_CompleteReport.pdf.

SB Morgen. (2020, May). Nigeria's Kidnap Problem – The Economics of the Kidnap Industry in Nigeria.

Schakel, H. C., Wu, E. H., & Jeurissen, P. (2018). Fiscal Rules, Powerful Levers for Controlling the Health Budget? Evidence from 32 OECD Countries. *BMC Public Health*, 18(300), 1–17. Retrieved from https://bmcpublichealth.biomedcentral.com/track/pdf/10.1186/s12889-018-5198-y.

Schnitzer, M. C. (1994). *Comparative Economic Systems*. Cincinnati, OH: South-West Publishing Co.

Schultze-Kraft, M. (2017). Understanding Organized Violence and Crime in Political Settlements: Oil Wars, Petro-criminality and Amnesty in the Niger Delta. *Journal of International Development,* 29(5), 613–627. Retrieved from https://onlinelibrary.wiley.com/doi/abs/10.1002/jid.3287.

Schlesinger, A. Jr. (1958). *The Age of Roosevelt: The Coming of the New Deal.* Boston: Houghton Mifflin Company.

———. (1960). *The Age of Roosevelt: The Politics of Upheaval.* Boston: Houghton Mifflin Company, 1960.

Sertoglu, K., Ugural, S., & Bekun, F. V. (2017). The Contribution of Agricultural Sector on Economic Growth of Nigeria. *International Journal of Economics and Financial Issues*, 7(1), 547–552.

Shapiro, R. J., & Ross, D. (1993). Enterprise Economics: Rebuilding the American Economy. In W. Marshall & M. Schram (Eds.), *Mandate for Change*. Progressive Policy Institute. New York: Berkley Book.

Shapiro, R. J. (1993). Enterprise Economics and the Federal Budget. In W. Marshall & M. Schrain (Eds.), *Mandate for change.* The Progressive Policy Institute. New York: Berkley Books.

Shaw, T. M. (1975). The Political Economy of African International Relations. *A Journal of Opinion*, 5(4), 29–38.

———. (1982). Beyond Neo-colonialism: Varieties of Corporatism in Africa. *The Journal of Modern African Studies*, 20(2), 239–261.

Shaxson, N. (2005). New Approaches to Volatility: Dealing with the 'Resource Curse' in Sub-Saharan Africa. *International Affairs*, 81(2), 311–324.

———. (2007). Oil, Corruption and the Resource Curse. *International Affairs*, 83(6), 1123–1140. Retrieved from https://projects.iq.harvard.edu/gov2126/files/shaxson_2007.pdf.

Sherk, J. (2010, July 6). Government Jobs: Bloated Pay, Benefits Cost Us All. *USA Today*.

Shils, E. (1958). The Concentration and Dispersion of Charisma: Their Bearing on Economic Policy in Underdeveloped Countries. *World Politics*, 11(1), 1–19.

Shimeles, A., & Nabassaga, T. (2017). Why Is Inequality High in Africa? Working Paper Series. African Development Bank Group. Abidjan: Côte d'Ivoire. Retrieved from https://www.afdb.org/fileadmin/uploads/afdb/Documents/Publications/WPS_No_246_Why_is_inequality_high_in_Africa_A.pdf.

Shin, D. C. (1994). On the Third Wave of Democratization: A Synthesis and Evaluation of Recent Theory and Research. *World Politics*, 47(1), 135–170.

Shuaib, I. M., Augustine, O. E., & Frank, A. O. (2015). Balance of Payments: Nigerian Experience: 1960–2012. *British Journal of Economics, Management & Trade*, 7(4), 298–305. Retrieved from http://www.journalrepository.org/media/journals/BJEMT_20/2015/Apr/Shuaib742014BJEMT14638.pdf.

Shuaibu, M., & Oyinlola, M. A. (2017). An Empirical Analysis of Nigeria's Current Account Sustainability. *The Journal of Applied Economic Research*, 11(1), 54–76. Retrieved from http://journals.sagepub.com/doi/pdf/10.1177/0973801016676015.

Shultz, T. W. (1961). Investment in Human Capital. *American Economic Review*, 51, 1–19.

Siollun, M. (2009). *Oil, Politics and Violence: Nigeria's Military Coup Culture (1966–1976)*. New York: Algora Publishing.

Sklar, R. L. (1963). *Nigerian Political Parties: Power in an Emergent African Nation*. Princeton University Press.

Smith, A. 1776 (1991). *An Inquiry into the Nature and Causes of the Wealth of Nations*. New York: Prometheus Books.

Smith, B. (1981). Federal-state Relations in Nigeria. *African Affairs*, 80 (320), 355–378.

Smith, D. J. (2007). *A Culture of Corruption: Everyday Deception and Popular Discontent in Nigeria*. Princeton University Press.

Smithsonian National Museum of African American History. (n.d.). Retrived from https://nmaahc.si.edu/.

Solis, M. (2016a). The Trans-Pacific Partnership – The Politics of Openness and Leadership in the Asia Pacific. Asia Working Group, Paper 6. Brookings Institution. Washington, DC.

———. (2016b). The Case for Trade and the Trans-Pacific Partnership. Brookings Institution. Washington, DC.

Subair, G. (2013, September 18). Nigeria's Unemployment Rate Hits 22% - World Bank. *Nigerian Tribune*.

Soludo, C. C. (2008). Preface. In P. Collier, C. C. Soludo, & C. Pattillo (Eds.), *Economic Policy Options for a Prosperous Nigeria*. New York: Palgrave Macmillan.

Souza, J. P. (2019). The Nigeria Near-Miss and Maternal Death Survey: Collaborative Research Generating Information for Action. *BJOG*, 126(S3), 5–6. Retrieved from https://obgyn.onlinelibrary.wiley.com/doi/full/10.1111/1471-0528.15749.

Soyinka, W. (1997). *The Open Sore of a Continent: A Personal Narrative of the Nigerian Crisis*. Oxford University Press.

———. (1994). Culture Memory and Development. In I. Serageldin & J. Taboroff (Eds.), *Culture and Development in Africa*. Proceedings of an International Conference. World Bank, Washington, DC. Retrieved from http://documents.worldbank.org/curated/en/303951468203676341/pdf/multi0page.pdf.

———. (2014, March 2). The Canonization of Terror. *Vanguard*. Retrieved from http://www.vanguardngr.com/2014/03/canonisation-terror-wole-soyinka.

———. Soyinka, W. (2019, October 9). Lessons from Nigeria's Militarized Democratic Experiment. *The New York Times*. Retrieved from https://www.nytimes.com/2019/10/09/opinion/nigeria-militarized-democratic-experiment.html.

Stanford Encyclopedia of Philosophy. (2017). Colonialism. Retrieved from https://plato.stanford.edu/entries/colonialism/.

State House. Office of the President. Federal Republic of Nigeria. State House Medical Center. Retrieved from http://www.statehouse.gov.ng/index.php/government/the-state-house/departments/state-house-medical-centre.

Stelter, B. (2019, November 11). Bill Moyers: 'Do Facts Matter Anymore? I Think They Do'. *CNN Business*. Retrieved from https://www.cnn.com/2019/11/11/media/bill-moyers-reliable-sources/index.html.

Stiglitz, J. (2006). *Making Globalization Work*. New York: W. W. Norton & Company.

———. (2015). Rewriting the Rules of the American Economy: An Agenda for Growth and Shared Prosperity. Roosevelt Institute. Retrieved from https://rooseveltinstitute.org/wp-content/uploads/2015/05/RI-Rewriting-the-Rules-201505.pdf.

———. (2002). *Globalization and Its Discontents*. W. W. Norton Company.

Strange, S. (1988). *States and Markets: An International Political Economy*. New York: Basil Blackwell.

Stevens, P. (2015). The Resource Curse Revisited. Chatham House. The Royal Institute of International Affairs. London: United Kingdom. Retrieved from https://www.chathamhouse.org/publication/resource-curse-revisited.

Stockholm International Peace Research Institute (SIPRI) (2020). Military Expenditure Data. Retrieved from https://www.sipri.org/databases/milex.

Storey, B. (1953). *Report of the Commission of Inquiry into the Administration of the Lagos Town Council*.

Suberu, R. (2010). The Nigerian Federal System: Performance, Problems and Prospects. *Journal of Contemporary African Studies*, 28(4), 459–477.

———. (2018). Strategies for Advancing Anticorruption Reform in Nigeria. *Dædalus,* 147(3), 184–201.

Suberu, R. T., & Diamond, L. (2002). Institutional Design, Ethnic Conflict Management, and Democracy in Nigeria. In Andrew Reynolds (Ed.), *The Architecture of Democracy: Constitutional Design, Conflict Management, and Democracy*. New York: Oxford University Press.

Taiwo, O. (2010). *How Colonialism Preempted Modernity in Africa*. Bloomington and Indianapolis: Indiana University Press.

———. (2014). *Africa Must Be Modern*. Bloomington and Indianapolis: Indiana University Press.

Taiwo, J. (2004, September 28). Nation's Varsities Deplorable, Says Panel. *This Day*.

———. (2008, November 12). FEC Approves ₦12.2bn Loan for Health Projects. *This Day*.

Tanzi, V., & Davoodi, H. R. (1997). Corruption, Public Investment, and Growth. International Monetary Fund Working Paper No. 97/139. Retrieved from https://papers.ssrn.com/sol3/papers.cfm?abstract_id=882701.

Tanzi, V. (1998). Corruption Around the World: Causes, Consequences, Scope, and Cures. *Staff Papers (International Monetary Fund)*, 45(4), 559–594.

Temenos and NetGuardians. (2017). *A-Z of Financial Crimes in Africa*. Retrieved from https://www.temenos.com/globalassets/mi/rep/a-z_fin_crime_africa-final_1609.pdf.

Tell (1993, December 20, p. 17).

The Economist. (1993, August 21). *Survey of Nigeria*.

———. (2012, September 29). Free Exchange: An Incurable Disease. Retrieved from https://www.economist.com/node/21563714/all-comments.

———. (1995, May 20). Survey of South Africa.

———. (1996, June 8, p. 46).

———. (1996, June 29, p. 19).

———. (2000, May 13). Hopeless Africa. Retrieved from https://www.economist.com/news/leaders/333429-hopeless-africa.

———. (2015, April 6). How Nigeria Won Its First Democratic Power Transfer. Retrieved from http://www.economist.com/blogs/economist-explains/2015/04/economist-explains-2.

———. (2019, November 20). Economic Intelligence Unit. Nigeria. Retrieved from https://country.eiu.com/nigeria.

———. (2011, April 14). Democracy 1, Vote-Rigging 0. Retrieved from http://www.economist.com/node/18560577.

———. (2013, April 13). Nigeria – Lurching Ahead. Retrieved from http://www.economist.com/node/21576135/print.

———. (1994, May 1, p. 44).

———. (1992, p. 8). Nigeria. Economist Intelligence Unit (EIU) Country Report, No. 3.

———. (2012, March 3).

———. (2014, April 7). How Nigeria's Economy Grew by 89% Overnight. Retrieved from http://www.economist.com/node/21600330/print.

———. (2011, December 3). Corruption in Nigeria: Dragon Slayers Wanted.

———. (1993, August 21).

———. (2013, October 3). Oil Theft in Nigeria – A Murky Business.

———. (2007, September 27). Reforming the Oil Industry.

———. (2015, June 20). Buhari's Chances – Can He Do It? Retrieved from http://www.economist.com/node/21654605/print.

———. (2015, June 20). Nigeria's Moment – How Africa's Most Important Failure Can at Last Come Right. Retrieved from http://www.economist.com/node/21654605/print.

The Europa Yearbook 1997, vol. II. London: Europa Publications Limited.

The Guardian. (2013, November 25). National Conference: Matters Arising. [Editorial].

———. (2017, January 26). Nigeria's Way Out of Economic Meltdown. Retrieved from https://guardian.ng/opinion/nigerias-way-out-of-economic-meltdown/.

———. (2014, February 1). NASS Orders Suspension of Import Waivers, Concessions.

———. (2007, August 10).

———. (2006, June 6).

———. (2012, January 26). Fuel Subsidy: Cost of Governance. [Editorial].

———. (2004, October 27).

———. (2004, October 29). [Editorial].

———. (2015, May 15). The National Assembly and the Cost of Governance. [Editorial].

———. (2016, July 13). No to Life Pension for Senators. [Editorial]. Retrieved from http://guardian.ng/opinion/no-to-life-pension-for-senators/.

———. (2011, December 15). Ghost Workers Cause of High Overhead, Says Okonjo-Iweala.

———. (2012, April 26).

———. (2020, March 26.) Stripping Elected Officials of Immunity. [Editorial]. Retrieved from https://guardian.ng/opinion/stripping-elected-officials-of-immunity/.

———. (2016, February 10). In Search of a True Nigeria. [Editorial]. Retrieved from http://www.ngrguardiannews.com/2016/02/in-search-of-a-true-nigeria/.

———. 2013, February 13). Nigeria and Ezekwesili's $67 Billion Waste. [Editorial].

———. (2011, November 23). The Scourge of Corruption. [Editorial].

———. (2016, January 25). Whither Nigeria's Political Class? [Editorial]. Retrieved from http://www.ngrguardiannews.com/2016/01/whither-nigerias-political-class/.

———. (2016, August 2). Nigeria and the Ruins of Military Rule. [Editorial]. Retrieved from http://guardian.ng/opinion/nigeria-and-the-ruins-of-military-rule/.

———. (2013, May 29). Nigeria Democracy: Fourteen Years On. Retrieved from http://thecitizenng.com/public-affairs/nigerias-democracy-fourteen-years-on-the-guardian/.

———. (2017, October 1). Nigeria: A Glimmer of Hope at 57!. [Editorial]. Retrieved from http://guardian.ng/opinion/nigeria-a-glimmer-of-hope-at-57/.

———. (2017, September 24). Equip Nigerian Hospitals Like Uk's. [Editorial]. Retrieved from http://guardian.ng/opinion/equip-nigerian-hospitals-like-uks/.

———. (2016, April 1). On the Poor State of Public Hospitals. [Editorial]. Retrieved from http://guardian.ng/opinion/on-the-poor-state-of-public-hospitals/.

———. (2011, October 17). Mixed Results Trail ₦29b Teaching Hospitals' Project.

———. (2011, June 26).

The Nation. (2008, August 15). States Get ₦21b from UBEC.

The New York Times. (2000, June 20).

The Street Journal. (2012, December 22). Immunity Clause: Nigerian Leaders' License to Loot.

The Sun. (2013, February 27). The Scourge of Ghost Workers.

The Tide. (2007, October 4). UBEC Receives ₦72bn in Nine Years.

This Day. (2007, August 31).

———. (2005, August 5).

———. (2010, October 20).

———. (2014, December 15). CBN Boss: Nigeria Loses ₦20 Billion Annually to Palm Oil Importation. Retrieved from http://www.thisdaylive.com/articles/cbn-boss-nigeria-loses-n20-billion-annually-to-palm-oil-importation/196754.

———. (2009, May 18).

———. (2003, August 30).

———. (2009, June 15). The Stolen ₦285 billion.

———. (2015, July 13). Nigeria Spent ₦813bn on Sugar, Wheat, Others in 2013. Retrieved from http://www.thisdaylive.com/articles/nigeria-spent-n813bn-on-sugar-wheat-others-in-2013/214423.

———. (2008, August 21). FG Earmarks ₦6bn for Free Medicare.

———. (2007, February 11). Federal Government Moves to Revive Public Schools.

———. 2009, February 26). Teachers' Strike Paralysis Schools in Lagos, Ogun, Oyo.

———. (2009, May 18). Kogi Teachers Call off 6-month Old Strike.

———. (2009, January 13). UBEC Disbursed ₦20.4bn to States in 3 Years.

———. (2008, October 2). FG Spends ₦2.4bn Debt Relief Fund on Education – W'Bank.

———. (2007, October 24). Nigeria Accounts for 0.7 % Share of Global Exports – EU.

Thomas, S., & Canagarajah, S. (2002). Poverty in a Wealthy Economy: The Case of Nigeria. International Monetary Fund. IMF Working Paper 02/114. Retrieved from https://www.imf.org/external/pubs/ft/wp/2002/wp02114.pdf.

Thompson, H. et al., (2017, September). Developing Businesses of Scale in Sub-Saharan Africa: Insights from Nigeria, Tanzania, Uganda, and Zambia. Chatham House.

Thorbecke, E. (2013). The Interrelationship Linking Growth, Inequality and Poverty in Sub-Saharan Africa. *Journal of African Economies,* 22(1), i15–i48. Retrieved from https://academic.oup.com/jae/article-abstract/22/suppl_1/i15/762013.

Tignor, R. L. (1993). Political Corruption in Nigeria Before Independence. *The Journal of Modern African Studies*, 31(2), 175–202.

Tijani, J. O. (2014). Empirical Analysis of Balance of Payment Adjustment Mechanisms: Monetary Channel in Nigeria, 1970–2010. *Mediterranean Journal of Social Sciences*, 5(14), 67–76.

Tilley-Gyado, R., Filani, O., Morhason-Bello, I., & Adewole, I. F. (2016). Strengthening the Primary Care Delivery System: A Catalytic Investment Toward

Achieving Universal Health Coverage in Nigeria. *Health Systems & Reform*, 2(4), 277–284. Retrieved from https://www.tandfonline.com/doi/pdf/10.1080/23288604.2016.1234427?needAccess=true.

Tilley, H. (2016). Medicine, Empires, and Ethics in Colonial Africa. *AMA Journal of Ethics*, 18(7), 743–753.

Tipps, D. C. (1973). Modernization Theory and the Comparative Study of Societies: A Critical Perspective. *Comparative Studies in Society and History*, 15(2), 199–226.

Transparency International. (2018). *Corruption Perception Index 2017*. Retrieved from https://www.transparency.org/news/feature/corruption_perceptions_index_2017.

———. (n.d.). Corruption: Costs to Developing Countries.

———. (2015). Nigeria's Corruption Challenges. Retrieved from https://www.transparency.org/news/feature/nigerias_corruption_challenge.

———. *Promoting Revenue Transparency – Report on Oil and Gas Companies*. Retrieved from http://www.euractiv.com/sites/all/euractiv/files/TI_PRT_2011_report_FINAL_EN.pdf.

———. (2015). *Nigeria: 2015 Country Summary*. Government Defense Anti-Corruption Index. Retrieved from https://government.defenceindex.org/downloads/docs/nigeria.pdf.

Trapp, L.; Lienert, I.; & Wehner, J. (2016). Principles for Independent Fiscal Institutions and Case Studies. *OECD Journal on Budgeting*, 2015(2), Paris: OECD Publishing. Retrieved from http://personal.lse.ac.uk/wehner/ifis.pdf.

Thurow, L. C. (1985). *The Zero Sum Solution*. New York: Simon & Schuster, Inc.

———. (1999, June). Building Wealth: The New Rules for Individuals, Companies, and Nations. *Atlantic Monthly*.

Tukur, S. (2017, November 3). Buhari's Govt Has Created Seven Million Jobs – Minister. *Premium Times*. Retrieved from https://www.premiumtimesng.com/news/more-news/248186-buharis-govt-created-seven-millions-jobs-minister.html.

Tullock, G. (1967). The Welfare Costs of Tariffs, Monopolies and Theft. *Western Economic Journal*, 5, 224–232.

Tuokuu, F. X. (2012). www.modernghana.com/news. Retrieved from http://www.modernghana.com/news/421515/1/africas-dutch-disease-theway-forward.html.

Turner, T. (1980). Nigeria: Imperialism, Oil Technology and the Comprador State. In P. Nore & T. Turner (Eds.), *Oil and Class Struggle*. London: Zed Press.

Turshen, M. (1977). The Impact of Colonialism on Health and Health Services in Tanzania. *International Journal of Health Services*, 7(1), 7–35. Retrieved from https://pubmed.ncbi.nlm.nih.gov/319069/.

———. (1984). *Political Ecology of Disease in Tanzania*. New Brunswick, NJ: Rutgers University Press.

Tyler, G. (2002). Nigeria - Public and Private Electricity Provision as a Barrier to Manufacturing Competitiveness. World Bank. Retrieved from https://openknowledge.worldbank.org/bitstream/handle/10986/9746/multi0page.pdf?sequence=1.

Uchegbu, A. C. (2009, June 9). Gov, Ministers, MPs Steal ₦285bn – EFCC, *Vanguard*.

Udeaja, G. (2011, January 21). Orji Appoints 457 New Aides. *The Guardian*.

Udeh, J. (2002). Petroleum Revenue Management: The Nigerian Perspective. Paper Presented at World Bank/International Finance Corporation Petroleum Revenue Management Workshop, Washington, DC. October 23–24. Retrieved from http://documents.worldbank.org/curated/en/252901468763835613/pdf/296760Petroleu1ue0ESMAP0tech0no1051.pdf.

Udo, N. S. U. (2014). Dividends of Democracy in Nigeria (1999–2010): The Paradox and Need for a Re-Focus. *Journal of Studies in Social Sciences*, 8(1), 46–60. Retrieved from http://infinitypress.info/index.php/jsss/article/viewFile/353/346.

Udo, B. (2018, March 26). Over 80,000 'Ghost Officers' Uncovered in Nigerian Police. *Premium Times*. Retrieved from https://www.premiumtimesng.com/news/headlines/263052-over-80000-ghost-officers-uncovered-in-nigerian-police.html.

———. (2014, April 11). Nigeria Ranks Third Among Countries Having Extremely Poor People, World Bank Says. *Premium Times*. Retrieved from http://www.premiumtimesng.com/business/158554-nigeria-ranks-third-among-countries-extremely-poor-people-world-bank-says.html.

Udoh, E. (2013). *The Nigerian Factor: The Unseen Force in Action*. Trafford.

Udogu, E. I. (2014). [Review of the book *Ibrahim Babangida: The Military, Politics, and Power in Nigeria*, by Dan Agbese]. *Africa Today*, 61(2), 127–131.

Udoko, N. J. (1993). *Colonial Capitalism and Politics of Underdevelopment in Post-colonial Africa: The Case of Nigeria, 1960–1990*. (Published Ph.D. dissertation). Clark Atlanta University. ETD Collection for AUC Robert W. Woodruff Library. Paper 1495. Retrieved from http://digitalcommons.auctr.edu/cgi/viewcontent.cgi?article=3076&context=dissertations.

Ugbe, A. U., & Agim, J. I. (2009). Influence of Teachers' Competence on Students Academic Performance in Senior Secondary School Chemistry. *Global Journal of Education Research*, 8(1/2), 61–66. Retrieved from https://search.proquest.com/openview/82973d6f2cd14ecb910dc371cb3c10fb/1?pq-origsite=gscholar&cbl=105791.

Ugwoke, F. (2006, October 26). UNICEF Laments Poor participation in Pre-School Education. *This Day*.

Ugwu, H. U., Nwankwojike, B. N., Ogbonnaya, E. A., & Ekoi, E. J. (2012). Energy and Economic Losses Due to Constant Power Outages in Nigeria. *Nigerian Journal of Technology*, 31(2), 181–188.

Ujah, E. (2017, June 5). 55 Top Govt Officials, Businessmen Stole ₦1.4trn Under OBJ, Yar'Adua, Jonathan. *Vanguard*. Retrieved from http://www.vanguardngr.com/2017/06/55-top-govt-officials-businessmen-stole-n1-4-trn-obj-yaradua-jonathan/.

Ujah, E. et al. (2014, April 7). $510bn GDP: Nigeria Now Africa's Largest, 26th Globally. *Vanguard*. Retrieved from http://www.vanguardngr.com/2014/04/510bn-gdp-nigeria-now-africas-largest-26th-globally.

Ukiwo, U. (2005). On the Study of Ethnicity in Nigeria. Center for Research on Inequality, Human Security and Ethnicity (CRISE). Working Paper No. 12. Queen Elizabeth House, University of Oxford, pp. 1–21.

Ukuma, S., & Ochedikwu, J. O. (2013). Re-engineering Vocational and Technical Education in Nigeria for Greater Quality Service Delivery in the 21st Century for Sustainable Development. *Academic Journal of Interdisciplinary Studies*, 2(6), 97–102.

Ukwueze, E. R. (2015). Determinants of the Size of Public Expenditure in Nigeria. *SAGE Open*, 1–8. Retrieved from http://journals.sagepub.com/doi/pdf/10.1177/2158244015621346.

Ulasi, I. I., & Ijoma, C. K. (2010). The Enormity of Chronic Kidney Disease in Nigeria: The Situation in a Teaching Hospital in South-East Nigeria. *Journal of Tropical Medicine*, 2010, 1–7.

Umezurike, C. (2008). Globalization and Labor in Africa: Ethnic Identity in Nigeria and Cross Border Migration in the Republic of South Africa. *Globalizations*, 5(4), 599–619. Retrieved from https://www.tandfonline.com/doi/abs/10.1080/14747730802500422?mobileUi=0&journalCode=rglo20.

———. (2009, July 12–16). The Divergence of Economic Reforms and Democracy in Nigeria. Paper Presented at the 21st World Congress of the International Political Science Association (IPSA), Santiago, Chile. Retrieved from http://paperroom.ipsa.org/papers/paper_203.pdf.

———. (2012). Globalization, Economic Reforms, and Democracy in Nigeria. *Africa Development*, 37(2), 25–61.

Umukoro, N. (2013). Poverty and Social Protection in Nigeria. *Journal of Developing Societies*, 29(3), 305–322. Retrieved from https://journals.sagepub.com/doi/abs/10.1177/0169796X13494281?journalCode=jdsb.

———. (2013). Governance and Public Health Care in Nigeria. *Journal of Health Management*, 14(4), 381–395. Retrieved from https://journals.sagepub.com/doi/abs/10.1177/0972063412468970.

Umoru, H., & Erunke, J. (2014, April 23). NNPC is a Cult – Nwobodo. *Vanguard*. Retrieved from http://www.vanguardngr.com/2014/04/nnpc-cult-nwobodo.

Uneke, C., Ogbonna, A., Ezeoha, A., Oyibo, P., Onwe, F., & Ngwu, B. (2007). *The Internet Journal of Health*, 8(1), 1–5. Retrieved from https://print.ispub.com/api/0/ispub-article/6444.

Ungar, S. J. (1989). *Africa: The People and Politics of an Emerging Continent*. New York: Simon and Schuster.

Usman, O., & Agbede, E. A. (2015). Government Expenditure and Economic Growth in Nigeria: A Cointegration and Error Correction Modeling. *Munich Personal RePEc Archive*. Retrieved from https://mpra.ub.uni-muenchen.de/69814/1/MPRA_paper_69814.pdf.

U. S. Centers for Disease Control and Prevention (CDC) (2021). Malaria's Impact Worldwide. Retrieved from https://www.cdc.gov/malaria/malaria_worldwide/impact.html.

Umar, H. (2020, March 24). 50 Nigerian Soldiers Killed in Deadly Boko Haram Ambush. *The Washington Post*. Retrieved from https://www.washingtonpost.com/world/africa/50-nigerian-soldiers-killed-in-deadly-boko-haram-ambush/2020/03/24/23c87e98-6dee-11ea-a156-0048b62cdb51_story.html.

United Kingdom Parliament. (n.d.). Frequently Asked Questions: MPs. www.parliament.uk.

United Nations Development Program. *Human Development Report 2020*. Retrieved from http://hdr.undp.org/sites/default/files/hdr2020.pdf.

United States Agency for International Development. (2015). *Nigeria - Country Development Cooperation Strategy 2015–2020*. Retrieved from https://www.usaid.gov/sites/default/files/documents/1860/Nigeria_CDCS_2015-2020.pdf.

United States Bureau of Economic Analysis. (2007, September). *An Introduction to the National Income and Product Accounts*. Retrieved from http://bea.gov/scb/pdf/national/nipa/methpap/mpi1_0907.pdf.

———. (2014, October). *Measuring the Economy – A Primer on GDP and National Income Product Accounts*.

———. GDP by State. Retrieved from https://www.bea.gov/data/gdp/gdp-state.

———. Regional Data. GDP and Personal Income. October 2, 2020 update. See also *Statista*. Retrieved from https://www.statista.com/statistics/248023/us-gross-domestic-product-gdp-by-state/.

United States Department of State. Bureau of Diplomatic Security, Overseas Security Advisory Council (OSAC). *Nigeria 2012 OSAC Crime and Security Report*. Retrieved from https://www.osac.gov/Pages/ContentReportDetails.aspx?cid=12090.

———. Bureau of Democracy, Human Rights and Labor. *Country Reports on Human Rights Practices for 2014* – Nigeria. Retrieved from https://2009-2017.state.gov/documents/organization/236604.pdf.

United States International Trade Administration. (2020, September 14). Nigeria - Country Commercial Guide. Market Overview. Retrieved from https://www.trade.gov/country-commercial-guides/nigeria-market-overview.

United Nations Children and Educational Fund (UNICEF). (2018). The Reality of Malaria: The Largest Killer of Children. Retrieved from https://www.unicef.org/health/files/health_africamalaria.pdf.

———. (2017). *UNICEF Nigeria: Country Program Document 2018 – 2022*. Retrieved from https://www.unicef.org/nigeria/reports/unicef-nigeria-country-programme-document-2018-2022.

United Nations Conference on Trade and Development. (1998). Overview. In *Trade and Development Report 1998*. United Nations. New York and Geneva. Retrieved from http://unctad.org/en/docs/tdr1998_en.pdf.

———. *The Economic Development in Africa Report 2017: Tourism for Transformative and Inclusive Growth*. Retrieved from http://unctad.org/en/PublicationsLibrary/aldcafrica2017_en.pdf.

United Nations Development Program. (2006). Niger Delta Human Development Report. Retrieved from http://hdr.undp.org/en/content/human-development-report/.

———. (2017). *African Economic Outlook: Entrepreneurship and Industrialization*. Retrieved from http://www.africa.undp.org/content/dam/rba/docs/Reports/African_Economic_Outlook_2017_EN.pdf.

———. (2016). A Comprehensive Analysis and Review of Investment, Production and Export Incentives in Malawi. Retrieved from https://info.undp.org/docs/pdc/Documents/MWI/Final_report_%20Fiscal%20Incentives%2019-12-2016.pdf.

———. (2003). *Human Development Report 2003.* Millennium Development Goals: A Compact Among Nations to End Human Poverty. New York: Oxford University Press.

———. (2018). *Human Development Indices and Indicators: 2018 Statistical Update*. Retrieved from http://hdr.undp.org/en/2018-update.

United Nations Economic Commission for Africa & Organization for Economic Cooperation and Development. (2009). *Mutual Review of Development Effectiveness in Africa: Promise & Performance.* A Joint Report by the Economic Commission for Africa and the Organization for Economic Co-operation and Development. Retrieved from https://www.oecd.org/dac/MRDE_2009_English.pdf.

United Nations Educational, Scientific and Cultural Organization (UNESCO). (1989–1999). *General History of Africa.* Eight vols. Paris: UNESCO.

———. (2000). *State of Education in Nigeria.* Retrieved from http://unesdoc.unesco.org/images/0014/001495/149503eo.pdf.

United Nations Office on Drugs and Crime & National Bureau of Statistics. (July 2017). *Corruption in Nigeria – Bribery: Public Experience and Response.* Retrieved from https://www.unodc.org/documents/data-and-analysis/Crime-statistics/Nigeria/Corruption_Nigeria_2017_07_31_web.pdf.

———. (n.d.). UNODC's Action Against Corruption and Economic Crime. Retrieved from https://www.unodc.org/unodc/en/corruption/index.html?ref=menuside.

———. (2008, November 30). Nigeria's Corruption Busters. Retrieved from http://www.unodc.org/unodc/en/frontpage/nigerias-corruption-busters.html.

United Nations News Center. (2017, September 29). Over Half of Schools Remain Closed in Epicenter of Boko Haram Crisis in Nigeria – UNICEF. Retrieved from http://www.un.org/apps/news/story.asp?NewsID=57773#.Wc8fZ2hSzcs.

United Nations. UNAIDS 2016–2021 Strategy. *On the Fast-Track to End AIDS.* Retrieved from https://www.unaids.org/sites/default/files/media_asset/20151027_UNAIDS_PCB37_15_18_EN_rev1.pdf.

———. UNAIDS 2016. *Global AIDS Update 2016*. Retrieved from https://www.unaids.org/sites/default/files/media_asset/global-AIDS-update-2016_en.pdf.

United States Department of State. (1997, April). Bureau of International Narcotics and Law Enforcement Affairs. Nigerian Advance Fee Fraud. Retrieved from http://www.state.gov/documents/organization/2189.pdf.

———. Bureau of Democracy, Human Rights and Labor. *Country Reports on Human Rights Practices for 2013* – Nigeria. Retrieved from http://www.state.gov/j/drl/rls/hrrpt/humanrightsreport/#wrapper.

United States Institute of Peace. (2019, Jun 1). The Current Situation in Nigeria. A USIP Fact Sheet. Retrieved from https://www.usip.org/publications/2019/06/current-situation-nigeria.

United States National Science Foundation. (2018). National Science Board. *2018 Science & Engineering Indicators.* Retrieved from https://www.nsf.gov/statistics/2018/nsb20181/assets/nsb20181.pdf.

Ushie, V. (2010). Implementing the Fiscal Responsibility Act at the State Level in Nigeria. Center for the Study of Economies in Africa (CSEA). CSEA Working Paper WPS/10/002.

Utomi, P. (2007, October 8). Politicians, Lifestyles and the Nigerian Condition. *The Guardian*.

———. (2007, May 30). Electoral Fraud: Of Meaning and Consequence. *The Guardian*.

Uwazurike, C. (1996). Ethnicity, Power, and Prebendalism: The Persistent Triad as the Unsolvable Crisis of Nigerian Politics. *Dialectical Anthropology*, 21(1), 1–20.

van de Walle, N. (2009). The Institutional Origins of Inequality in Sub-Saharan Africa. *Annual Review of Political Science*, 12, 307–327. Retrieved from https://www.annualreviews.org/doi/pdf/10.1146/annurev.polisci.11.063006.092318.

———. (1999). Economic Reform in a Democratizing Africa. *Comparative Politics*, 32(1), 21–41.

van der Ploega, F. (2012). War and Natural Resource Exploitation. *European Economic Review*, 56(8), 1714–1729.

———. (2017). Political Economy of Dynamic Resource Wars. *Journal of Environmental Economics and Management*.

———. (2011). Natural Resources: Blessing or Curse? *Journal of Economic Literature*, 49(2), 366–420.

Vanguard. (2018, November 21). Boko Haram Kills Nigerian Army Commander, Dozens of Soldiers. Retrieved from https://www.vanguardngr.com/2018/11/boko-haram-kills-nigerian-army-commander-dozens-of-soldiers/.

———. (2007, January 4).

———. (2004, September 2). UNN Facilities Are Rotten – Panel Chairman.

———. (2012, November 4). I Pray for Our Oil to Dry Up, Ezekwesili.

———. (2017, October 16).

———. (2015, November 11).

———. (2011, July 18). Ghost Workers Don't Exist, Criminals Do.

———. (2016, April 19). EFCC Detects 37,395 Ghost Workers in Federal Civil Service, Says Magu. Retrieved from http://www.vanguardngr.com/2016/04/efcc-detects-37395-ghost-workers-federal-civil-service-says-magu/.

———. (2014, March 16). Nigerians are Corrupt - President Mugabe of Zimbabwe. Retrieved from http://www.vanguardngr.com/2014/03/nigerians-corrupt-president-mugabe-zimbabwe.

———. (2013, January 28).

———. (2013, January 28). Oil Revenue: I am Resolute – Ezekwesili. Retrieved from http://www.vanguardngr.com/2013/01/oil-revenue-im-resolute-ezekwesili.

———. (2019, January 15). Non-Asset Declaration: CCB to Prosecute Civil, Public Servants. Retrieved from https://www.vanguardngr.com/2019/01/non-asset-declaration-ccb-to-prosecute-civil-public-servants/.

———. (1998, November 9).

———. (1998, November 10).

———. (2014, March 11). Adesina Advocates Halal Beef System to Crop, Cattle Farmers Crisis.

———. (2014, February 15). Improving Our Hospitals. [Editorial]. Retrieved from http://www.vanguardngr.com/2013/02/improving-our-hospitals.

van Handeren, R. C., & Kolthoff, E. (2017). Noble Cause Corruption Revisited: Toward a Structured Research Approach. *Public Integrity*, 19(3), 274–293.

van Klaveren, J. (1970). The Concept of Corruption. In Arnold J. Heidenheimer (Ed.), *Political Corruption: Readings in Comparative Analysis*. New York: Holt Rinehart and Winston. Retrieved from http://www.cics.northwestern.edu/news/2010/05-Nigeria-Joseph.pdf.

Veblen, T. [1899] (1979). *The Theory of the Leisure Class*. New York: Penguin Books USA Inc.

Verter, N., & Becvarova, V. (2016). The Impact of Agricultural Exports on Economic Growth in Nigeria. *Acta Universitatis Agriculturae et Silviculturae Mendelianae Brunensis*, 64(2), 691–700. Retrieved from https://acta.mendelu.cz/media/pdf/actaun_201606402069l.pdf.

Vigoda, E. (2003). From Responsiveness to Collaboration: Governance, Citizens, and the Next Generation of Public Administration. *Public Administration Review*, 62(5), 527–540. Retrieved from https://onlinelibrary.wiley.com/doi/abs/10.1111/1540-6210.00235.

Vogl, F. (2012). *Waging War on Corruption: Inside the Movement Fighting the Abuse of Power*. Lanham, MD: The Rowman & Littlefield Publishers, Inc.

Volpato, C., & Licata, L. (2010). Collective Memories of Colonial Violence. *International Journal of Conflict and Violence*, 4(1), 4–10.

Wahl, R. (2014). Justice, Context, and Violence: Law Enforcement Officers on Why They Torture. *Law & Society Review*, 48(4), 807–836.

Wallace, A. (2012, October 6). The Case for Calm Over Rising Health Costs. *The New York Times*. Retrieved from https://www.nytimes.com/2012/10/07/business/cost-disease-offers-a-case-for-health-care-calm.html.

Wallace, P. (2016, September 22). Nigerian Lawmakers to Probe Claim $17 Billion of Oil Stolen. *Bloomberg*.

Walkenhorst, P. (2007). Distortions to Agricultural Incentives in Nigeria. World Bank. Agricultural Distortion Working Paper No. 37. Retrieved from http://documents.worldbank.org/curated/en/403481468336719555/pdf/560410NWP0NG0v1LIC10Nigeria10708rev.pdf.

Wall Street Journal. (2015, February 1). Africa Loses $60 billion a Year Illegally, Report Says. Retrieved from https://www.wsj.com/articles/africa-loses-60-billion-a-year-illegally-report-says-1422794047.

Wallis, W. (2012, June 26). Nigeria Losing $1 billion A Month to Oil Theft. *Financial Times* (London).

Watts, M. (2004). Resource Curse? Governmentality, Oil and Power in the Niger Delta, Nigeria. *Geopolitics*, 9(1), 50–80. Retrieved from https://www.tandfonline.com/doi/abs/10.1080/14650040412331307832.

Weber, M. (1947). *The Theory of Social and Economic Organization*. Translated by A. M. Henderson and Talcott Parsons, New York: Oxford University Press.

Wei, S. J. (2003). Corruption in Developing Countries. Brookings Institution. Washington, DC. Retrieved from https://www.brookings.edu/on-the-record/corruption-in-developing-countries/.

Welch, E. W., Hinnant, C. C., & Moon, M. J. (2005). Linking Citizen Satisfaction With E-government and Trust in Government. *Journal of Public Administration Research and Theory*, 15(3,1), 371–391. Retrieved from https://academic.oup.com/jpart/article/15/3/371/941130.

Welcome, M. O. (2011). The Nigerian Health Care System: Need for Integrating Adequate Medical Intelligence and Surveillance Systems. *Journal of Pharmacy & BioAllied Sciences*, 3(4), 470–478. Retrieved from https://www.ncbi.nlm.nih.gov/pmc/articles/PMC3249694/.

Wengraf, L. (2017, June 16). How Europe Underdeveloped Africa: The Legacy of Walter Rodney. *Review of African Political Economy* Blog Post. Retrieved from http://roape.net/2017/06/16/europe-underdeveloped-africa-legacy-walter-rodney/).

———. (2015, February). Digital Divide: Improving Internet Access in the Developing World Through Affordable Services and Diverse Content. Brookings Institution. Washington, DC. Retrieved from https://www.brookings.edu/wp-content/uploads/2016/06/West_Internet-Access.pdf.

———. (2011, October 19). Technology and the Innovation Economy. Brookings Institution. Washington, DC. Retrieved from http://www.brookings.edu/research/papers/2011/10/19-technology-innovation-west.

West Africa. (1995, January 23–29, p. 94).

———. (1996, March 11–17, p. 381).

———. (1983, September 12).

———. (1995, January 23–29, p. 99).

West, C. (2004). *Democracy Matters*. New York: The Penguin Press.

Williams, G. (1994). Why Structural Adjustment Is Necessary and Why It Doesn't Work. *Review of African Political Economy*, 21(60), 214–225. Retrieved from https://www.tandfonline.com/doi/pdf/10.1080/03056249408704057?needAccess=true.

Williamson, J. (1998). Globalization: The Concept, Causes and Consequences. Keynote Address to the Congress of the Sri Lankan Association for the Advancement of Science. Colombo: Sri Lanka. Peterson Institute for International Economics, Washington, DC, USA. Retrieved from https://piie.com/commentary/speeches-papers/globalization-concept-causes-and-consequences.

Wilson, S. Y. (1990). Africa the Development Challenges of the 1990s. *The Review of Black Political Economy*, 19(2), 5–16.

Wilson, W. J., & Aponte, R. (1985). Urban Poverty. *Annual Review of Sociology*, 11, 231–258.

Winseck, D. (2017). The Geopolitical Economy of the Global Internet Infrastructure. *Journal of Information Policy*, 7, 228–267. Retrieved from https://www.jstor.org/stable/10.5325/jinfopoli.7.2017.0228#metadata_info_tab_contents.

Winthrop, R., & McGivney, E. (2016, May 20). Skills for a Changing World: Advancing Quality Learning for Vibrant Societies. Brookings Institution, Washington, DC.

Wolfe, P. (2006). Settler Colonialism and the Elimination of the Native. *Journal of Genocide Research*, 8(4), 387–409.

Wong, P. N. (2012). Discerning an African Post-colonial Governance Imbroglio: Colonialism, Underdevelopment and Violent Conflicts in the Democratic Republic of Congo (DRC), Liberia and Sierra Leone. *African and Asian Studies,* 11, 99–94.

World Bank. *World Development Indicators 2017.*

———. (1994). *Nigeria Structural Adjustment Program: Policies, Implementation, and Impact.* Report No. 13053-UNI.

———. (2016). *World Development Report 2016. Digital Dividends.*

———. (2016). Digital Dividends. *World Development Report 2016.*

———. (1987).*World Debt Table of Developing Countries.*

———. *World Debt Tables 1980.*

———. (1997). *World Development Report.*

———. (2010). *The World Bank in Nigeria 1998–2007: Nigeria Country Assistance Evaluation.*

———. (2006, November 28). Foreign Aid Effectiveness: Easterly vs. Radelet Debate. Growth and Crisis Blog. Retrieved from https://blogs.worldbank.org/growth/foreign-aid-effectiveness-easterly-vs-radelet-debate.

———. World Bank Atlas, 1992, p. 19.

———. (2017). *Nigeria Bi-annual Economic Update: Fragile Recovery.*

———. (2013, May). *Nigeria Economic Report.* No. 1. Retrieved from https://openknowledge.worldbank.org/bitstream/handle/10986/16568/776840WP0Niger0Box0342041B00PUBLIC0.pdf?sequence=1&isAllowed=y.

———. (2013). *Transforming Arab Economies: Traveling the Knowledge and Innovation Road.* Retrieved from http://documents.worldbank.org/curated/en/664441468059651205/pdf/827360ESW0v10P00Box379869B00PUBLIC0.pdf.

———. (2001). *Nigeria University System Innovation Project.* Report No. PID9528. Retrieved from http://documents.worldbank.org/curated/en/155791468760224988/pdf/multi0page.pdf.

———. (2015). *Sri Lanka: Innovation, ICT and Competitiveness.* Retrieved from http://documents.worldbank.org/curated/en/686541468179086023/pdf/97683-WP-P146575-OUO-9-Box391483B.pdf.

———. (2017). *2017 Private Participation in Infrastructure Annual Report.* World Bank. Retrieved from http://ppi.worldbank.org/~/media/GIAWB/PPI/Documents/Global-Notes/PPI_2017_AnnualReport.pdf.

———. (2010). Infrastructure and Economic Growth in Egypt. Policy Research Working Paper No. 5177. Retrieved from http://web.worldbank.org/archive/website01241/WEB/IMAGES/WPS5177.PDF.

———. (2003). *Nigeria: Policy Options for Growth and Stability.* Report No. 26215-NGA.

———. (2014). Diesel Power Generation: Inventories and Black Carbon Emissions in Nigeria.

———. (2010). D. Brady & M. Spence. In D. Brady & M. Spence (Eds.), *Leadership and Growth.* Commission on Growth and Development. Washington, DC: World

Bank. Retrieved from http://www.worldcocoafoundation.org/about-cocoa/history-of-cocoa/.

———. 2019 World Development Report. *The Changing Nature of Work*. Retrieved from http://documents.worldbank.org/curated/en/816281518818814423/pdf/2019-WDR-Report.pdf.

———. (2019). *FY2019 Nigeria Country Opinion Survey Report*. Washington, DC.

———. (2012). *Fighting Corruption in Public Services: Chronicling Georgia's Reforms*. Retrieved from https://elibrary.worldbank.org/doi/abs/10.1596/978-0-8213-9475-5.

———. (2015). *Mind, Society, and Behavior*. World Development Report 2015. World Bank. Washington, DC. Retrieved from http://documents.worldbank.org/curated/en/645741468339541646/pdf/928630WDR0978100Box385358B00PUBLIC0.pdf.

———. (2008). Governance, Growth, and Development Decision-Making. Reflections by Douglass North, Daron Acemoglu, Francis Fukuyama, Dani Rodrik. Retrieved from http://documents1.worldbank.org/curated/pt/373891468314694298/text/441860WP0REPLA1rnanceandgrowth0test.txt.

———. (2020, June 23). Nigeria to Keep the Lights on and Power its Economy.

———. (2009). *Accelerating Catch-up: Tertiary Education for Growth in Sub-Saharan Africa*. Washington, DC. Retrieved from http://siteresources.worldbank.org/INTAFRICA/Resources/e-book_ACU.pdf.

———. (2018). Stolen Asset Recovery Initiative. Annual Report January -December 2017. Retrieved from https://star.worldbank.org/sites/default/files/star-annual-08.pdf.

———. (2007). Stolen Asset Recovery (StAR) Initiative: Challenges, Opportunities, and Action Plan. Retrieved from https://www.unodc.org/pdf/Star_Report.pdf.

———. (2020, December 14). Brief. Combating Corruption. Retrieved from https://www.worldbank.org/en/topic/governance/brief/anti-corruption.

———. (2020). Sub-Saharan Africa Total Population. Retrieved from https://data.worldbank.org/indicator/SP.POP.TOTL?locations=ZG.

———. (2008). Commission on Growth and Development. *The Growth Commission Report*.

———. (2017). Nigeria: Fiscal Governance and Institutions Project (P163540).

———. (2016, January 5). Improved Access Roads Change Social and Business Dynamics in Nigeria's Kaduna State. Retrieved from https://www.worldbank.org/en/news/feature/2016/01/05/improved-access-roads-change-social-and-business-dynamics-in-nigerias-kaduna-state.

———. GDP (current US$). Accessed March 2021. Retrieved from https://data.worldbank.org/indicator/NY.GDP.MKTP.CD.

———. (n.d.). Social Protection. Retrieved from https://www.worldbank.org/en/topic/socialprotection.

———. (2020). Foreign Direct Investment, Net Inflows (Balance of Payment – BoP, current US$) – Nigeria. Retrieved from https://data.worldbank.org/indicator/BX.KLT.DINV.CD.WD?locations=NG.

———. (2019, November). *Electric Power Consumption (kWh per capita)*. Retrieved from https://data.worldbank.org/indicator/EG.USE.ELEC.KH.PC.

———. (2021). GDP (Current US$). Retrieved from https://data.worldbank.org/indicator/NY.GDP.MKTP.CD.

———. (2021). Current Health Expenditure (% of GDP). Retrieved from https://data.worldbank.org/indicator/SH.XPD.CHEX.GD.ZS.

———. (2020). Foreign Direct Investment, Net Inflows in Reporting Economy (current US$). Retrieved from https://databank.worldbank.org/reports.aspx?source=14&series=BX.KLT.DINV.CD.DT.

World Bank and United Nations Office on Drugs and Crime. Fact Sheet on Stolen Asset Recovery. Retrieved from https://www.unodc.org/pdf/Star_FactSheet.pdf.

World Cocoa Foundation. (n.d.). *History of Cocoa*. Retrieved from http://www.worldcocoafoundation.org/about-cocoa/history-of-cocoa/.

World Health Organization. (2020). *World Malaria Report 2020: 20 Years of Global Progress and Challenges*. Geneva: Licence: CC BY-NC-SA 3.0 IGO. Retrieved from https://www.who.int/publications/i/item/9789240015791.

———. Nigeria. (n.d.). Retrieved from https://www.who.int/violence_injury_prevention/road_safety_status/2015/country_profiles/Nigeria.pdf?ua=1.

———. (2016, December). 10 Facts on Malaria. Retrieved from http://www.who.int/features/factfiles/malaria/en/.

———. (2020, November). Malaria. Retrieved from https://www.who.int/news-room/fact-sheets/detail/malaria.

———. (2019, June 25). Maternal Health in Nigeria: Generating Information for Action. Retrieved from https://www.who.int/reproductivehealth/maternal-health-nigeria/en/.

World Economic Forum. *The Global Competitiveness Report 2017–2018*. Retrieved from https://www.weforum.org/reports/the-global-competitiveness-report-2017-2018.

———. (2015). *The Case for Trade and Competitiveness*. Retrieved from http://www3.weforum.org/docs/WEF_GAC_Competitiveness_2105.pdf.

World Trade Organization. *World Trade Statistical Review 2020*.

Wraith, R., & Simpkins, E. (1964). *Corruption in Developing Countries*. Routledge.

———. (1970). Nepotism and Bribery in West Africa. In Arnold J. Heidenheimer (Ed.), *Political Corruption: Readings in Comparative Analysis*. New York: Holt Rinehart and Winston.

———. (1963). *Corruption in Developing Countries*. London: George Allen & Unwin, Ltd.

Yagboyaju, D. A., & Akinola, A. O. (2019, July 24). Nigerian State and the Crisis of Governance: A Critical Exposition. *SAGE Open*, 9(3). Retrieved from https://journals.sagepub.com/doi/10.1177/2158244019865810?icid=int.sj-full-text.similar-articles.3.

Ying, T. Y., Eng, A., & Robinson, E. (2010). Perspective on Growth: A Political Economy Framework – Lessons from the Singapore Experience. In D. Brady & M. Spence (Eds.), *Leadership and Growth*. Commission on Growth and Development. Washington, DC: World Bank. Retrieved from https://openknowledge.worldbank

.org/bitstream/handle/10986/2404/527080PUB0lead101Official0Use0Only1.pdf?sequence=1.

Ynalvez, M. A., & Shrun, W. M. (2015). Modernization Theory. In *International Encyclopedia of the Social & Behavioral Sciences*, 2nd Edition, Elsevier, https://www.sciencedirect.com/topics/social-sciences/modernization-theory.

Young, C. (1994). *The African Colonial State in Comparative Perspective*. New Haven and London: Yale University Press.

Young, T. (1999, March). *The State in Africa: The Politics of the Belly by Jean-François Bayart: Power in Africa: An Essay in Political Interpretation* by Patrick Chabal: *Rethinking Third World Politics* by James Manor: *Citizen and Subject: Contemporary Africa and the Legacy of Late Colonialism* by Mahmood Mamdani. *Journal of Southern African Studies*, 25(1), 149–154.

Zabbey, N., Sam, K., & Onyebuchi, A. T. (2017). Remediation of Contaminated Lands in the Niger Delta, Nigeria: Prospects and Challenges. *Science of the Total Environment*, 568, 952–965. Retrieved from https://www.sciencedirect.com/science/article/pii/S0048969717303169.

Zalanga, S. (2016). Julius Nyerere: Leadership Insights for Contemporary Challenges. In E. Obadare & W. Adebanwi (Eds.), *Governance and the Crisis of Rule in Contemporary Africa*. New York: Palgrave Macmillan.

Zartmann, W. (1995). *Collapsed States: The Disintegration and Restoration of Legitimate Authority*. Boulder, CO: Lynne Reinner.

Zenith Economic Quarterly. (2016, April). Youth Unemployment: Creating the Job Creators. Zenith Bank Plc (Nigeria). [Editorial]. Retrieved from https://www.zenithbank.com/media/2258/zenith-economic-quartery-vol12-no2-april-2016.pdf.

Zhang, X., & Chen, S. (2013). A Systematic Framework for Infrastructure Development Through Public Private Partnerships. *IATSS Research*, 36(2), 88–97. Retrieved from https://www.sciencedirect.com/science/article/pii/S0386111212000337.

Zhang, H. (2000). Corruption, Economic Growth and Macroeconomic Volatility. Retrieved from http://www.karmayog.org/anticorruption/anticorruption_913.htm.

OFFICIAL PUBLICATIONS

Publications of the Government of Nigeria.

1999 Constitution of the Federal Republic of Nigeria.

Anya, Anya O. et al., (2011). *Report of the Technical Committee on Review of Budgetary Allocations to Ministries and Agencies.* Abuja, Nigeria.

Danjuma, Theophilus Y. et al., (2010). *Report of the Presidential Advisory Council.* Abuja, Nigeria.

Federal Republic of Nigeria. *Third National Development Plan 1975–1980.* Lagos: Federal Government Printer.

Federal Republic of Nigeria. Fiscal Responsibility Act, 2007. Retrieved from https://www.cabri-sbo.org/en/documents/fiscal-responsibility-act-2007.

National Assembly of the Federal Republic of Nigeria. Nigerian Communications Act, 2003. *An Act to Establish the National Frequency Management Council and the Universal Access Fund and to Reform the Nigerian Communications Commission and Repeal the Nigerian Communications Commission Act 1992; and Related Matters.* Retrieved from https://www.ncc.gov.ng/data/html/NCA2003.html?ml=1.

Nigeria House of Representatives. *Report of the Ad-hoc Committee to Verify and Determine the Actual Subsidy Requirements and Monitor the Implementation of the Subsidy Regime in Nigeria.* Resolution No. HR.1/2012, Laid on Wednesday April 18, 2012. Retrieved from http://www.letemps.ch/rw/Le_Temps/Quotidien/2012/10/06/Economie/Images/FUEL_SUBSIDY_PROBE_REPORT.pdf.

Oronsaye, Stephen. et al., (2012). Report *on the Restructuring and Rationalization of Federal Government Parastatals, Commissions and Agencies. Abuja, Nigeria.*

PricewaterhouseCoopers (PWC) (2015). *Auditor-General for the Federation Investigative Forensic Audit into the Allegations of Unremitted Funds into the Federation Accounts by NNPC.* Retrieved from http://www.wgei.org/wp-content/uploads/2015/10/Full-report-20billion-dollars-missing-oil-money_SAI-Nigeria.pdf.

Revenue Mobilization Allocation and Fiscal Commission (RMAFC). *Remuneration Package for Political and Judicial Office Holders,* Effective Date July 1, 2009. Retrieved from http://rmafc.gov.ng/LEGISLATIVE%20ARM3.PDF.

Ribadu, Nuhu. et al., (2012). *Report of the Petroleum Revenues Special Task Force.* Retrieved from http://www.channelstv.com/home/wp-content/uploads/2012/11/REPORT-OF-RIBADU-LED-PETROLEUM-REVENUE-SPECIAL-TASK-FORCE-2012.pdf.

Index

About the Author

Ucheoma Nwagbara is an economist, policy analyst, and public servant. He received his PhD in public policy from Southern University and A&M College, Baton Rouge, Louisiana, USA. In addition to public service, he is adjunct professor of Public Policy, Health Policy, and Urban Policy at Southern University and A&M College, Baton Rouge, Louisiana, USA. His research and writing interests are on health policy and economic development, public policy as well as Nigeria's political economy, economic development, leadership, governance, governmental reform, innovation, bureaucracy, globalization and, above all, modernization.

CPSIA information can be obtained
at www.ICGtesting.com
Printed in the USA
BVHW030823140122
624249BV00015B/10

9 781793 633750